The Disputing Process—Law in Ten Societies

THE DISPUTING PROCESS— LAW IN TEN SOCIETIES

LAURA NADER
AND
HARRY F. TODD JR.,
EDITORS

NEW YORK COLUMBIA UNIVERSITY PRESS 1978

Library of Congress Cataloging in Publication Data

Main entry under title:

The Disputing process—Law in ten societies.

Bibliography: p.
Includes index.
1. Arbitration and award. 2. Negotiation.
3. Courts. 4. Customary law. I. Nader, Laura.
II. Todd, Harry F.
K2400.D5 347'.09 78-8729
ISBN 0-231-04536-0
ISBN 0-231-04537-9 pbk.

NEW YORK COLUMBIA UNIVERSITY PRESS GUILDFORD, SURREY

PRINTED IN THE UNITED STATES OF AMERICA

To Elizabeth Colson—
friend and teacher

CONTENTS

PREFACE

THIS BOOK constitutes an experiment in collaborative research between a teacher and her graduate students. It is an attempt to bring into focus a major area of interest and exploration in the anthropology of law—the disputing process—as the first step in a wider inquiry. These essays concentrate on disputes between people of the same culture, disputes between people who for the most part know each other and who expect to interact in some fashion in the future regardless of the outcome of the dispute. A second study of the disputing process, concentrating on people who are strangers to each other, will result in a companion volume which will deal with alternatives to the judicial system in the United States. The present volume and the one forthcoming together cover the range of relations that are found between disputing parties the world over, the range of sources of dispute, and what is done about disputes.

During 1963–64, while a fellow at the Center for Advanced Study in the Behavioral Sciences in Stanford, California, I reflected about the directions in which anthropological research on law should be pointed. The ideas for a project on comparative village law emerged as a result of a seminar held that year at the Center in conjunction with a group of students from Berkeley and colleagues at the Center (Paul Bohannon and Herma Kay) on the methodological problems involved in comparing the law-ways of different people.

This project, which was to be called the Berkeley Village Law Project, had several aims: ethnographic, comparative, and pedagogical.

Although in 1964 there were already several excellent descriptions of the law of different peoples, many of which had appeared during the previous decade (Hoebel 1954, Howell 1954, Smith and Roberts 1954, Gluckman 1955, Bohannan 1957, Pospisil 1958, Berndt 1962, and Gulliver 1963), I felt that the ethnographies reported on such different organizational and cultural levels, using quite different methodologies, and had such varying intellectual aims that for comparative purposes the available data base was not sufficient. In a survey of developments in the anthropological study of law (1965b) I began to outline a perspective for our work. Several assumptions informed our approach at the beginning: (1) there is a limited range of dispute within any particular society; (2) a limited number of formal public procedures are used by human societies in the prevention or handling of grievances (e.g., courts, contests, ordeals, go-betweens, etc.); (3) the disputants have a choice in the number and modes of settlement (e.g., arbitration, negotiation, mediation, adjudication, coercion, and avoidance); (4) the range of manifest and latent functions of law vary cross-culturally. We were interested in understanding the conditions that defined the presence and use of specific dispute-resolving procedures. We would concentrate on one function of law—the management of disputes. Because the modes of settlement are limited in number, dispute processes would offer a good starting place for comparison.

Our description of law was to be cast in the context of the broader patterns of social control, though not to be equated with social control, and our understanding of social control was to be cast in the broader framework of the culture and social organization of the societies under study. We agreed that the core material for comparison would come from a quantitative and qualitative sampling of dispute cases in each society.

The dispute case, unlike any particular form of dispute processing or any particular class of disputes, is present in all societies. Universally such cases share most of the following components, depending on what stage the dispute is in: that which is disputed (property, custody of children, theft, homicide, marital obligation, and so on); the parties to the dispute (sex, age, rank status, and relation between parties); presentation of the dispute (before a remedy agent such as a judge, go-between, lineage head); procedure or manner of handling the dispute; the outcome; the termination of the grievance; and the enforcement (or nonenforcement) of the decision. Mapping the component parts of a case had been attempted using materials from my Zapotec fieldwork (Nader 1964a), so that the sociological aspects of conflict could be systematically discerned; the results were useful as springboards for comparative work (Nader and Metzger 1963, Nader 1965b).

The work was to be intensively comparative. Each fieldworker was to attempt an intrasocietal comparison before any general attempt to compare the various societies one with the other. In order to permit comparison across society, the data had to be collected in as systematic a way as possible, which meant that prior to departure for the field the fieldworkers needed to agree upon what they would collect and within what framework the collection of data would be undertaken. I wanted to train students who would contribute to the development of a general theory about behavior as it pertains to law. I was concerned with forms of dispute management and styles of dispute management as they relate to questions of rank, status, stratification, and cultural diversity.

Originally my intention was, in addition, to contribute to the way in which research might be conducted by graduate students so that individual contributions had cumulative impact. Anthropological fieldwork had clearly benefited throughout the previous five or six decades from a pattern of individual fieldworkers choosing a topic of their interest which they then pursued in independent fieldwork. In the early days this was, I think, an appropriate mode. But in recent years, I felt, anthropology seemed to be rediscovering itself: the work was becoming more redundant than cumulative. I asked myself if something more valuable might not be gained by cooperation. The Harvard values study (Vogt and Albert 1966) and the pioneer work on child rearing by John and Beatrice Whiting (J. W. M. Whiting et al. 1953; B. Whiting 1963) were models of such cooperation. In training students in the anthropology of law I believed we would accomplish what needed to be accomplished at that point in time if we worked as a group with a formal designation. Calling it the Berkeley Village Law Project would, I believed, increase the chances that students would communicate with each other, and with their teacher. In addition, irregular group meetings and the assigning of younger graduates to the dissertation committees of the older graduate students insured a variety of interchange. However, such an effort needed to be systematic and rigorous if the impact was to be cumulative. At the same time, I was aware that to be overly rigid and insistent upon common modes of data gathering, given the state of knowledge in 1964, might cause us to lose something. For the most part the fieldworkers were quick to say when an approach or method was inappropriate. For example, it soon became clear to our first fieldworker, Klaus Koch, that the case method as first defined was not as ideal a unit for comparison as it had been thought. I had worked in a society where the presence of a court system made clear when a case began and ended. But among the Jalé of New Guinea, as Koch correctly observed, it was not clear when a case began and when it ended. The extended-case method as illustrated by Colson (1953) was more appropriate there.

The fieldwork reported upon in this book took place over a ten-year period, from 1965 to 1975. The fieldworkers in this project chose where they wanted to go, a trade-off on the agreement that we would look at comparable types of material within a common framework. The societies ranged geographically. In Asia, Klaus Koch (1967) worked in Indonesian New Guinea. Nancy Williams (1973) worked in Australia. Four students went to Europe: Barbara Yngvesson (1970) to Scandinavia, Harry Todd (1972) to Germany, Julio Ruffini (1974) to Sardinia, and Carl McCarthy to Liechtenstein (only to later complete his dissertation on O.E.O. legal services in the United States [1974]). Bruce Cox (1968) worked among the Hopi Indians of the United States. Three worked in the Middle East: June Starr (1970) in Turkey, John Rothenberger (1970) in an all-Muslim Lebanese village, and Cathie J. Witty (1975) in a Lebanese village with an almost equal proportion of Muslim and Christian inhabitants. Two worked on opposite sides of the African continent: Michael Lowy (1971) in Ghana and Richard Canter (1976) in Zambia. Two students went to Latin America: Sylvia Forman (1972) to Ecuador, and Philip Parnell (1978) to Mexico. Of these fourteen studies, all of which have been completed as Ph.D. dissertations at the University of California, Berkeley, ten are represented in this volume.

At the outset a primary research interest was in social morphology—the forms used for dispute processing and their concomitant interrelation with specific forms of social groupings (Nader 1964b, 1965a). A geographic distribution was not necessary to achieve the range of variation in types of dispute-resolving agencies. Theoretically, we could have stayed within a single continent or perhaps even within a single culture area to achieve such a sample. Epstein's *Contention and Dispute* (1974) is such an attempt for Melanesia. The papers in this volume represent the known range of types of remedy agents. There is an absence of third parties and direct confrontation among the Jalé of New Guinea. Courts are present and are the predominant remedy agents in Zambia, Ghana, and Mexico. Societies in which other third-party forms are preferred to courts at the local level are described for Turkey, Lebanon, Bavaria, Sardinia, and Scandinavia, even though courts were available and were sometimes used by the villagers.

As the studies proceeded it became clear that if we wished to understand choice—if we wished to understand why one remedy agent is preferred over another, or why certain forms had developed in the first place, or why certain outcomes and strategies were prevalent—we needed to describe and analyze our data in the context of an ongoing process. Focus on the process meant that disputing in the context of social groupings had to be understood in its various phases or stages both before and after it reached a recognizable public forum. Hyperactivity in legal behavior has to be understood in the context of rapid social change, similar to findings in the religious sphere (Wallace 1966) that suggest that an increase in religious activity may often accompany periods of rapid change. Indeed, there is strong evidence that social change may induce behavior characterized by involuted legal activity—although that activity, from the point of view of a monopolistic nation-state's legal system, is sometimes characterized as illegal.

We hope that our contributions will be of interest and of use to a world wider than that of the anthropologist-scholar. There is much talk of law in the governance of people in the world today. In the developing nations law is seen as a means of entrenching power positions. The people of these developing nations are experiencing difficulties traceable to using conflicting and changing systems of law. Imposition of centralized, professionalized, nation-state law is decreasing traditional access to law.

In the United States, as well, there is a crisis that is challenging the position of law as defense, as protection, as orderly change. We hope there will come a time when the anthropological understanding of law in the United States is at least equivalent to our understanding of customs surrounding law among the peoples described in this book, and that the barriers to implementing our knowledge will decrease.

Laura Nader
Berkeley, California
December 1977

ACKNOWLEDGMENTS

WE ARE grateful to the many organizations who have supported our research. The National Institutes of Health and of Mental Health supported the independent work of Richard Canter, Sylvia Forman, Michael Lowy, Philip Parnell, Julio Ruffini, June Starr, Harry Todd, and Nancy Williams. Klaus Koch's work was supported by the Social Science Research Council and the Wenner Gren Foundation. Carl McCarthy and John Rothenberger were supported by the Ford Foundation.

In 1964 funds for the overall project were requested of and denied by the National Institutes of Mental, Health, in part, they informed me, because of the young age of the principal investigator. I am particularly grateful to the Center for Advanced Study at Stanford, California, for being most supportive and willing to bet on a young anthropologist during the incipient period of planning. We thank the Wenner-Gren Foundation for support of a mini-conference held in Amherst, Massachusetts, in the fall of 1973 in an effort at preliminary assessment of our work. The results of this conference were presented in a special session at the annual meetings of the American Anthropological Association in November 1973.

I am especially appreciative of my colleagues at the University of California, Berkeley; in particular, Professors Elizabeth Colson and Eugene Hammel played important roles in what was always cooperative supervision of many of these young anthropologists as graduate students. Professor Herma Hill Kay of Boalt Hall Law School also provided continuing support and advice.

With all this help this manuscript could not have been completed without a support staff. Dr. Harry Todd helped me initiate the process of outlining the expectations for these contributions; he collected the essays, genially hounded the contributors until work was in, and helped edit the volume. I give special thanks to Grace Buzaljko, our much appreciated and respected editor. Mrs. Buzaljko's task was particularly onerous at times as she struggled with the writing of young scholars. All too often such work is not recognized as a totally indispensable part of the training of a scholar; Mrs. Buzaljko was teaching the newly initiated the art of precision in the use of language and of simplicity for communication's sake. Belinda Johns, my research assistant, typed and checked and double-checked the final manuscript with me with persistence, good cheer, and the care that comes from being interested in the substance as well as the task.

Finally, I would like to thank my family; it was my parents who very early trained me to think about law and justice; it was they who cared for the children while I was away visiting researchers at their field sites. My siblings and my husband continually contributed to the substance and methodology in my thinking about law in culture and society. The children contributed a good deal to morale; they more than anyone else protected my time so that I could get my work done.

As I have said, this has been an experiment in collaborative research, which includes the contributors to this volume and as well those four members of the Berkeley Village Law Project not specifically represented here; Bruce Cox, Sylvia Forman, Carl McCarthy, and Nancy Williams always enlivened and enriched discussions. For us as individual participants the experience has been rich although not always smooth. Whether the substantive work results in the cumulative impact I had earlier envisioned I leave for others to judge.

L.N.

CONTRIBUTORS

Richard S. Canter received his B.A., M.A., and Ph.D. in anthropology from the University of California, Berkeley. His field research in the Appalachian area of the United States and in Zambia was supported by the National Institutes of Health (National Institute of General Medical Sciences). His major interests are in legal and political anthropology as they relate to local-level and national-level change. He is currently an Assistant Professor of Anthropology and Co-Director of the Law and Society Program at Boston University.

Klaus-Friedrich Koch began his studies in ethnography, psychology, and philosophy at the universities of Bonn and Tübingen. A Fulbright Fellowship brought him to the University of California, Berkeley, where he obtained a B.A. and Ph.D. in anthropology. He did fieldwork in New Guinea and in the South Pacific, where he directed a four-year project involving comparative studies of law in the polyethnic nation of Fiji and in the kingdom of Tonga.

From 1967 to 1974 he taught at Harvard University, where he also spent a year as a Fellow in Law and Anthropology. Following a year's residency as a visiting scholar at the Center for Interdisciplinary Research at Bielefeld University in Germany, he taught at the University of Virginia (1975–76). He is currently an Associate Professor of Anthropology at Northwestern University.

His publications deal with law, conflict management and warfare, kinship and social organization, and comparative psychology.

Michael J. Lowy has a B.A. from the City College of the City of New York, an M.A. from Hunter College, and a Ph.D. from the University of California, Berkeley. He has published articles on his field research among Native Americans in northern California, and on the people of a southern Ghanaian town. His research in Ghana was funded by the National Institute of Mental Health. He has taught anthropology at the University of Pittsburgh, and has been a Visiting Professor at the University of Wisconsin, Stanford University, the State University of New York at Buffalo, and the University of California, Berkeley. In 1973–74 he was a Law and Modernization Post-Doctoral Fellow at the Yale Law School. He is currently a J.D. student at Stanford Law School, where he is a Russell Sage Foundation Resident in Law and Social Science.

Philip Parnell received his B.A. in sociology and anthropology at Princeton University and his Ph.D. in anthropology at the University of California, Berkeley. He has conducted research on dispute settlement in Mexico and the United States, having received traineeship grants from the National Institute of Mental Health and the Center for the Study of Law and Society at Berkeley. He is an Assistant Professor of Forensic Studies at Indiana University in Bloomington, teaching in the areas of law, anthropology, and social control.

John E. Rothenberger received a B.A. in English literature from Lehigh University and a J.D. from Yale Law School. He served in the U.S. Army and practiced law in San Francisco before studying anthropology at the University of California, Berkeley, where he received his Ph.D. in 1970. He has done fieldwork in Mexico and Lebanon. He is presently an Associate Professor of Anthropology at California State University, Hayward.

Julio L. Ruffini received his B.A. in International Relations from San Francisco State College in 1960, worked as a social worker for several years thereafter, and then obtained his Ph.D. in anthropology from the University of California, Berkeley, in 1974. During 1975–77 he was a Post-Doctoral Fellow in Social Gerontology and Medical Anthropology at the University of California, San Francisco. His fieldwork has been with San Francisco Bay Area Samoans, and in Sardinia. His research in Sardinia was sponsored by the National Institutes of General Medical Sciences, the Department of Anthropology, University of California, Berkeley, and the Wenner-Gren Foundation. He is currently an Adjunct Assistant Professor of Anthropology in the Medical Anthropology Program, Department of International Health, School of Medicine, University of California, San Francisco, where he is engaged in research on the legal needs, problems, behavior, and perceptions of the elderly in the Sunset District of San Francisco.

June Starr holds a B.A. in philosophy from Smith College, an M.A. in general anthropology from Columbia University, and a Ph.D. in social anthropology from the University of California, Berkeley. She spent 1969–70 as a Fellow at the Middle East Center, Harvard University, and 1973–74 as a Fellow at Yale Law School, in the Law and Modernization Program.

She received a summer grant for Turkish language study from the Committee for Middle Eastern Studies, University of California, Berkeley, in 1966; was awarded National Institute of Mental Health Pre-Doctoral Fellowships for the years 1966–69; and received an N.I.M.H. Grant for Field Research for 1966–68. She has written several articles on the impact of changing laws in rural Turkey, as well as a monograph entitled *Dispute and Settlement in Rural Turkey* (1978). Her current research concerns the division of labor, with special attention to women's roles, in pastoral nomadic societies in Iran. She is Associate Professor of Anthropology at SUNY—Stony Brook.

Harry F. Todd, Jr. holds both a law degree (J.D., George Washington University, 1965) and a Ph.D. in anthropology (University of California, Berkeley, 1972). He has done research in Mexico as well as in Bavaria (West Germany). In 1972–73 he served as Acting Assistant Professor in the Department of Anthropology, and concurrently as a Post-Doctoral Fellow at the Center for the Study of Law and Society, both at the University of California, Berkeley. In 1974–76 he was a lecturer and Post-Doctoral Fellow in the Medical Anthropology Program, Department of International Health, School of Medicine, at the University of California, San Francisco. He is currently Assistant Professor of Anthropology in Residence at that university, and since 1975 has been Co-Editor of the *Medical Anthropology Newsletter*. He is presently doing research on the legal problems, behavior, and perceptions of the elderly in San Francisco.

Cathie J. Witty received an M.A. in public administration from Harvard University and a Ph.D. in anthropology from the University of California, Berkeley. She has done fieldwork in the Middle East, where her work was supported by an N.I.M.H. Traineeship. Presently she is Assistant Professor in the Graduate School of Social Work and Social Research, and Adjunct to the Department of Anthropology, Bryn Mawr College, where she teaches in the areas of Middle Eastern studies, law, social policy, development, minorities, and administration.

Barbara B. Yngvesson holds a B.A. degree from Barnard College in religion and philosophy and a Ph.D. from the University of California, Berkeley, in anthropology. She has carried out research on dispute management in Scandinavia and in the United States, supported by grants from the Institute for International Studies. She is presently Associate Professor of Anthropology at Hampshire College, Amherst, Massachusetts, and a member of the Undergraduate Legal Studies Faculty there. The author of several articles on dispute processing, she is concluding a study of the use of a community forum in the processing of criminal cases in an eastern seaboard district court.

INTRODUCTION

Laura Nader and Harry F. Todd, Jr.

THE LAW has many functions. It serves to educate, to punish, to harass, to protect private and public interests, to provide entertainment, to serve as a fund-raising institution, to distribute scarce resources, to maintain the status quo, to maintain class systems and to cut across them, to integrate and disintegrate societies—all these things in different places, at different times, with different weightings (Nader 1965b: 17–21; Nader and Yngvesson 1973: 908–15). Law may be a cause of crime; it plays, by virtue of its discretionary power, the role of definer of crime. It may encourage respect or disrespect for itself.

The title of this volume, *The Disputing Process—Law in Ten Societies*, was selected to reflect its dual focus on disputes and on the processes used by people around the world to deal with these disputes. In all human societies there are persons who have problems of debt, of theft, of infidelity, of employment, of consumption, and of personal injury. Many of these people seek to do something about their problems, and in so doing resort to remedy agents that the society has previously developed to deal with them; and, if no satisfaction can be obtained through these traditional means, they create new forums through which they seek to obtain "justice," however they may perceive it.

In any society there are alternatives or choices to be made when disputes arise. Anthropology has a large and very good body of cross-cultural materials on formally recognized institutions of dispute settlement (see, for example, Nader, Koch, and Cox 1966). Anthropologists have written about judges, councils, go-betweens, crossers, duelers, and so forth. They have also compared negotiation with mediation, arbitration, and adjudication techniques. Thus we have a pretty fair idea of the range of variation in patterns of formally recognized rules or institutions relating to the settlement or at least to the management of disputes in specific societies. The contribution of this volume is to distinguish the components of processes of dispute in order to better understand the conditions underlying them and the consequences following from them.

In the world of developing nations there is much talk of law—as an instrument of social engineering, as a vehicle for consolidating nationalist movements and homogenizing heterogeneous populations, and as a means of entrenching power positions, both indigenous and foreign. There are problems in using conflicting and changing systems of law, often imported wholesale, often based on an alien value system. Those who regularly profit from sudden changes in the law are the growing classes of legal and paralegal professionals, and the political entrepreneurs responsible for the sometimes devastating melting-pot approach to nation building through the law. Those who often suffer are the preliterate, the illiterate, the common people closest to urban centers—people whose indigenous systems of law are sabotaged under pressures for modernization. For such people the imposition of centralized, professionalized law has decreased their traditional access to law, at least until they learn by various means how to manipulate or use the newly introduced system. Many of the essays in this book document or at least adumbrate the problems and frustrations experienced, and the adaptations made by individuals faced with modern legal orders.

In the United States there is also concern with law. In recent years political speeches have been riddled with talk of law and order, and much attention is given to the new weaponry and surveillance techniques that may be used to maintain law and to enforce order. We are experiencing a time when the poor and underprivileged are no longer the major focus of law enforcement, which is increasingly concerned with more affluent groups. Public interest lawyers are voicing the view that law enforcement should apply not only to the lower and middle classes, but also to the more powerful in this country, whose known violations of the law have widespread effect on American society. At the same time, the problem of access to the legal system is ever more acute, the use of legal means is spreading. Minorities—ethnic groups, women, homosexuals—are actively seeking to use it to improve their civil status. We are living at a time when citizens are awake to the possibility that they can protect themselves by means of the law, defend themselves by means of the law, and change the system by means of the law.

In the meantime there is also a growing movement in the United States to manage individual and group interests outside the formal legal system. Voluntary complaint committees, arbitration boards, toll-free hot lines, newspaper action lines, and other such mechanisms now serve in the dispute management process. Within one of the most professionalized systems of law in the world we have voices crying out that the legal system is overburdened, that extrajudicial systems must be developed. We have come full circle; there has been overdependence upon the law, some say. In this context it is crucial that we look at smaller societies to see how things as a whole work. In particular, it is important to see how things work in societies where the boundaries between formal and informal systems are often blurred, and can be crossed when convenient by participants who understand and use the total system for specific ends, and where law often plays a secondary role in the mangement of disputes.

Our approach is eclectic. It represents an amalgam of a number of diffrent theoretical and conceptual approaches found in prior anthropological research on law and on general issues of organization and structure (see, for example, the summaries in Nader 1965b, Moore 1969, Cox and Drever 1971, Pospisil 1971, Nader and Yngvesson 1973, and Collier 1975). In terms of contemporary work, there is much that our approach has in common with the work of sociologist Donald Black (1976). Black has consistently interested himself in law as a social phenomenon, and has suggested a number of interesting propositions linking variations in law-ways with variations in culture, social organization and stratification, as they are reflected in social control. He has been concerned with the spread and direction of law and with the decrease in other social control systems in culturally differentiated and socially stratified societies. His work on the style of law is particularly pertinent to many of the essays in this volume. Whether law has a penal style, a compensatory or therapeutic style, or a conciliatory style depends on the rank-relations between litigants and their degree of intimacy.

In addition, Colson's 1953 article, "Social Control and Vengeance in Plateau Tonga Society," contains in a condensed form the principal elements of the processual approach as we have used it. By focusing on one detailed case of homicide, Colson shows how members of this society handled a breach of prescribed rules, and she demonstrates through careful analysis how a complex network of cross-linkages in social relations serves to hold in check a potentially escalatory situation. She also touches on considerations of strategy, pointing to the choices open to the parties involved. Colson's emphases on the processes of control, the relation of these processes to structural considerations, and the importance of litigants' strategies for manipulating the structure, and her use of detailed case materials, are also prominent features of our approach.

This volume represents one perspective in the anthropological study of law. In the first portion of this Introduction, we attempt to provide a background to both methodological and theoretical approaches to the anthropological study of disputing. Here, we discuss the impact of the "trouble case" approach on theory and method, provide a typology of procedural modes utilized worldwide in dispute settlement, and discuss the structural-functionalist model of disputing behavior which permeated legal anthropology for at least two decades. The second part of this Introduction provides a different perspective, on law as a social process. The emphasis in this second section goes beyond the static, equilibrium model of structural-functionalist studies, toward a more dynamic, processual one; here we examine the implications of this shift from structure to process in the cross-cultural study of law. Particularly salient here is the focus on time and on the role of individual choice making in disputing. A number of "dimensions" which we have found to be intimately associated with the form and manner of disputing are discussed. The third part of the Introduction is a brief overview of some of the directional patterns resulting from the evolution of the dispute mechanisms under the aegis of the nation-state as part of the increasingly centralized industrialization process that is sweeping the world.

BACKGROUND

The first task of any anthropologist is to provide a basis for comparison and generalization through adequate description, or ethnography. Perspectives on what should go into a description are intimately related to methods used, and vice versa. In part because many anthropologists, like lawyers, have invested their energies principally in understanding dispute settlement and litigation in general, we have for the past several decades found the case method particularly useful. Indeed, when our study group began this collaborative effort, the case was the unit of analysis upon which we focused.

The Case Method in the Field of Law

In 1941, in *The Cheyenne Way,* Llewellyn and Hoebel outlined three approaches to the exploration of the law-stuff of a culture: in their own words, rules, practice, and trouble cases.

> The one road is ideological and goes to "rules" which are felt as proper for channelling and controlling behavior. Students of ethics and legal philosophers are likely to call these felt standards for proper behavior "norms." Students of modern law, accustomed to clothing such norms in words, and to meeting them chiefly in verbalized form, speak of them as "rules" for behavior. In any event, they are ideal patterns, "right ways" against which real action is measured. The second road is descriptive; it deals with practice. It explores the patterns according to which behavior actually occurs. The third road is a search for instances of hitch, dispute, grievance, trouble; and inquiry into what the trouble was and what was done about it (Llewellyn and Hoebel 1941: 20–21).

These three approaches are, of course, related. Norms are generally reflected in behavior, and to some extent become active in patterning individual behavior to guard against potential deviance. Nevertheless, for Llewellyn and Hoebel (1941: 29), it was the trouble case that was to be the unit of analysis: "The trouble-cases, sought out and examined with care, are thus the safest main road to the discovery of law. Their data are most certain. Their yield is richest. They are the most revealing."

The collecting of trouble cases has provided anthropologists with a focus apart from law as a set of rules or customs. It has caused the fieldworker to look at the actual workings of law in society, and in so doing, has turned the focus to the examination of disputing.

Of course, all ethnographic fieldworkers collect cases, no matter what their focus of interest, simply in the process of examining particulars prior to, or as part of, generalization. In the anthropological study of law, the word "case" has, however, usually referred to the gathering of materials about disputes. Anthropologists have used the case method in the search for systematic aspects of procedural and substantive law, for uncovering important jural postulates, for abstracting values important to a society. These cases have been varied in form and content, and even in the names anthropologists have given them: the trouble case, the extended case, the social drama.

There are four basic types of case materials which the anthropologist of law utilizes: observed cases, cases taken from recorded materials, memory cases, and hypothetical cases. Probably the preferred type of case for our purposes is that which is directly observed or recorded by the fieldworker. The best case documentation is usually achieved when the anthropologist is able to record the genesis of a grievance or a conflict before it becomes a dispute. (These terms are defined on pp. 14–15 below.) The opportunity to observe ongoing grievances, conflicts, or disputes (outside of an institutional setting such as a court) depends on a combination of circumstances and luck; it means that the anthropologist has to be in the right place at the right time.

Even when the anthropologist is fortunate enough to be able to observe the genesis of a conflict or dispute, there is the question of the representativeness of the case. Is the observed case a typical or normal response to the situation under observation, or is it in fact atypical? This consideration is especially salient if the anthropologist is interested in inferring norms or rules of proper conduct from the case materials.

One way in which the anthropologist has attempted to resolve problems of sampling is to supplement the observed cases with other kinds of case materials, particularly with "memory cases." In eliciting a memory case, the researcher asks his informants about instances of confict or dispute which occurred in the past. This approach, too, has its pitfalls, for memory cases, unlike observed cases, tend to be tainted by selective recall: informants tend to remember events which have impressed them in some way and tend to forget others. This is certainly true of the New Guinea materials, as evidenced by comparing Klaus Koch's memory cases with his observed field cases. "Screen memory" may operate; things or events may be recalled, but may be cast (or judged) in terms of the present situation and present standards, instead of those prevailing at the time of the dispute.

The use of the "hypothetical case" raises the problem of ideal as opposed to actual behavior. In this kind of elicitation, the informant is not asked about what *did* happen, but rather what *might* happen if a certain act occurred. At the very least, known cases will be used comparatively, in "hypothesizing" about other cases. For this reason, the hypothetical case is subject to the same limitations as the memory case.

In the last decade or so there has been a change in the way cases are used in the anthropology of law. Llewellyn and Hoebel (1941), for example, viewed a case as a means for discovering the "law jobs" of a society and the "administrative machinery" available for handling them. Barton (1919, 1949), who utilized the case method in his work in the Philippines considerably earlier than did Llewellyn and Hoebel, used cases to provide data on offenses, on sanctions, and on the elements of "modern legal mechanisms" employed by the Ifugao and the Kalingas. He also used case materials (particularly in his book *The Kalingas*) as sources for rules of substantive law in the society he was studying. A more recent example of the use of cases to a similar end is Pospisil's *Kapauku Papuans and Their Law* (1958). In all these examples the authors' emphases were on the use of the case method to describe "law" as a domain in its own right in the societies they studied. There is a growing tendency now in studies of the anthropology of law to view the core of a "dispute case" as simply one part of a long-term case that may have begun many years earlier, with consequences that may continue to affect social relations in the group under study for some time. In this use of the case method the "law process," as seen throughout the developing case, is not viewed as separate from the case as a whole. The case becomes an arena in which various structural principles are brought into play through the operations or transactions of the principal actors involved. Thus utilized, cases may become diagnostic tools for pinpointing stress areas in the social structure of the community (Turner 1957), illustrating which issues the people involved perceive to be conflict-engendering and the relationship into which conflict is structured in that society. Cases utilized in this way have been called "extended cases" (Van Velsen 1967). An extended case may comprise a series of related cases through time, involving some or all of the same actors; or it may comprise one detailed case unsettled over a period of months or years. In each instance, the dispute in question is viewed within the social context in which it develops and is played out, allowing the analyst to trace developments and shifts in the balance of power between the individuals involved. Starr, Koch, Yngvesson, and other writers in this volume have used extended-dispute cases to focus on the strategies used by litigants in obtaining a desired end.

The Development of Legal Procedures

As we have said, all societies have developed procedures that can be called into operation when trouble arises. We shall not deal here with the question of whether these procedures are law or social control or "merely" custom. We will take a more neutral position and say that whatever we label these procedures, there are a limited number of them.

Most societies have access to several procedures to deal with trouble, and some of the total range of procedures is described below.

The crucial variables are the presence or absence of a third party and the basis of the third party's intervention, and the type of outcome (if any). The same basic procedural modes are used worldwide in attempts to deal with grievances, conflict, or disputes: adjudication, arbitration, mediation, negotiation, coercion (or conquest, in Boulding's [1962] terms), avoidance, and "lumping it."

"Lumping it," a term used by Felstiner (1974, 1975), and discussed by Galanter (1974) and Danzig and Lowy (1975), refers to the failure of an aggrieved party to press his claim or complaint. The issue or problem that gave rise to a disagreement is simply ignored, and the relationship with the offending party is continued. "This is done all the time," Galanter (1974: 124–25) writes, "by 'claimants' who lack information or access (to law) or who knowingly decide gain is too low, cost too high (including psychic cost of litigating where such activity is repugnant)."

Avoidance, on the other hand, or what Hirschman (1970) refers to as "exit," entails withdrawing from a situation or curtailing or terminating a relationship by leaving, by finding a new business firm to deal with, and so on. This is a common expedient in many instances of trouble and may serve as a sanction in itself. Avoidance entails a limitation on or a complete break in social relationships between antagonists; "lumping it," on the other hand, refers to the lack of resolution of a grievance, conflict, or dispute because one of the parties chooses to ignore the issue in dispute, usually basing his decision on feelings of relative powerlessness or on the social, economic, or psychological costs involved in seeking a solution. The relationship, however, continues, because avoidance, for one reason or another, is not a viable alternative. The individual must continue the relationship with the neighbors, the Welfare Department, and Social Security Administration, or the only merchant through whom he has access to a particular kind of goods. Thus, while the salient feature of avoidance is the reduction or termination of social interaction, lumping behavior involves ignoring the issue in dispute, but continuing the relationship. Both "lumping it" and avoidance behavior involve unilateral decisions on the part of at least one of the principals and have been described for societies as different as the Hopi (Cox 1968), the Scandinavians (Yngvesson 1970), and the Koreans (Hahm 1967).

A third procedural mode, coercion, also involves unilateral action. Here one principal imposes the outcome on the other. The threat or use of force often aggravates the conflict and impedes a peaceful settlement. Such "self-help" procedures are found everywhere, but have been described as generally characteristic of many New Guinea cultures (Epstein 1974, Koch 1974).

In the next procedural mode, negotiation, the two principal parties are the decision makers, and the settlement of the matter is one to which both parties agree, without the aid of a third party. In this situation the parties try to persuade one another. "They seek not to reach a solution in terms of rules, but to create the rules by which they can organize their relationship with one another" (Gulliver 1973: 2–3). Negotiation, then, is a dyadic arrangement.

Less documentation is available for negotiation patterns and for avoidance and lumping behavior than for third party procedures in spite of the fact that in industrialized countries like the United States negotiation, avoidance, and lumping behavior are the most frequent responses to dispute situations (Best 1976).

Mediation, in contrast, involves a third party who intervenes in a dispute to aid the principals in reaching an agreement. Regardless of whether the principals solicited the aid of a mediator or whether he was appointed by someone in authority, both principals must agree to his intervention. The mediator may be an institutionalized neutral, such as the Nuer leopardskin chief (Evans-Pritchard 1940), or he may be a person of acknowledged prestige, such as the Ifugao go-between (Barton 1919: 18–19). The *burgermeister* of rural Bavarian villages (Todd 1972, 1978) and the *mukhtaar* in Lebanese villages (Rothenberger 1970, Witty 1975) are examples of mediators in small-scale societies represented in this volume. Nader's work on the Zapotec *presidente* (1964a, 1969b) illustrates how a single person, the presidente, may be mediator, adjudicator, and arbitrator all in one day. Gulliver (1973) has analyzed in depth the kinds of mediators, their roles, and their rationale, pointing to the richness of the data on mediation in the anthropological literature.

Two other procedural modes that are used in attempts to handle trouble are arbitration and adjudication. In arbitration both principals consent to the intervention of a third party whose judgment they must agree to accept beforehand. When both parties agree to perform an ordeal or a divination and accept the outcome as a decision, the third party in the arbitration is a nonhuman agent (Koch 1974: 28, cf. Roberts 1965). When we speak of adjudication we refer to the presence of a third party who has the authority to intervene in a dispute whether or not the principals wish it, and to render a decision with means at his or her disposal, and furthermore to enforce compliance with that decision.

Why do we bother to distinguish among these procedures? It is not simply an exercise in classification. There are numerous implicit and explicit hypotheses about the range of options, the limitations of the various procedures, and the relation of procedure to outcome and consequences. The very fact that within the same society a variety of procedures may be used in the course of a single dispute suggests that people recognize that one procedure is not good for every kind of problem. Fuller (1968: 108) has noted the limitations of systems of adjudicative law in respect to their use as instruments of social order in dealing with certain types of problems. The aims of those involved also inform us. Do the participants in a case aim to restitute, retaliate, or prevent escalation, as discussed by Canter (below) for Zambia? Is the legal procedure used as a mechanism for social change—for disrupting status differences as with the Turkish cases described by Starr in this volume, or for restating village power and status relationships as noted by Rothenberger for a Muslim village in Lebanon or by Todd for a Bavarian village? If we recognize an even broader complexity we look not only at the range of options but also at the consequences of different levels of involvement: one person acting on his own through self-help has different consequences than two persons in face-to-face negotiation, or three or more persons, at least one of whom is acting as a mediator, arbitrator, or adjudicator. Much of the context for such variation is described in this volume in an effort to understand why the disputing process looks different from different vantage points (Starr and Yngvesson 1975).

Procedural Modes and the Nature of Social Relations and Groupings

Structural-functionalist analysis in anthropology has been concerned with form and structure, with the arrangement of persons in social relation to one another (Radcliffe-Brown 1952), as well as with the effect of increasing population density and social differentiation. In his monograph on *The Judicial Process Among the Barotse of Northern Rhodesia* (1955) Max Gluckman generalized that if one could determine the nature of the social relationships between the parties to a dispute, then one could predict the procedure that would be employed in the decision-making process. The nature of social relationships between disputants is stated in terms of a dichotomy, opposing single-interest (or simplex) relations to multiplex ones. Gluckman spells out this distinction in the following terms.

> In more differentiated societies a person is linked to a variety of different persons, with many of whom his relationship is formally confined to a single interest, as for example, that of a labourer with his employer, a bus traveller with the conductor, a housewife with a shopkeeper, even an invalid with a doctor, or a churchgoer with a priest. In Barotse society . . . nearly every societal relationship serves many interests. . . . The headman is related to his villagers by political as well as kinship bonds. By birth and by residence in a village a man acquires his civic status and is linked to a number of overlords. . . . This multiple membership of diverse groups and in diverse relationships is an important source of quarrels and conflict; but it is equally the basis of internal cohesion in any society (Gluckman 1955: 18–20).

Commenting on this statement, Van Velsen (1969: 138) notes that "where multiplex relationships prevail judges and litigants, and litigants among themselves, interact in relationships whose significance ranges beyond the transitoriness of the court or of a particular dispute. Today they are disputing in court, tomorrow they may be collaborating in the same work party." Thus, the nature of the relationships in which litigants or disputants are involved will affect the manner in which they attempt to manage the problem. Again, in Gluckman's terms, "the fact that the parties (and often the judges too) are normally involved in complex or multiplex relations outside the court-forum, relations which existed before and continue after the actual appearance in court, . . . largely determine(s) the form that a judicial hearing takes . . ." (Gluckman 1969: 22).

The structural-functionalist model, as applied to dispute processing, can be diagramed as follows:

Relationship between disputants	determines	Procedural form of attempts at settlement	and hence determines	Outcome of the dispute

The idea here is that the nature of relationships sets restraints on the settlement process. This hypothesis is usually formulated as follows: Relationships that are multiplex and involve many interests demand certain kinds of settlement, such as compromise, which will allow the relations to continue.

As Gluckman (1955) elaborated this theme, the crucial variable was the level of complexity of the relation. We summarize in the following model:

Disputants in multiplex or continuing relationships	will rely on	Negotiation or mediation in settlement attempts	which will lead to	Compromise outcomes
and				
Disputants in simplex relationships	will rely on	Adjudication or arbitration in settlement attempts	which will lead to	Win-or-lose decisions

The rationale for this model of dispute processing, if we may turn once again to Gluckman, is that the main task of the Lozi judge is to prevent the breaking of relationships, to make it possible for the parties to live together amicably. Gluckman argues further (1955: 20–21) that this task is related to the nature of the social relationships out of which spring the disputes that come before the judge. Actually, the crucial component probably has less to do with the nature of cross-cutting ties than it does with the need or desire to maintain continuing relations. Berman (1958: 474–75) illustrates this point in his description of the inadequacy of the judicial response to relations between labor and management in the early history of labor law in America.

In a comparable mode, Nader (1965a) illustrates the determinative quality of social groupings. In a comparison of Lebanese and Mexican villages, she argues that dispute settlement through law does not arise where there are no recognized social cross-linkages between parties in dispute. The Lebanese village, characterized by a sociological division into two parts, with marriage occurring only within the half one belonged to, had no third-party procedures for the management of disputes between members of these different halves. The Mexican village, typified by many cross-linked associations between people and between groups, had developed a lively court system for management of disputes. Dual division organization would appear to be incompatible with adjudication, arbitration, or mediation. In this model the types of extant social groupings determine the presence of one or another of the procedural modes discussed earlier.

A Note on Terminology

The fieldworkers represented in this volume (in particular those working in societies without formal courts) have collected data on the disputing process by documenting the course of life histories of disagreements between people or between groups. In general, we have tried to agree on the terminology for at least three distinct phases or stages of the disputing process: the grievance or preconflict stage, the conflict stage, and finally the dispute stage.

The *grievance* or *preconflict* stage refers to a circumstance or condition which one person (or group) perceives to be unjust, and the grounds for resentment or complaint. The offense may be real or imagined, depending on the aggrieved party's perception. The important thing is that he feels himself wronged or injured. The grievance situation is charged with potentiality: it may erupt into conflict, or it may wane. The path that it will take is usually up to the offended party. His grievance may be escalated by confrontation; or escalation may be avoided by curtailing further social interaction, by the second party's failing to pick up the gauntlet. This stage may be characterized as monadic.

The issue is joined and the disagreement enters the *conflict* stage if the aggrieved party opts for confrontation—if he throws down the gauntlet—and communicates his resentment or feeling of injustice to the offending party. Thus, both parties are aware that disagreement exists between them. The conflict phase, therefore, is dyadic. It is not the offender's move: he may escalate, or attempt to deescalate, through coercion of, or negotiation of a settlement with, the aggrieved party.

Finally, the *dispute* stage results from escalation of the conflict by making the matter public. A third party, a person or group, is now actively involved in the disagreement. As Gulliver (1969a: 14) puts it, "no dispute exists unless and until the right claimant, or someone on his behalf, actively raises the initial disagreement from the level of dyadic argument into the public arena, with the express intention of doing something about the desired claim." Thus, the dispute stage is at least triadic and involves a third party who intervenes either at the behest of one or both of the principals or their supporters, or on his own initiative.

These stages are not neat nor are they necessarily sequential: the aggrieved party may escalate his or her grievance directly to the dispute level without ever confronting the offender (i.e., without ever raising the grievance to the conflict level); for example, he or she may without warning file a court action. Similarly, deescalation to a lower level, or avoidance or lumping behavior, may occur at any time; one party may simply quit or concede at any stage in the disagreement. The disagreement may bounce back and forth among and between levels, and may become confused with other issues and disagreements, the original point becoming lost among the hydra-headed tangle of issues and events brought on by the lapse of time and the exacerbation of other hostilities and enmities between the principals and their supporters.

DIMENSIONS OF THE DISPUTING PROCESS

A thorough examination of case material within the full sociocultural context of the dispute case produces a view of law as process. This view involves a substantial alteration of the equilibrium principle inherent in structural-functional studies, in favor of a more dynamic approach that treats the dispute as but one event in a series of events linking persons and groups over time and possibly involving other disputes. Disputes are social processes embedded in social relations. The focus of attention shifts "from the dispute itself (and the techniques for handling it) to the social processes of which the dispute is a part" (Starr and Yngvesson 1975: 562–63, 564). Disputing does not always have a happy ending. The official Reconciliation Agency in Bavaria has not been completely successful; the Jalé of New Guinea have difficulties in finding peaceful settlement of their disputes; the competition between village- and district-level courts often impedes justice in Mexico, Zambia, and elsewhere.

The shift from structure to process, stemming from the works of Colson (1953), Turner (1957), Bailey (1960, 1969) and Gulliver (1971), brings with it a shift in the level of interest from institutions and social groups, to the individual and the choices which he or she is forced to make in disputing. In any dispute (or grievance or conflict) situation, people are interacting. They are involved in the process of making decisions about how best to maximize their own advantages, how best to obtain the results they seek. The processual model, unlike the structural-functional model, focuses on people enmeshed in networks of social relations, on people making decisions that are based on a number of competing factors. The going is not always smooth, although the tensions involved in disputing mechanisms have not always been clear. As has been noted by Starr and Yngvesson:

> The literature . . . reflects a bias which has characterized much anthropological research, both in law and other areas, until the past decade. A Durkheimian emphasis on harmony of interests and shared goals has heavily influenced our thinking and seems to have shaped the ways in which anthropologists have perceived the handling of disputes, particularly among people in multiplex, ongoing relations. . . . multiplex, ongoing relations are frequently not harmonious. . . . Ongoing relationships may be based on conflict or have elements of conflict structured into them, and the ongoing aspect may or may not be voluntary. Examples of such conflict-based relationships are those based on

> *debt* (e.g. sharecropper/patron relationships) or debt relations between affines in regard to bridewealth [Van Velsen, 1964], ***inheritance*** (e.g., certain son/father relations in patri-primogeniture inheritance systems, sibling relations in other agnatic or cognatic systems), ***marriage*** . . . and others (Starr and Yngvesson 1975: 559, 564).

Structure of Social Relationships

There have been numerous studies documenting the part that social relationships play in the disputing process. Some of them point out that where continuing relations are important to individuals everything is done to see to it that the paths chosen reinforce such goals. In a now classic paper Stewart Macaulay (1963) describes the avoidance of the law as a way of building and keeping good business relations; businessmen prefer not to use contracts in their dealings with other businessmen, and even prefer not to use the criminal law in dealing with criminal business activity (Sutherland 1949: 248). There are a number of other examples of avoidance of the law, particularly when zero-sum (all-or-nothing) operations would militate against continuing relations (van der Sprenkel 1962: 112–23; Hahm 1967: 19–20). Collier (1973), in her work on the Zinacantecans of southern Mexico, suggests that Indians who wish to preserve a valued relationship will seek a settlement procedure that promotes reconciliation, and she notes that although these Indians use Ladino legal procedures when necessary, a decision to take another Zinacantan to a Ladino court is "like a decision to go to war." Among the Jalé of New Guinea (Koch 1974), members of the same patrilineage usually mediate and participate in reconciliation rituals, but geographic distance, even among kin, increases the likelihood of broader confrontation.

While all the writers in this volume illustrates the point that the nature of relationships between parties is a significant factor, all of them, as is suggested by Koch's use of geographic proximity and distance, are aware that continuing relationships are but part of the picture. It is not enough to state that because litigants wish to continue their relation they will seek negotiated or mediated settlements with compromise outcomes. Starr, for example, found that ties within the family itself may give rise to disputes over inheritance among siblings, or arguments between young males and females over the males' attempts to control the behavior of their unmarried sisters.

The structure of social relationships among and between litigants not only may give rise to conflict and disputing but may act as a constraint on escalation. Yngvesson in her description of a Scandinavian fishing village clearly demonstrates that *what is done* is often less important than *who did it,* so long as the actors involved are members of the insider category in that community.

Rothenberger makes the point that the relationship between Lebanese litigants and remedy agent is crucial too. This point is backed up by Canter, who notes that one of the four reasons for a Zambian headman's rejecting a case in the village moot is either that it involves close relations between disputants who have had a long history of conflict between themselves or that it involves a headman from another village or a member of the political elite.

It is no longer sufficient to generalize that in a face-to-face society disputes between two members of such a society will be resolved through some kind of compromise or reconciliation mechanism. The ties between and among litigants, and among litigants and remedy agents, may be rooted in a variety of principles: kinship, residence, patron-client, friendship, competition. It is this variety that must inform a dynamic understanding of the social relational dimensions of disputing.

Control of Scarce Resources

It is in relation to control over resources—particularly over scarce resources—that the subject matter in dispute becomes salient. In situations in which scarce resources form the basis of a dispute, individuals may rank the resource higher than they rank the relationship, and may be willing to sacrifice the social relationship with their opponents in order to gain access to, or exclusive use of, the resource (Starr and Yngvesson 1975). Litigants are forced to rank-order their priorities.

In her description of disputing in an Ecuadorian village, Forman (1972) analyzes into separate categories cases involving people who have multiplex, ongoing relationships and who are disputing specific kinds of issues. She argues that different issues generate the strategies employed by the disputants regardless of type of relationship, and that the apparently desired outcomes were also different. The noncompromise outcomes involved land and other important property, and prestige and access to power and influence within the community—all dealing with scarce resources. Forman points out that there is no reason to believe that people involved in these zero-sum strategies fail to recognize the potential, or actual, damage of their strategies to their relationships with their adversaries. Again, in situations in which the object of the dispute is most highly valued, the social relationship will be sacrificed. A cost-benefit accounting approach, as outlined by Forman, forces one to view the justice motive from the perspective of the litigants, rather than from that of the third-party decision maker solely.

Scarce resources have generally been defined in material terms (e.g., land, money, control over women). But as Rothenberger, Starr, Ruffini, and Todd all note in this volume, nonmaterial resources may also be considered scarce: honor, pride, prestige, power, valor. Here we are dealing with a rank-ordering of priorities in the cultural dimension. Certainly, in the Ghanaian setting described by Lowy, money is in short supply; but this factor is balanced by another scarce resource, put into context in the saying that "A good name is worth more than money."

We can predict that the level of conflict will probably increase with real or perceived scarcity. Certainly the response or forum that is used to achieve a solution will vary with actual conditions of scarcity or abundance. The Hopi Indians could use avoidance as a technique to handle Navajo expansion as long as there was plenty of land to move into (Cox 1968). The situation changed significantly when Navajo population figures rose. Avoidance was no longer an adaptive way for the Hopi to handle poaching.

Distribution of Power

It is perhaps obvious to note that power and control over scarce resources are interconnected and relevant to disputing, and yet there has been little systematic discussion of law and the distribution of power in either the sociological or the anthropological literature. This is surprising, since it is apparent that legal structures affect the distribution of power in so many societies, and since our own society is one in which the distribution of power so thoroughly affects the legal structure. We need to understand the processes whereby disputing mechanisms maintain and legitimize the distribution of power, and with the means by which the powerful control disputing mechanisms.

National law is a mechanism and a process that may be used to distribute or centralize power or to legitimate and maintain power groups. So too it is with law in economically simple, preliterate societies. In our studies of small-scale societies from New Guinea to Turkey and Sweden, we have found situations in which local law favors dominant parties. We have also come across tactics invented by local peoples to increase the possibilities for equity. Many years ago Barton (1919) described a system of fines among the Ifugao of the Philippines which was organized according to the ability of each class to pay. The Zapotec (Nader 1969b) require the powerful to be more responsible than the powerless and thus would penalize the rich who steal more severely than the poor. The weaker parties find avenues of redress that may be perceived as competitive with the disputing mechanisms controlled by the dominant parties. In the Ghanaian town of Koforidua, Lowy (1971) describes the varieties of access that people have, ranging from courts to supernatural processes.

What is important about plural or multiethnic societies is that one segment of the population imposes or endeavors to impose its norms on other segments that do not accept them but are coerced to conform. In monoethnic homogeneous communities, however, there is also use of power, and here we speak of relative power. The landowner father in rural Turkey may retain almost total control over his tenant-farmer son. In Lebanon the outcome of a dispute in a Sunni village may revolve about how people are related. The "insider" group in a rural Bavarian village or in a Scandinavian fishing village is composed of persons of higher status in the community, persons who control access to several remedy agencies in which conflicts and disputes may be processed. Among the Lenje in Zambia, Canter points out, women are treated as legal minors in marital disputes, but as nonminors in disputes which do not devolve about marital problems.

The degree to which law functions as a power equalizer depends on a number of factors, such as who controls the setting of norms or the court or moot organization, and whether there is easy access to adversarial representatives such as lawyers. There is in all societies some contradiction between the ideology governing legal structure and how such structures operate in reality. However, gross contradictions are most likely to appear in communities characterized by social and cultural diversity.

Clearly, law functions to equalize power, to ensure fairness, but also to legitimize the dominance relations of some cultures or subcultures over others. The examples in this volume, however, suggest that in isolated indigenous societies a variety of functions may appear, but that in societies characterized by stratification and cultural diversity the weight of law as equalizer appears light in comparison to the power derived by the already powerful from routine actions of law.

In small, homogeneous societies there is a kind of social control that stems from the fact that people in conflict know each other and share a broad range of interpersonal ties and consensus about power relations. Individuals are dependent on each other for their social welfare. In industrialized societies there is a general absence of the kind of community social control usual in isolated societies. When individuals are no longer dependent on each other for their welfare, the tendency is for the powerful to manipulate legal means for their exclusive advantage.

The motives in using disputing mechanisms are varied. Investigating the conflict resolution process from the point of view of the litigant forces us to think in terms of a variety of mechanisms. As Lowy puts it (personal communication): "We are forced to drop the assumption that litigants use remedy agents merely or even primarily to resolve specific incidents of conflict. We no longer see the court as an institution devoted to clearing up 'social messes,' but rather as an arena in which litigants are engaged in behavior with diverse meaning." It is, as we shall see, the quest for power that sometimes motivates people to use disputing forms.

Aims of the Actors

As part of our focus on interactional aspects, the Berkeley Law Project group has stressed that the perspective of the litigant must be treated as of at least equal importance to that of a third party—the judge, for example.

There is a special importance to be derived from treating the participants in the disputing process as deserving of equal sociological attention. People who write about the judicial process and the judicial decision as if the outcome were solely the product of a third party, a judge, miss the sociological relevance of the courtroom as an interactive arena. In Duane Metzger's examples from Mexico (1960) we see that decisions are of one sort when all courtroom actors are members of the same Indian community, but quite something else if one of the actors is a Ladino.

In examining the disputing process we can distinguish among the values, aims, strategies, and goals of the various actors or we can look at the actors as members of a group and analyze their coalition patterns (Metzger 1960). A litigant may be willing to lose a skirmish if, in the end, he wins the war. A judge may be willing to compromise a difficult case if the peace of the village is at issue (Nader 1969b). A decision maker may be a bureaucratic representative of the national government or, as in Parnell's description for Mexico, a local-level authority whose loyalties are bound into neither the national system nor the local system of relations, but into personal ambition.

"Going to court" may have different meanings for people in different status/role relations. Going to court in Ghana may ostensibly be to maximize the plaintiff's monetary payoff; but more importantly it may be a way to elicit an apology or a settlement out of court. In the Turkish village, a villager may go to court to "neutralize" rank differences between himself and his opponent.

The availability of alternative forums for dispute processing may help a litigant to maximize his ability to achieve his aims. Simply threatening to use the Italian legal system may force the disputant's opponent to settle through informal channels. Individuals and institutions participating in the transactional network described by Parnell for Mexico may activate this network when the formal legal structure does not serve their aims. The Lebanese in the villages described by Witty and Rothenberger have the state system to fall back on, as do the peoples in most of the other societies described here as part of the nation-states, though they may regard it as only a last resort.

Access to Forums

People all over the world who are sufficiently motivated by what they think is an injustice will go to great lengths to find a way to right a wrong.

We have been concentrating on understanding how people respond to situations which they feel are unjust. What one does about an injustice or felt injustice, whether it be vandalizing, ripping-off, or seeking compensation or punishment, is directly related to what forums are available and how they operate. Access then becomes a key concept.

Among the Zapotec of Oaxaca, Mexico, expectations of access are such that a Zapotec is irritated at having to wait a few hours to be heard in a court. In a Washington, D.C. "ghetto" a black woman was incredulous that the newly opened office of legal assistance expected her to wait a month for an appointment to discuss a consumer problem. Slow access is no access, and some say it is the fastest way to lose potential legal clients (Conn 1977). In addition, there appears to be no positive correlation between high standard of living and the availability of forums; witness the United States. If one is powerless in the courts, one may try elsewhere, as did the lady in the Washington ghetto. Among the Zapotec the disputing system is characterized by a series of interdependent mechanisms, but access to or success in one system does not determine access to the others (Nader 1977).

Political organization plays an important role in limiting or increasing the availability of forums. The organization of government into ever more "inclusive" levels (cf. Pospisil 1958) is a familiar model in the West. Such organization not only has an impact on the availability of alternative remedy agencies to hear the same kinds of complaints, either originally or through appeal process, but it also has an impact on the costs of utilizing such a system.

Canter points out that the Lenje of Zambia use a range of remedy agents in a hierarchical order, and that this order is established by the remedy agents themselves, who insist on hierarchical dispute processing. The Ghanaians, Lowy points out, also have a hierarchical arrangement in the court system, but other nonhierarchical alternatives are also present. In Sardinia (Ruffini 1974), shepherds have to choose between two competing political systems—the Italian and the Sardinian. Though the Sardinian shepherds prefer to avoid use of the formal Italian system, and most choose to resort to the informal, local-level system, the threat of escalating disputes by bringing them to the attention of the Italian police and courts provides the shepherd with an additional bargaining tool that can be used to achieve a more advantageous settlement.

The absence of forums may be crucial. The lack of third-party institutional arrangements for disputing among the Jalé of New Guinea leaves the question of peace or escalation dependent on the effectiveness of kinship and residential networks. When these break down, intravillage conflict often degenerates into intervillage warfare.

Time

The dimension of time is the essence of process. Several "functions" of time in the disputing process can be identified: the delay to either avoid decision making or to cool out a case, and the delay that culiminates in a number of "saved up" cases to increase the strength of a case on which action is finally taken. The first views time as a strategy for delaying decision making, or for avoiding it entirely. In some societies a defendant in a civil case may repeatedly request, and receive, continuances of a case as part of his overall strategy for winning. Starr (1968) has shown how continual delay in Turkish court proceedings may increase the cost of these proceedings to such an extent that capitulation by one of the parties is inevitable. Years of delay in American court cases leads one to believe that an improved standard of living does not extend to quick justice.

Delay may also provide litigants with time to reexamine their respective strengths and weaknesses. In the community studied by Yngvesson (1970) action on disputes and conflicts was repeatedly delayed until a general consensus could be achieved among members of the community (cf. Frankenberg 1957). Disputants may be able to utilize additional time to redefine the issues in dispute or to achieve a catharsis by "talking the problem to death."

Timing is crucial for the individual fisherman, since it involves a choice as to whether to proceed to the next step of the process. Among the Australian aborigines, Williams reports (1973) their belief that "time should . . . mediate an offense and an act of retaliation or of resolution; immediate reaction is at the least inappropriate, and in some situations may constitute an offense in itself. Aborigines regard 'rushing' or any indication of haste as bad form . . ." (p. 171).

Still another function of time is pointed out by Canter in this volume. Delays in prosecuting cases, in this instance, may be the result of a litigant's "saving up" grievances and conflicts in order to be able to build a stronger case for future prosecution. When the situation appears ripe, the claimant comes into battle armed with all his "saved up" cases.

Time is also a factor in terms of the amount of it allotted for hearing cases in a particular forum. Lowy contrasts the time given to hearing cases before the Reconciliation Commission with what the Ghanaian courts afford, and the impact of this difference on the decisions. Here we are dealing with *enough* time to air the issues, to get at the basis of a complaint.

Costs

The question of the costs involved in pushing an action has been noted in our discussion of the structure of social relationships. On a more general level, however, costs pure and simple—outside the domain of scarce resources and social relationships—may be considered separately. Costs may be sociological, psychological, or economic in nature. Physical distance from the court or remedy agent may be an important factor. Greater distance requires greater outlay of economic and time resources in order to present a dispute before a remedy agent; and this cost may increase almost exponentially if to it is added the cost of transporting witnesses and/or supporters to the forum, the costs of obtaining evidence, or the costs of the proceedings themselves (if the litigant should lose).

The possibility of further escalation as a cost must also be considered. The simple airing of a grievance may engender others, and lead directly to escalation. If an individual takes another to court, or goes to the police or some other remedy agent, he must be able to predict with some certainty that he will not lose more in the long run than he gains in the short run. According to Ruffini (1974) the Sardinian shepherd who has lost sheep to a thief may find that his chances of recovering part or all of his flock are practically nil if he reports the theft to the police. Instead, he prefers to utilize more informal channels—the *baracelli,* comprising an island-wide network of informal social relationships—in an effort to get his sheep back. Going to the police might well result in feud; and the shepherd who utilizes that channel may find that he loses status within the community or, worse yet, that he is ostracized entirely (sociological and psychological costs), with no hope of ever recovering his animals.

Koch (1974: 89) provides another example, noting that in Jale society, "property damage—including the wounding of dogs and pigs—initially calls for repair or restitution by the responsible party. If such claims remain unsatisfied, the grievance can precipitate a confrontation that may lead to injuries and even killings. As the scope of a conflict enlarges, support and alliance structures determine the involvement of more people in the dispute and lead to the participation of the parties' kinsmen, men's house groups, neighbors, and trading friends from other villages."

Psychological costs have thus far proven difficult, if not impossible, to measure, although they be the most important, just as the impact of stress on bodily health has been recognized to be crucial, yet problematic to measure. Lowy notes that going to court in Ghana may not only involve direct costs of filing an action but may also result in confusion and great psychological costs to court users. This cost may further be exacerbated by the plaintiff on appeal, who incurs further debt if he loses. The other side of the coin is reflected in the title of a classic paper (Gibbs 1963), "The Kpelle Moot: A Therapeutic Model for the Informal Settlement of Disputes." In this society the costs of not going to moot would be great.

The Cultural Dimension

When we speak about the cultural dimension we are referring to the domain of ideology, values, and attitudes, all within the realm of perception and cognition. With the exception of a few studies, such as Hoebel (1954), Gluckman (1965), Graburn (1969), and Spradley (1970), work on disputing has mostly dealt with social relations, social structure, and social networks. The cultural perspective on the study of law requires that we discover the native or "inside" point of view, and sometimes this means a redefinition of the very domain we are looking at. As Graburn (1969) points out for the Eskimo, "no law, no crime." This same value is expressed in Western law—from Roman through Anglo-American common law (and statutes, too)—in the legal maxim *nulla poena sine leges* (without a law, there is no crime).

Practically all of the essays in this volume point out that every disputing action has its ideological or cultural component. Deviant acts themselves are culturally defined, while acceptable behavior centers around particular social norms. How far an individual or group may stray from norms is dependent on the structure of the culture. The Bavarians use the concept of character to explain social and economic failure and the consequences and accompanying frustrations of such failure. The Sard believe that livestock theft is an act of valor rather than the crime that Italian national law takes it to be, and they negotiate such theft. The Lenje of Zambia have measures of competence which inform us of their standard for legal institutions: "If the magistrates' courts were working they would have decreased the frequency of cattle rustling." The villages of Loani, Mexico, measure their own competence in dispute settlement in contrast to the state legal system and they resort to involuted tactics to resist the involvement of outside judicial agencies in village affairs. Such evaluations are based on cultural values which measure competence in terms that the consumers of law can understand—for example, an award of restitution to the offended. Among the Atlantic fishermen in our sample the example of the burning down of the station people's property bears this point out. The "insiders" in this fishing community had much wider latitude in breaches than the "outsiders" had.

Many of the papers in this volume refer to the insider/outsider dichotomy which describes the dualistic arrangement of categories or groupings of individuals found in the communities studied. Most of these categorizations are based on emic categories—"fishermen" (Yngvesson), "character" (Todd), "child of the place" (Witty), "shepherds" (Ruffini)—categories which cut villages into "we's" and "they's." Each category has its own normative/symbolic system, its own standard for the right and proper behavior. Canter's discussion of ethnicity as a factor in achieving a mediated settlement is informative here, for it links a number of the other studies in addressing the question of access to remedy agents. In his paper Canter notes that to be Lenje in a district with a Lenje majority is to have a wide network of kinship, social, and residential ties. To be Lenje is to have an advantage—not only an advantage in language, in higher social status, in personal knowledge of others' past behavior but, most importantly, an edge in access to conflict-resolving forums. This same advantage is found to exist among all members of the "insider" or "we" category in dually organized societies, for they are part of the "haves," and because they are, they come out ahead (Galanter 1974).

Ghanaian proverbs reveal the ideology of disputing in the town of Koforidua: "You should not achieve ten before your neighbor achieves nine"; "if you pull a string to hard it will break"; "if you pursue your own sweet case you do bad"; "a good name is worth more than money."

Symbols lie at the very basis of dispute processing. Family loyalty, obligation for past care, sentiment, and shame are often used in arguments in which family decisions are framed among the Zambian Lenje. Qualities such as courage, revenge, sagacity, wiliness, and acuteness help to define the Sard shepherd as a capable man or a brave man, one who is not foolhardy; and it is the brave, the capable, person who is able to call upon his kinship and friendship networks for help in solving problems. As Rothenberger points out in his essay, land, a premium resource in the village he studied, is less a basis for dispute than honor and shame. As with other peoples described in this volume there is a cultural constraint against airing grievances outside the community. In fact, taking a dispute outside informal village channels, i.e., out of the hands of local indigenous dispute-processing mechanisms, can lead to ostracism, censure, and an even wider range of negative sanctions.

Discovery of the cultural dimension, whether through folk categories like "character" (Todd), "honor" (Rothenberger), or "valor" (Ruffini) or through distinctions like that which Lowy uses between "argument" and "case," or which Yngvesson, Witty, and Todd use between "insiders" and "outsiders," opens a door to reveal how informants perceive the world, including the way in which they see and evaluate the machinery for processing disputes and decide on their course of action. Through this door we enter into the whole symbolic domain and into the manipulations that are used by peoples to minimize their risk of maximal loss.

Incorporation into National Legal Systems

Each one of the peoples in this volume lives within the boundaries of a nation-state, whether a new or an old nation. They all feel the power of a national legal system and choose to use it or not where they have a choice, or find ways of coping with it.

We have placed these descriptive essays in a sequence that ranges from societies that have virtually no contact with nation-state law (the Jalé of Indonesian New Guinea) to societies that exemplify increasing incorporation of local, traditional law (the villages of Zambia) or the increasing incorporation of state law into the local traditional system (the Zapotec and other Indian groups in Oaxaca, Mexico). It may come as a surprise that a Scandinavian fishing village should follow the Jalé of New Guinea or that a Bavarian village should follow shortly after that. However, throughout many industrialized nations we still find economically self-sufficient enclaves that either do not need or actively avoid contact with the national system. The last four essays, all concerned with active contact between local peoples and different parts of the national legal system, indicate the need for discussion of the direction of law.

THE DIRECTION OF LAW

What will the lives of the peoples in developing countries be like if they are increasingly integrated into state and national frameworks, but if proportionately more of their grievances result from contact with larger-scale impersonal organizations rather than from contact with their neighbors? A major problem for nations in the future will be that one of their most powerful tools for integrating and cementing national goals may be despised and rejected by the majority of the common folk. The reasons are manifold. There is intolerance which characterizes social and cultural pluralism; there is unequal power which becomes more pronounced in differentiated and stratified society; there is professionalism which alters the patterns of access to major dispute mechanisms; there is the problem of legal competence. Sometimes these life matters are all rolled into one cluster of variables—the distribution of power.

In all the societies described in this volume where the presence of the nation-state was predominant there are varying degrees of conflicting interest. Everywhere examples are plentiful of the members of national elites using the law to dominate and control. The law at points of intersection between national and local systems is not one that often serves the interests of local peoples. In many of the developing countries the least qualified legal personnel are sent to the hinterlands. In many, national law runs roughshod over customary law, and even worse, uses national law to legitimate acts of conquest and imperialism (Hahm 1967).

Much of the trouble in administering the law has arisen from a total ignorance or avoidance of the question of pluralism. Indeed, it is not unusual in history for the prejudices of the dominant ruling class to prevail over a society as law. As Pound stated the problem:

> Justice, which is the end of the law, is the ideal compromise between the activities of each and the activities of all in a crowded world. The law seeks to harmonize these activities and to adjust the relations of every man with his fellows so as to accord with the moral sense of the community. When the community is one in its ideas of justice, this is possible. When the community is divided and diversified, and groups and classes and interests, understanding each other none too well, have conflicting ideas of justice, the task is extremely difficult (1906: 339).

This ignorance or avoidance of pluralism is also intimately related to misuses and nonuses of the law that result in widespread negativism and disrespect for the law or in conflict between systems (as evidenced in the United States or in any young nation in which the law is in a "developmental state"). P. C. Hahm (1967: 146–66; 1968) discusses the development of attitudes of disrespect for the law in Korea as a result of traditional expectations of the political structure as well as of the initial encounters that Korea had with foreign law. In China (van der Sprenkel 1962) such negative attitudes towards the law and law courts resulted in village "antilitigation societies," even though in China

> . . . the major control over individuals is in the hands of the immediate groups to which they belonged. . . . Matters would first be dealt with by those best able to know both the facts of the case and the local law, and the majority of cases would go no further. This was one way of providing for the great diversity of custom throughout the area of China, whereas to have charged the official courts with the whole burden of applying law would have required much more costly administration and given rise to problems of elaborate codification (van der Sprenkel 1962: 119).

Antonio Pigliaru (1959) describes the conflicting system of law found in Sardinia, where the vendetta is a legal system in competition with the state. The traditional system does not incorporate laws of the state that are not coherent with its system. It behooves the anthropologist to query under what conditions diversity is tolerated by the state. Ehrlich (1936: 14) provides us with one hypothesis: "It is only when the state has grown extremely powerful and has begun to tend towards an absolute form" that the idea arises "of making the state the authoritative, and in course of time the sole, source of law."

The simple recognition of pluralism has sometimes helped us to "make sense" of behavior defined as deviant by the state. Whyte's early study (1955) makes sense of gang behavior by viewing the gang not so much as a deviant group but rather as a subculture whose members are conforming to the norms of that subculture. In a similar vein Sutherland develops his theory of crime (1949) by means of the concepts of homogeneity and vertical pluralism: "criminal behavior is learned in association with those who define it unfavorably . . . a person engages in such criminal behavior if, and only if, the weight of the favorable definitions exceeds the weight of the unfavorable definitions" (1949: 234).

The greatest bulk of the literature on pluralism and law has dealt with the "problem" of pluralism in the new nations—societies whose legal systems reflect their former colonialism. Under colonialism pluralism was considered a way to block or control by dividing and conquering. Western colonial administrators with little or no training in local, traditional law were sent to colonial outposts and were expected to oversee courts and moots operating according to local law where that local law did not conflict with the law of the colonial power. After the demise of the colonies and the creation of new states, the power supporting plural legal order was replaced, for the most part, by a "national" centralized government whose explicit aims were to use the law as a means of resolving the "pluralism problem."

The motivation of new states is of a different sort from that of the colonial powers and has its roots deeply planted in a hypothesis that, although largely untested, is treated as if it were God's Truth. The hypothesis is that national success (which is taken to mean economic development), indeed, national existence, depends on creating a homogeneous people and that the best way to do this is by means of the law, usually law imported from the West. There is also something that smacks of sympathetic magic here, the idea that if these nations import a legal system or code from a progressive country, they too will have at least the seeds of progress and modernity. L. Friedman (1969) presents a challenging critique of this position, which is based largely on "belief" rather than evidence.

It may well be that in a more realistic view the engineering of legal development would be seen as a dominant/subordinate acting out of conflict resulting from disparate values and from competition for power. In the new nations new loci of power are developing and consolidating, and the law is often used as a means to consolidate power positions. As Friedman points out, "importance of law is sometimes part of a political revolution" (1969: 47).

It has not been uncommon for scholars to accept the premise that a society must have one law controlling the behavior of all its members (in spite of the fact that no society does, most emphatically not the societies whence these scholars come). Pospisil comments on the history and validity of this idea (1967). There is very little in the literature, however, on the consequences of such an idea, on the impact that it has had on dealing with practical problems faced by the new nations and even here in the United States. The validity of the notion that homogeneity, the state, success, and progress, all go hand in hand can be challenged only by charting the consequences in particular case studies. In a stratified society the ruling elite have much to gain by invoking homogeneity, since it is their culture, or that to which they have adapted, which sets the standard for homogenization.

The question of what constitutes illegal behavior becomes debatable in societies where peoples of differing ways of life, with differing expectations and priorities, live under one central "legitimate" political authority. One part of the population of such a society is usually attempting to assert its authority over other parts. The situation we have described for colonies or new nations is not unlike that in the more technologically "advanced" countries where those with technological education may come to feel, unconsciously or consciously, that they have the right to make decisions affecting the welfare of all in their society. In any society, then, we have subcultures with their own systems of law, and the various subcultures may be in conflict with one another, one segment usually imposing, or trying to impose, its values on others who are forced to conform to them (Barnes 1961). It is not, as Hoebel (1954) would have it, that in a society some individual or group is recognized socially, that is, by the society as a whole, as having the privilege of applying physical force.

In the development of law, at least that part that is consciously engineered, the "realities" of the situation are most often *not* absorbed as part of the data crucial to realistic planning. It is one thing to recognize that law is not, in fact, a monopoly of the state; it is another matter, and one that desperately requires cognizance of the "realities," to agree on the consequences of the objectives of a centralized state monopoly, for example, the assurance of the speed of justice, and the access of people to the legal forums. Rights without access to forums are no rights at all.

Sardinia is a place where state law functions as the legitimate law and where alongside this state law we have a working de facto Sard shepherd system of law. The Italian state views the Sard shepherds as lawless. The shepherds view the state law as something foreign and not responsive to their daily needs (Ruffini 1974). State law seems unnatural, as it is imposed from without, while their own law emerges from their own setting and seems natural. The shepherds argue that state law is not attuned to their reality, and in describing that other system of law Sards use adjectives such as arbitrary, expensive, time-consuming, corrupt (Ruffini 1974). They are more generous in describing their own system.

Ruffini's work deals mainly with how cattle theft is handled by the two systems, both of which the anthropologist can afford to call legal. What is it to steal cattle? What is theft to these Sards? The responses stress the element of distribution; perhaps the element of distribution is a necessity in a system where scarcity rather than abundance is the norm. As stated by one Sard (Ruffini 1974), "The providence of God being merciful to all his creatures, how would he allow it that the shepherds of Gallura possess 500, 800 or 1000 sheep, while we have little flocks of a hundred? Wherefore, if we, through deceit or bravery, can steal from them some hundreds, we help, at least in part, to [distribute property]."

In another response from a shepherd (Brigaglia 1971:186–88) we learn, "If somebody steals my flock, he steals my flock, he does not offend me. It depends, depending on who he is, he offends me, and how he steals, and why . . ."

Cattle theft is not an offense; it is, in Brigaglia's terms, "only a movement of something from one place to another." Ruffini (1974) concludes that to the Sard shepherd "cattle theft is not regarded as a crime, but as the source of a dispute, which should be settled amicably without resort to the state." It seems obvious that such attitudes would influence the forms and styles of justice that are used, whether in Sardinia or elsewhere.

An understanding of how justice operates in the context of native attitudes and values is crucial to any constructive analysis of the consequences of certain directions of legal development. Canter (1976) describes cattle-rustling cases which took place in the chieftaincy of Mungule in the Central Province of Zambia. Mungule, a multiethnic area, is the home of the matrilineal Lenje-speaking people. In this area there exists a sharp dichotomy between the settlement processes applicable to civil and criminal cases. Civil cases, such as divorce, adultery, petty theft, land disputes, and the like, have been left to the local court, which settles disputes primarily by unwritten and yet changing customary law elaborated by statutes and legislation. In contrast, criminal cases must be heard at magistrates' courts in the urban centers. Such hearings follow a form dictated by the unified criminal code, a code imposed originally by the British. For at least the past twenty years the people of Mungule have taken cattle-rustling cases out of the community to the magistrates' court in the urban center, and during this period cattle-rustling cases have increased. By 1970 the increase in the number of such cases and the concomitant lack of deterrence by the judgments of the magistrates' court precipitated a local demand that cattle rustlers should be tried by the local court, not taken outside the community.

Under customary law situations, if an action does not work another solution is sought. What was happening here was that local standards of workability could not apply in measuring the competence of the national legal system, which like our own has no rigorous way of measuring competence. In the Lenje courts two procedures to effect a just decision were in conflict: those of proof and those of sanction. The local moots and courts perceived the burden of proof to be distributed between the litigants, each of whom represented himself. In the magistrates' courts the use of solicitors placed the burden of proof heavily on the plaintiff. The second point of contrast and misunderstanding was in the area of sanctions. The local system was primarily based on compensation and group responsibility, in the normal course of events. Self-help was not part of the usual proceedings. The magistrates' courts, on the other hand, used punitive sanctions, involving years in prison at hard labor; compensation for the theft was perceived as only a secondary consideration and often was postponed for years. The way the local peoples measured the success or failure of magistrates' courts was simple: if cattle rustling decreased in frequency, the national court was a success; since it did not, it was a failure. The response of the locals was increased self-help, resulting in solutions which were often devastatingly damaging and disruptive. The national officials responded in turn by increasing the maximum penalty for convicted cattle rustlers from seven to fifteen years at hard labor.

The situation of pluralism need not always result in negative effects on local peoples, and indeed may be manipulated by local folk to their own advantage. Witty (1975) conducted research in a small Lebanese village of 900 people, a community which contains both Christians and Shia Moslems. Both groups use the national court in a nearby town as a means of changing local norms and behaviors without involving themselves too much in the formal legal system. According to Witty, the presence of the court here is incorporated into the means by which an individual may settle his problems locally. He may use the procedures outside the village to humiliate his opponents and to change alliances and power patterns in the village. In the situations she describes, national law is used in an active attempt to gain power within the village. Such procedures are usually not followed in cases of violence, however, because court manipulation produces no valued results; they are also avoided in cases in which it is important to the villagers to achieve ideal patterns of social justice. These ideals are often frustrated in the national courts for reasons common to Americans: no money, no access, and no legal expertise. One Lebanese villager who was unable to collect 7,000 pounds from an urban shopkeeper waited seven years to collect, until his son completed law school.

Canter tells us that among the Lenje a dispute can be handled through the dispute settlement process, which follows all expected procedures and laws, and the process can still be considered "unjust" because social expectations and cultural presumptions of dispute processing have been ignored. The action of "judging well" is informed by social context. In the Lebanese example presented in Witty's paper, the litigant was trying to manipulate the political and the social context in an attempt to change existing power relationships and his position vis-à-vis lawmen and other villagers. The man who would wait seven years to collect a debt was motivated by a strong sense of justice, made effective only by self-help of a different sort than among the Lenje.

It is not simply heterogeneity which brings about legal pluralism. Even within more homogeneous cultures alternative justice systems are usually available. The variety of motives for pursuing a dispute—to gain power, to obtain scarce resources, to gain justice, to compensate for a wrong—almost ensures that this will be so. It does seem that whenever two or more legal cultures apply to the same group, there is what Bohannan (1957, 1965) refers to as a "working misunderstanding." In all these pluralistic situations it appears that fairness or something called "justice" is difficult for the national legal system to achieve; the local litigants usually do not understand what is going on or why one decision was chosen over another. It is all the worse when the dispute involves litigants of unequal status or different group membership, for in such situations the grievance is usually heard within the legal sphere of the dominant culture, a culture whose values are usually quite alien to one of the parties. Equitable decisions, some would argue, are impossible in highly stratified areas, and certainly justice as a motive in decision making is not possible if the law sees legal justice (or "the law") rather than social justice as its end.

Law between Strangers

The disputes described in this volume are for the most between people who know each other or who at least share some common social and political linkages. The social situation may remain stable for years or even decades, but in nations where industrialization grows, where not only production patterns change but consumption patterns as well, there are dramatic effects on dispute resolution (Berthoud 1972). In a nation such as the United States there is an increase in the contact between strangers of unequal power. When most of the actual and potential disputes are between strangers rather than between parties who know one another, certain structural changes occur in the law. Courts decline in personnel relative to population and growth and need; their function shifts from dispute settlement to the arrangement of economic transactions, access decreases, the true plaintiff becomes the victim, the state becomes the plaintiff, the function of law as a power equalizer diminishes, and the role of law is reduced relative to issues that affect the quality of everyday life. Extrajudicial processes will develop in direct response to these trends; so will self-help procedures.

The problems of order in a face-to-face society are both similar to and different from those in a modern, industrialized, faceless society increasingly dominated by large multinational corporations, by technologies with broad impacts over time, and by large governmental bureaucracies. The differences are reflected in the general absence of the kind of social control by which order is traditionally maintained: people in dispute know each other and share a broad range of interpersonal ties. When people in dispute do not know each other, when there is an imbalance in power, and when professionals are heavily on the side of powerful plaintiffs, formal institutions cease to serve the needs of the many.

There are various ways of measuring the adequacy of a national legal system—whether the needs of the consumers of justice are met in the handling of individual or block complaints. First, there is the measure of fairness which Pound (1906) pointed to as difficult to achieve in a stratified heterogeneous society, particularly if the plaintiff becomes a victim and is not a recipient of restitution. Another measure of adequacy is access. Professionalism, lack of information, cost, time, distance, shame, and bias are some of the factors which account for access and use patterns in complex societies. More important than access is reception. Does the court continue to receive dispute cases, or will the change in the courts from being predominantly dispute settlement agencies to being routine administrative agencies become commonplace in the developing world as well as in the United States except for matters of divorce, custody, and so on (Friedman and Percival 1976)? If we look at the developing countries we can see that the changes that must have taken place in the West over the last hundred years or so are happening in a matter of decades. In addition to the issues of fairness, access, and reception, we in the West have had changes over time in the status and relationships of litigants, such as the change from plaintiff to victim status, from an active to a passive role for the plaintiff, which also affects and enhances in some ways the role of defendant.

In the Western world, law is generally considered something independent of other aspects of social life, or at least not assimilative of other aspects of life, and as R. Abel notes (1973) it is important to recognize how this separation has come about as well as that it is intrinsic to Western notions of law. Sir Henry Maine (1963) spoke about the gap between the law and social needs and opinions. Islam traditionally recognized this gap and attempted to close it by recognizing customary law. Sudanese Muslim judges worry about applying national law in areas where customary law has prevailed. How, they argue, can a judge resolve a Dinka marital case if he does not understand Dinka customary law? Few Italian judges worry about similar problems in Sardinia—Sard law is not really law at all.

Western law, whether in code form or some other form, has affected practically all the countries of the world. We are likely to have further expansion of the idea that law is something independent of the social system in which it is set. Young lawyers of the developing nations who are trained in Western-type law schools and versed in the custom of legal precedent will be part of this expansion. These specialists will extend the misunderstanding that Bohannan (1957, 1965) speaks about, as the oppositions are argued about—efficiency versus fairness, unintelligibility versus intelligibility, context-insensitive versus context-sensitive. People will react to a national legal system that does not respond to the needs of its customers: frustrated Turks will circumvent, the Lebanese will manipulate, the Ghanaians will elaborate, the Zambians will adopt self-help procedures—and so will Americans who feel that their access to law and justice is blocked. Our ghettos are full of examples: no access and lots of self-help. A self-help orientation will encourage an elaboration of alternatives; self-help will also increase violence and ripping-off the system.

One of the consequences of professionalism is the segregation of professionals from their clients, from the people they are supposed to serve. When this separation occurs the profession develops a life of its own, independent of its clients. There is no longer need to prove competence to clients, nor is there reason to communicate with them. For example, Aubert (1966) illustrates that the need for law professionals to communicate with each other is greater than their need to communicate with clients. In the case he wrote about, Norwegian housemaids could not themselves understand the housemaids' law which was designed to protect them.

The papers in this volume reveal the breadth of what is possible in law. Those who believe that order cannot be achieved without law in the Western sense will find that clearly this is not so. Those who believe that homogeneity by means of law is the best road to modernity will be disenchanted by the evidence. Those who believe that Western law best provides for equality before the law should watch the operation of law in a village court. Those who believe that small societies have no difficulties in devising peaceful settlements for disputes will find that the evidence contradicts them. What should be a hopeful sign for the future is the role that modern peoples have played in consciously designing constructive forums for justice. Engineering a legal system requires first that we listen to the needs of the participants, and second that we increase our tolerance for diversity. It requires further an understanding of power and conflicting interests. The world provides us with a laboratory of experiments in its forums for dispute.

ONE

PIGS AND POLITICS IN THE NEW GUINEA HIGHLANDS: CONFLICT ESCALATION AMONG THE JALÉ

Klaus-Friedrich Koch

AMONG THE Jalé people of Western New Guinea any conflict can escalate into a war. The original incident may be a quarrel among relatives, a disagreement about a boundary between neighbors, the abduction of a wife from a man in another village, or the failure to provide compensation for injuries in the form of pigs. In theory almost any conflict can be settled by restitution or indemnification rendered to the aggrieved party. In practice the political realities of interpersonal and intergroup relations often make it difficult to settle conflicts by peaceful means. I will explain these difficulties by describing a particular case that illustrates the main features of Jalé conflict management rather well.[1]

THE SETTING

The Jalé people, speakers of a language belonging to the Dani family (see Bromley 1967), have settled in compact villages along the valleys of the Jalémó region in the Central Mountains of Western New

Guinea, an area roughly delineated by the geographical coordinates of 138°15′ and 139°30′ east longitude and 4° and 4°20′ south latitude. Their subsistence depends on pig raising and on cultivating a variety of root crops and greens commonly found in the New Guinea Highlands. To supplement this diet they gather forest products and hunt birds and marsupials. Though land resources are plentiful, the prolonged fallow periods necessary for a recovery of the soil require periodic shifts of residence. Given an average crop season of eight to ten months, the Jalé leave their base villages about twice every year and take up residence in dispersed hamlets, which are usually the settlements of people from a particular ward, a demarcated section of the village.

Most villages are divided into two or more wards. These residential compounds consist of a cluster of domiciles, the largest of which is invariably the men's house. The men's house, also called the "sacred house," is the home of all initiated males of the ward. As the locus of much ritual activity, entry into this house and passage through its courtyard are prohibited for females and uninitiated boys. Only "men of knowledge" (who have passed a secondary initiation) can occupy one particular section of the house, the sanctum, where nets holding ritual paraphernalia are stored.

A family hut is primarily the home of a married woman and her uninitiated sons and unmarried daughters. In a polygynous marriage cowives with their children may maintain a joint household, but more frequently they live in separate huts. Other coresidents of a woman are likely to be her own or her husband's widowed mother, as well as her recently married daughter, her daughter-in-law, or her husband's brother's wife, who may stay with her until the husband of each has built his own family hut.

SOCIAL ORGANIZATION

The people divide their population into named exogamous moieties, each comprising a number of named sibs, whose members are widely dispersed over several valleys. A single men's house may be the home of several lineages belonging to different sibs. Agnatic descent defines membership in both moiety and sib and the right of residence in a ward. The solidarity of the corporate agnatic lineage and, by extension, that of the whole men's house group, is ritually reinforced through the initiation of its "sons." Rank relations are structured by prestige gained through the acquisition of ritual knowledge, age, and successful pig exchanges to the benefit of junior agnates and nonconsanguineal coresidents.

Marriages and compensatory payments made in connection with warfare represent the main occasions when so-called "big men" can advance their positions by providing pigs on behalf of their relatives and neighbors. The political role of the "big men" is limited. They serve as orators for their men's house at dances and at peace ceremonies, and they take a prominent position in dispute orations between neighboring wards. They do not, however, hold any judicial office that would oblige or enable them to settle disputes, either among members of their own ward or between wards and villages.

An Omaha type of kin classification and the prohibition of marriage with a member of one's mother's patrilineage produce a fourfold categorization of a person's relatives outside his family (Koch 1970). The first category comprises ego's own agnatic relatives; the second contains his mother's agnates; the third contains his sister's children; and the fourth consists of two sets of affines, one comprising a man's wife's agnates and the other his sister's husband and the husband's lineal kinsmen. Diverse jural relationships attach to the different roles a person maintains in this quadrifocal kinship web, which in polygynous marriages extends to additional lineages. Marriage, then, establishes a distinct set of affinal relationships with the agnatic descent group of the linking spouse. A woman's postnuptial home is normally in the ward of her husband's men's house. Thus, a viripatrilocal residence separates a married woman from her natal ward except in rare instances of ward endogamy or uxori-patrilocal residence.

The strict residential segregation of the sexes not only results in very different processes of socialization for boys and girls but also correlates with the rigid separation of men and women in political and jural affairs and in ritual life. The residents of a men's house constitute a political as well as a ritual community. In fact, the wards are the most inclusive political segments in Jalé society and form the principal war-making units in both intravillage and intervillage conflicts. In the absence of political and judicial offices, self-help—often in the form of violent retaliation—is an institutionalized method of conflict resolution when negotiation fails. If a confrontation develops into a fight between the parties' supporters and someone suffers an injury, the skirmish may mark the beginning of a round of battles and retaliatory raids lasting for weeks, months, and even years. Whether or not a dispute reaches this state of hostility depends largely upon relations of kinship and residence between the principal parties.

CONFLICT MANAGEMENT

In disputes within the patrilineage, the coresidents of the principals can exert a mediating pressure toward a peaceful settlement as long as the parties continue to live together. The intervention of coresidents and formal avoidance tactics between the principals tend to prevent forceful retaliation. The performance of a reconciliation ritual can repair the solidarity of a lineage if the parties have formally severed their relationship. However, when an agnatic descent group has moved to separate locations, the diverging territorial alignments of the principals impede peaceful procedures, and revenge actions become a likely choice for an injured party seeking redress. The involvement of two residence groups in a conflict weakens lineage solidarity, and acts of violent retaliation and countervengeance resemble the patterns of confrontation between villages or different wards, especially when a previous conflict has resulted in the residential separation of the parties. Furthermore, the absence of daily interaction delays or even precludes a final reconciliation of the principals.

Unlike conflicts within the lineage, conflicts between husband and wife endanger their conjugal relations but not the solidarity of a whole group. However, severe marital conflict also involves the woman's kinsmen because it threatens to disrupt the affinal exchange relationship that the marriage established. The wife's kinsmen share an interest in the continuation of the exchanges with the husband

and his agnates—who may have participated in the reciprocative gift transactions that validated the union—and thus both sides may seek a reconciliation of the spouses. In this situation the transfer of pigs and other gifts within the context of the existing exchange pattern represents a functional equivalent to the reconciliation rite terminating conflicts among agnatic kinsmen.

In conflicts between husband and wife, people other than the spouses' closest consanguineal relatives rarely intervene. On the other hand, in direct confrontations between affines each party can rely on the support of his men's house group. If the dissolution of the linking marriage severs the principals' affinal relationships, pig seizures become a common method of redress.

Conflicts between nonkin members of a ward can be managed peacefully as long as they actually live together in the same place and, especially, if hostilities with other groups demand concerted military action. But—as in conflicts within the lineage—a spatial separation of the parties inhibits negotiations and may encourage them to resort to force, which then tends to precipitate a chain reaction. However, if a person absconds from his ward to escape punishment after he has committed an offense, his departure may mitigate the injured party's wrath and thus alleviate the danger of revenge.

In disputes between unrelated members of neighboring wards, two factors may restrain the parties from resorting to forceful retaliation: the mediating efforts of a principal's coresidents who have affinal links to his opponent or to members of the opponent's men's house group, and the recognition that undisturbed garden work and effective defense against an outside enemy requires amity among neighbors. The relatively greater jeopardy experienced by foreign residents in interward conflicts signifies the importance of amicable relationships between autochthonous lineages for maintaining peace within the village community.

Unless a person has suffered bodily injury, a dispute between neighbors remains amenable to a compromise settlement through negotiation. Altercations, usually after dusk, bring a conflict to public attention and give the two sides a chance to express hostile sentiments in nonviolent fashion. In this situation "big men" have a chance to intervene, and, regardless of their residential association, they unfailingly appeal to both parties to exercise restraint. However, bodily injury in a retaliatory action tends to elicit a revenge attack, which often initiates a war. Yet the same factors that inhibit the outbreak of violence continue to operate in reducing the virulence of armed combat. If someone has been killed, one revenge death normally ends the fighting. Emigration of the person responsible for the war, like an offender's temporary abscondence in intraward conflicts, decreases the chance of further vengeance.

Although parties belonging to different villages may succeed in peacefully settling a conflict over, for example, an abduction, mistaken pig seizures, or rights to garden land, an unsuccessful verbal confrontation in these cases often leads to forceful retaliation, which is the usual method of seeking redress for adultery, wanton pig theft, and pillage of crops. Since in intervillage vengeance anyone's pig may be seized from the foraging grounds of the opponent's village, every dispute between strangers jeopardizes not only a party's coresidents but also his neighbors in other wards. Consequently, an unresolved conflict between individuals from different villages affects the political relationship between whole communities and often prevents any negotiation whatsoever if a new dispute arises between different persons in the two villages.

The probability that a confrontation will result in armed combat is generally greater the greater the geographical distance and the fewer the affinal relationships between the local groups involved. These same conditions also impede an early settlement when villages in different regions participate in a war. In this situation alliances are created by default rather than by considerations of affinity and traditional amity, and unsatisfied claims to compensatory pigs among allied wards greatly inhibit the conclusion of a peace treaty that all parties will honor.

The management of conflict among the Jalé cannot be understood without knowing how they establish a person's liability for harm caused to others. Jalé jural ideology deduces liability from a doctrine of "effective action." This means that the Jalé do not distinguish between intent, negligence, inadvertence, and accident as aggravating or extenuating circumstances. In evaluating only the consequences of the injurious act, they do not question a person's guilt or innocence—his psychological state—when they establish his formal liability, that is, his obligation to provide restitution or indemnity to the injured party. The recognition of personal responsibility influences merely the procedure by which the injured party seeks to obtain redress. In particular, kin and residential relationships between the parties determine if and how a person's responsibility for causing harm is translated into liability to provide indemnification. For example, the man who invites a neighbor to accompany him on a trading trip on which the neighbor falls from a cliff, or the husband whose wife dies in childbirth are as liable to pay indemnification in the form of "guilt pigs" as the man who kills somebody in a fight. In the first situation the Jalé reason that the fatal fall would not have occurred if the victim had not been induced to make the trip. The unhappy husband is held to have caused his wife's death by his penis, for if he had not copulated with her she would not have become pregnant and thus would not have died.

Although all three men are liable to provide the same compensation, the enforcement of the sanction will vary according to the social relationships involved. The kinsmen of the victim will be most lenient with the husband and will allow him more time to provide the required pig, especially if they are interested in continuing the exchange relationship that the marriage had established. They will insist on immediate indemnification from the neighbor on the trading trip, a man with whom they share less tangible interests. And they may not even accept a "wergild pig" from the slayer or his kinsmen—if, indeed, such an offer is made—and instead may contemplate blood revenge.

The same reasoning assigns blame for any injury or loss in the course of war to the parties to the original dispute. These two individuals, called the "men of the arrow's stem," are held responsible for every injury, loss, and death suffered by their allies, even if it was one of their supporters who inflicted the initial injury that triggered the war. Furthermore, a "man of the arrow's stem" is obligated to compensate his allies for their help with pork cut from a special pig, called a "parsley pig," which sometimes is also given to supporters in confrontations that ended in a scuffle.

In Jalé law, liability is not only absolute but is also corporate; that is, it is shared by the agnatic kin group of the party whose action caused the injury. Both concepts appear to correlate with the necessity of settling disputes by coercive self-help. If, in the absence of jural authorities, abscondence of the offender and alleged or actual accidents were to confer immunity, the maintenance of regulated social life would become precarious.

The following case illustrates how precarious a single conflict can be for continuing peaceful relations within a community and between villages. In spite of its complexity I have chosen to discuss it in detail because it deals so clearly with three important aspects of Jalé conflict management. First, it explains how a particular dispute generates new grievances between parties who were not involved in the original dispute. Second, it outlines the process by which alliances are created which draw other people into a conflict. And third, it elucidates the mediating effect of cross-cutting affinal relationships. (Numbers in parentheses identify the principal participants by their genealogical connections as shown in fig. 1.1. Names of places appear in fig. 1.2.)

ESCALATION: A CASE IN POINT

In 1959 Lóló (1), of the Womikma ward in Pasikni village, lived at a homestead away from the village together with his third wife, Óngkómen. Nearby, at the small hamlet of Suaxéi, an outlier of Womikma in the Walingkama area, lived his sons by his deceased first wife, Wielu (7), Talala, Esetmena, and Nalek (8), and his son by his divorced second wife, Jóxóliangke (6). One day Wielu, Lóló's eldest son, returned to Suaxéi from a trading trip, bringing pandanus kernels, which he shared with his father, brothers, and half-brother. Lóló felt that Wielu had given him the less delicious marginal sections of the fruit. They had an argument about the matter and parted in anger.

The following day Wielu harvested a fruit from another kind of pandanus tree which grows locally. Since Wielu was still angry with Lóló, he did not invite him to the meal, even though he had received the tree from

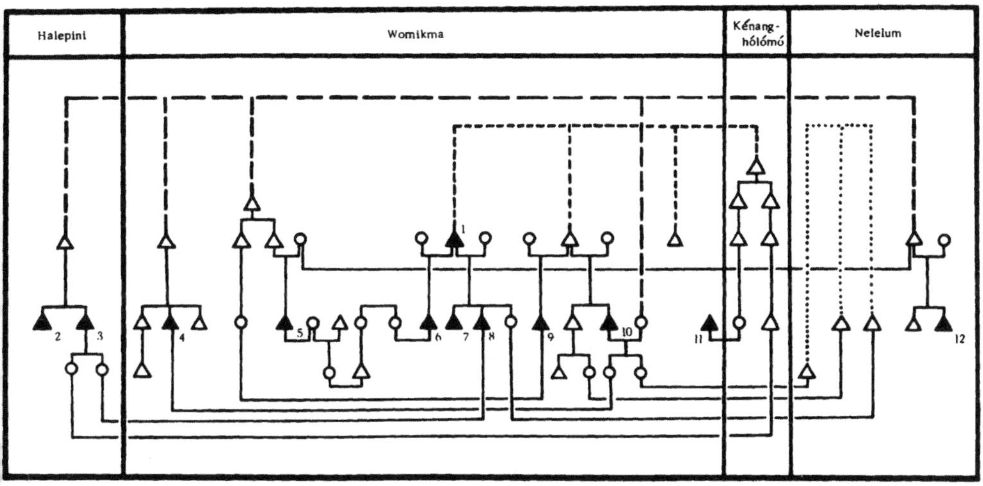

Figure 1.1. Genealogical relationships of participants from four Pasikni wards. Solid lines indicate marriage ( ) and descent ( ) links; broken lines indicate common sib membership. 1. Lóló, 2. Kuron, 3. Muriek, 4. Silóxóp, 5. Uluon, 6. Jóxóliangke, 7. Wielu, 8. Nalek, 9. Póve, 10. Ngajóxók, 11. Ésangko, 12. Jénguruk.

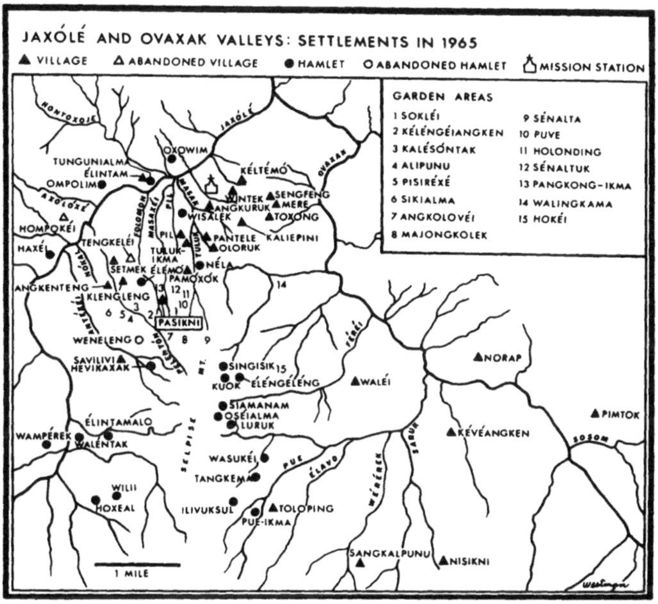

Figure 1.2. The Central Jalémó region, showing settlements in the Jaxólé and Ovaxak valleys in 1965.

his father. This demonstration of filial neglect so angered Lóló that he cut down the tree from which his son had taken the fruit, together with two others that he had given to him. He brought the remaining ripe fruits to his maternal kinsmen living in the village of Savilivi, who gave him in exchange the same kind of kernels that Wielu had obtained on his trading trip.

Back at his homestead, Lóló roasted the kernels in the company of a friend from Kaliepini, a nearby village. While the two men were busy at this task inside Lóló's men's house, Wielu appeared in the doorway and rebuked his father for cutting down the trees "instead of just taking the fruits if you got 'cramps in your stomach' " (a metaphor denoting extreme anger). Father and son cursed each other. Suddenly Wielu drew an arrow and shot at his father but missed him. Then, before Wielu could escape beyond reach of the arrows of his father and his friend, an arrow shot by the latter hit his thigh.

Wielu told his brothers about this encounter, and they decided to avenge the wound. At sunrise the following morning they hid in the vicinity of Lóló's homestead. When the unsuspecting Lóló appeared outside, his sons dashed forward and shot some arrows at him, forcing him to retreat into his house. Curious about the clamor, his wife Óngkómen looked out through the entrance of her own hut. When she began shouting, Esetmena shot her in the arm.

When the brothers had stalked off, Lóló and his friend, who was still with him, called for help from the villages of Mere, Toxong, and Sengfeng. Lóló had two main reasons for asking for support from these villages: his long, solitary residence in a homestead away from Pasikni had made him a frequent visitor at some of the men's houses in these other villages and, as an expert hunter, he had provided sacrificial marsupials for the initiation of several boys into these men's houses (as their "father" he could now depend on the boys' help). That same day a battle took place between Lóló's supporters and his sons, who were assisted by a few kinsmen of Talala's and Wielu's wives, both women from Toxong.

The following day Pasikni men joined the fight on both sides. The conflict between father and son had escalated into a war. On the third day of fighting Sangkéak, a man from Mere who had supported Lóló, was seriously wounded by an arrow shot by Jóxóliangke.

When he died the following morning, the people of Suaxéi immediately evacuated their hamlet and, carrying all their possessions, made their escape to Pasikni by a long, devious trek through the forest. They had hardly reached the village when a war party advanced toward it along the stream.

While the Pasikni men banded together for a battle outside the settlement, a single man by the name of Pólépóléjok from the village of Angkenteng appeared in the village and shot dead the Womikma man Póve (9). With this killing Pólépóléjok avenged the death of Sangkéak, who had sponsored his secondary initiation. Except for a few men with affinal links to Lóló, all Pasikni men who had originally supported him now helped their neighbors to drive the enemy from their village land. Póve's killing contributed to a fast retreat of the invaders.

For several years an uneasy truce existed in the valley, but by 1964 Esetmena, Nalek, and Jóxóliangke had resettled at Suaxéi. Talala went to live with his wife's kinsmen in Toxong, and Wielu built his own homestead at a place not far from Suaxéi. Lóló moved to Savilivi, where he and his wife lived with a distant maternal kinsman. In early 1964 a new war broke out in the valley between the villages of Pasikni and Savilivi. Lóló, as "man of the arrow's stem" and a resident in a hostile village, feared retaliation for the unrevenged death of Póve, and he returned to Suaxéi, where Esetmena, Nalek, and Jóxóliangke welcomed their father. They exchanged pigs and asked a medicine man to perform the reconciliation ceremony. Talala also participated in the rite, but Wielu refused to end his avoidance relationship, which had begun five years earlier with the pronunciation of a curse against his father during their ill-fated conflict.

Wielu also failed to provide a "guilt" pig to Póve's half-brother Ngajóxók (10) of Womikma, who could claim such indemnification from the "man of the arrow's stem" on his side. When, six years after the "pandanus war," as the conflict had become known in the Jaxólé Valley, Wielu still owed the pig, Ngajóxók decided to seek redress by force.

On July 29, 1965, Ngajóxók went to Suaxéi and seized a small pig belonging to Nalek. Ngajóxók was already cooking the animal inside his garden shed, located about halfway between Suaxéi and Pasikni, when Nalek began searching for it. Later that day someone told Nalek that, some time previously, Ngajóxók had stolen and eaten another one of Nalek's pigs. (The Suaxéi people had always thought that this pig had drowned in a river or fallen off a cliff.)

Nalek set out for Pasikni accompanied by his father-in-law, Muriek (3) of the Halepini ward in Pasikni, another Suaxéi resident. On their way they discovered thick smoke emanating from Ngajóxók's shed. While Nalek stayed behind, Muriek approached the place. Squatting down near the shed, Muriek asked Ngajóxók for a piece of ember to light his cigarette. Ngajóxók told him to wait a moment as he was just taking sweet potatoes from the oven. After a while Ngajóxók handed some of the food to Muriek through the entrance and gave him the desired piece of ember. Muriek pretended to walk off, but soon sneaked back to the shed and, peeping through an aperture in the wall, watched Ngajóxók remove meat from the oven and hide it on the logs stored above the fireplace. He walked back to Nalek and told him his discovery. Nalek now went straight to the shed, entered it, grabbed a pig's leg from the hiding place, and left without speaking a word to the surprised Ngajóxók.

The two men continued toward Pasikni, where they arrived in the late afternoon. Near the Womikma ward they found a pig that belonged to Najóxók. As Nalek struggled to tie a rope to its front leg, he was discovered by a small boy, whose father's brother had married one of Ngajóxók's daughters. The boy immediately informed Ngajóxók's wife, who rushed to the place where the two men were still struggling with the pig. She attacked Nalek with her digging stick. Muriek pushed the woman to the ground. Attracted by her screams, several Womikma people came to her help.

The noise of the fight drew men from other wards to the scene, among them Muriek's younger brother, Kuron (2) of Halepini. Soon the brawling developed into a tumultuous fight, with bows and arrows being used as lances, between Womikma men and their supporters from the Nelelum ward and several Halepinians, who assisted the two Suaxéi raiders.

As I watched the medley and listened to the altercations, I could not detect any reason for the particular composition of the two factions. However, a clear pattern later emerged when I discussed the case with informants and examined the genealogical relationships among the participants.

The most active fighters on Ngajóxók's side were his son-in-law, Silóxóp (4), and his brother, both of whom actually injured Muriek and Kuron. Affinal links also called for Ngajóxók's support by Nelelum men. One of them was betrothed to Ngajóxók's second daughter, and another had married the daughter of his deceased brother. Although Ngajóxók's wife came from Halepini, she had been the adopted daughter of a man who himself had settled there as a war refugee. Therefore, the Halepini men aligned themselves with Ngajóxók's opponent Muriek. The decisive role of affinity in conflicts extending beyond ward lines becomes even clearer during the next phase of the conflict.

The scuffle was still going on when Nalek suddenly ran away. When someone shouted, "He is going to kill Ngajóxók," many of the men pursued him. His opponents wanted to prevent the attack, and his supporters wanted to come to his defense. Ngajóxók had meanwhile hidden the pig meat in a thicket and had observed the fight from a ridge bordering the village. He decided to return to Womikma, but when he reached the path leading to the village, he was attacked by Ésangko (11), another Womikma man. The fight between the two men ended when Silóxóp and his brother intervened to escort Ngajóxók home.

Ésangko came late to join the scuffle because he happened to be visiting another men's house in the village when the fighting started. He had two reasons to side with the Suaxéi party: he had married the agnatic cousin of a man from the ward of Kénanghólómó, who was the husband of one of Muriek's daughters. These links involved him with Nalek in one intricate exchange network. Moreover, Ésangko held a grudge against Ngajóxók because he had never reciprocated a pig that he had once received from Ésangko's father.

Muriek and Nalek soon heard that Ésangko was in trouble because he had sided with them. They returned to Womikma and the inevitable altercation again evolved into a scuffle. Several elders from Halepini and Nelelum urged the fighters to stop and reminded them that Nalek was, after all, a Womikma boy and not just a stranger. They also warned that the dispute might turn into war. None of the men engaged in the scuffle heeded their admonitions.

Finally, Uluon (5), a Womikma resident and a sib brother of both Muriek and Silóxóp, ended the fight by a dramatic show of anger. Keeping his bow at the ready, he pointed the arrow toward the opponents as he stepped rapidly between them in repeated back-and-forth movements. His half-brother, Jénguruk (12) of Nelelum (whose father had married Uluon's widowed mother as his second wife), joined him in this performance. At the top of their voices the two men shouted again and again, "Stop the scuffle, don't go on!" They reprimanded the Womikma men for beating each other in front of their own men's house, for which Jénguruk's elder brother had once killed an enemy in revenge for the slaying of a Womikma man. Now that their own brother had been slain and eaten by the enemy, they should seek to revenge his death and bring a body to Nelelum instead of fighting among each other.

Meanwhile it had become dark, and everybody drifted back to his ward. Ésangko, who had stood aside from the scuffle weeping and complaining that nobody else from Womikma had helped Nalek, went to Kénanghólómó, his wife's natal ward, where he had built his family hut. He slept in the Kénanghólómó men's house for several weeks. When he returned to Womikma, his coresidents welcomed him and called the incident "something that has always happened."

Given the failure of the elders to end the scuffle, the successful intervention of Uluon and his brother, Jénguruk, both younger men, needs to be explained. Certainly the unrevenged death of their brother gave their complaints a considerable weight. However, I believe that Uluon's position as an affine to both parties was a more important factor. Póve, whose killing had caused the whole conflict, had married the daughter of Uluon's father's brother; and after Póve's death Uluon had generously invited his widowed cousin to live with her two children in his family hut. His relationship to Nalek derived from the betrothal of his adopted daughter, the child of his second wife, to a sister's son of the wife of Jóxóliangke, a man who was a uterine half-brother of Nalek. Since Jóxóliangke had adopted the boy after his father's death, he participated in the affinal exchanges between Nalek and his agnates and Uluon.

Jóxóliangke's position in the conflict prompted him to intervene when he heard of the fight after Nalek and Muriek returned to Suaxéi late in the evening. At that time he happened to be at his garden hamlet, located near Suaxéi, but he was the only member of Lóló's lineage who had retained his permanent residence at Womikma. Therefore, he had a personal interest in the settlement of the conflict. He could not defy his brothers, nor could he afford to jeopardize his place in the Womikma ward.

The following afternoon, Nalek returned to Womikma together with Jóxóliangke and Wielu. A discussion took place inside the men's house and lasted for several hours. Ngajóxók defended his seizure of the pig because of his rightful claim to compensation for the death of his brother, and he refused to make restitution. In vain Jóxóliangke and Wielu urged him to return a pig to Nalek. The three brothers left with the threat to harvest Ngajóxók's garden near Suaxéi.

A few days later Nalek delivered portions of a "parsley pig" to Halepini. Ésangko received the largest share.

Ngajóxók shared with his Womikma men's house group the meat of Nalek's pig, which he had hidden on the day of the fight.

On December 20, 1965, the Womikma men initiated the son of Ngajóxók's deceased brother into their men's house. Ngajóxók, who had adopted the boy, gave one of the pigs he received from the initiate's maternal kinsmen to Nalek. This gift settled the case.

To understand the obstacles to the settlement of a dispute without violent confrontation requires a comprehension of two critical problems in Jalé conflict management, which the events in this case elucidate with particular clarity.

This first problem is the "snowball effect" of inadequate procedures to deal with grievances. The absence of an authority capable of adjudicating conflicts creates situations in which even minor disagreements among agnates, such as a quarrel over a few nuts, may escalate the conflict into war between whole villages. The second problem is the potential of every retaliation to generate new grievances. Since a "man of the arrow's stem" incurs a liability for compensating all injuries and deaths suffered by his supporters, he may, by refusing to comply with this obligation to pay "guilt" pigs to the agnatic kinsmen of the victims, create a conflict between himself and his allies. This new enmity, in turn, entails a definite chance that forceful seizure of pigs will lead to further violence.

Whether or not one side resorts to armed combat depends entirely on the outcome of the confrontation following the seizure. As long as nobody is seriously injured in an ambush or a scuffle, an intraward conflict can still be settled in face-to-face negotiations between the principal parties. In the original dispute between Lóló and his son Wielu, the possibility of a peaceful settlement was eliminated when one of Lóló's friends wounded Wielu with an arrow. By contrast, in the ensuing conflict between Nalek and Ngajóxók, a fierce fight did not prevent a meeting of the opponents on the day after the brawl. Although the discussion failed to achieve an immediate settlement, the aggrieved party abstained from its threatened retaliation. Undoubtedly this restraint influenced the other side to make the demanded restitution. Significantly, the initiation of a boy into their common men's house—a ritual act that reaffirmed and consolidated the unity of its membership—provided the occasion for the settlement.

Other important aspects of Jalé conflict management evident in this case are the influence of sib affiliation, affinity, and common residence in dispute processes. In intraward conflicts, the main support lines to residents of other men's houses follow affinal links rather than sib affiliation. The reason for this dominance of personal linkages through marriage over putative kinship through descent is obvious: interests in the maintenance and enhancement of affinal exchange relationships have no counterpart in the mere recognition of common sib membership. The intervention of the men who terminated the fight also reveals that conflict with an outside enemy functions in the management of local disputes. Their reprimand reminded the opponents of their collective duty to avenge the death of their own sib brother and appealed to their sense of solidarity in the presence of an ongoing war with villages in a distant region.

In Jalé society every dispute that cannot be settled by direct or mediated negotiation may escalate to forceful retaliation. Retaliation has two consequences. On the one hand, it creates opposing factions composed of lineages, whole men's houses, or villages, depending upon the territorial range over which the hostility extends. These alliances enhance the solidarity of the groups involved and may mitigate current conflicts among their members. On the other hand, any vengeance suffered by supporters creates a new conflict between the party responsible for the hostilities and those of his allies who fell victim to it. This situation may then lead to a series of reprisals and counter-reprisals which rupture existing alliances and realign former opponents.

The same process occurs on every structural level. Consequently many seemingly discrete conflicts represent merely a distinct phase in the history of a long-standing conflict. The quarrel between Nalek and Ngajóxók is an example of an intraward conflict that arose in the context of an inter-village war that, in turn, had developed from a quarrel between agnates. Similarly, many interward conflicts that I recorded in the field can be understood only as a by-product of a previous intervillage war. Thus, when a conflict has extended beyond the locality of the two parties, every forceful retaliation against nonkin neighbors of the "man of the arrow's stem" generates new hostilities within smaller territorial ranges (see fig. 1.3).

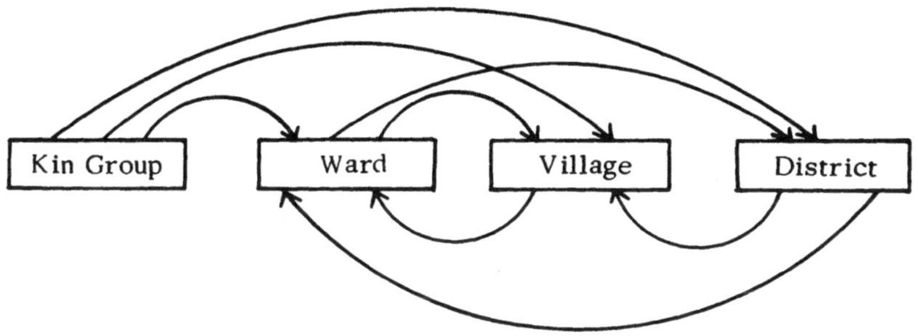

Figure 1.3. Extension and repercussions of conflicts.

CONCLUSIONS

The Jalé have very few and very ineffective methods to transform a dyadic confrontation into a triadic relationship which could secure a settlement by the intervention of a third party. Instead, the conditions that restrain an aggrieved party from seeking redress by retaliation depend entirely upon common interests of the opponents: (1) in conflicts among agnates and nonkin coresidents, the need to maintain the solidarity of a men's house group for the protection of its common political and economic interests; (2) in conflicts between spouses and affines, their mutual interest in the preservation of exchange relationships; and (3) in conflicts between wards or neighboring villages, the necessity for these local groups to form military alliances against an enemy from wider territories—other villages or regions. In addition, the liability of a principal and his agnates to compensate their supporters for damages or injuries suffered in the course of any conflict may dampen a party's desire for revenge. However, although kinship and residence provide certain brakes that deter escalation, these constraints are not strong enough to prevent forceful retaliation in any particular conflict. Especially if the parties belong to different villages, conflicts often escalate into warfare.

NOTE

1. The author worked among the Jalé between October 1964 and July 1966, while holding a Wenner-Gren Foundation predoctoral fellowship. His field research was supported by a grant from the Social Science Research Council. This article is adapted by permission of the publishers from *War and Peace in Jalémó: The Management of Conflict in Highland New Guinea,* by Klaus-Friedrich Koch, Cambridge, Massachusetts: Harvard University Press, © 1974 by the President and Fellows of Harvard College.

TWO

THE ATLANTIC FISHERMEN

Barbara B. Yngvesson

ON ROCK ISLAND, disputes are focused less on *acts* than on *people*. *What was done* is less important than *who did it*. An act considered normal when done by a kinsman or fellow community member may generate an entirely different response when done by an "outsider." Although some disputes arise out of specific acts (e.g., theft, lying, trespassing) and are settled by restitution, many disputes emerge from relationships (e.g., that of community member to outsider) and can only be "settled" by removing the source of the dispute (the outsider) from the community. The settlement process used in disputes of the former type (those focused on acts) is characterized by a quick response to the offending behavior, use of an outside remedy agent, and settlement by restitution or indemnification. By contrast, in disputes within the community, the response is typically drawn out over a period of months or years, the dispute is handled locally, and the aim of the process is either denial that a dispute exists (i.e., maintenance of the previous relationship) or termination of the relationship.

This paper will analyze the ways in which interpersonal grievances of Rock Island fishermen become, or fail to become, disputes of concern to the fishing community at large; and it will discuss the ways in which disputes of public concern are handled.[1] In particular, consideration will be given to (1) the importance of ongoing relations (as against the desire for control over scarce resources) as a factor influencing the course of disputes and (2) mechanisms through which interpersonal grievances are "cooled" and disputes avoided.[2] The analysis is based on case materials spanning a forty-year period.

THE SETTING

Rock Island is a fishing community of 314 persons, located off the Atlantic coast of an industrialized Western nation. The distance of the island from the nearest mainland city (an hour's trip by passenger ferry and another hour by boat) contributes to the islanders' concern over their isolation from, but dependence on, the services this city provides. Local facilities for water and sewage disposal are inadequate, and connection to town services is planned, but the distance involved has caused delays in laying the pipeline. All major shopping must be done in the city, although one grocery store struggles to maintain itself on the island. An island grammar school is maintained, but there is constant anxiety that it will be moved to the mainland if the number of island children becomes insufficient to justify its existence.

Rock Island is linked both politically and economically to the mainland and to other islands in the area. The island is part of a municipal district, and sends representatives to the municipal assembly; islanders also sit on several local government committees (which meet on other islands). Thus, most political activities are based elsewhere.

There is no official governing body on Rock Island, but in 1967 islanders formed an unofficial island council, the purpose of which is to "safeguard the interests of the island and to be of help in solving its problems" (Statutes of the Rock Island Council, 1967). The council is headed by an executive committee, consisting of a chairman, vice-chairman, secretary, and treasurer, who are elected annually. All voluntary associations on the island are represented on the council (Red Cross, Pentecostal Church, Library Association, local chapter of the Fishermen's Association), and all islanders are encouraged to attend its meetings. The council serves as a public forum where issues affecting the interests of the island as a whole are discussed, and where recommendations are made and decisions reached on how these issues should be dealt with. The council enforces its decisions by public pressure, which may be of considerable influence when applied on the island itself. When decisions are made regarding the relations of the island to the mainland or to some other outside force, the council serves mainly as a symbol of the unanimity of island opinion on the issue in question.

Economically, the island is heavily dependent on the activity of its fishermen. While other occupations are represented (teachers, painters, carpenters, store owners, and previously, lighthouse keepers), 67 percent of the wage earners are engaged in full-time or part-time fishing. Most of the fishing is carried out in international waters, and the fish are marketed nationally or internationally, rather than on the island itself.

Most islanders are considered locally to fit into the category "fishermen" or "members of the fishing community."[3] This category is a complex one, in that criteria for inclusion in it are not occupational, but are based on birth and behavior. It includes most people, whether or not they fish for a living, who were born into the fishing community on the island and subscribe to its norms.

An understanding of relations between "fishermen" or "members of the fishing community" requires some familiarity with the social organization of fishing teams, through which all professional fishing on the island is carried out. Teams usually have seven or eight members, two or three of whom (traditionally members of the same family) own the boat and the equipment. Other members of the team, who frequently are kin of the owners, are in no way considered to be employees of, or hired by, the owners of the boat. Basic to the operation of the fishing team is the norm that all members of the team are "equal," and that all operate on the idea of maximum profit for the whole team. "Equality" means that status distinctions (owner/nonowner) and tasks are not ranked; the catch is distributed equally to all members of the team, although two shares are allocated "to the boat" for capital expenses; no direct orders are given; team decisions are reached by consensus; and all members of the team are considered honest and to be trusted. Teams tend to be quite stable, and many fishermen have worked together on the same boat their whole adult lives.

Many of the structural features and values characteristic of team relations can also be found within the fishing community. All 194 persons of the category "fishermen" are said to be related by ties of kinship, and genealogical records indicate that in fact many fishermen are descendants of three men who lived on the island in the eighteenth century and founded the island's three principal cognatic descent groups. Islanders say that a considerable amount of intermarriage has occurred within and between these descent groups, and genealogical records substantiate this.

As is true of the teams, there is a strong sense of identity among members of the fishing community, in part related to their perception that "everyone in the community is related to everyone else." Linked to this sense of identity is a philosophy of equality markedly similar to that on which team relations are based. One might almost say that community relations are patterned on a team model. Specifically, this means that the following values are maintained for intracommunity relations: (a) No differences in prestige based on occupational or educational status are recognized within the fishing community. (b) Differences in authority in the community are based solely on age, and are associated primarily with nuclear family organization; adults who do not stand in the relationship of parent/child to each other are not viewed as having more or less relative authority or power and are assumed to be uninterested in striving for such power. All "real" members of the community are expected to be oriented principally toward the good of the community and not toward their own personal benefit. (c) All decisions affecting the entire community are reached by consensus (specifically by representatives of the community on the island council). (d) Everyone in the community is equally trustworthy. If any dishonesty occurs in the community, it must be an outsider who is responsible. Dishonesty is an inherited trait. If a community member evidences this trait, "it is an illness" for which neither he nor the community is responsible.

In contrast to relations between members of the fishing community, which are characterized by close kin linkages, multiplex ties, trust, and a strong sense of mutual interdependence, are those between members of this community and "outsiders." Technically speaking, the category "outsiders" includes only the fifty-six persons living on the island who were not born there. Potentially, it may be extended to include any one of the sixty-four native but "fringe" persons who are not linked by descent or marriage to one of the fishing community's three core descent groups. Whether a "fringe" member of the fishing community is or is not labeled and treated as an outsider is dependent on how he behaves; if such a person does not conform to fishing community norms, his behavior is attributed to outside ancestry (which may be several generations removed) and he is referred to as an outsider. Birth outside the fishing community is associated with nonconformist behavior, which the fishermen feel powerless to control. For example, present-day islanders who are descendants of a nonnative eighteenth-century lighthouse keeper on the island are potential outsiders due to their ancestry. The lighthouse keeper's descendants (see case 3 below) are considered to be primarily interested in improving their own welfare at the fishermen's expense. The fishermen feel incapable of influencing their behavior, since their roots are on the mainland and their loyalties are seen as oriented there and not toward the island. Because of their large landholdings they are regarded as particularly threatening. Yet it is only these specific lighthouse keeper's descendants who are regarded as behaving in a deviant manner and who are labeled outsiders, and not others. Similarly, there are many persons on Rock Island today who are technically classified as outsiders because they were born elsewhere, and who in principle will never be completely absorbed into the fishing community. But most of these people have affinal kin on the island and are linked by ties of friendship to members of the fishing community. The only real outsiders are persons born elsewhere (or with ancestors born elsewhere) who do not conform to fishing community norms.

DESCRIPTION OF GRIEVANCE BEHAVIOR AND REMEDY AGENTS

Grievance Behavior

Any act by one person or group which another person or group views as an infringement of its rights may be considered a *grievance*. Such acts include a wide variety of behavior, such as an unfriendly glance or the absence of a greeting, gossip, failure to return borrowed money, or taking another's property. Most of these acts are private and do not concern the community at large. Fishermen agree, however, that other acts potentially constitute a serious breach of community norms. Acts defined as theft, breach of contract, property damage, physical assault, or sexual molestation, for example, are considered to be serious breaches and are punished by the community. Any act regarded as a threat to the further expansion and development of the community—and thus threatening its welfare—is also considered a serious breach of the norms. Particularly threatening are any attempts to expand or maintain control over land on which the community is dependent for survival.

However, rules regarding the conditions under which a particular act is to be considered "theft," "breach of contract," and so on, are fluid, allowing for a range of interpretations and definitions. For example, fishermen consider theft to be the worst offense that a person living on the island could commit, and theft is defined as "taking the property of another." It is stressed that "theft is always committed by a person from the outside," and, in fact, all cases of theft I collected, with one exception (which was considered serious), were committed by persons defined as "outsiders." Yet several instances were reported to me in which persons who were not "outsiders" had taken the property of another. These acts were not called "theft," but rather were referred to as "borrowing" or as acts committed by "someone who isn't so careful to distinguish what is mine from what is yours." "Borrowing" and "failure to distinguish my property from yours" are considered by the fishing community to fall in the range of normal acts, although ideally some kinds of borrowing should not occur. Some people may feel that such acts are cause for grievance, but the grievance is considered a private matter, to be settled between the individuals involved.

Another example involves the act of "walking on the property of another." Right of passage over private property is guaranteed by national law, with certain restrictions, and this right is recognized on the island between all members of the fishing community. However, people referred to as lighthouse keepers consider it a breach if persons of the category "fishermen" or nonislanders walk on their land. The fishermen say, "If a person walks on his [a lighthouse keeper's] property and bends a blade of grass, the grass will unbend again when he has passed, but he regards this as property damage."

A third example is also related to the concept "property damage." I was told that young boys like to set fire to grass on the island, and several instances of this were reported to me. These acts, which were at times done in spite of direct orders to the contrary by the boys' parents, were always laughed at and called "mischief." I was told that "they do it because they are boys, and they see their fathers doing it in the spring" (on their own land).

These examples suggest that from the point of view of the fishing community as a group, the domain of grievance behavior can be subdivided in the following ways: (a) normal acts (which private individuals may consider to be grievances); and (b) breaches (which are of concern to the community). The decision to label a particular act as a breach or as normal behavior is partly determined by the nature of the act (only certain kinds of acts are potential breaches), partly by its degree of importance (e.g., the amount of property taken), and to a large extent by the relationship of the parties involved.

Responses to Grievance Behavior

Fishermen maintain that the ideal means of resolving any grievance is an amicable settlement on a one-to-one basis. In this kind of settlement the claim is not disputed; the offender admits his guilt, and full restitution is made for the offense committed. In spite of this ideal, many cases are not resolved in this way, but are handled by government remedy agents on the mainland, or by the community in an unofficial way.

Official remedy agents include a system of courts and other government agencies located in the nearest major city on the mainland. The courts include the rural district court, special courts, and the court of appeal. Most civil and criminal cases may be taken, in the first instance, to the rural district court for settlement. Certain categories of cases, such as those over ownership and subdivision of land, may be handled by special courts or judges. Many government departments also function as remedy agents for grievances that arise within their domain: cases of adverse possession of land, for example, may be handled by the regional surveyor's office; problems involving children under eighteen may be handled by the child welfare committee of the municipality; and so on. In all these agencies, a formal and regular procedure is followed, the aim of which is an unbiased investigation and judgment of the case.

In marked contrast to this official system, in which codes and formal hearings play an important role, is a purely local and unofficial system on the island itself. When a grievance is handled locally, there is (except for the island council, discussed below) no person or agency through which the offended party can register a complaint, as would be the case on the mainland. Rather, a notable characteristic of the "local system" is precisely the absence of mechanisms through which private grievances can be formalized or ritualized. Local mechanisms for handling grievances consist not so much of a variety of remedy agencies (courts, legal aid centers, child welfare committees, and so on) but of a series of developmental stages through which a grievance progresses, any one of which may serve to terminate the grievance.

Briefly, the local response pattern to grievances is as follows: An offense or series of offenses is followed by a period of apparent inaction (i.e., there is no confrontation with the offender and no overt attempt to prevent the grievance from continuing). The inaction period may last several years, during which time the offense is discussed, or gossiped about, in the community at large. Some grievances terminate or appear to terminate during this stage, thus remaining, at least nominally, in the category of private grievances ("normal acts" from the perspective of the community). In other cases, this period is followed by a confrontation between the offender and the offended person. The confrontation may or may not lead to an "amicable settlement," the ideal means of resolving any grievance. Evidence suggests, however, that most cases which reach a confrontation stage do not terminate amicably but result in the fictive or actual expulsion of the offending individual from the community. The principal mechanisms involved are ostracism and the classification of an individual or group as an "outsider."

There is one exception to the local pattern I have described. Some grievances (to date, two) which threaten the further expansion and development of the community are taken to the island council, rather than being handled in the ways discussed above. In choosing to take a grievance to the council, however, the parties to a grievance are choosing a process structurally similar in many respects to more diffuse local settlement processes. The council is in no sense an adjudicative body and bears no similarity to the courts of the state legal system. It serves rather as an arena for the airing of island problems. (Most council members are fishermen, but technically all islanders can be represented on the council.) If a grievance involves two persons or groups resident on the island, the aim of the council is to help the parties reach a negotiated settlement. If a problem is one in which the community (or a group of community members) is involved with a nonresident party or parties (such as representatives of the regional or federal government), the council serves as an arena in which the islanders can discuss possible courses of action. A decision to follow one or another course is based on a majority vote. The council is never used to consider purely interpersonal grievances among the fishermen. A notable characteristic of the grievances which to date have been taken to the council is that both involved the issue of control over a scarce resource (land) that is essential to the continued existence of the fishing community.

Three cases will be presented and analyzed in the following pages, providing the basis for a discussion of response patterns used by Rock Island fishermen and the sociocultural factors influencing choice of one or another of these.

The Three Cases

1. *The Case of the Deviant Mechanic.* This case has been in progress since at least 1955–56, and is still unresolved.

Although cars are for the most part prohibited on Rock Island, some islanders who have special need for motor vehicles (such as carpenters, the store owner, and the Red Cross workers) own trucks, most of which are very old and frequently in need of repair. Albert Cooper, a fifth-generation fisherman, is a self-trained mechanic who has been repairing the trucks since he was a teenager (he is now forty). There is only one main road, which runs the length of the island, and he can frequently be seen near the store working on "The Golden Palomino" or some other old truck, pausing to chat with young people as they pass along the road. He is very popular with children on the island, and particularly with young girls, who enjoy hitching rides on the back of one or another of the trucks he is currently working on. The island is about one and one-half miles long, and Albert often offers to take a group of children in one of the trucks to a favorite pebble beach on the northern tip of the island. Some of the younger girls (eight or nine years old) say that he is teaching them to swim.

During the year I was on the island, girls of twelve and thirteen began complaining that Albert was pestering them to go swimming out at Pebble Beach, where he insisted that they bathe without their swimsuits. He had apparently been doing this for several years, but the children had not previously found it objectionable. One day in 1967 Martha told him at the beach, "We can swim any way we want," and he stopped bothering her. The next time he suggested that she and some friends go swimming, she told him not to ask them again and he did not. The children said that he became very angry, however. The daughter of an informant stated that when she was in school (in 1955), Albert had become very angry when she and her friends once refused to go swimming with him. In the early 1960s, Albert gave swimming lessons to a daughter of a carpenter on the island, and they used to go swimming together from a skerry nearby. The situation eventually became known to the girl's parents, who put a stop to it. But they allowed their youngest daughter to go with her friends to Pebble Beach with him.

In 1968 all the girls over twelve on the island decided to stop talking to him, and their parents did not object; but I was told that it was the girls' decision, not the parents'. By the time I left, the island's two nine-year-old girls had become friendly with him and sometimes accompanied him to Pebble Beach.

My principal informant for this case stated that the parents had known about the situation all along and yet did nothing. (She had learned of the situation from her own daughter.) She had talked about it to one mother, who simply said, "He is that way." Another woman said, "It is an illness," and appeared interested in Albert's behavior, but took no action. Another informant, born elsewhere, pointed out that had he arrived on the island and begun behaving in such a way, it would not have been accepted; this informant said the fishermen were familiar with Albert's ways: "They have known him since he was a child, and have seen how he ran naked" in the rocky uninhabited areas of the island. At the time I left Rock Island, several mothers were expressing concern about the situation, but there was no indication that they were planning to take action against Albert.

Although no overt action was being taken against Albert in this particular situation, open objection to other deviant behavior on his part was expressed by members of the community during 1968. I was told that infidelity is "judged severely" by the fishermen, and yet Albert, who was married, had more or less openly established a liaison with another woman, the owner of an island cafe. I heard this situation commented on critically by the fishermen, and it was impossible to miss the open distaste with which Albert and the woman were regarded when they appeared in public together.

More serious from the fishermen's point of view was Albert's public dissent from the general stand of the fishing community against a forest preserve, proposed by concerned ecologists for a large portion of the island's land area. Albert's dissent was noted and commented on publicly by a prominent fisherman on the island during an island council meeting: "There is only one person in this room who is against us and for the preserve, and he is sitting right behind me!"

Albert has openly expressed the opinion that people should be free to do and say as they wish, and has made it clear that he finds conventional opinions and behavior distasteful. After an island council meeting, a fisherman repeated that only one person opposed the island's stand on the preserve. The fisherman's twelve-year-old daughter said immediately, "That must have been Albert—he's always against everything."

There is a small group of persons on the island of which Albert seems to be the focal point; they socialize together and are believed by the fishing community to share Albert's liberal views and behavior. This group includes Albert's wife, the woman with whom he has established a liaison, a young house painter on the island and his wife, and a teacher on the island.

2. *The Case of the Stolen Goods.* A respected fisherman on Rock Island, Harris Jenks, married a woman from a neighboring island. They had a

daughter, Anne, who married and settled down on Rock Island. During the course of approximately a year, Anne was observed shoplifting by employees of the Rock Island cooperative. She hid the goods from the cashier as she went to pay. Employees of the store discussed among themselves and informally with other members of the community what they should do about the thefts, but they took no action for several months. Toward the end of the year, Anne was accused by the store manager and confessed to the thefts. She begged the manager not to take the case to court, and said she would repay the full amount. The case was thus "settled amicably." Later discussion among the islanders revealed that Anne's mother's brother had also been known to steal. It was said that Anne's son was not "completely trustworthy" either. Informants on the island stated that it was clear that the "thief trait" in Anne's family did not come from Rock Island, but from her mother's kin (i.e., from that part of the family from the neighboring island).

It was reported to me during my fieldwork period that Anne had gone to the hospital with a nervous breakdown. She told my informant that people on the island were so harsh and unfriendly to her that she could no longer stand it.

3. *The Case of the Lighthouse Keepers' Homestead.* This case includes twenty-three separate grievances. Most of them occurred during the period 1938–40, but two were resolved later (1945 and 1957). Events leading up to the case can be traced as far back as the eighteenth century, but the immediate background to the grievances begins in 1900.

Rock Island was a lighthouse and foghorn station from approximately the mid-eighteenth to the early twentieth century. In August 1900 the station was transferred to the Vineyard, another island, although station personnel living on Rock Island at the time were permitted to complete their remaining years of service there. The last of these people retired in 1933, and in 1934 lighthouse and foghorn responsibilities for Rock Island officially ceased.

During the century and one-half during which the station was located on the island, approximately 23 percent of the land on the island was used by lighthouse and foghorn personnel and their families, allegedly as a partial reimbursement for their services. The land is known on the island as the lighthouse keepers' homestead. The land was government property, however, and when the station was moved, plans were made to dispose of it in accordance with the needs of the island's inhabitants.

A report by an official from the Department of the Interior in August

1932 notes the following: A map was drawn up in 1893 subdividing the homestead among the six lighthouse and foghorn personnel then in service. Records of land transactions indicated that this informal partitioning was not legal. Twenty-six houses, belonging primarily to fishermen, were later constructed in the area, and a former lighthouse keeper reported that these were built with the permission of the station personnel, to whom a yearly sum was to be paid by each homeowner. The fishermen had no legal right to be on the land because the station personnel had no legal right to subdivide the area in the first place. The report suggested: (1) that the areas built on by the fishermen be sold to them; (2) that a suitable amount of land be sold to the lighthouse and foghorn personnel remaining on Rock Island; and (3) that the remaining land be used for the needs of the island community as a whole. The report stressed that the land in question was government land "under general disposition" and thus that it had not previously been of the type which could be purchased by the user.

In 1934, following a government order, the area was surveyed and a plan drawn up for a legal subdivision, in accordance with the recommendations in the 1932 report. The committee in charge noted that "the fishing population on Rock Island, due to the present less favorable situation in fishing, has poor earning possibilities and correspondingly small resources for purchasing the land plots on which they have for several years had their houses, free of charge [sic]." With this analysis in mind, together with the small likelihood that there would be need for government installations in the area in the near future, the committee was generous in determining the size and value of the plots.

In 1935, four children of one of the last of the station personnel, George Trafalgar (d. 1931), wrote to the Department of the Interior maintaining that personnel of the station had inherited rights to use of the land for an unlimited period, and that they also had been granted the right to purchase the land, should it be sold. They maintained that this right had been passed down in their family from generation to generation, beginning in the eighteenth century: "For as far back as it is possible to follow lighthouse keepers in the census records, responsibility for the lighthouse and rights to the land have been inherited in accordance with the provisions in the . . . government order [of July 9, 1928]. The very fact that the conditions of entitlement to the land have been followed for well over a century must in itself provide sufficiently strong proof that the land is of the type which can be purchased." They pointed out that before the mid-nineteenth century, the lighthouse and foghorn personnel on Rock Island had received no salary and after that date had been paid a lower wage than such officials on other islands, and they maintained that the reason for this differential could lie only in their use and purchase rights to the land.

The Department of the Interior denied the request of the Trafalgar descendants that they be allowed to purchase the land, but the descendants appealed this ruling. In 1938 their appeal was granted, and they were allowed to purchase their homestead land for approximately sixty cents. Approval of the Trafalgar petition meant that all other descendants of lighthouse and foghorn personnel on the island were also given purchase rights to their homestead land, and by June 1939 almost one-quarter of the total land area of the island was legally in the hands of six persons, representing the descendants of four of the island's early station personnel. The driving force behind the acquisitions, and the person exercising greatest control over the land once it was purchased, was one of the descendants of George Trafalgar, Thomas Trafalgar.

Informants in the island fishing community tell me that immediately after the purchase, the station people, led by Thomas Trafalgar, insisted that the fishermen who had built within the homestead purchase the plots on which their houses stood. The subdivision plan drawn up by government surveyors in 1934 was used in calculating the size of the plots, but the station people demanded a much higher amount per square meter than the government had asked of them. The fishermen took the matter to court in 1938, and by mid-1940 most of them had acquired legal title to their plots on the basis of squatters' rights, or adverse possession. One of the conditions laid down by the court was that the houses on the land should have been built before January 1, 1919. In most cases the fishermen were able to prove this, but in a few instances the houses had been built at a later time; in those cases title to the plot was and still is held by station people.

This series of grievances together with six other instances in which fishermen successfully sued in court for condemnation of land areas that were owned by station personnel but were essential for the functioning of the community—such as the school, the fishermen's cooperative, and the harbor—split the inhabitants of the island into two factions, the outlines of which had underlain island social organization for generations.

The fishermen consider the station people, and particularly Thomas Trafalgar, as obsessed with power and the desire to improve their own welfare at the expense of that of the fishing community. The fishermen consider that the station people have broken a verbal contract made by their predecessors, on which the fishermen had relied. In turn, the station people—and here I am voicing the opinion of Thomas Trafalgar—regard the fishermen as liars and thieves, who stole land to which station people were entitled by virtue of decades of demanding work in government service. I am told that the positions of both sides have only hardened over the years. According to an informant in the fishing community who is related to Thomas Trafalgar, "He would do almost anything to get back at the fishermen." Trafalgar continues to own a considerable amount of land on the island, but will not sell plots "because he does not want any fishermen living on his land." His own accounts to me confirm this stance. Since 1959 he has sold only one plot, to a fisherman from another island. The fishermen tell me that they are desperately in need of land if the community is to progress.

Thomas Trafalgar has complained to me that members of the fishing community (often children) constantly trespass on his land and damage it. He says that when he complains to their parents, retaliatory acts are carried out against him. Twice in the 1960s children set fire to parts of his property after such a complaint, and he maintains that it was their parents who were behind it. An informant in the fishing community told me that "children may have set fire to his property and he probably thinks it is because it was *his* property, but children do that kind of thing all the time."

A few years ago, the fishermen set up a lamppost along a path bordering the lighthouse keepers' homestead. I am told the lamp was needed because the path was dark, and that it was a benefit both fishermen and station people who used the path. The station people objected to the lamp, however, on the basis that it was on their land, and they would not allow the fishermen to connect it. At a council meeting during which the matter was discussed, the fishermen decided to leave the post standing anyway, "as a shame to the station people," and it was still there in 1968.

It is interesting to note that although marriages have occurred between station people and fishermen, no member of either group is regarded as neutral. A husband or wife must be either station person or "fisherman." Thomas Trafalgar's wife was the daughter of a fisherman and the sister of one of the founding members of the fishermen's cooperative store on the island. When the fishermen/station people grievances began, Trafalgar was removed from the board of directors of the cooperative on the basis that "he could not possibly be loyal to both sides." His removal infuriated Trafalgar, and he has only harsh words for the cooperative and anyone connected with it. The present manager of the cooperative is married to a woman whose mother was the daughter of a station official, but the marriage of the younger woman to a member of the fishing community (and particularly her ties to the cooperative) make her highly suspect to the station people. There is one man on the island, a descendant of a lighthouse official, who has tried to keep a foot in both camps, but "no fisherman would trust him."

FACTORS IN THE CHOICE-MAKING PROCESS

Patterns in Grievance Development

Two perspectives can be brought to the analysis of case materials from a society. The cases can be examined for evidence of a persisting structure of relations, and the influence of this structure on the handling of disputes. Cases can also be examined for evidence of patterning in their development, linked to what Stanner (1966: vii) has termed "the ways in which persons 'work' or 'operate' on other persons, or on things, even on themselves, to obtain valued objects in life." In the case materials from Rock Island, the persisting structure (e.g., roles of insiders and outsiders, fishermen and lighthouse keepers; types of grievances linking these roles; types of mechanisms used in handling grievances) recurs and can be noted. Beyond these features of content are other, more subtle likenesses in what might best be described as the rhythm[4] and flow of cases as they develop over time. I analyzed the cases with a view to discerning the rhythm more clearly, and the analysis suggested that it was linked both to case duration and to the quality of exchange over a case (as determined by aim of the exchange, the social context within which it occurred, and the conceptual model underlying the exchange).

The cases presented here are illustrative of rhythm patterns in the development of Rock Island grievances. In the analysis below (see table 2.1) the cases are broken down into sequences of development, as a means of focusing on differences in rhythm. The analysis indicates that two patterns occur. One of these is illustrative of responses in which local processes are used; the second illustrates a response pattern using state remedy agents.

In pattern A, an offensive action by one individual against another (stage I) is followed by a reaction at a private or informal level (stage II). A period follows in which, although the recognition of a

TABLE 2.1
GRIEVANCES ANALYZED AS A SEQUENCE OF OPERATIONS

	Pattern A		*Pattern B*
Stages	*Case 1*	*Case 2*	*Case 3*
I. Action (potentially a breach)	Albert begins taking girls to Pebble Beach, suggesting nude swimming	Anne begins taking goods from coop	Station people buy homestead, charge high price for plots
II. Reaction—informal	12-year-olds begin objecting, stop going to the beach, tell parents	Employees notice theft, discuss it with others	
III. Discussion among community members—"nonaction" period	Parents aware for years of Albert's behavior but take no action "because he is from here and people know his ways"; behavior continues; gossip; public but indirect criticism regarding other behavior toward end of period	No action to apprehend Anne for nearly a year, while she continues taking goods	
IV. (a) Reaction—formal		Coop personnel confront Anne with evidence	Fishermen take issue to court
(b) Settlement		"Amicable" settlement	Adjudicated settlement
V. Sanctions		Self-exile, ostracism (thefts blamed on inheritance; classified as outsider)	Fishermen's children burn station people's grass; lamppost left as protest

grievance is tacit, no direct action to remedy the situation or to prevent its recurrence is taken by adults in the community. During this time the grievance is discussed on the island (stage III). This period may last several years, and may or may not be followed by stage IV, in which a breach is openly recognized; this stage may culminate in an "amicable" settlement (denial of a breach). The final stage (V) involves action by the community to sanction or remove the offender from the community.

In pattern B there is a sequence in which an offensive action is immediately recognized as such publicly, and a formal complaint is lodged with an external remedy agent. There is no "nonaction" period of discussion, and the case is settled by adjudication through an official government agency, such as a court. In some pattern B cases, a court settlement is followed by an attempt at community sanctions, as in case 3.

Analysis of cases collected during my fieldwork period (in which the offenders were adults) indicates that each case can be described by using one of the developmental patterns outlined here. It should be stressed, however, that although the breakdown of each case followed closely the statements of informants and my own observations, no Rock Islander would suggest such a breakdown, nor would he conceive of a case as developing according to any particular pattern. The breakdown is useful in that (1) the emphasis on form enables the analyst to note similarities between apparently dissimilar grievances and to isolate those points in the development of a case at which dissimilarities are present, and (2) the emphasis on developmental stages means that the cases are presented as ongoing processes (or "developing structures") rather than as separate events. Each stage of the process influences the further development of a case, and it is only in certain instances that a particular mode of settlement can be predicted simply on the basis of issue involved or category of offender.

Factors Influencing Grievance Development

One of the main differences between the patterns is the relatively long "nonaction" period which is present in pattern A but is lacking in pattern B. Analysis of case materials (archival materials from the district court and from the surveyor's office for the periods 1948–68 and 1930–68, respectively, and locally handled cases covering the period 1958–68) indicates that "nonaction" is a characteristic feature of locally handled grievances involving two adult members of the Rock Island fishing community. Of the seven recorded cases[5] involving two adult members of the fishing community, six were handled on the island using "nonaction."[6] This finding suggests that two members of the fishing community will typically attempt to muffle a grievance by avoiding a public airing. Such grievances may remain latent for years and eventually be forgotten; if they do become public they are handled by redefining the relationship of the offender to the community (see below). In contrast, all thirty-three cases in which an outsider offended a member of the fishing community evoked rapid reactions. Response involved immediate public accusation or confrontation, and the case was taken to an external agency for resolution. Gossip and discussion among community members might have also occurred, but they were never a substitute for a more formal reaction to the grievance.[7]

The case materials suggest, then, that a significant factor influencing the way in which a Rock Island grievance will develop is the nature of the relationship between the parties involved. The one case which seemed to be an exception to this rule involved a grievance between two members of the fishing community over land ownership; this case was taken to court for resolution. Although information on the details of this case is limited, other research (Starr and Yngvesson 1975) suggests that cases involving control over scarce resources are likely to go to court; parties to such cases often seem more interested in winning the case than in muffling a grievance (with a view to maintaining their previous relationship). It is significant that there is no case involving control over land on Rock Island in which the nonaction mechanism was used or which was resolved amicably. As the discussion of case 3 indicated, however, almost all these cases involved offenders who were classified as "lighthouse keepers" (i.e., nonmembers of the fishing community). It might be argued, however, that opposition raised by the lighthouse keepers to the use of their land by the fishing community was a significant factor barring them from acceptance into the fishing community. Thus, *who you are* (i.e., social identity in the fishing community) may be the main issue determining the way a grievance in which you are involved is handled; but ***what you control*** and ***how this control is administered*** may determine your social identity.

Handling Intracommunity Grievances: Becoming an Outsider

Ideally, there is no interest among members of the Rock Island fishing community in acquiring wealth or power that would accrue principally to their own benefit rather than to that of the community as a whole; nor would any member of the fishing community be guilty of behavior which was a "serious breach of community norms" (theft, property damage, physical assault, breach of contract, sexual molestation). Such traits are only evidenced by "outsiders." Yet case materials indicate that some persons with deep roots in the community are in fact suspected of and sanctioned for such behavior. The principal mechanism through which offenses by such persons are handled is that I have termed "nonaction."

I developed the concept of a "nonaction" period in Rock Island grievances as a result of my inability, in the process of questioning informants, to find out "what happened" after a deviant act had occurred. Questions regarding response or reaction to a grievance were continually met with silence or puzzled looks or with the answer "Nothing was done." I found this response mystifying and a little irritating (on the assumption that some vital aspect of a case was purposefully obscured), until I began to notice, first, that there were similar periods when "nothing happened" in other domains of island social life (periods of nonaction in decision making on teams and at island meetings), and second, that in fact things did "happen" to individuals who had been involved in local grievances but that what happened was not so much a discrete act of punishment as a process of reclassification, of fictive or actual exclusion from the community.

In case 1, discussion of Albert's behavior involved a consideration of whether his actions were "normal," not only by general community standards but in the light of what was expected of him as an individual whose patterns of behavior had been known and accepted in the community for many years. Other factors involved in this assessment included: (1) The context in which his actions were being performed at any given moment. During my stay on the island this meant that his behavior with young girls was viewed as one of several deviant or potentially deviant stands—opposition to the fishing community on the issue of a forest preserve on the island, and his adultery—each of which influenced the process of deciding whether his behavior could be considered "normal" within the general range of deviation expected of him. Many people simply said, "He is like that," remembering his behavior as a child when he ran naked in the rocky hills of the island. (2) His network position on the island as a "real" member of the community with deep roots there, making it difficult for any one (or more than one) individual to take action against him without alienating a large segment of the island population.

In the second case (the stolen goods), the long period when "nothing was done" was again a time during which the offender's behavior was assessed in the light of what was known of her family history on the island and elsewhere. The fact that her mother was born elsewhere and that other members of her family were considered untrustworthy, led to a consideration of her behavior as not normal and subject to strong community sanctions, and to a classification of that part of her character which led her to steal as an "outside trait."

In effect, then, "nonaction" is a period of assessment in which the circumstances surrounding a deviant act, the history of the individual, his or her ties in the community, and the consequences in the community of a formal reaction to the grievance are considered and weighed against one another. The fact that during this period the behavior of a deviant is formally "ignored" for several months or years provides deviants with an opportunity to change their behavior; alternatively, the relationship of offender and offended may develop in such a way that an "act of grievance" is no longer viewed as such. Rather, a potential deviant may be viewed as "sick," and the deviant act may be classified not as "theft" but as an "inability to distinguish between mine and yours," an illness from which some persons suffer but which must be tolerated and humored.[8] The case of the stolen goods provides an example of a "nonaction" process which led to the fictive and ultimately the actual exclusion of an islander from the fishing community, because of a combination of deviant behavior and the fringe status of the offender. In the case of the deviant mechanic, there was evidence that the social identity of the offender was beginning to shift toward outsider status, although at the time of my departure most people still described him as "sick" or simply "that way."

Two Models

Up to this point I have discussed conceptual schemes used by the members of a fishing community in handling situations that could potentially give rise to a grievance. One scheme is characterized by (1) a concern with contextual aspects of the grievance, in terms of time perspective, as an event with a past and a future; in terms of social space, as an event viewed in the light of its effects in a field where an alteration in one relationship may trigger a series of secondary changes; (2) a tolerance for a wide range of behaviors around an ideal norm; (3) a concern with maintaining the fiction that no change (in the form of a grievance) has occurred, or with redefining the nature of the relationship of deviant to community in such a way that the grievance (or potential grievance) is structured into the new relationship.

This conceptual scheme for handling grievances can be found within the bounds of a relationship or complex of relationships which is conceived by those involved in it as being "ongoing." Such relationships need not be "multiplex," nor need they be based, along traditional anthropological lines, on ties of kinship, friendship, or affinity. Business relations, for example, which may involve single-stranded as well as multiplex links between persons involved, may also be ongoing: "Not only do the particular business units in a given exchange want to deal with each other again, they also want to deal with other business units in the future. And the way one behaves in a particular transaction, or a series of transactions, will color his general business reputation" (Macaulay in Aubert 1969: 204).

When a commitment to maintain a valued relationship—whether business or other—exists, settlement of a grievance must entail a consideration of the offending act and a decision regarding the offender in which the history and future of the relationship between offender and offended plays a key role.

In contrast to the style of handling grievance behavior within the bounds of an ongoing relationship, encounters across such boundaries occur within the context of an entirely different set of rules for behavior: (1) The encounter occurs in what might be called a social vacuum (from the point of view of the offended party) in that it happens outside the bounds of relevant social space and time. Reaction to the encounter need only involve a consideration of its immediate effects, and not the repercussions of the act in a field of enduring social relations. The encounter itself may have no past, present, or future, or if it does have a historical dimension, maintenance of the relationship in the future is not of concern. (2) In this kind of encounter, tolerance for a range of behaviors deviating from the ideal is low. (3) The problem of maintaining a particular quality of relationship between deviant and community (or between offender and offended party), or of restructuring the relationship in the light of the encounter, is of no consequence, since no enduring relationship is involved. The aim in such encounters, from the point of the offended party, is simply to bring an end to and mitigate the effects of the confrontation as quickly as possible.

The contrast I have described in styles of handling deviant behavior within and across the boundaries of enduring relationships can perhaps best be illustrated by an analogy drawn from the fields of law and medicine, in which the legal conception of the criminal is compared to the medical conception of a sick person (Aubert 1963a: 50):

> The sick and the criminal are constructed [conceived] as members of two different worlds, and do not only represent variants of a common category of roles. The sick person is constructed as someone with characteristics along a dimension of time, while the criminal is constructed without any time perspective. The defining characteristics of the criminal, partly because of this discontinuity, have no location in space either.

Within a field of enduring social relations, the conceptual scheme for treatment of a deviant is similar to that of the medical construction of a sick person, as described by Aubert; treatment of a deviant who is not involved in a process of ongoing relations follows a "criminal" model in which the time perspective is lacking. In the latter context, the use of a remedy agency—such as a court—that deals with past events as discrete happenings may be a satisfactory way of handling a grievance. In the former situation, events can only be evaluated and given meaning if considered as part of a developing process of relations: reaction to them should be cautious and should allow sufficient time to place the events in proper perspective (see Aubert 1963a: 56).

CONCLUSIONS

Much of the literature to date in the field of legal anthropology, including that empahsizing legal processes, has been oriented toward explaining the use of particular institutions (courts, moots, negotiation proceedings) or mode of dispute settlement (negotiation, adjudication, arbitration) within societies and cross-culturally (see Moore 1969, Nader 1969b, Nader and Yngvesson 1974, for discussions of this literature). In reference to this focus, Nader suggested in 1969 that "style of dispute settlement . . . [might] be viewed independently of its formal expression as court or agency" (1969b: 88). In such analyses, the features of style rather than the types of agencies (court/noncourt) become the central focus and form the basis for comparative work. Aubert's analyses (1963b, 1969) of types of conflict, and of the forms of conflict resolution to which these correspond, provide an example of an investigation of "style" in Nader's sense, in that Aubert defines the components of what he calls the legal and bargain models of conflict resolution, enabling other researchers to consider these features independently of the agency involved.

In this paper, I have also been looking at style (or what I have termed rhythm), but I have focused not on style of dispute settlement, but on the broader concept of style of response to grievance behavior. Analysis of case materials from a small Atlantic fishing community suggested that two response styles or modes were used, one characteristic of a locally based response, the other found when response involved use of mainland remedy agents. Significant features of the response process were the following: time involved in responding to an offense (cooling period/rapid response), aim of the response process (healing/punishment or restitution), focus of the process (person/act); strictness with which actual behavior is measured against the ideal, and structure of the process (dyadic/triadic).[9]

I attempted to explain choice of response by examining the ways in which parties to grievances were related and their perception of the significance of these relationships. My data suggested that an important factor influencing mode of response on Rock Island was the time context within which a relationship was viewed. The following hypotheses were suggested as an explanation of response patterns there and for testing on a wider range of data: Within the context of a situation in which enduring relations are important I would expect the use of "informal" and diffuse settlement processes, a style in which healing is the aim, the focus is on the person, actual behavior varies widely around the norm, and the structure of the process is dominantly dyadic. A marked "cooling" period will occur, since an event that in some way alters the nature of the relationship must be considered not as a discrete act but as part of a developing process which should be allowed to play itself out.

In contrast, modes of handling grievances in encounters where past and future aspects of the relationship are not important will be characterized by a rapid response, focus on the act, actual behavior strictly judged in reference to the ideal, with punishment or restitution as the aim, and a response process that is dominantly triadic in structure. An exception to these patterns might be expected in cases in which the control of scarce resources is at issue. Evidence from several studies indicates that in such cases response to the grievances will focus on the act rather than the relationship, and that both parties will strive to win even if the relationship has been of long duration.

Aubert has suggested that "law is not concerned with causal processes nor with phenomena that have a dimension in time" (1969: 28). My data suggest a corollary to this: that breaches in relationships which have a time dimension are not amenable to handling through the law (i.e., courts) or, in my terms, through a process in which time is ignored. They must be dealt with in time, and not by stopping a relationship at the arbitrary point at which a grievance was committed.

NOTES

1. Research on which this article is based was carried out in an Atlantic fishing community in 1967–68 and was supported by a research training grant from the Institute of International Studies, Berkeley, California. Names of persons and places in the article are fictitious. It is written in the ethnographic present, but refers, except where otherwise noted, to the period 1967–68. This is an altered version of "Responses to Grievance Behavior: Extended Cases in a Fishing Community," reproduced by permission of the American Anthropological Association from the *American Ethnologist,* 3(2) 1976.

2. By "grievance" I mean an act by a person or group which another person or group views as an infringement of its rights. "Dispute" has been defined by Gulliver (1969a: 14) as a disagreement that has been raised from the level of dyadic argument into the public arena. In this paper, I am dealing with both grievances and disputes, in that I am interested in the process through which certain kinds of grievances become matters of public concern. Because my interest is as much in the development of relationships over time as in the way disputes (which are issue-oriented) are handled, I will use the concept "breach" rather than "dispute" for grievances which become matters of public concern.

3. Throughout the paper, the terms "fishermen" and "members of the fishing community" are used interchangeably and distinguish persons who are included in the fishing community to the exclusion of other islanders. The term "fishermen" will not be used as an occupational category, unless specified.

4. "Rhythm" is defined in the *American Heritage Dictionary of the English Language* (1969) as "any kind of movement characterized by the regular recurrence of strong and weak elements." For my purpose I have adapted this definition to mean the regular recurrence of action (strong) and nonaction (weak) stages in the grievance response process.

5. The number of local cases is small. This is partially a function of the way I have defined "a case," which usually involves several separate grievances, but is also related to the kinds of issues included in my sample, which is limited to grievances actually or potentially of community concern. See above for a discussion of this point. The small number of cases is also related to the fact that Rock Islanders are markedly oriented toward the suppression of open conflict, and few grievances surface above the purely interpersonal level.

6. The seven divorce cases are not considered here because no alternative to an official remedy agency was available.

It is difficult to estimate how complete a sample I have of locally resolved cases. My data indicate that the cases are clustered approximately within a ten-year period (1958–68), although one case can be traced back to the early 1950s. Informants ranged in age from thirteen to eighty (although my principal informants were in their mid-fifties) and included lighthouse people, nonislanders, and fishermen. A few cases, which were in progress during my fieldwork period, were personally observed. It is clear that accuracy of my data is heavily dependent on the reliability of my informants. That the data are accurate is suggested by the fact that they were cross-checked with several informants, and that information collected from local informants on cases resolved off the island was duplicated by the twenty-year and thirty-eight-year samples from official sources, with only one exception. (My informants did not know that I was also conducting archival research.)

7. Attempts were made to handle two cases through the island council during my fieldwork period. One case involved an outside group that was interested in converting a large portion of the island into a forest preserve; this case was eventually taken off the island for settlement. The other case was a grievance over land involving two local groups, and was just beginning when I left the island. This case had been simmering for several years, but this was the first overt attempt either party had made at handling it.

8. The distinction drawn by Gusfield (1967) between the sick deviant and the enemy deviant is useful here. Gusfield points out that "acts which we can perceive as those of sick and diseased people are irrelevant to the norm," whereas the acts of those who publicly define themselves or are publicly defined as enemies are seen as threats to the norm (1967: 312–14). Gusfield writes further that "deviance designations are not fixed. They may shift from one form to another over time. Defining a behavior pattern as one caused by illness makes a hostile response toward the actor illegitimate and inappropriate. 'Illness' is a social designation, by no means given in the nature of medical fact. . . . Hence the effort to define a practice as a consequence of illness is itself a matter of conflict and a political issue" (1967: 313).

9. The dyadic/triadic distinction made here is not to be taken literally, as meaning that only two parties or only three parties are involved in the process, but is meant as a description of the underlying structure of the process. Some dyadic responses may involve a third party who mediates or otherwise aids the two principals in negotiating a solution; in triadic processes, in contrast, the third party is not merely a mechanism for easing the exchange between the principals but has a distinct role and set of interests unrelated to theirs. Triadic processes can be represented in the form

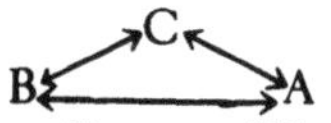

while dyadic processes look this way: B←→(C) A.

THREE

LITIGIOUS MARGINALS: CHARACTER AND DISPUTING IN A BAVARIAN VILLAGE

Harry F. Todd, Jr.

GOTTFRIEDING is a small, rural village lying deep in the Bavarian Forest of West Germany.[1] The pseudonym I have given it, which translates as "the place of God's peace," together with the village's sylvan location among high, rolling hills and lush forests, conjures up an image of a tranquil, serene peasant community—one in which people go about their everyday activities in a spirit of friendship and cooperation. Indeed, this is the picture that is received by the casual visitor passing through the village, or by the vacationer spending a few days. It is a picture, however, which is illusory; for like other villages of its kind, despite the outward trappings of community, Gottfrieding is not a unified whole. Rather, it is a conglomeration of individuals who continually interact and who, in the course of this interaction, must repeatedly choose among alternative courses of behavior.

These choices, however, are rarely unconstrained; individuals are seldom free to choose from among all competing alternatives. It is my aim in this paper to elucidate some of the sociocultural parameters which impose limitations on choice in Gottfrieding, particularly as these constraints affect the decisions that individuls in a marginal, or deviant, position in the village are required to make at various stages in the disputing process.

THE SETTING

Gottfrieding is located in the northeastern section of Lower Bavaria, a few miles north of the Danube River. The village exhibits the characteristics of a clustered village (*Haufendorf*), with its houses grouped around four major social centers: the general store, the church, the school, and the public house. The tight clustering of residential units around these public places ensures a great amount of interaction within a small, well-defined area.

The public house[2] is the prime locus of male interaction. At the same time, however, it plays a much wider role in village social life, providing a setting for many of the events which are celebrated at various points in the individual's life cycle (birth, confirmation, marriage), as well as for those festive occasions associated with the seasonal cycle of the village itself (dances at Christmas and carnival [*Fasching*]). One portion of the public house, the *Gastzimmer*,[3] or public drinking room, will be of particular interest to us later in this paper; for it is in this arena that many grievances and conflicts which occur among male community members are effectively managed.

Politically, the civil parish (*Gemeinde*) is the lowest administrative level in the West German governmental hierarchy. In the civil Parish of Gottfrieding, which had a total population of 743 in 1970, there are twelve villages and hamlets, ranging in size from the village of Gottfrieding itself (the parish seat), with 371 people, to the smallest of the hamlets, presently comprising only one household of six persons. The parish is administered by a mayor (*Bürgermeister*) and a parish council (*Gemeinderat*) composed of eight councilmen (*Gemeinderäte*). The mayor is the parish's chief administrative officer, as well as its major representative to the governmental bureacuracy lying outside the parish. Both he and the parish councilmen are elected for four-year terms.

The whole northeastern region of Lower Bavaria lies in a border area (*Grenzgebiet*), since it shares a common boundary with Czechoslovakia. Lower Bavaria (and the Bavarian Forest region in particular) has long had a reputation for being the backwater of Germany, and its people have been thought of as crude, illiterate peasants—a reputation which, in the past, was not completely undeserved. This picture has gradually changed, however, as the village and parish have been increasingly drawn into the wider industrialized society of West Germany. The village is not, in reality, a traditional "peasant" community any longer. In the economic sphere, for example, occupational patterns are radically different from those of yesteryear. In 1970, of the eighty-one employed men in the village, only 2 percent relied exclusively on agricultural pursuits as the sole source of income. The remaining 98 percent derived most of their income from employment in industrial or commercial enterprises located, for the most part, outside the village. Twenty-five percent of these men worked at both: they are the "worker-peasants" of modern-day Europe (see Franklin 1969)—men who are able to supplement cash wages earned in industry or commerce with income from part-time agricultural activities. The remaining 73 percent worked exclusively for cash wages or salaries—as skilled, semiskilled, or unskilled workers or laborers, or as craftsmen, tradesmen, or professionals—and had nothing at all to do with agriculture.

Thus, economically, today Gottfrieding is a strongly heterogeneous community in which peasants, worker-peasants, and wage earners live side by side. The heterogeneous nature of village life is underscored even more forcefully when it is recognized that 58 percent of the men in the worker-peasant and worker categories commute daily or weekly to their place of employment. Only 43 percent of the male labor force remains in the village during the workday (or workweek).

The occupational picture for the women of the village has also changed, though hardly to the extent that it has for men. Thus, while most (63 percent) of the women still report their primary employment as "housewife" (*Hausfrau*), and a few (3 percent) as "agriculturalists" (*Landwirtin*), others are assuming new responsibilities outside the home and family farm. Women who have taken jobs—

primarily as seamstresses in a dress-making factory in the village (17 percent), or as professionals or domestics (16 percent)—are able not only to supplement their family's income but, through this medium, to increase their influence in the family. In families with working wives, the "traditional" roles of the woman—her nearly exclusive involvement in the three *Ks*, *Kinder*, *Kirche*, and *Küche* (children, church, and kitchen)—is presently undergoing radical change. Wives are increasingly being viewed by their husbands as "partners in the marriage" and are accorded as great a voice, if not a greater one, in the running of the household and in the family's decisions as the man.

THE VILLAGE COMMUNITY: STRUCTURE AND NORMS

Thus, with the changes engendered by industrialization of the countryside and the latter's increasing involvement in the nation-state, the patterns of village life—both behaviorally and perceptually—have also changed. These seemingly disruptive socioeconomic forces, however—manifested, for example, in the restrictions that have been placed on male interaction by the exigencies of earning a cash wage—have not been so strong as to fragment the village's perception of itself *qua* community; there are a number of equally powerful integrative forces that have tended to counteract these potentially destructive ones. These integrative forces are bascially cultural in nature, deriving from shared perceptions of the world and manifesting themselves in a number of cultural symbols that Gottfriedingers use to define themselves as belonging together, to a community.

Paramount among these symbols is common residence, derived from the geographic and economic isolation of the village, which sorts villagers out from nonvillagers. A man is identified not by name, but by whether he is or is not a Gottfriedinger. Furthermore, Gottfriedingers clearly recognize that their speech patterns and usages are unique, even in the immediate area. They take pride in pointing out how different their "dialect" (*Dialekt*) is from that found ten miles in any direction.

A number of other socioeconomic parameters, also stemming from common residence, aid in providing villagers with symbols of identity. These include a shared history and agricultural heritage; cross-cutting ties of neighborhood, friendship, and kinship; a common religious creed; and continual, intensive interaction over the entire life span with the same people in the same arenas—in institutionalized meeting places such as the gastzimmer. All these factors have operated to counter the disruptive social pressures created by war and economic exigency. At the same time, they have acted to reinforce a sense of community, of sameness and belonging, among Gottfriedingers.

The notion of community, then, plays an important role in the definition of an individual as a Gottfriedinger, as an *insider*. It is an aspect of social life which derives, ultimately, though not exclusively, from coresidence, a symbol which serves to mark off insiders from *outsiders*. A second variable, however, provides another indispensible ingredient for community, and goes beyond common residence to cut across the seemingly monolithic and homogeneous grouping that coresidence would alone define. This all-important component of community is the village's normative system, for it is the individual's subscription or nonsubscription to village norms which acts to classify him *within the village* as an insider or as a noninsider.

Thus, there are two screens or filters through which an individual must pass in order to be classified as a member of the village community. The first is defined simply in terms of physical residence in Gottfrieding: no person residing outside the village can ever be included as a community member. The second screen is defined by subscription to village social norms. Individuals, even though they reside within the village's boundaries, may be sifted out from other villagers and barred from inclusion in the community if they do not subscribe to and support these social norms.

In Gottfrieding, subscription or nonsubscription to these social norms is defined in terms of the folk category of character (*Charakter*). Those persons in the village who conduct themselves in a manner antithetical to village norms are considered to be without character and are, by virtue of this lack, relegated to low statuses in the village's social structure. This conceptualization, however, is rooted in the social norms and norms of common consent[4] of only one segment of the village population—namely, in the norms of those persons who are considered to have character. Those who are considered by this segment to be characterless would not necessarily so classify themselves.

Those persons who are conceived of as having character belong to the central core of community life and interact on a frequent, regular basis in particular institutions. This grouping may be conveniently referred to in Gottfrieding as *insiders*, or as members of the village *social cluster* (cf. Epstein 1969: 111), the latter term referring to that dense portion of the village network in which there are multiple, cross-cutting ties between and among individuals. While the limits of such a cluster in any social situation are necessarily vague, they nevertheless are clear enough to define recognizable differences among villagers. This concept is used here, then, to indicate a grouping of people—an *exclusive* grouping to which one definitely does or does not belong (cf. Barnes 1954: 44).

The two attributes of community (coresidence and character), come together to define the social cluster, and to provide a picture of Gottfrieding's social structure. This structure may be represented schematically by two concentric circles. The inner cirle represents the cluster, the insiders—that part of the village network which is composed of people who live in the village *and* who subscribe to the social norms and norms of common consent held by most other villagers. These people are held together structurally by a series of mutiplex ties (based on kinship, friendship, neighborhood, and occupation), and culturally by subscription to a common normative system. These structural and cultural components combine in, and the ties and norms among insiders are constantly reinforced through, the continuous interaction that occurs among insiders in their institutionalized meeting places.

In the outer circle surrounding this inner core are the characterless individuals, or *marginals*. Like those in the cluster, marginals are tied into the village network in terms of coresidence and in terms of varying ties of kinship and neighborhood; but unlike insiders, they do not share in the community's normative system. Rather, their relationships with one another, and with those in the cluster, are based more on pragmatic, personal considerations rather than on normative ones (cf. Bailey 1969; Bott 1957). These people are seen by those within the cluster to be socially marginal to the community because of their characterlessness, and are consequently excluded from many village activities.

These marginals possess no institutionalized meeting places of their own, and rarely enter into those of the insiders—and even then, only on specific village-wide occasions. There are few cross-cutting ties among persons in this marginal category, or between them and insiders; those that do exist tend to be transactional in nature. Generally, the marginal is bound most closely with one neighbor or one friend instead of with a number of neighbors, friends, or work mates. There are a few kinship ties among the marginals, and between them and insiders, but where these exist they tend to be deemphasized. In their occupations, some of these people share very little with their fellow villagers who are insiders. They are itinerant workers, are out of work (either unemployed or unemployable), or are pensioned. These occupational factors, particularly, in the folk view, reflect strongly and negatively on the marginals and reinforce the characterless label that has been applied to them by insiders.

Character, then, is a folk concept used by villagers to differentiate between two categories of Gottfriedingers—insiders and marginals. As such, it is intimately bound up with the system of status and prestige in the village. Those without character, the marginals, can never hope to achieve or be accorded a high status by village insiders. In this situation, characterlessness per se is sufficient reason for relegation of an individual to a low status. Other considerations, however, may enter to cloud the picture; for the relationship between character and status is primarily a negative one. If one does not have character, he is automatically doomed to a low status. However, even if an individual has character, he is not automatically accorded a high status; it would be difficult if not impossible for a man with a small income and little or no property to claim for himself a high status. But his being of good character might well help him to raise his status above that which is accorded his fellow villager who is in similar economic circumstances but who is characterless. Further, it is extremely unlikely that an individual with a large amount of money, or with extensive property holdings, would ever be categorized as characterless and assigned a low status.

The folk category of character is not the sole source of the definition of villagers as marginal. There are several socioeconomic determinants that also partition the set, and that the analyst may enlist in identifying village marginals.

These socioeconomic criteria may be used to define two general types of marginals. The first is the *economic marginal*. He is distinguished primarily on the basis of several economic indicators and is generally referred to in the village as a *Taugenichts*, here meaning a "ne'er-do-well." This type of marginal is a person who cannot hold down a regular or a prestigious job. He usually has little or no money, and even that which he has is unwisely expended. He is a man, I was told, who even if he were given 10,000 marks today, would have nothing tomorrow. Such an individual is unable to feed and clothe his family in a manner considered appropriate by insiders; and the children of such people are living symbols of their parents' failings. In addition, these individuals are constantly in debt and continually appear in the local court in answer to suits for debt, garnishment of wages, or attachment or repossession of goods.

The second kind of marginal may simply be called the *troublemaker*. He, too, is referred to as a *Taugenichts* in its "good-for-nothing" connotation. This person, generally, over time, has acquired a reputation for getting into trouble, for causing problems. He is a person who simply cannot get along with others: he is either insulting or insulted, attacking or attacked, complaining or complained about. He is an individual who, at one time or another, finds himself filing the answering complaints in the village reconciliation agency (see below) or in the court for slander, malicious gossip, insult, or rumor mongering; or who files nuisance actions in the district court against fellow villagers for minor debts or other issues.

While these two marginal types are analytically distinct, in actuality the economic marginal is almost invariable a troublemaker also.

His marginality is enhanced by his economic woes, many of which act to exacerbate an already bad situation.

Two additional general points must also be made here with reference to marginality. First, movement from the marginal category into the insider one, or vice versa, is possible, though generally the tendency is for a person to move toward the outer zones rather than to migrate inward. Inward migration takes times and requires effort; one must not only make a claim to character but must establish this claim through a long, slow process of proving himself acceptable to insiders.

Second, marginality tends to run in families, though it does not invariably do so. Affiliation with marginals, particularly with marginals who are relatives and who live in the same household, may cause a nonmarginal individual also to be so classified. To escape this categorization, that individual must make a claim to character in his own right and must, through interaction with insiders, constantly validate this claim.

On the basis of the folk category, village insider informants consistently placed thirteen individuals, representing five families, in the marginal category. Opinions on seven other individuals, however, differed. By applying the socioeconomic criteria to the same population, I defined as marginal the thirteen persons unequivocally named by informants using the folk category. In addition, four other persons, all of whom had received equivocal informant ratings, were located. Three other persons who had received equivocal informant ratings but who did not meet the socioeconomic criteria for marginality, were excluded from further consideration.

The two listings, then, identified thirteen "hard core" marginals, and four "quasimarginals"—those who were on the skids, moving into the marginal zone, or on the upswing, entering the cluster area. For analytical purposes, however, these seventeen people, representing 7 percent of the village adult population (eighteen years old or older) of 244, will be considered here to constitute the marginal population of Gottfrieding.

recting, or sanctioning, mechanisms which may be activated to restore the status quo ante. These restrictions on interaction are embodied in a number of *rules of the game,* which are called into play throughout an evening. During this period the stammtisch will experience several shifts in personel: some men will leave, others will take their places. The only requirement for joining in is that the entering person must know these game rules, and abide by them.

There are three basic kinds of game rules found in this setting: rules that define who is eligible to join in (rules of personnel), rules that deal with how those interacting should behave (rules of behavior), and rules that state what should be done when a rule is broken (sanctions). It must be noted, however, that most of these rules lie at the analytical level only; most participants would not be able to verbalize many of them. In addition, these rules are not of the same analytical order: some are of a lower level of abstraction than others and are more specific restatements of other higher-level rules.

a. Rules of Personnel. The gastzimmer is a place in which *men* interact. In this setting, further, interaction ideally occurs among equals; those who are considered unequal are perforce excluded from participation. Thus, the institution is a place in which *male insiders* gather; and village women, village male marginals, and outsiders (whether tourists or other representatives of the outside world) have only a tangential role, if any, to play in interaction here.[6]

b. Rules of Behavior. As the primary locus of male interaction, the gastzimmer is the main village arena in which consensus can be achieved on norms. The frequency of interaction in this environment serves to correct idiosyncracies of ideology and behavior (cf. Bott 1957: 212) by providing a place in which reality testing can occur.[7] Reality testing in this setting simply means that the individual is provided with an opportunity to question whether his thoughts and actions are in line with those of the other men present. It means that he is given a chance to reassess his position, to rethink his ideas, to rephrase his arguments in light of the criticism of others. It does not permit him, however, to question the norms themselves; for there is a crucial difference between questioning whether there is indeed consensus on a particular norm, and challenging the validity of the normative system or of a particular norm itself. Indeed, it is because marginals question the norms, and not the consensus, that they are segregated from the remainder of the community.

Thus, gastzimmer behavior that challenges one or more norms of the cluster is inappropriate (antinormative itself) and disallowed. Furthermore, while interaction here is necessarily interpersonal, it must be based on an issue, not on a personality. Once an issue becomes personalized, once a man's reputation is attacked, the bounds of permissible interaction have been exceeded; all too frequently, these kinds of interaction provide the basis for grievances that quickly mushroom into conflicts, often into disputes.

Because of the requirement of equality among participants, each man has a right to be treated as a peer and to express his views. To deny a man these rights is to deny that he is equal. Even though his opinion on an issue may not be concurred in by (and indeed may be highly unpopular among) other participants, the individual still has a right to express it, within the limitations noted above. Political affiliation, for example, provides one basis for differences of opinion here. Yet no man is denied the right or opportunity to express his views on political issues, even if he be a lone Social Democrat at a table full of Christian Socialists.

This right to be heard, however, carries with it a correlative duty to participate. Equality among those present is based on face-to-face interaction; and if a man does not join in discussions, if he does not actively participate, he may be in danger of losing his right to participate at all.

Another outgrowth of the right to be heard is the duty of participants to defend their viewpoints. This consideration does not imply, of course, that a man may not modify his views in the light of criticism by others. On the contrary, the reality-testing function of the gastzimmer is based precisely on the opposite premise: that opinions will be modified in order to bring them into consonance with those of the wider community. If modification of an unpopular opinion should prove necessary or desirable, however, such modification should never take the form of capitulation, at least not of obvious capitulation; rather it should occur slowly, by way of small compromises and gradual concessions.

Finally, if an attack is made by a person claiming equality—a claim which is felt by participants not to be acceptable—then no response need be forthcoming, particularly when the attack assumes a personal character. The offended party may opt simply to ignore the charge, and thus refuse to escalate the matter; indeed, this may be the only viable course open to them. To pick up the gauntlet in such a case would be to acknowledge that the offender was of equal status, or that his remark was worthy of consideration.

Infrequently, a grievance or conflict degenerates into physical action. When this occurs, every effort is made by others present to break it up. In general, if the antagonists insist on fighting, they are sent outside. Fights have no place in the gastzimmer, for they represent a physical threat to other participants, as well as a threat of economic loss to the owners of the establishment.

These rules, then, generally define the manner in which men are expected to behave in this setting. Not infrequently, however, one or more of them is broken. To take care of such situations, a number of procedures have been developed.

First, a general preference is manifested here toward avoidance of conflict altogether. If behavior which gives rise to a grievance can be ignored (or if it cannot be ignored, an excuse can be found for it), then no conflict or dispute will result. One common excuse is that the offender is "speaking through beer" (*er spricht durch Bier*), that is, he is too drunk to know what he is saying. Although this excuse is frequently used to mitigate or even excuse the offense, the offended party is still expected to be properly aggrieved, and to protect his honor by confronting the offender, thus escalating the grievance. It is then up to another man, usually a friend of the aggrieved, to assure him that the offender is "speaking through beer." The matter is then generally permitted to deescalate through the offended party's acquiescence in this judgment.

There are occasions, however, in which the infraction cannot be ignored or excused, and a dispute (which may involve physical action) cannot be avoided. In this situation, a third party not directly involved is expected to intervene in the dispute in an attempt to separate the antagonists, and to mend any ruptures in social relations which have occurred. Thus, physical intervention by a third party is almost invariably accompanied by verbal attempts at deescalation. If either or both attempts fail, however, and physical aggression continues, then the dispute must be removed from the premises.

The person who assumed this conciliator or mediator role may coax, cajole, importune, shame, wheedle, and exhort (even extort) either or both parties; he may attempt to avoid the issue by changing the subject through which the grievance, conflict, or dispute was given rein; he may threaten one or both of the antagonists with physical expulsion from the arena, if he is the publican (*Gastwirt*); or he may join in the argument himself, offering a middle road which both parties can adopt without losing face. If he should fail in these attempts, the recalcitrant party may find that he is subject to one of the several sanctions available to the gastzimmer group.

c. Sanctions. When an individual, despite repeated warnings from other participants, continually ignores or breaks the rules, or habitually acts as if the rules do not apply to him, he may be excluded from further participation in gastzimmer interaction. This sanction may be imposed either by the men at the stammtisch or by the publican; and it may be complete or partial, temporary or permanent.

Expulsion by the publican is considered an extreme sanction, and is rarely invoked. Nevertheless, the owners of gastzimmers are keenly aware of the necessity of segregating troublemakers; they realize that these people threaten the orderly course of interaction in their institution, hence their own economic security. A gastzimmer that acquires a reputation as a place where fights frequently occur will be shunned by many.

There is a more subtle way of excluding a person from gastzimmer interaction, this one effected by the men at the stammtisch themselves. A person, over a period of time, may find that he is pushed off into a corner, that he is not listened to, that no one will move over to allow him to pull a chair up to the table. In this way, he is gradually isolated—first socially, and then physically—and made to feel unwelcome if he intrudes himself. Over time, he may take up a position permanently at another table, away from the stammtisch; and afterwards, he may appear less and less frequently, perhaps at the same time beginning to frequent establishments in neighboring villages. He has not been told not to return, and yet his visits come further and further apart, until finally he is not seen at all.

The gradual isolation and ostracism of the repeated rule breaker has one major advantage over the other exclusionary mechanisms: it is possible for the renagade to stop the exclusionary process at almost any time, and even to reverse it; for an actor may be reinstated by mending his ways.

Reinstatement may be achieved by way of apology or other atoning action, and may be made directly to the offended party or group or indirectly through a third party. With an apology, the offender explicitly recognizes his mistakes; he recants. Further, he reaffirms the validity of the norms he once challenged. The apology, however, need not be explicit; actions may suffice. In either case, the atoning party may be put on probation until the members of the group decide that he is indeed sincere and ready for readmission.

The following incident, observed in the gastzimmer, illustrates the operation of a number of these rules of the game.

Drivers for the Gottfrieding brewery work on a commission basis, so that the more beer they deliver, the greater is their income. One of these drivers, Karl, made an arrangement with the foreman of a nearby textile factory to deliver several cases of beer each week for the consumption by the workers. On his latest trip, however, he learned that Xaver, a villager who works in the factory, had complained about the beer and had suggested to the foreman that another brand be bought. The foreman agreed, and so informed Karl, who thus lost a customer and income.

Early that afternoon, Xaver entered the gastzimmer and took a place at the stammtisch, where several men were already seated. Shortly thereafter, Karl appeared with a friend who had accompanied him on that day's rounds. Both Karl and Xaver were already visibly drunk.

As Karl entered, he looked over at Xaver, and muttered under his breath "You *Hammel* [castrated ram]!" [8]

Conversation at the stammtisch ceased, and there was a noticeable tension in the air. Xaver tried to ignore the remark, as did the other men at the table, all looking down into their beers.

Karl and his friend sat down at one of the other tables. He began slowly and softly at first, berating Xaver, building up in audibility and voice tone until his comments could clearly be heard by everyone in the room. Finally, he shouted across the room: "You had no right to do what you did, and you know it, you *Saubär* [literally, sow-bear]!"

Xaver, continuing to stare into his beer, responded quietly, "It's none of your business."

"What do you mean, it's none of my business?" Karl demanded. "You're a saubär!"

"What did you say?" Xaver demanded, turning to Karl for the first time, his face in a snarl.

At this point, one of the men at the stammtisch, Franz, intervened, turning to Karl, lifting his head and chin high in censure, and saying, "Hey! Wait a minute." But his remark failed to stop Karl.

"I said, hammel! saubär! You *Dreckhammel* [filthy castrated ram]!"

Xaver turned to one of the men at the table, asked him for a pencil, took a beer mat, and began to write on it.

"You want to make a complaint [for insult in the village reconciliation agency]?" Karl demanded. "Okay. I'll give you something to complain about. Can you remember them all?" he asked, referring to the animal names he had earlier called Xaver. "Dreckhammel. Saubär. Let's see. Have I missed anything?" he shouted defiantly.

Xaver turned sharply to face Karl. At this point, Franz again tried to intervene, aided by the grumblings of others at the table. "Come on," Franz demanded. "That's enough!" But again, his remarks failed to deter the protagonists.

Suddenly, Karl jumped up and rushed Xaver, catching the man—and everyone else—off guard. He pushed Xaver off his chair, and onto the floor. "You *Scheiss'* [shit]!" he growled.

Franz jumped up and grabbed Karl, pushing him back toward his seat with a roar of disapproval. One of the other men helped Xaver back onto his chair.

Karl continued, "Go ahead and write them down. Write them all down if you can." (This latter reference was to the fact that Xaver is functionally illiterate.) "Go ahead!" he challenged. "Make a complaint!"

After a few moments of silence, Karl continued. "Let's see what you've written down," he demanded.

"It's my business," Xaver retorted. "I've got it all down here," he said indicating the beer mat.

Again, Karl charged Xaver, grabbing at the beer mat.

"You scheiss'!" Karl shouted, grabbing Xaver from his chair and throwing him several feet against a bench and the wall. The men at the table jumped to their feet, but were too late to prevent the action. Xaver's head hit the wall, and he fell to the floor motionless, blood flowing from a cut in his scalp. Had Franz not then intervened, Karl would have continued the attack.

"You stupid ass!" Franz shouted, pulling Karl to the other side of the room. "Now look what you've done!"

"It's not my fault," Karl insisted. "It's his own fault."

Xaver was out cold. A doctor was called by the publican, who then proceeded to berate Karl thoroughly for his actions.

Even after Xaver and two others left to see the doctor, Karl kept insisting that the affair was not his fault, that Xaver "had it coming," that he was not sorry about what he had done. No man in the gastzimmer made any move or comment which would affirm these statements or lend approval to his actions. Instead, they turned their backs on him, ignoring him.

A few days later, I learned that Karl had paid the medical bills that Xaver had incurred, and in addition, had given Xaver money for "pain and suffering." Xaver, in return, never filed a complaint, and the matter was, for all intents and purposes, dropped. Karl was retained as a driver by the publican, but only after he had been thoroughly castigated for his actions, had made full restitution to Xaver, and had promised never to take such action again.

From this case, we see that while some conflict may be tolerated within the gastzimmer (even though disapproved), all conflict is not. The initial response of the men present was to try to quiet Karl by calling attention to the inappropriateness of the personal names he was using against Xaver. One may disagree with another in this setting, but he may not attack the individual by calling him names or by physically assaulting him. When Franz's verbal admonitions failed to calm the principals, after the first attack he tried to prevent further action by separating the two. It was only by moving quickly that Karl managed to catch everyone unprepared the second time and succeeded in injuring Xaver.

Karl's payment of Xaver's medical bills, together with the added sum for pain and suffering, kept his job for him. Furthermore, it foreclosed Xaver's filing of a complaint in the reconciliation agency.

At the same time, it was taken by the group as an apology; and as such, it prevented exclusionary action against him.

Up to this point, we have considered only the operation of the men's social arena in the management of grievances, conflicts, and disputes. I now want to consider briefly a parallel institutionalized meeting place that serves many of the same functions for women as do the gastzimmers for men, viz., the village *information center.*

2. *The Information Center*

The women of Gottfrieding do their marketing practically every day and are thus provided with an excuse for visiting with other women. They pause for a few minutes before and after shopping to exchange a tidbit of news with others whom they have met in the store or on the street; or they drop in at one of the information centers in the village for a more formal and lengthy exchange. The woman who depends on the first route runs the risk of frequent interruptions and exposure, if she is gossiping, and this path is limited essentially to quick exchanges.

On the other hand, the woman who wants the whole story, or who has a particularly juicy bit of information to contribute, adopts the second route: she visits an information center. Such centers are simply the homes of information brokers—women who act as a central clearing house to receive and pass on information.

By far the most popular of the three village centers is the one across the street from the centrally located grocery store. Although each center has its regulars, the criteria for admission to one particular center are not generally so restrictive as to exclude nonregulars.

The flexibility of the rules defining who may participate in particular information centers, however, should not be taken to imply that everyone is eligible; for, as Gluckman (1963: 313) points out, "the right to gossip . . . is a privilege which is extended to a person when he or she is accepted as a member of a group or set. It is a hallmark of membership." In Gottfrieding, this requirement is operationalized by defining the centers as places in which *insider* women gossip and exchange other information. It translates as a rule exluding marginal women from participation, and in so doing underscores once again the social differentiation found in the village.

The organization of female information interchange is simple once the existence of these centers and brokers is known. Women drop by a center alone, or in pairs, to exchange news and gossip with the broker—perhaps over a beer or a cup of coffee. When more than two or three women gather together, however, particularly in public, the conversation rarely includes gossip—or at least not much gossip. There is always a danger involved in such open gossip with too many people; the gossip becomes too public, and the gossip monger may well open herself up to charges of slander and defamation of character, as well as rumor mongering, and thus to actions in the reconciliation agency. Private gatherings of two, even three, on the other hand, are relatively safe, particularly if they occur within the confines of a center.

An additional safeguard against exposure is built into the system. A person who feels himself aggrieved by a village gossip is faced with the paradox of either bringing a charge of gossiping against the monger in a public forum (and in so doing, publicizing the gossip even further) or doing nothing. This paradox is not easily resolved, since neither course is particularly attractive; and its resolution will depend on many factors, including the status and reputation of the injured individual, as well as that of his opponent.

Thus, like interaction at the beer table among men, information exchange among women has its own game rules. One visits with equals, and exchanges news and gossip with equals, just as one drinks and argues with equals. Women are excluded from the gastzimmer, men from the information centers, and marginals from both. Procedurally, too, the two institutions manifest quite similar patterns: the right to receive gossip and other information imposes a duty to supply it from time to time Furthermore, by gossiping, women aid in the redefinition and reaffirmation of community (cluster) norms; for the information contained in gossip may itself act as a sanctioning mechanism, providing an outlet through which a transgressor is told that her behavior is inappropriate. In addition, long-term hostilities may be avoided through the use of this mechanism, by providing the aggrieved party with a channel—similar to the one provided by the gastzimmer—through which the abreaction of hostilities can be achieved without confrontation (hence, without escalation).

There is a major difference, however, between these two institutions, particularly in terms of the content of interaction permitted in each. Whereas talk at the beer table ideally never involves attacks on personalities, gossip ideally inevitably does. This course of action is made somewhat safer in the information center, despite the fact that more sensitive and potentially explosive topics are dealt with there, simply because the exchange occurs within small groups of two or three women. Interaction at the beer table, on the other hand, is polyadic, and generally involves six to twelve men. In the gastzimmer, a confrontation—either immediately, if the party under attack is present, or at a later time—is almost inescapable, and escalation almost unavoidable. Thus, gossip in this public arena is discouraged not only normatively but also pragmatically; there are simply too many potential witnesses to the attack who could be called to testify against the gossiper.

In the information center, on the other hand, the dyadic or triadic nature of the conversation makes it extremely unlikely that either confrontation or widespread publication will occur. Even if they do, and the issue is escalated to a dispute, it is very unlikely that action will be taken against the gossip monger, or that the other who participated in the gossip will testify against her, even if they are called on to do so; for to do so might well mean their future foreclosure from the center. This is not to say, however, that gossiping is completely foolproof, even in the Gottfrieding centers; for if it is carried out in front of the wrong people at the wrong time, gossip can backfire on its purveyor and cause her serious problems.

3. *Insider Mechanisms: Summary and Consequences*

We have seen within the Gottfrieding cluster strong normative constraints against confrontation and escalation. There is a marked reluctance to promote grievances to conflicts, and conflicts to disputes—a reluctance reflected in the stress within the cluster on maintaining grievances, conflicts, and disputes within the community. Taking a dispute to a remedy agency outside the village for resolution is a form of escalation that may be normatively disapproved and negatively sanctioned; for it means that resolution may well be achieved by reference to norms other than those which prevail within the community. If a dispute should arise, it should normatively be mediated by a third party drawn from the community, not by strangers or outsiders.

The strong adherance to this normative proscription against taking cases outside the village for settlement is reflected in the fact that very few disputes with an insider complainant left the community for resolution. Those disputes that did go beyond the boundaries of the gastzimmer and information centers into the village-centered reconciliation agency (*Sühneversuch*) were usually resolved there; or, if they were not, the claim was usually abandoned. This situation contrasts sharply with that obtaining in cases in which village marginals were complainants. Marginals, lacking access to arenas like the gastzimmer and information centers—village social centers in which the early stages of the disputing process can be contained and managed—must take their cases to agencies in which they too are eligible to compete. In the village, this means they must go to the priest or mayor (as confessor or mediator) or to the reconciliation agency; if these agencies fail, marginals must go outside Gottfrieding, to governmental officials or lawyers, or to the courts.

PANVILLAGE MECHANISMS: THE RECONCILIATION AGENCY[9]

Village marginals with grievances have only three choices open to them: they may choose simply to lump it; they may choose to confront their opponent directly, with the intention of seeking redress of the grievance; or they may choose to escalate the grievance or conflict to a dispute by bringing an action in a public arena or by involving a third party. Confrontation, in the absence of constraints (such as those that exist among insiders in the gastzimmer or information center) almost invariably leads to escalation and to disputes. In the discussion that follows, we will be dealing exclusively with this escalated phase and with the village reconciliation agency—open to both insiders and marginals—which is specifically designed to handle these disputes.[10]

Bavarian law provides that a private criminal complaint (similar to an Anglo-American tort action) may be filed in court only if the injured party has first undertaken an "attempt at reconciliation" (*Sühneversuch*) with the offending party at the parish level. The agency was set up primarily as a means of controlling court loads and of preventing frivolous and nuisance actions from reaching the courts. Included in the list of actions that must first be heard in this agency are breach of peace, insult, slander, light intentional or negligent bodily injury, threat, destruction of property, and malicious gossip.

The proceedings are headed by the mayor. After a complainant files a charge in the parish hall, a date is set for a hearing, usually one which is agreeable to both parties. Although the statute provides that the respondent's attendance may be compelled, the mayor has indicated that such action would not promote reconciliation. Thus, frequently, only the complainant appears; and the mayor has no choice but to issue a certificate (*Zeugnis*) which states that the hearing was held but was without result due to the nonappearance of the respondent. The complainant is then free to file an action in court. Similarly, if both parties appear at the hearing, but no settlement is reached, the certificate is also issued. Frequently, however, even though the certificate has been obtained, no suit is ever filed.

When both parties appear, the hearing begins, the mayor asking each party to state his side of the dispute. Since the mayor is acting as a conciliator trying to get the parties back together rather than trying to find fault with one or the other; since the issues and questions of fact involved are rarely clear-cut, and are almost always in dispute; and since the mayor has no power to enforce a decision, even if he made one—his role is simply to listen attentively and to try to persuade both parties that a reconciliation is in their best interests. Thus, after talking with the disputants and with other villagers who have information bearing on the problem, he points out the rights and wrongs and the strengths and weaknesses in each position, and tries to suggest a compromise. Thus, he coaxes the parties by logic, condemns them for their obstinance and unreasonableness, shames them for their intransigence. He cites prior friendship or common economic interests and suggests that the village welfare would better be served by their reconciliation. With all these tactics, he aims for an amicable resolution of the problem.

During the 1960–69 period, a total of 51 cases were heard in this agency. Intravillage disputes accounted for 22 (43 percent); an additional 11 (22 percent) were disputes between a villager and a nonvillager who was, nevertheless, coresident in the parish (hereinafter referred to as "parishioner"); and the remaining 18 (35 percent) were disputes between two nonvillage parishoners. Since no villagers were involved in this last category of cases, this corpus has been omitted from further consideration here.

Of the corpus of 33 cases involving villagers, 32 (97 percent) of the actions were brought for insult or slander. The thirty-third case was a personal injury action, involving money damages. Although the agency, therefore, is authorized to hear a variety of complaints—including breach of the peace and threats to life or property, as well as actual property damage and personal injury—in actuality, it deals with relatively few complaint types, and practically all of the cases brought to it revolve around the question of one's good name, his character.

TABLE 3.1
INCIDENCE OF ACTIONS IN RECONCILIATION AGENCY BY COMPLAINANT-RESPONDENT PAIRS

Complainant-Respondent	N	%
Marginal-Marginal	9	27
Marginal-Insider	6	18
Insider-Marginal	3	9
Insider-Insider	4	12
Marginal-Parishioner	8	24
Parishioner-Marginal	1	3
Insider-Parishioner	0	0
Parishioner-Insider	2	6
TOTALS	33	99*

* Rounding error

If these 33 cases are broken down in terms of complainant-respondent pairs, some interesting patterns can be discerned (see table 3.1). Examination of the figures reveals that in 27 of the 33 cases under consideration here (82 percent), marginals were involved: in 23 cases (70 percent) they were complainants, in 13 (52 percent) respondents.[11] In addition, in those 23 cases with marginal complainants, resolution was achieved in only 8 (35 percent). Of the 15 cases remaining unresolved, 10 (67 percent) were taken on to court.

These figures contrast with those for cases in which insiders were complainants. Insiders appeared in 15 of the 33 cases (45 percent): in 7 (21 percent) as complainants and in 12 (36 percent) as respondents. The major difference between them and marginals, however, comes in when resolution rates are considered. In the 7 cases with insider complainants, 4 were of the insider v. insider type and 3 of the insider v. marginal type. All insider-insider cases were resolved amicably here. In contrast, in none of the insider-marginal cases did the respondent appear; hence, in none was resolution achieved. Yet even though all 3 of these insider-marginal cases were taken to court, a compromise settlement was reached in each before a decision was handed down by the court. These data, then, should be read as directly supporting the viability of the (insider) normative proscription against appealing cases to the outside for resolution.

The evidence from the reconciliation agency can be summarized as follows:

1. The disputes brought to this agency were almost exclusively those involving honor and reputation—in a word, character—a scarce resource here.

2. These disputes were brought primarily by those in marginal positions within the village social structure: 6 percent of the village's adult population brought 70 percent of the actions here.

3. In cases in which marginals were involved—whether as complainants or respondents—reconciliation was generally not achieved here, and more frequently than not the case wound up in court.

4. Insiders seem loath to take cases into this agency for resolution.

5. In cases in which insiders were involved, resolution and reconciliation was usually achieved, provided that the respondent was also an insider or a nonmarginal parishoner. If the respondent was a marginal, resolution and reconciliation could not be expected.

As I have suggested elsewhere (Todd 1978), it is doubtful that the Reconciliation Agency was ever very effective in the area of dispute management in this village, particularly in disputes involving marginals. In a broader context, however, the agency has provided a convenient forum for marginals in which claims to character could be lodged and status fought for. It has provided an arena for institutionalized "prestige contests," and a procedure that allows the Gottfrieding marginals to establish a pecking order among and between themselves, as well as to try to establish a status claim vis-à-vis village insiders. In this respect, then, it has acted to supplement and complement the other options open to marginals in grievance situations—avoidance (or lumping), face-to-face negotiations (with the attendant risk of escalation and even violence if or when tempers flare), or seeking a decision in court—by providing an institutionalized procedure that not only deals with the manifest problem (the grievance itself), but also reflects the underlying structural conflict and social dissonance as well.

EXTRAVILLAGE MECHANISMS: THE COURTS

The reconciliation agency data provide only a part of the picture in Gottfrieding, for the agency is designed to handle only particular kinds of disputes. There are instances in which village institutions are not able—because of the subject matter of the dispute—to contain the problem and in which a villager, if he is to obtain satisfaction, must utilize outside agencies. The individual, in such instances, is not penalized for ignoring the general proscription against recourse to outside agencies, but only if his actions meet several criteria.

First, the issue must be one that cannot be handled satisfactorily within the village by village institutions and personnel. Second, it must involve a scarce resource, usually real property or money. Third, the claimant must have made some effort to settle with the respondent within the village context, utilizing acceptable procedures. Cases involving honor and reputation (scarce resources for some segments of the village population), for example, should not be taken outside the village for resolution, since normatively these issues can be effectively dealt with by village institutions and personnel. A boundary dispute, on the other hand, may ultimately be resolvable only by recourse to the surveying office, the county offices, or the court.

There are a number of resources outside Gottfrieding upon which an individual may draw in seeking to resolve or manage his problems. His choice among these agencies, however, is limited, primarily by the nature of the problem itself, secondarily by economic considerations. Even with these constraints, however, a number of outside agencies remain, including governmental administrative agencies, lawyers, the police, and the courts. In the following section, the discussion is limited to one of these: the district court that has jurisdiction over the region in which Gottfrieding is located.

The district court (*Amtsgericht*) is the lowest level in the West German ordinary court hierarchy. It has original civil jurisdiction over most cases in which the amount in controversy does not exceed 2,000 marks (approximately $700 in 1975), and original criminal jurisdiction over most petty offenses and misdemeanors. In looking at both civil and criminal records from this court for 1960–69, we shall once again see that it is the marginal population of Gottfrieding which turns to this court with problems; and that insiders, when they do appear here, do so under one of the subject-matter exceptions to the general proscription noted above.

1. Civil Cases

Civil cases heard before the court dealt with (1) claims arising out of *economic rights* (debt, eviction, personal injury, property damage) and (2) actions requesting *executions on judgments* that were based on these economic rights (attachments, garnishments, repossessions). Thus, the "economic rights" actions represent original court proceedings; the "executions" are actions deriving from a judgment in an "economic rights" case with which the defendants have yet to comply.

This latter situation arises frequently in civil suits against marginals in Gottfrieding, since in most cases the original judgment against the defendant is obtained in a court far away from the village—in Berlin, in Hamburg, in Munich. Judgment is usually for the plaintiff by default, the defendant, because of the distant location of the court, not appearing to respond. This default judgment, however, is worthless unless and until the plaintiff can locate some of the defendant's property that lies within the jurisdiction of the court rendering the judgment. If this is not possible, then the plaintiff must go, with his default judgment, to another court that does have jurisdiction over the defendant and his property and ask this second court to execute the judgment of the first court by attaching the defendant's property, by garnisheeing his wages, or by repossessing the goods giving rise to an unpaid debt. These execution actions, therefore, almost invariably wind up in the court having jurisdiction over the area in which the defendant has his primary residence.

In the court having jurisdiction over Gottfrieding, 59 original "economic rights" cases involving Gottfriedingers were heard between 1960 and 1969. Debt cases were the most frequent (21 actions, or 36 percent of the corpus), followed by actions for increases in (illegitimate) child support payments (16 cases, 27 percent), back rent and eviction (9 cases, 15 percent), cease and desist orders (5 cases, 8 percent), property damage (4 cases, 7 percent); personal injury (2 cases, 3 percent), and recovery of goods (2 cases, 3 percent).

Of these 59 cases, 27 (46 percent) were of the villager-villager type, 12 (20 percent) villager-outsider, and 20 (35 percent) outsider-villager. In villager-villager cases, marginals were involved in 21 (78 percent): in 18 (67 percent) they were plaintiffs, in 13 (48 percent) defendants. (This closely parallels information from the reconciliation agency, which showed marginals as plaintiffs in 70 percent of the actions.) Insiders, on the other hand, were plaintiffs in only 33 percent of these villager-villager cases, though they were defendants in 52 percent. As plaintiffs, they also sued other insiders in 6 cases (22 percent), marginals in 3 (11 percent).

These 27 cases, then, reflect the total corpus of original economic rights suits brought by one villager against another. The other two kinds of cases appearing in the 59-case corpus (villager-outsider and outsider-villager), however, do not represent such a total corpus: we are seeing in these latter instances only those actions that a Gottfrieding or outsider plaintiff chooses to bring in this particular district court; and these actions are only a portion of the total number of economic rights cases brought by these plaintiffs. We miss completely, for example, those cases in which an outsider plaintiff sues a Gottfriedinger in a court outside the immediate area and gains a default judgment. Similarly, we miss those actions in which a Gottfriedinger plaintiff chooses to sue an outsider defendant in a court which has jurisdiction over him. The data, then, for the villager-outsider and outsider-villager suits are incomplete, and for this reason are of interest to us only in connection with the discussion of the "execution" cases.

Of the 80 "execution" cases involving a villager that were heard by this court, 68 cases were brought by an outsider; and an additional 9 of these 80 cases were brought by a Gottfriedinger against a fellow villager. The remaining 3 cases were of the villager-outsider type. Thus, in 77 cases (96 percent of the corpus) Gottfriedingers were defendants; and in 85 percent of these latter cases the suit was brought by an outsider. Most of these outsider plaintiffs were retail companies located throughout West Germany which were trying to recover money for goods sold on the installment plan, a default judgment for which had already been obtained in another court. In these 77 actions, marginals responded in 57 (74 percent). Only 7 of the 17 village marginals, however, were found to be associated with these execution suits. These 7, representing 3 households, were all economic marginals.

In these outsider-villager economic actions, suits against insiders were settled as soon as the court having jurisdiction over the defendant's property agreed to execute the original default judgment. Suits against the economic marginals, on the other hand, did not usually result in such a settlement. Instead, these marginals threw up a number of legal roadblocks to the executions. It would not be unfounded to assert that these economic marginals, through years of dealing with the system, have developed a very definite expertise in handling actions of this kind, and are able to manipulate them to their own ends. One way is simply to let an execution judgment go by way of default. When the plaintiff tries to find goods to attach or repossess, or wages to garnish, he comes up empty-handed; either the goods are gone or are now worthless, or the defendent is out of work, hence judgment-proof.

There is a second favorite ploy, which works more to the economic advantage of the marginal defendant, and which is consequently preferred by many because it permits them to keep the goods while at the same time deferring or escaping payment on them. This mechanism is the pauper's oath (*Offenbarungseid*), a response in which the defendant fills out a form, swearing that, because his liabilities exceed his assets (each category being itemized), and because of family needs and other current financial obligations, he is unable to pay the debt at present. The acceptance of such an oath by the court acts to suspend payment on the debt (or to modify the terms of payment), while at the same time preserving the plaintiff's right to recover at a future date. Of the 77 execution cases, 29 (38 percent) involved the filing of a pauper's oath; and marginals accounted for 24 of these 29 instances (82 percent).[12]

In their continual involvement in these kinds of cases, the economic marginals of Gottfrieding present to village insiders a clear confirmation of their inability to handle money wisely, a failing that acts only to perpetuate their marginal classification.

2. *Criminal Cases*

For the 1960–69 period, 185 criminal cases in which a Gottfriedinger was defendant were heard in this court. These 185 cases involved a total of 86 different individuals, though the distribution was not a random one. For example, two of the village's leading businessmen accounted for 24 (13 percent) of the total (12 cases each). Their involvement in criminal matters, however, was limited to misdemeanors—primarily infractions of police regulations or violations of the weight laws for transport operations on public highways.

By far the largest concentration of criminal cases is in this area of minor violations: traffic offenses comprise 33 percent of the corpus, followed by other petty violations of miscellaneous regulations (23 percent). Marginals are more or less randomly distributed throughout these categories, the number of marginals being in line with their incidence in the general population. We may, therefore, dismiss these categories of cases as noninformative for our present purpose. Similarly, we may disregard three other categories of cases as well, because of the small number of instances in each: offenses against the State or the public, and offenses in office, comprised 6 percent of the corpus, while offenses against morality and acts dangerous to the general welfare stood at 1 percent each.

Thus, we are left with two major categories: offenses against the person (21 percent) and economic delicts (15 percent). Offenses against the person involve two basic types of action: those dealing with bodily injury and those dealing with honor and reputation. While marginal involvement in the first of these subcategories is high (25 percent), it is hardly high enough to warrant special consideration. The insult subcategory, however, presents a different picture, for here we find that marginal involvement is up to 84 percent.

Insult cases are of two major types, depending on the kind of complaint that is filed in the court. The first is the private complaint (*Privatklage*), which is similar to an Anglo-American tort action. In Bavaria, however, as noted above, no action can be filed in court until an attempt at reconciliation has been made. The private complaints which reached this court, therefore, represent unsuccessful reconciliation agency cases. In the Gottfrieding agency, reconciliation was achieved in only 12 of the 33 cases (36 percent). Of the remaining 21 unresolved cases, 14 (42 percent) were taken on to court—3 (21 percent) with insider plaintiffs, 1 (7 percent) with an outsider plaintiff, but 10 (71 percent) with a marginal plaintiff. It is clear, then, that it is overwhelmingly the marginal population of the village which brings insult cases to the courts.

The second type of insult case arises out of a criminal complaint (*Strafantrag*). This type of complaint is comparable to the Anglo-American lawsuit for criminal libel or slander, and is distinct from the private complaint in that a jail sentence or fine may result. Four such cases—3 involving marginals—were filed in the district court. In 2 of the 3, a marginal was the plaintiff.

In both kinds of insult cases, we find that the involvement of the marginal is more than random. Of the total of 18 cases filed involving offenses against honor or reputation, a marginal was found as plaintiff in 12 (66 percent). Insiders, by contrast, filed only 2 (11 percent), both of them private complaints. Outsiders made up the balance.

Turning now to those offenses involving economic delicts, we find 27 cases, or 15 percent of the corpus of criminal cases. These cases involved a variety of offenses, such as fraud and deception, falsification of deeds, poaching, and theft and conversion—all of which carry the moral disapprobation of the community. In the 27 cases here, marginals appeared as defendants in 12 (44 percent), a figure which is well beyond their incidence (7 percent) in the general population, and yet which is in line with their involvement in civil cases. This corpus, however, was generated by only 11 of the 15 village marginals—all but 1 of the 8 troublemakers contributing, along with 4 of the 7 economic marginals (3 of whom are in the same family).

The data suggest that marginals become involved in criminal actions only to the extent that these cases reflect their inability to get along peacefully with their fellow villagers. When only the interpersonal cases or cases which carry a moral stigma or which reflect on the individual's character, honesty, or reputation are considered, then, indeed, the marginal population does stand out. On the other hand, when the remaining cases are examined—that is, those in which there is little or no moral disapprobation attached to the act for which the case was brought—then the marginals are found to be no more prevalent in the sample than their proportion in the general population would indicate.

This observation suggests that the marginal classification is a label that is applied because of the inability of the persons who make up the marginal population to get along with their fellow villagers, rather than because the marginals represent any pervasive or prevalent criminal element in the population. Their quarrel is with their fellow villagers and their normative code—not with the state or its law. They are social misfits, social deviants on the village scene; but they are not criminals as that label is defined by federal and state laws.

CONCLUSIONS

The examination of the criminal records brings us back to our starting point: character. I suggested that while court involvement does not necessarily imply marginality, nevertheless marginality does imply court involvement in the management of interpersonal disputes. This conclusion has been substantiated by the evidence drawn from the records of the reconcilation agenc' and the district court. In each of these agencies, we have seen that the marginals of Gottfrieding—only about 7 percent of the total adult population—account for a disproportionately large number of cases.

The implicit obverse of this phenomenon—the relatively low degree of involvement of village insiders in cases heard before these agencies—suggests that selective access to the various grievance, conflict, and dispute management mechanisms within the village is closely tied up with the position which an individual occupies within the social structure of the community, and with his ascription to its normative system. Marginals, lacking access to these agencies and mechanisms in the village, are forced to use agencies that are available to them, most of which lie outside the village.

In the village institutions that manage grievances and conflicts, there is a strong emphasis on avoidance, negotiation, and mediation. Opportunity for negotiation, mediation, and conciliation is also available in the operation of the reconciliation agency. In the courts, however, mediation takes second place to adjudication, to an imposed settlement that may be to neither party's liking.

The question of access to village institutions, then, has important procedural implications, particularly for marginals. Lacking access to the gastzimmer and information centers, marginals must (1) avoid the issue, (2) confront the other party in an attempt to negotiate a settlement directly, (3) go to the reconciliation agency to try for a mediated settlement, or (4) go outside the village for an adjudicated (or, possibly, a mediated) one. The first path is not always possible, nor is it universally desirable. The second is also undesirable, since the constraints imposed by the presence of others in a structured situation are absent, and confrontation, taking place on the street or over a fence, is much more likely to be escalated into something more serious than it is to be deescalated. The third path is not always open, since the jurisdiction of the reconciliation agency is limited by statute to certain issues. The effective foreclosure of these three paths, then, leaves the marginal with only one viable alternative in most cases: to break the (insider's) normative proscription against outside involvement and take the dispute into an extravillage forum for settlement.

The arrangement and normative content of village relationships, therefore, impose on the villager a number of constraints that directly bear on his choice of remedy agent and procedure in attempting to manage grievances, conflicts, and disputes. These constraints, however, work against the members of both social categories in Gottfrieding, for neither the marginal nor the insider is free to choose from among all available remedy agencies or procedures. Restraints on insiders' choices arise because of their membership in the cluster, and are primarily normative in nature; restraints on marginals' choices arise because of their nonmembership, and are mainly structural.

Thus, the case for the litigious marginal is clear. If he is to achieve satisfaction, the social structure of the community effectively forces him to escalate his grievances and conflicts into disputes, and requires him then to take these disputes outside the village. At the same time, the community's normative system decries escalation and proscribes recourse to agencies and mechanisms lying outside the village's boundaries. Marginals perforce, are caught in a double bind: no matter which way they turn, they lose. If they try to assert that they have character by bringing an action against an insider in the reconciliation agency (an "approved" agency by community standards)—for example, for insult (an action which comprises a symbolic claim to character)—not only will the claim to character be denied but, given the community's normative emphasis on avoidance and deescalation, the simple act of lodging the claim may itself be regarded as a characterless action; and because of this, the marginal may be subject to further censure.

The result, then, is a self-perpetuating system—a system due partially to the marginals' own actions in both the social and economic spheres, but also partially ascribable to the stereotype that has developed among insiders of the characterless marginal. The more the marginal tries to deny his characterlessness, the more he reinforces the characterless stereotype. If any relief from this paradoxical situation is to be found, it must be in a social environment in which this stereotype is absent. This, in turn, means a social setting outside Gottfrieding—a setting in which villagers have little or no input; a setting in which insiders have little, if any, role to play; a setting in which the game is played by a different set of rules.

NOTES

1. The research upon which this report is based was carried out in 1970–71. It was supported by the U.S. Public Health Service, under N.I.H. Training Grant No. GM-1224. I gratefully acknowledge the help of my colleague, Dr. Julio Ruffini, in the preparation of this manuscript and in the clarification of some of the ideas which appear here and in other sections of this volume. Further explication of many of the points raised here can be found in Todd (1972) and Todd (1978).

2. The term "public house" is a translation of at least three different German words which are used alternatively: *Gastwirtschaft*, *Gasthaus*, and *Wirtshaus*. The public house is usually divided into several distinct areas, the most important being the public drinking room (the *Gastzimmer*); a public room (*Nebenzimmer*), which is usually reserved for village-wide or life-cycle occasions; a ballroom (*Saal*); and several bedrooms that are rented out to tourists or casual visitors. It was in such a rented room that I lived during my stay in Gottfrieding.

3. The German term *Gastzimmer* has no precise English equivalent. The term is used here to refer exclusively to the public drinking room within the public house (see n. 2 above). The plural is indicated herein simply by the addition of an "s" to the German form (i.e., *Gastzimmers*).

4. My usage follows that of Bott (1957), who distinguishes among "social norms" or "people's ideas about what behavior is customary and . . . right and proper in their social circle"; "norms of common consent" or "norms on which there is in fact consensus"; and "personal norms" or "those ideals and expectations that informants think are their own private standards, different from those they attribute to other people" (Bott 1957: 193–96).

5. The German term *Stammtisch* again has no precise English equivalent. It is simply the table (*Tisch*) in a public house which is reserved for regular guests. The German term is used herein for want of a satisfactory English term.

6. Further explication of the role of women and outsiders in gastzimmer interaction can be found in Todd (1972: chapter 4).

7. Not only is consensus on these norms achieved for village men but, by ex-

tension, it is also achieved for their wives and children. Photiadis's remarks about Greek coffeehouses apply to the Gottfrieding gastzimmer as well, when he writes, "The adult male demands that his family members behave in line with the expectations of the coffeehouse group, either because he likes to preserve his status in the coffeehouse group or because he actually adopts its attitudes" (Photiadis 1965: 50). This observation explains, to a large degree, why marginality in the village tends to run in families, for the exclusion of the marginal man from participation in the formulation and testing of these norms means—by extension—that his wife and children are also excluded from the process.

8. The use of animal names (such as *Hammel*, "castrated ram") in referring to an individual is one of the worst insults available to Gottfriedingers. In the absence of acceptable English terms that impart a similar flavor, the literal translations of these animal names have been provided here.

9. This agency is discussed in greater detail in Todd (1978).

10. Other pan-village mechanisms (i.e., those to which both insiders and marginals have access) include the offices of the priest and mayor. For an account of the functioning of these officials in processing disputes, see Todd (1972).

11. The sum of the percentages is greater than 100, since in nine cases a marginal appears as both complainant and respondent.

12. As noted earlier, poverty and marginality are not synonymous. Hence, the fact that an individual is forced by economic circumstances to sign a pauper's oath does not necessarily or automatically define him as a marginal. If this action is repeated, however, the individual may begin to find that his character is being called into question and that he is migrating into the marginal zone.

FOUR

TURKISH VILLAGE DISPUTING BEHAVIOR

June Starr

THIS PAPER attempts to suggest connections between conflict, social structure, disputant's choice of remedy agent, and dispute-handling institutions.[1]

In a Turkish village, certain important kinds of social relations are highly productive of conflict. Persons in conflict in paired status and role relations (such as father-son, sibling-sibling, husband-wife, patron-client) must then choose a remedy agency. There are different kinds of remedy agents available each of which have specific characteristics. When a person invokes informal, village, customary, or negotiatory methods of settling grievances, he is choosing flexible methods in which all interested parties can have input into the outcome, and in which there are ways of neutralizing (but not overturning) rank differences between disputants. A person may opt for formal court arbitration if he is dissatisfied with a negotiated village outcome; if he wants to undermine the social and political rank of his village opponent; if he wants to limit the area of conflict; or if he wants to dispute over resources.

There are two central points I wish to make. First, the state's methods for processing village disputes not only provide different outcomes (zero-sum as opposed to negotiatory) and different types of solutions than do the informal village methods, but also the use of one arena rather than another has consequences for the disputants' social relations and for the remedy agency itself. To use a village method of handling conflict is to accept the structure of enduring status relations in the village. To go to court, on the other hand, *may* be an attempt to disrupt or change existing power relations between people in different statuses. Or it may be an attempt to limit a disruptive, conflict-ridden social relation that is not amenable to village negotiation. This leads to the second point, which is that going to court has different meanings to different litigants in different status and role relations and in different types of disputes (such as those over land, marital obligations, debt, and the like). In attempting to account for both the patterns of village disputing and the reasons underlying these patterns, I do not claim any great originality for the concepts I use or the explanations I give. But I do hope that my analysis points toward an understanding of how change takes place in disputing behaviors, and institutions at the local level.

Other social scientists have found it useful to isolate the events occurring in particular disputes (this was a strength of the extended case method as used by Nader 1965a, 1965b; Van Velsen 1964, 1967; and Gulliver 1969a, 1969b); but a drawback is that it obscures how disputes between two persons connect with other disputing persons, since any disputing episode is usually classifed under one extended case only. It further obscures disputing behaviors which "push" the case forward to a new stage of resolution, but which, in themselves, remain *unmarked* as a stage in disputing (e.g., the threat of force, a violent argument). A disputing technique is defined as any attempt to communicate a grievance to an opponent. The technique may or may not make the complaint public.

To circumvent problems in the case method, all instances in which a villager used a disputing technique (e.g., public confrontation, private negotiation) or interacted with a dispute-handling institution were charted independently of the particular extended case in which the behavior was originally classified during my fieldwork or during the first analysis of cases in my dissertation (Starr 1970). This independent charting provided 104 instances of disputing behaviors. Of these, sixty-six, or two-thirds, took place in the village, and thirty-eight, or one-third, took place outside the geographic boundaries of the village. Of those handled out of the village, nearly one-half went to the Bodrum district court.[2]

What is most surprising about these data is that villagers in an area as remote as Mandalinci village in 1967–68 appealed to Turkish officials in provincial capitals and even in Ankara in attempting to find solutions to grievances (compare Nader 1965b). Such complaints concerned (1) the behavior of gendarmerie, (2) bias in award of local civil service jobs, and (3) court decisions. The picture we obtain from these data is not of the helplessness of naive villagers isolated from sources of power, but instead, of the ingenuity of *some* villagers in seeking solutions to problems in the face of increasing bureaucratic and administrative control.

When disputing incidents are placed in the context of social relations, roughly twenty-seven separate disputes[3] can be distinguished. By dispute, I mean nothing more than a social relation between two or more people who are in contact (or communication) and who choose to emphasize the conflict within their relationship.[4] The underlying cause of most disputes is conflict over control of scarce resources (a scarce resource is something people value which is in limited supply),[5] although ostensible claims are made on grounds of insults to honor, prestige, incorrect behavior, lying, or slander.

These twenty-seven disputes from Mandalinci village involve approximately sixty-six Mandalinci villagers as principals (forty-four males, twenty-two females). Nonvillage principals were one gendarme, one gendarme captain, one Bodrum lighthouse official, six residents of other villages, and five foreigners (citizens of other countries).

My data may not be a representative sample; in fact, the district court docket for the same period reveals that more Mandalinci villagers were involved in disputing at court than my village study reveals. The village-collected data do, however, point out trends in village disputing behaviors, and to some degree suggest the parameters of disputing techniques which Mandalinci people use.

THE SETTING

Mandalinci is a fictitious name for a village of 1,000 Turkish people (247 households) at the edge of the Aegean Sea on the Bodrum peninsula in the southwest corner of Turkey. Mandalinci, which means "tangerine grower," is one of thirty villages in the district of Bodrum, administered by Bodrum town (population 5,200).

At the time of my fieldwork, the trip by four-wheel-drive vehicle between Izmir and the village took about six hours; by Turkish transportation (jeeps, buses, cargo trucks) it was often much longer. At the end of August 1968 an all-weather bridge was completed on the Izmir-Milas section, and the road between Milas and Bodrum was asphalted. By coincidence, the ending of this district's isolation coincided with the end of my fieldwork.

Mandalinci village is dispersed over four miles of inland valley and seashore with houses grouped into six different nucleated neighborhoods or isolated at the edge of tangerine orchards. The villagers practice mixed agriculture and animal husbandry. Household food and cash crops (tangerines, tomatoes, squash, watermelon, artichoke, and several kinds of beans) are grown in fields, some of which are irrigated for spring and summer vegetables. All citrus fruits are grown in walled, irrigated orchards and sold between December and March. Cows, donkeys, and camels are grazed by villagers in the higher hills. Neither of the two boats owned by villagers are used for commercial fishing and rarely for sport fishing. Although the village has a seaside area and a deep-water harbor adequate for anchorage of large boats, the villagers are not seafaring people. They are essentially agriculturalists; the focus of their activities and interests is on crop growing and animal husbandry. Animals are necessary for plowing fields and transporting crops to roadside areas, where they can be loaded onto transport trucks. A few villagers raise cows for spring sale to slaughterhouses in Istanbul.

There are three residential units within the village: the household, the residence group, and the neighborhood. The household is the primary unit of social identity and socialization. A household occupies a one-room or two-room house and is an eating and sleeping unit, which typically contains a nuclear family (a husband, a wife, and their unmarried children). Sometimes a widowed parent (of husband or of wife) sleeps in a separate house nearby but eats with the family.

The "ideal" residence rule is patrilocal, but many considerations intervene in the decision by a couple concerning where to live, so that the resulting residence groups are in fact sets of kin, recruited with some patrilineal bias. These residential groups consist of two or three adjoining households that cooperate in food preparation, child care, and sometimes in cultivation of gardens, fields, and orchards. Such cooperating households contain married adults related to each other by sibling or parent-child ties. But patterns of mutual cooperation between households rarely continue more than one to three years, and not every village family is part of a residential kin group.

The third residential unit is the neighborhood (*mahalle*). There are six nucleated neighborhoods, four of which have names. Newer houses are isolated at the edges of the tangerine orchards. Nucleated neighborhoods typically contain older village houses in which live closely related kin. For reasons that will be discussed later, village marriages have tended to be endogamous, so that most people in each neighborhood have several kin ties to each other. Likewise, most village members (except for three in-migrating households) can trace a kin tie to each other. Neighborhoods are the sites of intensive interaction and visiting, but neighborhood membership confers no corporate advantages and has no additional "meaning" to members except as a setting for routinized daily activities. Households that own a tangerine orchard usually move out of a nucleated neighborhood when they can afford to build an orchard cottage. The demands of irrigating citrus orchards mean that someone has to determine on a daily basis, from June through November, whether or not the trees need watering. This "watering watchfulness" has drawn households from the nucleated neighborhoods to the comparative isolation of the orchards, but the patterns of visiting, by men to the coffeehouses and women to each other's hearths, continues.

The fourth residential unit is the village itself. Although Turkish administrators who visit the village consider it a corporate unit, Mandalinci residents do not conceive of it in this way. I found considerable disagreement among the villagers as to whether several households in a remote named area were part of the village. In discussions of village history with both villagers and Turkish officials, it became apparent to me that administrators had drawn village boundaries to fit administrative needs rather than village sentiment. Many of the world's people, however, live in nucleated groups and interact intensely with their neighbors without developing a corporate ideology, so that lack of corporateness in Mandalinci is neither typically nor atypically Turkish or Middle Eastern.

The Village and Its History

If an explanation need be found for the lack of corporate village-wide institutions, it perhaps lies in the diverse ways and reasons households came to settle the area. Until the increased animosity between Greece and Turkey in 1919 and after, the valley and seashore area were inhabited largely by Greek-speaking people. The Turkish population lived primarily in the high mountains (a forty-five minute hike from the present village center), and only three or four Turkish-speaking households had land and houses on the plain. Many Turkish and Greek-speaking households spent the summer in the Mandalinci area, and the winter in a variety of different locations elsewhere on the peninsula or nearby islands.

Households had maintained loose networks that gave them access to diverse land, brides, and information. Stretching up and down the entire Bodrum peninsula and to nearby islands, these networks linked the area together as households migrated between winter and summer pasturage. Some of the current Turkish households can remember times as late as the mid-1950s, when they still practiced biannual migrations with a few sheep between summer fields and winter pastures. All the Greek-speaking households left the area between 1919 and 1922, because of hostility between Greek and Turkish ethnic groups. It is from this period that the modern Turkish-speaking village of Sunni Muslims dates.

Under the *Shari'a* (Islamic family law and custom), daughters had rights to receive one-half the amount of land that sons did. The *Shari'a* had been collected and codified under Ottoman officials as the *Mecelle* of 1876, and it was essentially this body of law which was practiced and interpreted by rural Islamic judges, the *kadi*. The Ottoman Empire, which had allied itself with Germany and Austria, continued in form and substance until its demise at the Peace Conference at Versailles, held by the European powers to end World War I. (Ottoman inheritance law is and was irrelevant to Mandalinci villagers.) Ataturk's legal reforms included new Turkish Family Laws, incorporated in the Civil Code of 1926, which gave equal inheritance rights to all siblings for the first time in Turkish history.

With the development of cash cropping, beginning in the late 1940s, land became a valuable resource, and claims to exclusive ownership were advanced and upheld. Households settled near their orchards to protect their property, and in response to the work routines of citrus farming. Households owning citrus orchards began arranging marriages to other orchardist households in the village, so that more dense kin networks were forged within Mandalinci. This density of village networks resulted from decisions that households made as a way of focusing, collecting, and mobilizing resources.

By the late 1960s the following statements could be made about households permanently settled in the village: (1) at least five households represent members of local or regional elites, while the others do not; (2) women over forty years of age came from other areas and almost always from areas which differed from their husbands'; (3) some households came to the area as already established households; (4) village households lacking agnatic ties generally did not come from similar locales on the peninsula or islands and do not share similar household histories; (5) most household histories differ in details, such as place of origin of members, decisions concerning where to live, what mode of economic activity to pursue, and periods in the household cycle when these decisions were made; (6) many households of more than a twenty-year span have lived in several places, sometimes including cities (Milas, Izmir, or Aydin) for varying periods before deciding to come to (or back to) the village to practice citrus agriculture; (7) some foresighted fathers (now in their seventies) financed their male offspring in jobs or businesses in western Turkish cities, where the sons now are neighborhood storekeepers, taxi drivers, or restaurateurs in small neighborhood cafes; and (8) these same fathers married their daughters to Mandalinci youths and set up the couples as caretakers of their orchards, perhaps because it was easier to control a son-in-law than a son. In summary, households share generalized cultural values, but the accommodations and adaptations of specific households to changing economic and social circumstances vary according to their social class origins and to early decisions concerning land.

Village Social Structure and the Causes of Disputes

The Family. A family is based on the sexual union of a man and woman, who have usually obtained a civil marriage license (*nikah*) in Bodrum and have celebrated a wedding in the village. A nuclear family is the basic kin unit in Mandalinci, and is the core unit of any household. A family is tied to other families by kinship, marriage, residence, or contractual agreements. Contractual agreements between households are primarily economic in nature and are based on a tenant/landlord, landowner/day laborer relationship, or on another short-term work agreement.

Within the family, there is marked division of labor, and within the village there is marked segregation of the sexes. Adolescent girls and women do not go to a village store to buy staples, for to do so they would have to pass by men sitting at the coffeehouses, and such behavior would imply a curiosity about men or some kind of laxity and unchastity on their part. The highest compliment a Mandalinci man can pay a married woman is to say she is *temiz* (literally, clean), and most village women are careful to keep their virtue above question. The degree of goodwill and affection between married people varies considerably, but if a couple does not get along, the marked separation of the sexes allows them to interact only infrequently.

Type of Disputes Generated by the Village Social Structure

The older Turkish value system emphasized sibling unity and the quick resolution of discord between them. However, control of a tangerine orchard gives cash benefits, and hence power and prestige that are unavailable when that orchard is divided among heirs. Furthermore, Ataturk's "received, Western" inheritance laws, embodied in the Civil Code of 1926, stated that all siblings regardless of sex are to be given an equal share in the patrimony at the death of the father, after the widow has taken one-fourth.

Since the requirements of tangerine orcharding can be met by a single, nucleated household with two teenage children, some household heads wish to claim exclusive rights to an orchard and to find ways to undercut the inheritance claims of their siblings. Thus, orchards and land suitable for orchards become foci of two types of disputes: (1) those between siblings after the death of the father; and (2) those between father and adult sons over control of the orchard while the father is still living.[6] A father may keep his son—even a married son in his forties—in a tenant farmer position, and keep him there indefinitely until the father is so feeble or senile that he can no longer challenge his son's control. Conflicts between fathers and sons thus have to do with control of the land, and especially with such decisions as where to sell the produce, how much to spend in intensifying agricultural production, whether or not to diversify crops, and the like.

A second area of disputing concerns male honor and female chastity. Youths from poorer households cannot amass the cash to pay the bride wealth to marry at eighteen or twenty, and the moral standards of the village require that unmarried girls maintain not only modesty but discreetness and social distance between themselves and young men in order to enforce that chastity. Thus married women in their late twenties become the focus of seduction by unmarried but sexually interested youths. Such women have usually been married for ten or more years and, now sexually experienced, are either bored with or ignored by their husbands. Their husbands, men in their thirties to fifties, spend a great deal of day and evening time in the company of other men, because this ensures that when they have a crisis or problem, they will have access to other males for advice and strategy planning. The company of other males is crucial to maintaining the delicate balance of reciprocal relations, of obligations and favors, needed to gain information and to maintain social rank in a number of arenas necessary for survival in the political life of the village.

A wife who becomes involved in an adulterous liaison tarnishes not only her husband's but her brother's honor as well. Thus brothers continually guard their married sisters' behavior, and maintain a watchfulness over their sister's virtue, which the sisters (especially those involved in extramarital affairs) find tedious and loathsome. When a brother interferes, attempting to correct his sister's behavior, her refusal to admit the liaison or, if acknowledged, to break it off usually infuriates the brother, who may strike her, giving her grounds for a criminal case in court.

Thus social and structural features combine with the village value system to generate two types of relations that have intrinsic possibilities for prolonged conflict and disputing. The first is the father-son relationship after the son has gained adult status and thus is competing for rank in the village political arena of information sharing and reciprocal debts and favors, but is still unable to gain access to the sources of prestige and power, which can only come from making crucial decisions concerning the use of the family land. As long as his father makes these family decisions, any political maneuvering the son does is essentially on behalf of his father. Conversely, a son who can successfully negotiate decisions with his father, in order to gain income-producing property of his own (e.g., land, a store, a transportation vehicle), probably has become equally sophisticated in negotiating with other village men.

The second conflict-laden relationship is the one between siblings. Here the disputes are focused either on inheritance of property or on the sister's conduct. The longest and most intense disputes I witnessed in the village occurred between two sets of adult siblings: a pair of brothers and a brother and sister. The area of conflict and the basis of court cases involved insult, hitting, and slander, as well as contested rights to land. At least three land title cases occurred between the brothers, and at least two cases of assault between the brother and sister. As the Bodrum judges began to unravel the conflicting land claims, the intensity of violent interaction diminished, although neither set of siblings returned to warm and reciprocal relations during my village contact. Thus prolonged conflict over land tends to undermine older patterns of respect, loyalty, and obedience between siblings and between fathers and sons.

Village Factions and Patron-Client Ties

Two rival factions exist in the village, and these tend to be focused around patron-client rather than agnatic ties. One leader bases his authority on his status as a member of the regional elite and on his large land holdings, since he thus has diverse clients dependent on his patronage. He employs over fifty workers in his fields in summer, picking, weeding, watering, and transporting produce to his weighing and boxing areas at the seaside, where trucks, hired by him, load in summer and autumn. He often buys produce from his clients, paying them in cash and sending vegetables off to markets in Bodrum, Izmir, or Istanbul in hired trucks. He owns the only village olive press. He either buys olives directly from the villagers or presses their olives, keeping a fixed portion of the oil for his services. This oil he sells for profit in Bodrum. His household has such high rank in the village that no one dares dispute with him. In fact, the only gossip I ever heard concerning him or his household (outside of the information that his fifteen-year-old son was adopted) was that he was stingy because he charged high interest rates on loans. A member of his faction runs a small store at the seaside, where villagers purchase matches, kerosene for lanterns, cigarettes, rice, and sometimes flour, potatoes, eggs, and butter. These are usually bought on credit, to be paid off twice a year, after seasonal crops are sold.

The leader of the other faction is a "self-made" man, according to villagers. He dominates the central village area, and organizes landless village men, women, and children to collect snails, bay leaves, and other wild flora and fauna, which he buys for a few lira and sells for profit in Bodrum. Few nonkin work in his field and orchard, but he runs a competing village store, which has more items than the seaside one and also some manufactured clothing. Credit and cash are available at his store at no interest, and thus he has transformed a series of dyadic, asymmetrical ties into patron-client ties as his wealth and power have grown. He married his oldest son to the daughter of his best friend, an agnate of the village *muhtar*, or headman. This alliance gives the patron access to all official information concerning the village, and he acts as host when Turkish officials visit Mandalinci. At the time of my fieldwork he was solidifying his position. Although his prestige is not as high as his rival's, his effective power is greater, since his candidate has won the elective position of village *muhtar*.

The following example demonstrates his sophistication in dealing with important outsiders to the village. It also illustrates how a client uses a patron when he is in dispute.

A youth of about twenty-four years had had a long-term liaison with a married woman who was known in the village for promiscuity. One day he forced her to have intercourse when she did not want to, and to punish him she sent one of her children to her husband, who was at the seaside, with the news that Hasan was "injuring her." The husband passed Hasan on the path to his house, but the two avoided eye contact. The youth had assumed that the husband knew of the affair and had been ignoring it, but he knew now that there would be trouble. Therefore, he went to the home of his patron (he was one of the patron's day laborers at this time) and told him of the incident, asking his intervention.

It so happened that a gendarme captain was visiting the village that day. The patron told Hasan to hide in the shed in his orchard, and then arranged a feast for the gendarme. In his role as host, the patron recounted the history of the liaison and the ways the husband had ignored its existence for four years. Thus, he tactfully arranged to have the captain intervene to mediate the dispute between the husband and lover, in order to prevent the husband from opening a court case against his adversary for "rape."

In the interview with the youthful Hasan, the captain asked if he was carrying any "tokens" from his love. Hasan showed two love letters, a headscarf, and an old photograph. The captain showed these to the husband, advising him of how foolish he would seem in court, bringing charges against a man for rape when there was clear evidence of a long-term love affair. The captain advised the husband to take a firmer stand with his wife and stop being a "pimp." Thus the patron arranged that the youth would be cleared of charges and the husband embarrassed. He thus demonstrated his ability to protect those who remained loyal to him.

THE PROCESS OF DISPUTING

A brief overview of the disputing process in Mandalinci might read as follows: When a villager in Mandalinci gets into a dispute with another villager, he has a wide choice of social mechanisms and institutions by which he can attempt to handle his grievance. He can talk to the other individual directly. He can talk to the head of the household in which the other person lives. He can discuss the problem with a person he knows (kinsman, affine, friend, or patron) and ask him to see the other person. He can bring the issue to the attention of the village headman, the village council, or the gendarmes stationed in the village to keep peace. He can take the dispute out of the village by going to the subdistrict gendarme, the *kaymakam* (administrative director) of Bodrum, the Bodrum civil police, the Bodrum gendarme, or the Bodrum law court.

An examination of the cases of dispute I collected in the village indicates that some methods of dispute processing are used frequently, while others are rarely invoked or totally ignored. Most individuals choose among alternative processes in an attempt to maximize their own position and advantage. A choice of an in-village technique relates to two factors: (1) how a person views his rank vis-à-vis his opponent, and (2) the stage his dispute has reached (which in turn relates to methods he has used previously and why he thinks these have failed).

But, we need to note, Mandalinci villagers have customary ways of dispute management in which there are no specific individuals who act as judge, arbitrator, mediator, intermediary, go-between, or the like. In this village any household head can fill the role of representative, if a third party is to be brought into the dispute. Unlike most African and European communities, in Mandalinci there is no special setting or special time for discussion of disputes. Although a village council and a village headman are elected every four years on secret ballot by all adult members of the community, and are endowed with authority to hear and arbitrate certain types of disputes, the villagers do not use them for airing grievances. There are no mass meetings in the village. Unlike other Middle Eastern communities described in this volume, in Mandalinci no lineages can be mobilized to back an agnate in dispute, nor is there a forum where two disputants can, in the presence of their relatives, friends, and covillagers, "talk out" their difficulties.

Instead, there is a method of using "personal networks" to handle all of life's problems. Every individual is at the center of networks of contacts to others. These relations are qualitatively diverse: with some he is in direct, immediate, and intimate contact; with others he is more impersonal. Some relationships are symmetrical, while others are asymmetrical because of rank and power differences. Through personal networks a person is in contact, or can be put into contact, with a great variety of others. The higher a person's rank and power in the village, the more likely he is to have contacts of importance and usefulness outside the village. Networks can be used to extend a person's range of contacts indefinitely, provided a person has the ambition and personality to do so. In this sense an individual's personal networks are "open-ended."

The use of personal networks involves social exchanges (see Mauss 1906). A person conceives of his relationship to another as made up of reciprocal exchanges of favors. In this sense one thinks of a debit-credit sheet, and to ask a favor of another is to accrue a debt to him, which he may collect whenever he wishes. This is the underlying cement of most village relationships and most relationships between villagers and outsiders.

The impartiality of an office holder is alien to much of Turkish thinking. A major way of dealing with Turkish officials and state agencies is by personal intervention on someone's behalf. Office holders in Turkish bureaus accrue a series of obligations and favors with others, and interveners with office holders become involved in exchanges of favors and debts. Despite knowledge of this system of personal networks, villagers are willing to write complaints to anonymous bureau directors when they think they have been mistreated by Turkish officials, gendarmerie, or bureaucrats, because they assume their complaint will be taken seriously.

Village-Based Remedy Agents or Institutions

Two-Party Negotiation. Two-party negotiation occurs whenever one individual attempts to deal directly with his opponent to resolve a grievance. It can take the form of confrontation or persuasion.

Whether a person chooses a public or a private setting has important implications for the negotiation process, since an aggrieved individual using a public setting (a coffeehouse, a wedding, a chance meeting on the road) invokes public opinion and community-held norms in support of his position. He also ensures that observers will intervene if the discourse becomes heated and a violent encounter seems imminent. He may choose a private setting, either to keep the conflict and the negotiations secret or to suggest the possibility of violence in order to force resolution. An aggrieved person may also take secret revenge by destroying property belonging to his opponent; self-help is used when someone feels he cannot negotiate for a better settlement.

Three-Party Negotiation: Representatives. On a continuum, representatives may range from a young messenger and errand runner to an elder in the community, who by entering into the negotiation process brings much of his rank and power to bear on resolving the situation. The features that distinguish Mandalinci representatives from nonvillage third parties are: (1) they are not impartial, but act in behalf of one of the disputants, and (2) they have no authority to enforce a resolution outside of the pressure they can bring by virtue of their rank, power, and personality. Representatives lend their weight to one side or the other (but one side only), although, of course, they usually are not as partial and short-sighted about a situation as the principal they represent. Thus, by their presence they tend to inject a certain amount of "good sense" into the process and sometimes enter into hard negotiation as well. In Mandalinci the case material reveals that an adult household head, either a male or a female, acts as the representative for someone defined as a minor (i.e., any unmarried household member) in his or her house. Females become heads of households upon the death or absence (due to migrant labor) of their husbands.

The following is an example of how a household head intervenes in a dispute when a household minor has been unable to gain satisfaction.

Some village women went in Turgot's boat to an island about forty-five minutes from the village to gather wild grasses to make *börëk* (Turkish pastry). As a fee for transporting the women, Turgot, an adult male, went to the seaside store and, without the women's knowledge, had the storekeeper charge each woman's account for two kilos of gasoline (about twenty cents). Several days later, one of the women, Inci, learned of this charge against her account. She was especially upset, because there was an old debt between Turgot and her son, Sadik. The previous summer, when Sadik was fourteen, he and Turgot had worked on the same sponge-diving boat. Turgot had borrowed money from Sadik and had not yet repaid him, although Sadik had asked for the money on at least two occasions.

Inci finds Turgot on the village road when others are present. She shouts at him: "Why are you making bills for me in that store?" Turgot becomes quite agitated. "Why are you asking me in front of other people?" They are both aroused. They walk back and forth in a jerky manner, confronting each other to ask questions or scream abuses, walking away when the other talks. Turgot turns to yell at her: "I did not owe more than eight liras [eighty cents] to your son." He paces more, thinking. He continues, "And one month ago I gave him twenty liras [two dollars] when he asked for it. Another time I gave him thirty liras [three dollars] in the coffeehouse—"

Inci, interrupting, angrily screams, "You are a liar. You are a liar." Turgot retorts, "Your son is a liar. He stole a pencil and says, 'I found this outside near a stone.' That's the way you raise your children." Inci, growing red in the face, says, "We will see how your children grow up also." They stare at each other a minute, and then each goes off in a different direction.

About a week later, Inci's son goes to Turgot in the coffeehouse and again asks for his money. Turgot is very angry, but he pays the debt of thirty liras to Sadik.

Inci's confrontation of Turgot on the road thus had the following effects: It publicized Turgot's recalcitrance in repaying a debt, thus providing additional information for villagers to assess his character, and it humiliated him.

Village Muhtar and Village Council. An interesting aspect of Inci's confrontation of Turgot on the road was that the village *muhtar* witnessed the encounter, and yet did nothing to stop the shouting, nor did he intervene later to find out what the problem was. Despite his nonintervention, the *muhtar* and the village council of seven elected members are invested with dispute-settling powers by the Turkish Village Law. But villagers during my fieldwork and earlier did not bring disputes to them. My best informants said that this was not the way they handled problems.

At first I attempted to explain nonuse of the council and *muhtar* as due to known alliances and loyalties in the village, which would ensure that the stronger or better connected would win (Starr 1970: 405–8), for villagers say they cannot expect impartiality from others in their village whose very election to office depends on maintaining close associations with those who elected them.[7] Later I explained nonuse as due to the fact that villagers resent the power of fellow villagers to enforce arbitrated outcomes, and that taking a case to the council acknowledges the superior rank of council members (Starr 1974). Now I formulate the process as follows: In disputing with other villagers, persons may start with informal customary methods or may opt for a court-arbitrated decision. When a person invokes informal, customary, negotiatory methods of settling conflicts, he is choosing flexible methods, in which all interested parties can have input into the outcome, and in which there are ways of neutralizing (but not overturning) rank differences between disputants. A person may opt for formal court arbitration when he is unsatisfied with a negotiated outcome; when he wants to *upset* the status quo of social and political rank of his village opponent; when he wants to limit the area of conflict; or when resources are in dispute. Multiple motives may determine court use, for the above reasons are not mutually exclusive. Conflicting claims to the same resource generate prolonged conflict within the village, and a negotiated village outcome over a scarce resource may leave a person unsatisfied with his share. Thus a villager goes to court because he wants coerciveness, limitations on the issues to be discussed, complete control over the resource, or a formal break in a relationship (Starr 1975).

Relation of Village Disputing Behavior to Law Processes

An individual's decision to disrupt the village disputing processes has clear consequences. Village dispute processes effectively preserve ongoing, multiplex, affectional relations and maintain the status quo in social, economic, and political rank, *solely* because techniques of village disputing behavior are based on the *social recognition* of the disputants' occupational status, rank, prestige, and power (Starr 1978). To take a case out of the village for the first time is a calculated risk. But villagers who begin disputing at court usually become quite knowledgeable about court procedures, what decisions to expect, and how to use the court to their advantage. As Galanter (1974) and others have shown, litigants who are "repeaters" at court have a strategic advantage over first-time users, because they have acquired knowledge of how to open and process a lawsuit, how judges reason and make decisions, what services lawyers give despite their high fees, and what aspects of Turkish law can be used to help a litigant win. If an individual is an opportunist, going to court for the first time is a new learning process, a new arena in which to compete with his rivals and adversaries, and a new exercise of his political and diplomatic skills. Furthermore, following his own case through its many hearings and watching the procedures of court personnel and judges in the courthouse gives a rural villager opportunity to see, hear, and learn the bureaucratic and ideological basis of the new Turkish state. For some villagers it is an overwhelming experience, and they do not want to venture into the courtroom again. For others, however, it opens up entirely new vistas and horizons. Thus a person who has once initiated a successful lawsuit will probably in time again seek court intervention in his local quarrels, since he has learned to use the legal system to his advantage. For instance, the leader of the central village faction eventually pursued his dispute against his brother over an orchard through the appellate court system in Ankara, where he attempted to use connections to gain information concerning the outcome of his case (Starr 1975). In contrast, however, approximately 75 percent of the adult population in Mandalinci have never been litigants in anything but routine matters (i.e., nondisputes) in the Bodrum court.

Turkish Rural Law Enforcement Agents

At least two aspects of village disputing behavior relate to Turkish law enforcement agencies and the national legal system. The first is a calculated risk taken by a villager that he will gain more by disputing at court than by doing nothing or by negotiating in the village. His other option concerns the use of the gendarmerie. I will discuss the gendarmerie first, since invoking them usually leads to criminal procedures at court.

Village-based Gendarmes. A gendarme station has been maintained in the village since about 1900. In recent years, its ostensible purpose has been to prevent smuggling between nearby Greek islands and the Turkish mainland. Gendarmes are never stationed in the region of their birth, and thus they are outsiders to the village social system. A characteristic of the sergeant and two soldiers stationed in Mandalinci is their interpretation of their mandate to intervene in situations which they classify as "potentially violent." Since there is not much for the gendarmes to do, they tend to enforce rather strictly the Turkish gun laws, which state that every person carrying a gun must have a gun permit. In the past, it had been village custom to shoot off guns at weddings and other celebrations. A few villagers use old guns to hunt small game, and villagers have been known to shoot off guns in a gleeful mood, all of which have led the gendarmes to investigate, and sometimes to make arrests, which involve interviews by the district prosecutor in Bodrum and sometimes trial for criminal activities in the Bodrum court.

On five occasions during my fieldwork, four different villagers asked a gendarme to intervene in a dispute on their behalf. And, when a serious wounding occurred in a fight between two village youths, the gendarmes were quickly informed, as they controlled the only village telephone, and the parents of one youth needed to summon a vehicle to take their son to the Bodrum hospital. In this dispute, the intervention of village gendarmes clearly acted to prevent retaliation and the spread of violence to larger kin or friendship units. But in another village dispute the intervention of the gendarmes escalated the dispute into the Bodrum court, where only the judge's careful sifting of events and claims eventually straightened out the underlying issues and so resolved the dispute (see below).

District Gendarme Officers. On several different occasions during my fieldwork, district gendarme officers came to Mandalinci on business. In two cases, they came to investigate claims made in letters about alleged misconduct on the part of a local gendarme. On a third, a captain was merely spending a leisurely off-duty day at a "scenic seaside" village, but his visit coincided with an erupting dispute between a man and his wife's young lover, for which he successfully negotiated a village resolution. All interactions between villagers and gendarmes do not have such beneficial outcomes, however. The following is a dispute which escalated while I was living in the village:

One of the married village women, known as a prostitute, also had special boyfriends. One of them, Erol, from a nearby village, brought her bags of vegetables and hid them under the sofa on her porch in return for her sexual favors. One night during a drunken visit, he shot off a gun in her house. Villagers heard the shots, but no one was hurt, and no villager thought further about it. When a village gendarme came the next day to investigate the shots, no one remembered hearing any. But the gendarme reported the shots to his captain in Bodrum, and a few days later the captain came to Mandalinci to investigate the "alleged" shots. Before proceeding to the house, however, he drank *raki* (Turkish hard liquor) at the harbor coffeehouse. He stayed there until very intoxicated. He then asked a respected old village man to take him up the hill to the house in question. The wife was at home, but the husband was not. The captain searched the house for bullet holes and bullets, staggering around and unpleasantly drunk, the villagers said. Several of the villagers surmised that he had come to the village to spend money on the prostitute.

When the woman's husband realized how long the captain had remained alone with his wife in his house in a state of intoxication, he was angry. He wrote a letter to the gendarme station in Muğla, the state capital (*vilayet*), claiming that the captain had molested his wife. Four days later, the director of the Muğla gendarme station arrived in the village with a retinue of three jeeps. He talked with the respected old man, with the husband, and with the wife, gathering evidence concerning the conduct of his subordinate officer. I never learned the outcome of this investigation, for a gendarme director can discipline a lower officer as he sees fit but his action is not made public.

The point I wish to underline, however, is that gendarmes play a complex role in keeping village peace. Their presence in the village clearly allays certain kinds of violence, but gendarmes also interact with villagers in ways which create new disputes between villagers, and between the gendarmes and certain villagers. Thus, integration into larger social units has both benefits and drawbacks for Mandalinci people. Benefits accrue from undercutting a value system which suggests that a man *ought* to actively retaliate within an eighteen-hour period against another adult male who has committed an offense against his honor. Disadvantages accrue from giving gendarmes "authoritative positions of power over villagers" (Starr 1978).[8] Villagers are virtually defenseless when gendarme behavior affronts their values. The only redress open to them is to make written complaints to a gendarme's superior officer, and hope that that officer will feel responsible for the behavior of his subordinate.

The Turkish Legal System. When a villager takes a grievance out of the village context, he has a number of arenas in which to seek justice, but some arenas are determined by the type of grievance. For instance, if he has a grievance over land he can take the case to be heard at the administrative office of the district director in Bodrum (the *Kaymakan*) or he can open a case directly at the lower or higher Bodrum civil law court, depending on whether the disputed land is over or under 1,000 liras ($100) in value. If he feels some type of crime has been committed against him or his property, he can report the alleged behavior directly to the village gendarme, to the subdistrict gendarme (stationed in a large nearby village), or directly to the public prosecutor. (See fig. 4.1 for a diagram of the chain of jurisdiction pertaining to civil and criminal cases that occur in the village.)

The Gendarmes. Village gendarmes exercise a degree of discretion in filing reports. I recorded at least three instances in which, after carrying out a village investigation, the gendarme did not make a written report, meaning the matter was dropped. On the other hand, the subdistrict gendarmes, being unfamiliar with village personalities, are more likely to make a written report immediately, which then leads directly to the public prosecutor's office.

The Public Prosecutor. The public prosecutor (whose office is located in the Bodrum courthouse rather than in the police station) is required to carry out his own investigation. He reads the earlier reports, interviews the principals, and interrogates witnesses to at-

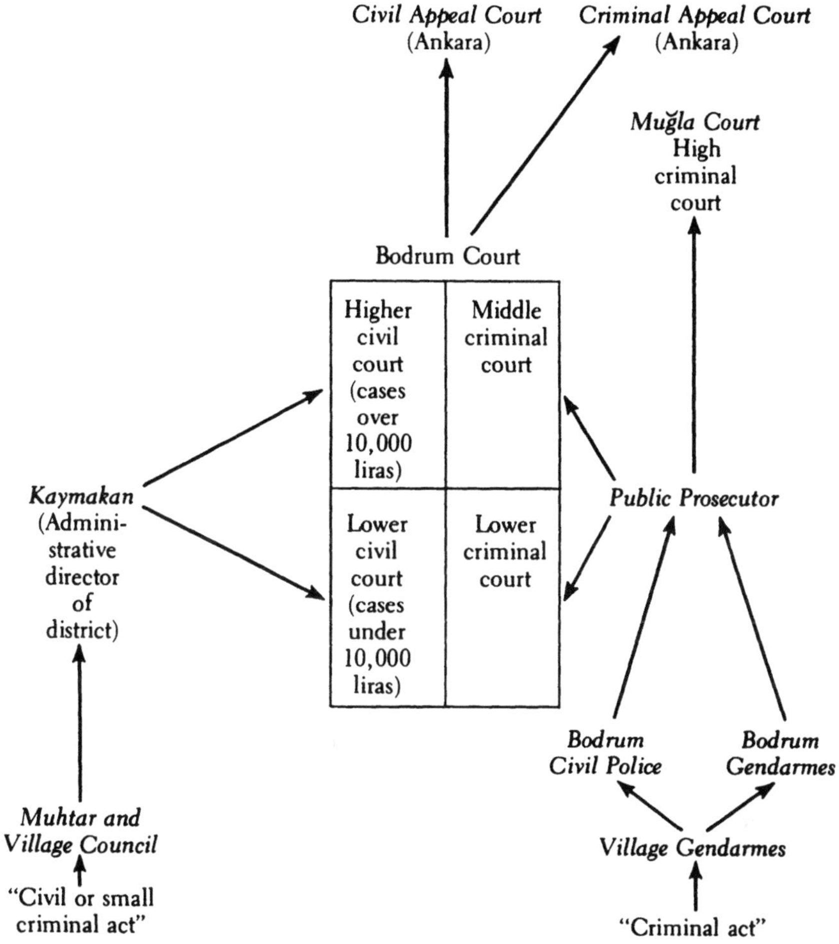

Figure 4.1. Chain of jurisdiction pertaining to civil and criminal cases. A case can be terminated at any level. Cases ordinarily do not go from lower civil or lower criminal court to the next higher court, although occasionally an administrative error places a case in the wrong court. If so, the judge has it transferred.

tempt to establish whether (1) any activity which could be considered lawbreaking has occurred, and (2) whether there is evidence which will stand up in court as "alleged criminal activity." Thus, the public prosecutor also has considerable discretion in deciding which cases to prosecute. However, his high salary, his training (which involves four years' study at one of Turkey's two law schools), his sense of professionalism, and the fact that his "record keeping" is subject to official scrutiny at least once a year, all act to keep him accountable to standards set by the national government and to national codes of criminal procedure and criminal law.

The Bodrum Law Court. The Bodrum courthouse stands in a residential neighborhood, isolated from other public offices, on an unpaved side street two blocks from the sea. The court has two judges and a public prosecutor. It is divided into four courts of law: the *sulh hukuk mahkemesi* (lower civil court), whose jurisdiction is civil cases involving up to 1,000 liras (in 1967, about $100) worth of property; *asliye hukuk mahkemesi* (higher civil court), whose jurisdiction is all other civil cases; *sulh ceza mahkemesi* (lower criminal court), which hears minor criminal cases as defined by the Turkish Criminal Code; and *asliye ceza mahkemesi* (middle criminal court), with jurisdiction over serious crimes up to and including involuntary manslaughter.

In theory, one of the two Bodrum judges presides over the lower civil and lower criminal courts, and the other is in charge of the higher civil and middle criminal courts. In practice, however, they often replace each other at the bench. The public prosecutor takes an interest in and follows all criminal cases, but he sits on the bench (to the right of the judge) only during the middle criminal court hearings. There is no jury for either civil or criminal cases.

People waiting for their case to be called sit or squat outside the courtroom, while inside a formal atmosphere is maintained. The judge and the public prosecutor wear black robes over pants and shirts, and the lawyers wear ties and Western suits. Women are expected not to cross their legs in court (even though they wear long dresses or baggy pants), and observers are required to be silent. Individuals giving testimony are required to stand. Only rarely is someone asked to give sworn testimony; the two instances I observed involved old people, one of whom swore on a Koran and the other on a loaf of bread. Judges told me afterwards that these two old people would believe in the efficacy of their oath.

One of the four male court stenographers sits at a table directly in front of the judge's bench during each court session. The judge questions the plaintiff, defendant, and witnesses, and after each testimony he dictates the answer himself to the stenographer, who types them on a standard, manual typewriter. Lawyers cannot directly cross-examine principals or witnesses, but must put their questions to the judge, who, if he considers a question relevant, asks it. After the first hearing, a lawyer may appear in place of a defendant in a civil case, but in criminal matters the defendant himself is required to appear each time.

One stenographer acts as head clerk, court treasurer, notary (the only one in Bodrum), and also as official debt collector, who oversees seizure and sale of goods when a judgment is executed. Another stenographer works mainly for the public prosecutor. A third is associated with both civil courts, while the fourth works with both criminal courts. Two other male employees are associated with the court: the younger, twenty-three years of age, acts as sergeant-at-arms during court hearings; the other, a man of about sixty, prepares and processes warrants, summonses, and billings. Both are sent for coffee and on other errands. Gendarmes deliver summonses and guard prisoners. A woman employed by the court acts as caretaker of the Bodrum jail and prepares food for the prisoners. The job is not sex-linked, however, for before her employment a man held this job.

Bodrum itself had no lawyers (*avukat*) at the period of my fieldwork, nor had any lived there previously. The nearest lawyers, of whom there were sixteen, lived in Milas, a city ninety kilometers away by an unpaved road. Usually lawyers appeared only in serious criminal cases and in cases with wealthy defendants. There were in Bodrum, however, four legal representatives (*vekil*), who lacked formal legal training but had become experts in civil litigation, especially concerning land. A *vekil* has the same prerogatives as a lawyer in a civil case; that is, he can prepare briefs, address questions to the judge, and appear in place of the defendant after the first hearing.

Court hearings are not continuous. The ideal form is for plaintiff and defendant to state their claims in the first hearing and to name witnesses. The witnesses are called and heard about ten days to three weeks later and, ideally, a decision is given in a third hearing.

Many different events and problems prolong disposition, however, so that an average case has approximately six hearings and extends over three to six months. Certain types of crimes, such as those which threaten the security of Bodrum town (e.g., smuggling, street brawling, possession of dynamite), fall into a special category which requires them to be heard promptly to completion.

The following case, involving four Mandalinci villagers and a village gendarme, illustrates how a husband used village gendarmes in a dispute to limit the area of discussion in the ensuing criminal case. It further illustrates how a judge in probing facts, evidence, motives, and goals to get at underlying causes of the conflict cleared up the difficulty and found a solution to the dispute which all principals considered equitable (Nader and Starr 1973) and which the judge himself felt was in accordance with Turkish law.

Ismail, a sixteen-year-old village youth, was going to Milas. Fatma, a married village woman with a reputation for prostitution, asked him to bring her a dress of a certain material from a Milas store. She said she would pay him when he returned. He bought the dress, which at least four villagers saw. "Is that dress for your mother?" they asked. Ismail laughed and said, "Would my mother wear that shiny thing?" According to villagers, the most beautiful material is metallic; such dresses are worn to weddings.

Ismail gave the dress to Fatma and asked for his seventy lira (about seven dollars), but she said, "I'll pay you later." Whenever he asked her, she always said the same thing. Finally, annoyed, he went to her, saying, "I am going after sponges. Can you give me my money now?" She thought a moment, and then said, "Come to my house at night. I will put a big copper pot outside. You can take it and sell it. If you get more than seventy liras for it, give me what is left over."

Late that night, as Ismail was carrying the pot away from her house, a friend of his, about his age, saw him. Ismail said, "Come, let's hide this somewhere. Later we will sell it and divide the money."

The friend helped him, but the next day he went to Adnan, Fatma's husband, and told him how Ismail had taken his pot and where it was hidden. The husband went to the village gendarme with the story. In the evening the gendarme and the husband waited together near the place where the pot was hidden. When Ismail came to pick up his pot, they captured him. They took him to the subdistrict gendarme station to question him and to make out a police report. Later a criminal case for stealing was opened against him in the Bodrum court.

Fatma was called to court as a witness. The judge asked her, "Do you owe Ismail any money?" "No," she said, "I have no debt to him." The judge then asked Ismail if he had any witnesses. "Not today," Ismail replied, "but material like her dress is not available in the village. Such material is not even sold in Bodrum." At a later hearing Ismail produced four witnesses. Each said, "We saw this material when he had it before he gave it to her, and in fact she is wearing that very dress in court today."

When the judge turned to Fatma to ask her to take an oath that Ismail had not paid for this dress, Fatma began crying. The judge said, "Don't spill tears on your new dress." Fatma asked that her pot be returned. The judge said, "Pay the money you owe and you can have your pot." After the court decision, Adnan paid Ismail 70 lira and took his wife's cooking pot back to her.

Many disputes which Mandalinci villagers take to the Bodrum court do not provide a decision satisfactory to *all* litigants and witnesses. (Witnesses may be principal actors in the village dispute, as Fatma was in the above case.) To achieve a satisfactory outcome takes time, skill, and patience on the part of the judge. The same judge usually sits for all hearings of a case, and he needs to engage in investigative work connected with the hearing and to review the court dossier at each hearing to see and evaluate past testimony. When the judge (or another official, such as a gendarme or civil policeman) probes social relations between litigants to find the underlying causes of specific events in the dispute, he frequently is successful in narrowing the focus of the conflict, in finding a way to resolve these narrower issues, and in giving a judgment which not only is binding but also is acceptable to both parties.

When judges are busy or pressed for time, they appear less interested in understanding the aspects of the social relations which have produced conflict than in applying "appropriate laws" in order to provide a judgment acceptable to the scrutiny of higher judges. In part, judges' schedules are full in the Bodrum court because of the way they define a workday and the hours they are willing to spend at the bench. This means that at times they ascertain "facts" as if "facts" were not embedded in the daily experiences of the litigants and thus were not susceptible to multiple layers of meaning. When this happens, judges may produce decisions which are in accordance with Turkish law codes and thus in a strict sense are legal but which leave one or more of the litigants unsatisfied because the narrow, legalistic decisions do not do what Llewellyn and Hoebel have claimed is an important job of law—to "clean up social messes" (1941: 20). When this happens the same litigants return to court, usually with a new complaint arising out of the same conflict-ridden social relationship. I have pointed out elsewhere (Starr 1975) that many Bodrum court decisions are not final in the sense that they resolve claims and disputes. Many court decisions only act to clarify a particular issue or claim in dispute; the clarification then becomes the basis of the next litigation between the same principals. Complex disputes may need two or more lawsuits to begin to resolve the controversy. One dispute over title to a tangerine grove entailed eight lawsuits in a six-year period. Given this situation, the counting of decisions that favor or go against the plaintiff yields little insight into the social effects of judicial decisions.

CONSEQUENCES AND CONCLUSION

1. Mandalinci village has customary processes of disputing in which no specific individual acts as judge, arbitrator, mediator, intermediary, go-between, or the like. If a third party is brought into the dispute, any adult household head can become a representative of one side or the other when necessary. In Mandalinci there is no special setting or special time for discussion of disputes; setting and context are left to the disputants to choose.

2. Despite the seeming randomness in site, setting, and context for the negotiation of disputes there are patterns that emerge from the disputes I recorded in a year and a half of village study which suggest how villagers select among competing modes (negotiation in the village or arbitration at the Bodrum court).

3. The village council and a village *muhtar* are both endowed with authoritative dispute-settling powers by the Turkish Village Law of 1924, but villagers do not take disputes to them to be resolved.

Villagers avoid and resent the "law powers" of their fellow villagers. They prefer to negotiate on an informal basis, since the outcomes are more flexible and negotiation as a process is part of everyone's daily, routinized behavior.

4. Furthermore, villagers say they cannot expect impartiality from others in their village whose very election to office depends on maintaining a support group. I take this to mean that villagers do not feel that the restraints of office (headman or council member) offset the personalities filling these statuses, since persons exercising official roles continue to maintain close and reciprocal ties to their supporters. This suggests that friendship and political networks take precedence over the restraints of impartiality which many Western social scientists claim prevent officials from exerting bias in job performance. In fact, the impartiality of an office holder is alien to much of Turkish thinking.

5. Thus, nonuse of the village *muhtar* and council is explained as follows. First, villagers do not want legal and hence binding decisions made by their fellow villagers, because more flexible, negotiated outcomes are available through informal, customary, village behaviors, and all disputants can participate in achieving a satisfactory outcome. Second, villagers have techniques of equalizing rank differences between disputants by their choice of representative. Third, taking disputes to the headman and council *masks* real social ties that the latter have, which are based on reciprocal debts and favors. Allowing the headman or council to hear disputes is to permit already powerful people (because of their office and their numerous and diverse dyadic ties) to gain additional power. Fourth, long-term disputes represent multiplex, affectional relations in which conflict repeatedly recurs because of the unsuccessful negotiation of past disputes. When individuals in such relationships focus their accumulated conflicts around a specific issue (such as inheritance, ownership of land or houses, unpaid debts) or when anger breaks into violence (insult, hitting), the push for resolution may become irresistible. Angry words or striking another may be translated into "criminal behavior" reportable to the gendarme or prosecutable at the Bodrum court.

6. Focusing the conflict in the relationship around an issue of inheritance or land ownership allows one or both persons to seek an arbitrated decision at the district court. Whether the judicial decision resolves the issues and restores the ongoing, multiplex relationship to a state of mutual help and affection, or results in mutual avoidance to prevent further disruptive encounters, depends in great measure on the amount of time and care Bodrum judges take in understanding the multiple levels of meaning each disputant attaches to the "facts" in the case.

7. When judges do not consider all aspects of a case which are important to the plaintiff and defendant and to their principal witnesses (who may have as active an interest in the court decision as the named litigants), then the judicial decision may not take into account the underlying grievances and issues, which frequently concern scarce resources and the distribution of power relations that the control of resources provides. This means that a principal to the dispute may be unsatisfied with the narrow legal decision, feeling his position has not been fully recognized. When this happens an unsatisfied claimant may either send the decision to appellate court in Ankara or open an ostensibly new case, focused around another legal aspect of the same issues.

NOTES

1. The fieldwork for this paper was conducted on a National Institute of Mental Health Traineeship and Field Grant for sixteen months in 1966–68, and I gratefully acknowledge this support. I want to thank Laura Nader, who continually pushed me to analyze and understand the connection between village disputing practices and the Bodrum law court; Richard Abel for his thoughtful criticisms; Michael Lowy for showing me that the "meanings" attached to court use are problematic; Grace Buzaljko for editing this paper; and finally, Elizabeth Colson, whose critical notes on my dissertation (Starr 1970) have led me into deeper study of the social relations between disputing parties and the ways in which disputes intertwine with village values.

2. This material is analyzed in Starr (1978: 258–62) and is not repeated here.

3. The twenty-seven cases of dispute are presented and analyzed in detail in my monograph (Starr, 1978). Category 1 consists of sixteen disputes between Mandalinci villagers (case numbers 8, 9, 12, 13, 14, 15, 16, 17, 21, 22, 23, 28, 29, 30, 31,

32); category 2 contains three disputes between Mandalinci villagers and villagers living in a twenty-five-mile radius (case numbers 4, 20, 25); category 3, five disputes between Mandalinci villagers and foreigners (i.e., citizens of other countries) (case numbers 5, 6, 18, 19, 27); and category 4, three disputes between Mandalinci villagers and Turkish officials (i.e., bureaucrats or gendarmes) (case numbers 25, 26, and example 2).

4. See also Abel (1973: 226–27); Starr and Yngvesson (1975: 559, 561, 564).

5. Barth (1966: 15) points out that "regardless of our initial evaluations—if something becomes dirt cheap, we may start treating it as dirt; in other words, we tend to revise our evaluations."

6. Compare Stirling (1974: 217–21) for changing relations between fathers and sons, and between brothers, under the impact of increasing knowledge and contact with wider Turkish society, including the possibility of working for wages.

7. Hunt and Hunt (1969: 124–26) document, in their article on rural Mexico, how lower officials are entwined in local social networks and thus lose their neutrality.

8. This supports two of Colson's (1974) assertions: first, that individuals in small-scale, face-to-face communities who know the disadvantages of minimal or diffuse governmental institutions might find greater security in incorporation into larger administrative units (1974: 6), and secondly, that leaders of nation-states, introducing unified court and administrative systems, are "less aware of the need to find a means whereby citizens can pursue grievances against the state and its agents" (1974: 7).

FIVE

THE SOCIAL DYNAMICS OF DISPUTE SETTLEMENT IN A SUNNI MUSLIM VILLAGE IN LEBANON

John E. Rothenberger

THERE HAS BEEN some discussion in the legal anthropological literature lately focusing on the question of scarce resources and the role that control over scarce resources plays in dispute processing. In general, these scarce resources have been defined in material terms—specifically, in terms of ownership of or control over land. When such disputes arise, the means used to process them are generally quite different from the ways in which disputes not involving a scarce resource are handled. In Qarya, a Sunni Muslim village in Lebanon, however, despite the fact that the village lies in a primarily agricultural region in which land is at a premium (hence, a scarce resource), I found that disputes over ownership of or control over land were nonexistent. Further, even in those instances in which a scarce resource *was* involved—either a material resource (e.g., rights of way across land, injury or destruction of property) or a nonmaterial resource (e.g., honor, prestige, or political or personal power)—I found that the procedures used in processing such disputes did not vary significantly from those instances that did not involve a scarce resource. More importantly, the position of the disputant—socially, politically, and economically—in relation to that of his opponent, and the position of both disputants to the remedy agent, determined both choice and course of procedure in the settlement process.

In this paper, I describe and analyze disputing and dispute settlement in Qarya by focusing on (1) the social, economic, and political environment of the disputing process; (2) the process of dispute settlement itself; and (3) the relationship of the disputing process to the social, economic, and political matrix of the village as illustrated by two contrasting cases involving the same parties. Specifically, I am concerned here with the relationship between the type and course of dispute settlement procedures, and the relative positions of the disputants vis-à-vis each other, and vis-à-vis the remedy agent or decision maker in any particular dispute.[1]

THE SETTING

Qarya is an all–Sunni Muslim village of about 1,100 people located at an altitude of about 3,500 feet (1,100 meters) in the mountains of Northern Lebanon.[2]

To get to the village, one drives north from Beirut along the Mediterranean coast, with the narrow Lebanese coastal plain on the east, until one comes to Tripoli, the capital of Northern Lebanon, a city of 200,000 people which is 90 percent Muslim. Tripoli is the political, legal, and trading center of Northern Lebanon. A few miles north of Tripoli, the road branches off northeast into the foothills and mountains leading to Mount Lebanon. Finally, one reaches the mountain bowl in which Qarya and several other communities are located.

The oldest and most densely built-up section of Qarya is on a flat area at the edge of a cliff, overlooking a river below and to the east. The houses, orchards, and fields continue west from this section up a hill from the top of which one can look west to the plains and the Mediterranean Sea.

Qarya is and probably always has been an agricultural village. It is not now a market town, although villagers say that in the past, when the road went along the river, the village was a market center for the area. Up until the demise of the silk industry with the invention of nylon and other synthetic fabrics, mulberry trees were grown on the terraced hills, as they were in much of the Levant. After that, the village subsisted on its own crops.

Since World War II, the greatest economic change has been the introduction of apples, and to a lesser extent apricots and peaches, as cash crops. Virtually everyone has at least a few fruit trees. Individual farmers generally sell their apples in the village to local merchants, themselves villagers and apple growers. Four or five of the village entrepreneurs travel to Iraq or Jordan each year to negotiate for sale of their fruit.

Apart from the cash crops, subsistence farming is still very important in Qarya. Crops include wheat, corn, potatoes, beans, tomatoes, onions, garlic, squash, cucumbers, peppers, and cabbage. Most of the agricultural work is hand done, because of the steep terrain. Major farm implements are the ancient Mediterranean ox-drawn scratch plow and the mule-drawn, stone-studded sled for threshing grain. Wheat and corn are ground by a village-owned water-driven mill, and bread is truly the staff of life. Yoghurt, burghol (cracked wheat meal), vegetables, and preserved fruits constitute the rest of the everyday diet. A chicken may be killed for a guest, and there may be a goat or lamb for religious festivals, but otherwise the villagers eat little meat.

Unlike some areas of the Lebanese plains, this is not a landlord village. Virtually every villager owns at least a little land. Every man is at least a part-time farmer, although the wealthy hire village day laborers to work the land with them. In addition, about a quarter of the men of the village, and almost 10 percent of the women, have nonagricultural work in the village, full-time on the part of some of the men, and part-time on the part of the women and the rest of the men. Also, approximately another quarter of the village men are employed outside Qarya, either seasonally or full-time.

NATIONAL POLITICAL STRUCTURE

Politically, Lebanon is a republic, with a president, premier, and a one-chamber Parliament. Lebanon as a nation was established on the assumption that there were slightly more Christians than Muslims in the population, an assumption that is no longer accurate. Lebanon has long been a refuge for religious minorities of all kinds, and all political and public offices are allocated by religious sect. The president is always a Maronite Christian, and the premier is always a Sunni Muslim. The number of members in Parliament and the number of members to be elected from each district are allocated by religious sect. Religion thus is the essential mark of personal identity in Lebanon.

There are four states in Lebanon. Tripoli is the capital of the state of Northern Lebanon. ᶜAkkaar, in which Qarya is located, is a district in Northern Lebanon, with its district capital at Halba.

The only formal government official in Qarya is the *mukhtaar*, or mayor, of the village. He is a villager, elected by the village and unpaid. Officially, he is only an administrative officer. The nearest central government installation is the military police post in the village on the eastern side of the river. The nearest courts are in the district capital and in Tripoli, each forty-five minutes' drive from the village.[3]

SOCIAL STRUCTURE

The Patrilineage

The Muslim Arab Middle East is an area of strong patrilineal ideology, and in Qarya the basic unit of social structure is the patrilineage. The patrilineage is composed of all the people who can trace their descent through males from a known, or in some cases, traditional, male ancestor. Even in cases where the original ancestor may be traditional rather than historical, all living members of the lineage are able to trace their actual genealogical relationships to each other.

There are also several clans in the village. A clan is a social unit composed of two or more lineages, claiming a common relationship and descent through a close, but unverifiable, relationship between the founders of the component lineages. For most social purposes, the component lineages of the clans may be considered as independent as are the independent lineages. But for most dispute settlement purposes, and more specifically for political purposes, the component lineages of the clans become united into a single unit or group.

The lineages and clans in Qarya are corporate in that they have a strong ideology of group unity and group responsibility. A dispute of a lineage member comes a lineage dispute. Current events and historical events are recalled and narrated as episodes involving the lineage rather than mere individuals. The lineages are thus the framework for social, dispute, and political action in the village.

Lineages are not corporate in the sense of owning corporate lineage property. However, land which is owned by individual lineage members, particularly by prominent lineage members, is often referred to as the property of the lineage rather than as property of the individual owner.

In addition to being social units for purposes of social action and dispute, lineages are also units of political action, on both the local and national levels. On the local level, the lineages of Qarya align themselves into one or the other of two opposing factions. On the village and national level, the lineages vote in elections as units and not as individuals. In the village, political representatives of "blocs" of national candidates distribute premarked ballots to lineage representatives, who in turn distribute them to the men of their lineages. Women are given marked ballots by their husbands, and so vote as part of their husbands' lineage groups. Women do not exercise an active, overt political role in the village.

Each lineage has a *wajiih*, or representative. He is not self-proclaimed, not elected, but rather is agreed upon by informal consensus of his lineage mates. Ideally, he should be relatively wealthy, so that he can maintain a guest room in his home, where he can entertain visitors. He should also be articulate, politically aware and active, and should have influential urban connections. The wajiih represents his lineage constituents in disputes, and acts as their "lawyer."

Social Classes

Villagers in Qarya divide the lineages into three groupings, or what I shall hereinafter call "social classes." Two of these social classes are named; the third is a residual grouping, unnamed, and composed of villagers who do not belong to either of the other two classes.

The upper social class is called the *mashaayikh*, or the shaykhs.

The lower class is the *fallaahiin*, or the peasants. The mashaayikh comprise about 55 percent of the village population, and the fallaahiin about 15 percent. The remaining 30 percent of the villagers fall into the residual "middle" class. No one ever speaks of a middle class, but only of the upper and lower classes. It should be noted at the outset that lineages, and not individuals, are assigned to one social class or another.

Three descent groups are recognized by villagers as being mashaayikh. There are formal criteria for assigning lineages to this class, but some lineages which meet the formal criteria are not considered to be, in fact, mashaayikh. The three recognized mashaayikh kinship groups are the three largest, wealthiest, and politically most active and most powerful groups in the village. The village genealogies of all three go back eight generations. All political and dispute settlement leaders are members of the upper social class.

There are five fallaahiin (peasant, or lower-class) lineages in the village. These are the descendants of people who came to Qarya fifty to 100 years ago from the neighboring northern Lebanese or southern Syrian villages to work as sharecroppers or tenant farmers. They now own land of their own, but they are still considered "peasants." These lineages are small, of middle economic status, and not politically active as independent groups. In calculating relative strength in village factional disputes, the five fallaahiin lineages are often considered to be a single unit, though they may not in fact act as such. If they ever acted as a unified group rather than as five small lineages, they would constitute a solid power bloc equivalent to all but the largest clan of the village.

There are two fallaahiin leaders who are welcome and whose opinions are considered in the councils and meetings of village leaders. In general, however, matters and disputes concerning only the fallaahiin are considered beneath the notice of the mashaayikh, especially by the young and more honor-conscious members of this class.

The rest of the lineages of Qarya, approximately 30 percent of the population, fall into an unnamed, undefined residual "middle" social class. It includes about ten lineages, of all sizes, but most being between the formally recognized mashaayikh and the fallaahiin lineages in size. In general, they, too, are of middle economic status. There are, however, two men of the middle social class who are of upper economic status. These two are in a position of being potentially politically active and powerful.

There are four named territorial sections, or quarters, in the village. While certain lineages tend to live in certain quarters, the quarters are by no means exclusive. They are not endogamous, and they are not politically united as they are in some Middle Eastern communities. Neither are the social classes endogamous, and marriages do occur between members of the upper and lower social classes.

Economic Status

In general, there is an egalitarian ideology in Qarya. People say, "We are all equal here." It is true that differences in standard of living are small. Everyone lives in about the same style. Houses may be new or old, but age is not a reliable indication of economic or social status. Everyone wears the same kind of clothes, although a poor man's clothes will be more faded and patched than those of a wealthy man. Everyone eats the same kind of food, although the wealthy may have meat once a week and the poor only on religious holidays. Every man owns at least a little land, although the wealthy may own many times the amount of the poor, and animals and other property as well.

There are no recognized economic classes as such. Economic status is an individual matter, and not a matter of lineage. With the prevailing egalitarian ideology of the village, it is difficult to get people to talk about differences of economic status. Eleven men were identified as being wealthy in the village. Most are of the upper social class, but two men of the residual middle class are included as well. By village standards, all own a considerable amount of land, many apple trees, and other property. All have somewhat larger and more elaborate houses than most of the other villagers.

Ten heads of household were identified as being poor. Being

classified as poor seems to result from unfortunate personal history and circumstances. The list comprises certain members of the middle social class, and two members of the upper class—one a younger son who did not inherit much land and who was sick and could not work for a period of years; the other a widow who was deserted by her husband and never remarried. Two widows without adult sons to support them were included in the category of the poor. It is significant that no one who could work as a day laborer on the land was included among the poor of the village. The list did not include any of the peasants or lower social class of the village.

Thus, Qarya follows the general Middle Eastern pattern described by Salim (1962). As Salim has pointed out, social class and economic status are not necessarily congruent in this area of the world. An individual may have a high economic status, for example, and yet belong to a low social class, and vice versa.

Factions

The Middle East is a traditional area of dual factionalism, and factionalism appears in various forms in different areas and communities. In Qarya the nucleus of one faction is the lineage of the mukhtaar (mayor) of the village. The nucleus of the other faction is the largest clan of the village. Around the two nuclei the other descent groups of Qarya ally themselves into two opposing camps. The two nuclei have been the cores of their respective factions for at least fifty years. The other lineages have been in a fairly stable, but somewhat shifting, pattern of alliances for a long period of time also.

The mukhtaar, who is recognized as the wajiih, or representative of his lineage, is also recognized as the head of the faction of which his lineage is the core. The core clan of the opposing faction does not have a single, strong, politically active chief. There are, however, three or four leaders of the clan who, in union or in opposition to each other, speak for the faction and lead its political activities.

The factions, along with the lineages, form the idiom or framework in which village history is created, remembered, and narrated.

The dual opposition is also the framework of village political activity. In matters or disputes of direct concern to the entire village, the two factions tend to mobilize against each other.

Social and Political Arenas

Coffeehouses. There are three coffeehouses in the village. The coffeehouses are the Middle Eastern equivalent of men's clubs. Most men patronize all three coffeehouses to some extent, but habitual attendance at a particular coffeehouse is a political statement. Each coffeehouse is primarily patronized by a particular political and social group or groups in the village. Habitual attendance is a sign of political allegiance. In the coffeehouses, news is exchanged, disputes are discussed and negotiated, honor is tested and reaffirmed, and political intrigue is hatched.

The coffeehouses also serve as schools for the art of politics and personal manipulation, both so important and typical of the life of the Middle East. In the coffeehouses, boys, particularly the sons of the wealthy upper class, gather and learn the skills of politics—arguing, persuading, negotiating, mediating, and listening. It is these sons who will in years to come be the political leaders and remedy agents of the village.

Guest Rooms. All the politically active and influential men of Qarya maintain guest rooms in their homes. These are the private equivalents of the coffeehouses. On almost every evening, most of the important men of the village hold a *sahra,* or evening party, in their guest rooms. As with the coffeehouses, habitual attendance of other men at the guest room of a particular individual is a sign of their social and political allegiance.

The Mukhtaar

The mukhtaar, or mayor of the village, is, almost of necessity, the wajiih of a wealthy, upper-class lineage, and wealthy in his own right.[4] He is not paid a salary, but it is his obligation to meet and entertain any official or unofficial guests to the village. Officially, the duties of the mukhtaar are administrative, not executive or judicial. He is responsible for recording births, marriages, and deaths; supervising the maintenance of village paths and roads; and reporting disorders to the military police. Beyond these duties, the extent to which a mukhtaar assumes executive and judicial prerogatives—the extent to which he becomes a dispute remedy agent and political leader—depends on his personality, intelligence, and ambition.

The mukhtaar in Qarya during my fieldwork had chosen to assume these unofficial duties, powers, and prerogatives. As a younger son of a previous mukhtaar, he had mastered the arts of local politics. He is a masterful politician and a persuasive yet subtle mediator and remedy agent. He has the weight of his socioeconomic position, in addition to his official position, behind his arguments and suggestions. In all but the most political or personal of disputes, he is trusted by the village as being neutral in his settlement efforts. He is by far the most important and influential remedy agent in the village.

A previous mukhtaar, Haajj Amiin, the wajiih of another upper-class descent group, is the second most important remedy agent in Qarya.

Military Police

There are no police in Qarya, but there is a military police post in the neighboring village, about a half-mile away. Whenever violence is reported or whenever a complaint is brought in a formal court, a Landrover with four military police with rifles appears in the village, and the usual result is jail, at least temporarily, for someone. The invocation, presence, or intervention of the police almost invariably adds to the intensity of a dispute and makes it harder to settle according to the preferred village mediation procedures.

In Lebanon there is also the "Maktab at Thaani," corresponding to the French Deuxième Bureau, the internal security police (see also n. 3). It is their duty to maintain peace and tranquility in the towns and villages and to prevent disruptive political activity. There are thought to be paid informants in the villages, primarily to report to the Maktab any local disturbance or political activity which might disrupt the peace of the area. The threat, implicit or explicit, of the Maktab at Thaani is a lever and weapon which can be used in local village political maneuvering.

THE PROCESS OF DISPUTE SETTLEMENT

For purposes of this paper, a ***dispute*** is a disagreement between individuals or groups in which one or more parties has taken steps to gain his ends by means of some recognized procedure "in the public arena" (following Gulliver, 1969a: 14). In this section of the paper, I will first explore the definitions and typology of dispute settlement procedures as they are applicable to Qarya. I will then list the elements of procedural style as they are evident in the village.

Definition of Processes

It is useful to distinguish between processes both descriptively—as they can be used to talk about individual disputes in a particular community—and analytically—as they can be used to compare categories of dispute cases.

Descriptively, there is a range or continuum of processes and related agencies and mechanisms which can be used when an overt dispute arises in Qarya:

(1) Nothing (perhaps then harboring a grudge)
(2) Argument or fighting without interference of a third person
(3) Negotiation between the parties without a third person
(4) Negotiation between the parties with the aid of a neutral go-between (often someone within the lineage), especially in marital disputes
(5) Mediation by a third party remedy agent (as defined in the Introduction to this volume)
(6) Appeal to the mukhtaar in his official capacity as pseudoarbitrator or adjudicator
(7) Invocation of the military police
(8) Appeal to the formal courts

In fact, any one dispute is likely to involve a range of processes and agencies—any or all of which may be called into action at the same time. It is therefore difficult to classify cases by the particular procedure being followed.

Analytically, dispute settlement procedures and processes may be classified in the ways noted in the Introduction to this volume.

These include negotiation, mediation, arbitration, and adjudication. In a village situation such as that of Qarya, however, it is often virtually impossible to distinguish among these procedures. In village dispute settlement, with a third-party remedy agent from the village, the procedure is by definition mediation, and not arbitration or adjudication. There is no one within the village with formal or legal authority to impose a binding decision upon the parties. The only exception to this is the *imam*, or prayer leader of the village, who has religious authority to make decisions in cases involving domestic matters, such as marriage, divorce, and inheritance, which fall under Muslim religious law as recognized in Lebanon within the Muslim community.

The imam of Qarya, however, is rarely appealed to for his decision. Most domestic disputes are settled within the lineage or lineages concerned by the wajiihs or by other local shaykhs or holy men chosen by the lineage or family heads. Purely religious questions, such as the validity and application of a religious oath, rarely arise.

A remedy agent such as the mukhtaar, however, may have de facto power—social, economic, political—over one or more parties to a dispute so that he in actuality may impose a settlement or decision. Thus the procedure in fact may be adjudication or arbitration, although in form it is still mediation. Such nuances are often impossible to sort out in a case analysis. (Gulliver [1969a: 21–22] also implies such overlap of procedures.)

Formal officials from outside the village, such as the military police and the central government, have authority and power to make decisions, but when they are operating in the village itself, they try to follow at least the form of the local mediation process. They attempt to arrive at a mutually agreeable compromise solution to the dispute at hand.

Adjudication occurs primarily when the villagers themselves go outside the village to the formal courts. Even then, the courts and influential members of the village generally urge that the parties return to the community and try to reach a settlement according to the village ideal of mediation and compromise.

Procedural Style

Laura Nader has defined "procedural style" as the continuous features that permeate court activities and constitute the form and manner of the court proceedings. I consider procedural style to be the manifestation in conflict resolution procedures, either directly or indirectly, of significant aspects and elements of the culture—ideals, morals, values, world view—as distinct from more materialistic or legalistic aspects of the procedure. These cultural elements are instrumental in motivating disputes, in choosing and carrying on the procedures for settlement of disputes, in determining the intensity with which the procedures are carried on, and in determining the settlements reached.

The cultural factors that seem most important in influencing procedural style in Qarya are the following:

1. The Muslim religion is the all-pervading environment within which life in Qarya takes place. God is all powerful; all events and all conditions are the result of the will of God. This belief can be used to avoid human responsibility or blame. Life, injury, misfortune, death are the will of God, and humans can do nothing to change them. Muslim religious law regarding marriage, divorce, and inheritance is recognized in Lebanon as legal for the Muslim community. The permission of polygyny, the ease of divorce by the husband, and male-oriented inheritance are part of the background of many disputes.

2. In Qarya disputes and disputing are public. Arguments are shouted from the rooftops, and listening to them is public entertainment. Negotiation and mediation sessions are usually public, often outdoors, with a general and vocal audience. These facts introduce an element of drama and "playing for an audience" into disputing and dispute settlement. On the other hand, there is also the custom of secret or semisecret coffeehouse or guest room intrigue in many disputes. At these sessions alliances are made, forces are mobilized, and tactics are discussed.

3. There is a decided preference for settling disputes within the village and by the mediation of a respected third party, with compromise between the parties and a generally agreed-upon settlement. It is felt that disputes should be settled within the village and not aired outside the community, in order to preserve the good name and honor of the village. Villagers know that when they take a dispute outside the village to a court or to the military police, the village loses control of the dispute and its resolution. Police are unpredictable, and the decisions of judges are often arbitrary.

4. There is a clear recognition of the importance and necessity of ongoing relationships within the community. The villagers of Qarya have known each other all their lives and will continue to deal with each other for the rest of their lives. All but a very few of the villagers handle their affairs in a way that indicates recognition of this principle.

5. The Middle East is an area of proud people. Honor, pride, prestige, impulsiveness, the readiness to do violence in defense of honor, the heroic ideal, and the grand gesture are all culturally valued.

6. There is a strong ideology of lineage and family unity. A dispute between individuals becomes a dispute between lineages. The respective lineage wajiihs represent their lineage members. An individual dispute, thus becoming a group dispute, means that the dispute is escalated to a higher and more intense level with a greater possibility of violence and further complications. On the other hand, the intervention of the wajiihs may also serve to insert an element of greater wisdom, experience, and restraint into the course of the dispute.

7. There is a social class structure in the village and an implicit economic status structure. These have an important bearing on the genesis of disputes, and on the process and final outcome of dispute settlement.

8. Dual factionalism in the village provides a further ideology or framework for escalation of a dispute beyond the lineage level, either implicitly, in the form of sympathy and indirect support, or explicitly, in the form of direct mobilization in political disputes. The dual factions of the village also provide a framework or idiom for the organization of village history, including the history of disputes.

There are three law systems in the Muslim Middle East: national law, with its formal court system; customary village law, with its emphasis on mediation within the village setting; and Muslim religious law, represented in the village by the imam or prayer leader. The village system and more particularly the court system often provide alternative remedy courses, and choices can be manipulated by people who are in advantageous positions.

Ongoing Relations versus Control of Scarce Resources

Some writers have stressed the importance of the recognition of and the desire to preserve ongoing relations in conflict resolution procedure (Gluckman 1955). Others have instead stressed the importance of the control over scarce resources, generally material resources

(Starr and Yngvesson 1975). But one must realize that nonmaterial resources may also be scarce resources that are competed for and are as, or more, important in conflict resolution procedures than are material resources. Honor, pride, prestige, and power may indeed be considered scarce resources and the motivation for competition.

Ongoing relations are undoubtedly of prime importance in a village such as Qarya. It is necessary that social life continue and that the village continue as a viable community. During serious disputes in Qarya there is no cessation of community life such as Siegel and Beals (1960) describe for their Indian community devastated by factionalism.

The necessity and desirability of preserving ongoing relations in the community is probably the basic reason why mediation and compromise within the village are the preferred means of conflict resolution. Out of my total of 108 cases, ninety-eight, or approximately 91 percent, were settled within the village by accepted village procedural means.[5] By compromise no one really wins, at least formally, and no one loses. The settlement is often marked by a formal peacemaking with ceremonial coffee drinking together. Peaceful relations are restored and community life proceeds.

Cases taken out of the village or settled by remedy agents from outside the village tended to be village factional or political disputes primarily, and also intervillage disputes, disputes involving violence and therefore the police, and disputes over land rights. However, the majority of all kinds of disputes, except factional disputes, were settled within the village.

A more interesting consideration is whether material or nonmaterial resources are the primary motivating factors in the instigation of disputes and the conduct of procedures for their settlement.

During the period of my research, most disputes were ostensibly and initially about material resources—rights of way across land, injury or destruction of property, conflicts over marriage contracts.[6] However, as I have said earlier, the Middle East is an area of proud people. Honor, prestige, and political and personal power are highly motivating factors. Although a dispute may be commenced for a material reason, the conduct of the dispute, the procedures followed, and the intensity with which they are pursued seem to be motivated by these nonmaterial scarce resource factors. Individuals continually compete for these scarce resources on their own behalf and on behalf of the lineages or factions they represent (cf. Campbell 1964). The conduct of disputes is one means by which this competition can be carried on and expressed.

This competition serves to further escalate disputes, because it gives additional motivation to win to all the parties concerned, including the remedy agents, who wish to enhance their prestige or political positions. Thus, material disputes about rights of way over land can become personal or group disputes with honor and prestige as the motivating factors.

My conclusions thus seem different from those reached by Starr and Yngvesson (1975) in that in Qarya it is socioeconomic-political position which determines the choice of procedures and not the material resources being disputed about. One possibly significant difference from the Starr-Yngvesson data is that I witnessed no disputes in Qarya involving the actual ownership or control of parcels of land. If there had been such cases, perhaps a different pattern might have appeared. The closest cases I found involved rights of way across land; these can be bitter and cause violence. But the general pattern of procedure for these cases does not vary significantly from cases with other subject matters.

Selective Use of Processes and Agencies

Anyone in Qarya in theory and in fact may use any conflict resolution remedy agent or agency. Actual and specific choices and results depend on the socioeconomic-political position of the disputant, his position vis-à-vis his opponent, and the positions of the disputants vis-à-vis the possible remedy agent.

The great majority of disputes are settled in the village according to preferred village mediation procedures. A dispute within a lineage is taken to and usually settled by the lineage wajiih. An interlineage dispute is taken to the mukhtaar, to Haajj Amiin (the former mukhtaar), to the imam, or all of them in consultation. The specific ramifications of the procedures and settlement depend on the relative positions of all the parties, including the remedy agents.

If a dispute involves violence that comes to the attention of the outside authorities, the military police intervene, the dispute is escalated, people are often put in prison, and a military court trial ensues. This is a process and agency not really desired or chosen by anyone in the village.

Formal courts are rarely resorted to. They may be used in intervillage disputes, in which village dispute resolution procedure is ineffective. An individual disputant may resort to the courts when he does not wish to conform to the mediation process for any one of a variety of reasons. Such a desire may be the result of the individual's position, or his position vis-à-vis his opponent, or his general attitudes toward the village.

THE RELATIONSHIP OF DISPUTES TO SOCIAL STRUCTURE

Two Cases

Case 1. Jamiil is a wealthy member of the "middle" social class and is one of the most active disputants in Qarya. He is a friend and political ally of the mukhtaar and, as wajiih of his lineage, is able to deliver votes in elections and to support the mukhtaar in factional disputes. He frequently flouts village standards of conduct and preferred dispute settlement procedures. He maximizes his own opportunities without concern for village opinion.

Jaabir is a member of a peasant or lower-class lineage, which has been in Qarya a short time relative to the upper-class lineages. He and his lineage still feel insecure within the social structure of the village.

Jaabir suffered several broken ribs in an accident while working as a day laborer at Jamiil's house. Controversy raged hotly as to responsibility for the accident. Jamiil promised to compensate Jaabir for his injury, expenses, and loss of wages. Jaabir consulted lawyers, who told him he could sue in court and collect damages.

However, Jaabir and his lineage commenced negotiations with Jamiil within the village framework and did not sue in court. Negotiations proceeded directly between the parties, conspicuously without the aid or intervention of the mukhtaar. When Jaabir threatened suit, Jamiil in turn threatened to bribe the judges or other officials.

Negotiations proceeded over four months within the village context. Finally, Jaabir told the mukhtaar that unless Jamiil paid a reasonable amount he would sue in court. At that point the mukhtaar became involved as a go-between, but not really as a mediator. Jaabir finally settled for forty dollars damages from Jamiil, equivalent to twenty days' wages as a day laborer, in addition to his actual medical expenses.

Case 2. In anger over Jamiil's recalcitrance in negotiating in good faith, Jaabir and his cousin Amiin cut the branches off a walnut tree that belonged to Jamiil, even though it was on the property of Jaabir's lineage. (It is possible for one party to own trees on land belonging to another.)

Jamiil immediately commenced a formal court suit, ignoring village mediation procedures. Before the case was heard, the mukhtaar and Haajj Amiin repeatedly scheduled mediation sessions between the parties. Jamiil consistently absented himself from the village and avoided the meetings. Jaabir, finally in exasperation, said that he also did not want mediation, but wanted the court to settle the matter. The court penalized Jaabir and his cousin about seventeen dollars damages to Jamiil and about the same amount as a fine to the court.

These two cases between the same parties but in reversed positions serve as clear, if not perfect, illustrations of the points to be made in this section, in which I will discuss the relationship of the village's social-economic-political system to the process of dispute settlement and political disputing.

Social-Economic-Political Background of Disputes

In Qarya, different kinds of people get into different kinds of disputes. The factors that influence or determine the kinds of disputes are biological, such as sex and age; social class; economic status; lineage representation; political position, influence, and affiliation; and personal knowledge and experience.

Biological Factors. Children dispute with parents, chiefly about overwork, or with siblings, as in cases of brothers stealing money from sisters. Remedy agents are rarely used, and there is usually no real resolution of the dispute.

Women dispute with other women about domestic matters, often at the public water taps or the communal pit ovens, or about the theft of minor crops. These, like the parent-child disputes, usually involve no remedy agents and no real resolution. Mother-in-law v. daughter-in-law disputes are frequent and usually take the form of long-term grudges, periodically eased by a nominal peace-making on religious festival days.

The most frequent form of women's dispute is the *zaʿlaana* case, in which a wife who feels mistreated by her husband leaves him and goes back to her parents' home. This is a culturally recognized way for a wife to express her grievance. In these cases the husband, usually after about a week, asks his or his wife's lineage wajiih, or perhaps another recognized village remedy agent, to act as mediator and make peace. There is a feeling that the remedy agent should be of the same social standing as the husband and wife.

Men dispute primarily among themselves, and most frequently about honor, politics, power, property, and women, not necessarily in that order.

Social Class. The upper-class lineages, the mashaayikh, are the wealthiest in the village. They have the most property to be concerned about, and thus they have more disputes than the other social classes.

The upper class disputes primarily with itself, with other members of the same lineage or clan, and with other upper-class lineages and clans. This is because the members of the upper class have similar social, economic, and political interests. It may also be that they disdain to dispute with members of the lower social class unless their own honor has been infringed upon or threatened.

The upper social class is also the "ruling class"—the politicians and political powers of the village. Upper-class lineages and their leaders are the nuclei and moving forces in the two opposing village factions. Thus, the upper-class disputes about politics and political control and power in the village.

In addition, the upper social class is also most concerned with its honor, prestige, and prerogatives. These concerns enter into disputes, particularly for young men of the upper class, who are quick to take affront for any real or imagined slight to personal or lineage honor or position, either from a member of their own class or more especially from a member of a lower class.

This trait is evidenced, for example, in their concern for "correct" conduct of courtship, marriage contract negotiations, and the wedding ceremonies and celebrations themselves. There is still a preference for patrilateral parallel-cousin marriage, to father's brother's daughter. The preference is present among all classes, but the rights and conduct of the marriage are particularly emphasized among the upper class.

The "middle" social class disputes primarily about property and material resources. Members of the middle-class initiate disputes relatively frequently with those of the upper class, perhaps indicating their resentment of upper-class prerogatives and their own rising aspirations.

The peasant class disputes most conspicuously about elopements and other marriage irregularities, and primarily with other members of the same class.

Economic Status. Economic status roughly corresponds to social class, but not entirely. There are poor members of the upper social class; there are rich members of the "middle" social class; and all the peasants, or lower social class, are considered to be of middle economic status.

Lineage Representation. The wajiih of the lineage represents individual disputants. If a lineage does not have an articulate, politically aware, and well-liked wajiih, an individual member of that lineage is on his own and at a disadvantage in competition with someone who has such a representative. A member of a lineage of higher social, economic, and political position is at an advantage over an opponent of lower position.

Political Position. When the two factions of the village are fully mobilized in opposition to each other in a political dispute, all the normally neutral remedy agents or mediators are also mobilized and active in one camp or the other. There are thus no neutral remedy agents in the village who can settle or mediate the dispute; no internal settlement is possible. In such disputes the village must call in outside remedy agents, or the outside remedy agents themselves—the military police or other government officials—take the initiative to intervene in order to restore peace (cf. Nader 1965a).

Some disputes are specifically political and factional. These are motivated by the desire for control, prestige, and power in and over the village. Many other disputes, particularly between members of the opposed nuclear lineages of the factions, develop factional and political overtones, even if the initial dispute is about property or other material resources and is not purely political. Such disputes are thereby escalated and complicated and made more difficult to settle within the village context.

Knowledge and Experience. It is the members of the upper socioeconomic stratum who have the knowledge and experience and the urban ties and influence to maximize their dispute and dispute settlement opportunities. These urban ties and influence arise as a result of kinship ties with powerful urban relatives; commercial dealings in marketing of the village crops; patron-client relationships with political, judicial, and military officials; and opportunities to act as host to visiting dignitaries in the village. Establishing these relations requires a fair amount of wealth and leisure time. Also important in acquiring this knowledge and experience is the coffeehouse school of politics, discussed earlier.

Access to and Use of Procedures and Agencies

Ideally, everyone in Qarya has access to any procedure for conflict resolution and to any agency. Anyone, regardless of age, sex, social class, or wealth, may go to the mukhtaar or other village remedy agent with a grievance and will be listened to. Anyone may appeal to the military police. Anyone may go to the courts, assuming he or she can pay the necessary fees. No lawyers are necessary.

In fact, however, access to and use of the procedures and agencies for conflict resolution are influenced and determined even more stringently by many of the same factors as were discussed above for the kinds of disputes in which people find themselves. Access to and use of procedures and agencies depend on personal and lineage position in the village, knowledge and experience, personality, and connections with or access to someone with power and political-legal awareness.

The specific processes do not necessarily vary between someone with little and someone with considerable power and influence. However, the force, intensity, and persuasiveness of presentation are often the deciding factors in the settlement reached. Someone with more political-legal awareness is usually able to present his case or have it presented with more force and persuasiveness than is a less aware disputant.

Within the village, women and children generally are not able to use remedy agents or mobilize effective representation. This usually means there are no effective means of dispute settlement available to them. An exception is the za^{c}laana case discussed earlier, in which a wife goes home to her parents, usually because of mistreatment by her husband. In this type of dispute, lineage and group interests in the marriage and the children are at stake. The case then develops as a case between men—the husband and the father of the wife. The husband, not the wife, summons a remedy agent. The remedy agent is a wajiih of one of the lineages, usually the wife's, or a shaykh or holy man, possibly the imam or the mukhtaar.

A member of an upper-class lineage with a powerful wajiih has a leader to go to to decide a dispute or to represent him in the settlement process with another lineage. The middle-class wealthy have ties with the upper-class leaders and so can invoke their help and representation.

Knowledge, personality, and political factors give access to out-of-village forums—police and courts, which are mainly the domains of the wealthy and upper social class. Wider perspectives, urban awareness, and connections result from wealth and social position.

Other people without politically aware and interested leaders must go to the upper-class leaders, but almost as "strangers," and ask for their help as mediators (but not as representatives). The upper-class leader is not closely involved on that person's behalf, but acts rather to settle the dispute for the sake of village peace and harmony.

Selection and Manipulation of Processes and Agencies

It is often difficult in a village situation to specify who is the "plaintiff" and who is the "defendant," who has the original grievance and who is the aggrieved.[7] It may be the "defendant" who commences the procedure as such.

A person who is sued in a court has not "chosen" the court as a procedure. A person arrested and put in jail has not "chosen" a military court. Sometimes a person is arrested and an entire dispute is plunged into a court process, when none of the parties desire such a proceeding.

Very often there are two or more procedures, such as a court trial and a village mediation process, going on simultaneously in a dispute. A disputant will often play one procedure against the other, hoping for an advantage in one or the other. Selection of procedures and agencies is dependent on one's perception of the possibilities and advantages. This choice in turn is dependent on the social-economic-political-personality factors discussed earlier.

A man of the upper social class, closely related to power figures in the village, has confidence and knowledge and sees relatively unlimited choice within the village and the court system. He has the ability to select so as to maximize his advantages without restriction. On the other hand, a man of the upper social class may consider himself to be a bearer of the village tradition, and thus may be constrained to conform to norms of mediation within the village.

A man from the peasant class knows of his lower position in the village and is sensitive to it. Jaabir is an example. He doesn't want to jeopardize his own position or that of his lineage. He is trying to improve the position of both in the community without antagonizing others. He tends to conform to the village mediation process conducted by village remedy agents from outside his own lineage.

A wealthy member of the "middle" social class—individualistic, opportunistic, urbanized, with friends in the influential upper social class, with knowledge and experience, and with an aggressive personality—maximizes his own advantage without the restriction of village norms and customs. Jamiil is an example. He is a person who seems most likely to use nonvillage mechanisms such as the courts. He may be contemptuous of the village and its traditional system. He may try to wreak punishment on his adversaries by his nonadherence to the traditional system, by going to the military police or to the courts.

The rest of the "middle" class, as well as the lower or peasant class, adheres to traditional village conflict resolution procedures.

Patterns of Disputants and Remedy Agents

The mukhtaar, Haajj Amiin, and the imam are the most important remedy agents in Qarya. The mukhtaar and Haajj Amiin are all-village remedy agents, acting on behalf of anyone in the village and in any kind of dispute except those which are specifically religious in nature. The imam acts in religious disputes, domestic disputes, and far less frequently in general village matters. Except when acting as the wajiihs of their respective descent groups, the three men employ very similar methods of mediating or settling disputes. In addition, the mukhtaar and Haajj Amiin often act together, and it is frequently said that the two can "speak for the village."

Harry Todd (1973: 20) has generalized on the type of conflict resolution procedure which tends to be used in disputes within and between groups or classes in segmentary and hierarchial communities. Inasmuch as Qarya is both segmentary and hierarchial, I generally accept but somewhat modify his conclusions and hypotheses.

In general, Todd hypothesizes that in a dispute between equals, the dispute will tend to be settled by mediation. I think it is necessary to consider the relative standing of the remedy agent vis-à-vis the parties. If the dispute is an intralineage dispute, the remedy agent will probably be the wajiih of the lineage, and hence of the same social and probably the same economic status as the disputants. In this case, the procedure will probably be mediation de facto as well as in form.

If the dispute is an interlineage dispute, the remedy agent is likely to be the mukhtaar, Haajj Amiin, or the imam—all wealthy members of the upper social class. If the disputants are also wealthy or are members of the upper social class, all the parties to the dispute, including the remedy agent, are again equals, and the procedure is again likely to be de facto mediation.

If the dispute is an interlineage matter, but the disputants are members of the lower class or of the nonwealthy segment of the "middle" social class, then the remedy agent is superior to the disputants. In this situation, the personal, lineage, and political power of the remedy agent, in addition to his wealth and the influence it can wield in the village, become factors in the conduct of the procedure. This informal power of the remedy agent may exert an influence on disputants to compel them to agree to the settlement he suggests. Thus, the procedure is still formally a mediation, but subjectively, on the part of all the parties to the dispute, it may actually be an arbitration or even an adjudication.

Todd correctly concludes that in cases of higher class v. higher class, there will tend to be mediation, but in cases of lower class v. lower class, there could be either mediation or adjudication. My addition is that the choice between mediation and adjudication depends on the position of the remedy agent vis-à-vis the disputants.

Todd's final conclusion is that in disputes between members of different classes in the hierarchy, there will tend to be adjudication. He does not distinguish between higher v. lower, and lower v. higher. My hypothesis is that in the case of lower v. higher, there will tend to be mediation, in form and in fact. For reasons discussed above, a member of the lower class is reluctant to violate village custom and go outside the village to court. Within the village, the upper-class remedy agent will probably be reluctant to alienate the upper-class opponent, who may be a political ally or potential supporter. Thus, the remedy agent will try to restore and keep peace by arriving at a compromise settlement agreeable to all concerned.

In the case of an upper-class against a lower-class disputant, the factors are reversed, and I suggest that there will tend to be adjudication, in form or in fact. An upper-class disputant or a wealthy middle-class "plaintiff" is more likely to go out of the village to the court or seek redress by some means of adjudication. If he decides to submit to village mediation process, the factors are now on his side. He is an equal of the remedy agent, and a political ally or potential ally. He is also ostensibly the aggrieved party. The remedy agent will put additional pressure on the lower-class "defendant" to agree to terms chosen by the remedy agent, and probably favorable to the upper-class "plaintiff." Thus, the result is still mediation in form but arbitration or perhaps adjudication in fact.

CONCLUSIONS

The units of social, political, dispute, and dispute settlement action in Qarya are lineages, rather than individuals. In political matters of general village concern, the lineages tend to mobilize into factions, which become the units of political action.

Political leaders and effective remedy agents in the village are a very few men of the upper social class, with wealth, intelligence, persuasive personality, political ambition, urban and influential connections, experience, and the inclination to engage in political and mediating activities.

There is a need for agreement on basic definitions in the study of law and conflict resolution. I have defined various conflict resolution procedures in a manner parallel to but not the same as the definitions of Gulliver (1969a: 17). With Gulliver, I pointed out that there is often an overlap and a continuum among the three procedures of mediation, arbitration, and adjudication. What is in form one procedure may in fact be another, as a result of differing socio-economic-political statuses among the disputants and remedy agents.

Although material resources are usually the initial cause of a dispute, the actual conduct of the dispute is determined more by nonmaterial scarce resources—honor, prestige, and pride. The value placed on ongoing relations in the community is the basis for the ideal of mediation and peacemaking within the village.

I suggested the importance of phenomena that escalate disputes and make settlement more difficult. When individual disputes become group disputes, or when government intervention intensifies or expands disputes, they escalate beyond their original bounds and become more difficult to resolve according to village procedures.

The pattern of the relationship among social structure, culture, and conflict resolution process probably varies with different societies. Cultural ideologies and preferences are as important as social structure in influencing the pattern of the processes to be followed, as indicated in the discussion of the factors of procedural style in determining processes in Qarya.

It is the social-economic-political position of the disputants, individually and in relation to their opponents, and also in relation to the specific remedy agents involved, which influences and determines the choice of and course of procedure in the dispute settlement process. We must consider not only the gross relationship of the parties as equal or unequal, but also the relative status of the "plaintiff" and "defendant," that is, whether the case is high status v. low status, low v. high, high v. high, or low v. low. Significant criteria for determining the procedures must be determined—social, economic, political, and other advantages or disadvantages. Furthermore, we must consider the varying pattern of relationships between the remedy agents and the parties to a dispute.

Building on Todd's materials (1973), I have suggested a series of hypotheses as to the pattern of these relationships as they occur in Qarya. Maximum choice in procedures and agencies lies with members of the upper social class who are also wealthy, who are in a politically favorable position, and who have urban knowledge and experience. Minimum opportunity lies with the poor, with members of the lower social class, and with women and children who are not politically aware and do not have the requisite experience, knowledge, and support.

Change is in the wind in conflict resolution mechanisms and procedures in many areas of the world previously governed by customary procedures, such as Qarya with its ideal of mediation. With increasing central government control and increasing diffusion of urban attitudes and experience, there will probably be a greater use of the mechanisms of the central government and of the courts, and less of the traditional mechanisms and agencies. The importance of honor, pride, group unity, and adherence to custom will decrease and individualistic and materialistic concerns will become more important in disputes and in the choice of dispute settlement procedures and agencies.

NOTES

1. The field research upon which this paper is based was conducted in Lebanon in 1966–67 with the support of fellowship grants from the Foreign Area Fellowship Program, New York. The primary report of that research is Rothenberger (1970). Thanks are again extended to all those mentioned in the Preface to that volume, especially to Laura Nader. I am grateful to the Wenner-Gren Foundation for Anthropological Research for supporting the September 1973 Conference of the Berkeley Law Project at the University of Massachusetts, Amherst, and for the opportunity that it provided for valuable exchange with other members of the project.

The discussion in this paper is based on 108 cases collected during my field research. The name of the research village and all personal names in this paper are pseudonyms.

The transliteration of Arabic words and names is basically the same as that used in Rothenberger (1970), but it has been simplified somewhat to bring it closer to everyday English spelling and the pronunciation of Arabic words.

2. The two main sects of the Muslim religion are Sunni Islam and Shii^c^a Islam. Sunni Islam is the majority sect in most of the Arab world. The name comes from Ahl as Sunna, or the community that follows the customs and words of the Prophet.

Shii^c^a Islam originated in a political conflict over who should succeed as khaliifa (caliph), or leader of the Muslim community, after the death of ^c^Ali, the fourth caliph and the Prophet's cousin and son-in-law. The Sunnites won, "establishing" the Sunni Umayyad dynasty in Damascus.

Shii^c^a Islam eventually developed theological as well as political differences from Sunni orthodoxy, and itself split into many sects. Shii^c^a Islam is the dominant religion of Iran, but in the Arab world it survives primarily in relatively isolated enclaves, such as Mount Lebanon and the shores of the Persian Gulf.

In Qarya the people recognized the two sects but said that there were few differences except that the Shii^c^a emphasized ^c^Ali more than they did. Shii^c^a visitors were welcome and treated as honored guests in the village (Gibb 1962: 120–21; Gibb and Kramers 1961: 30ff.; Hitti 1949: 75–77).

3. Lebanon has a national system of civil, criminal, and appeals courts, with codes based on European models. In addition, each religious community has legal jurisdiction over the domestic affairs of its members—marriage, divorce, and inheritance. There is thus a system of Muslim religious courts to deal with these matters within the Muslim community.

In the early 1960s, there were violent disputes over grazing rights in the mountain area northeast of Qarya. Since then the area has been under the equivalent of martial law. In cases involving violence, threat of violence, smuggling, possession of weapons, or disruption of the general peace and tranquility, the military police or the Maktab at Thaani, the internal security police—a branch of the army, intervene. In these situations the case is taken to the military court in Tripoli for resolution.

4. *Mukhtaar* is the Arabic word for village chief or mayor of a village. The word is from the Arabic root *ky-y-r* and the basic verb is *khaara*, "he chose" or "he presented." The Turkish word *muhtar*, used by Starr in this volume, is probably a derivative from the Arabic, as there has been much interchange between the two languages (see Wehr 1961: 266–67).

5. In a more restricted sample including only cases which occurred while I was in the village, and excluding memory cases, fragmentary cases with incomplete data, unfinished cases unless the ultimate procedure was clear, altercations without a third-party remedy agent and without more than incidental neighborhood interest, and cases directly involving my wife or myself, forty out of forty-six, or 87 percent, were settled within the village.

6. Out of my total of 108 cases, the most frequent principal subject matters in dispute were: rights in land, other than land ownership (eighteen); marriage disputes, concerning the proper conduct of a marriage (fifteen); honor and pride, primarily among young men of the upper social class (fifteen); marital disputes between husband and wife (twelve); and village politics and factionalism (eight). It should be noted that several "causes of action" or subject matters are often involved in the same dispute.

7. I have used the terms "plaintiff" and "defendant" in quotes, even though they are technical legal terms, because they are commonly understood in everyday English. I used them in the sense of the "person aggrieved" and the "person against whom one has a grievance." Alternative terms, specifically "complainant" and "respondent," also have technical legal meanings, primarily in the fields of equity and appellate law (Black 1951).

SIX

A GOOD NAME IS WORTH MORE THAN MONEY: STRATEGIES OF COURT USE IN URBAN GHANA

Michael J. Lowy

LITIGANTS in the town of Koforidua, Ghana, confront a wide range of agencies in the management of their disputes. Most ethnographic descriptions of law in villages throughout the world have accounted for preferred patterns of use of remedy agents by referring primarily to the social structural relationships between the parties. Preoccupation with this factor has obscured the facts that (1) a single agency is often used to accomplish diverse ends, and (2) the patterns of remedy agent use have ideological as well as strictly utilitarian import. I will explain the significance of these observations by describing how the court of lowest jurisdiction is used in a West African town.[1]

An analysis of seventy-four extended cases drawn from a total sample of 326 court cases shows a stronger association between the goal of a plaintiff and the way in which the court was used, than between the social relationships of the parties and the way in which the court was used. This finding may be generalizable to dispute settlement in other urban communities. The fact that these two aspects of a case are analytically separable means that strangers may be motivated to dispute out of the desire for economic gain or prestige, or out of a concern for the general welfare of the community. Likewise, litigants involved in ongoing social relationships exhibit the same range of goals in the use of the available remedy agents in their community. These possibilities have theoretical and applied import. Courts, as we now know them, may not have developed and flourished as a direct response to greater litigation between strangers over economic interest in the urban marketplace. Rather, they may have provided urbanites with an efficient forum for achieving prestige and status and a vehicle for formulating and disseminating ideas of correct behavior. Once the ideological basis for the use of remedy agents is understood, arguments against providing innovative dispute settlement agencies in some urban communities as well as arguments for eliminating those that do exist in some others, can be resisted, for they invariably rest upon social structural arguments.[2]

THE URBAN SETTING

The first settlers in Koforidua, fifty-three miles north of Accra, were refugees from a civil war between Juaben and Kumasi, two towns of the Ashanti confederacy, in 1874. From a population of 1,406 in 1901, Koforidua had grown to a city with a population of 40,000 crowded into one square mile by 1968. Koforidua, also known as New Juaben, is the fifth largest town in Ghana and a major center of transportation, administration, commerce, and cocoa marketing.[3]

Since the rapid population increase between 1921 and 1931, due in part to the completion of the railroad and motor roads, the town's population growth has slowed considerably.

The 1911 demographic imbalance of males over females (fifty-three males to every forty-seven females), usually associated with rapidly growing urban populations, has been reversed. In 1968 the ratio was forty-eight males to every fifty-two females. Men are now more likely than women to leave for the attractions of wage labor and "night life" of the two largest cities in Ghana: Accra and Kumasi. In addition, swollen-shoot disease has decreased the yield of cocoa grown in this part of Ghana, and thus has discouraged the usual influx of male migrant farm laborers into the area. While these factors have tended to reduce the number of adult men in the population, the growth of commerce and administration has attracted women. Young women are sent to Koforidua from neighboring villages to work as housegirls and assist older women in trade, often in exchange for the opportunity to attend school.

In 1968, over 40 percent of the population were born outside Koforidua. Fifty-seven ethnic groups were reported in a census that I conducted with student help that year. The results of this census are presented in Lowy (1971). Ashanti represented one-third of the total, and other Akan groups (mainly Twi-speaking peoples of southern Ghana) made up almost another third. The proportion of immigrants in the population has been declining since the 1930s as other regions of Ghana became more economically attractive and immigrants' children added to the nonmigrant population. Generally, there are more immigrants from nearby areas than from distant ones. However, Nigerians, Togolese, and Dahomeans account for about 8 percent of the migrant population.

Immigrants hope to accumulate enough money to be able to retire to their hometowns. Members of the same ethnic groups cluster together in the compounds (four-sided dwellings with a large open space in the middle) and neighborhoods of Koforidua. The Juaben Ashanti as "owners" of the town have the support of their families, elders, and leaders (chiefs) during times of stress and joy. The other ethnic groups form associations, which vary in organizational complexity. Generally the farther away from their homes, and the lower their position in the socioeconomic hierarchy, the more complex and important the ethnic association is in the affairs of its members.[4] Members of almost all ethnic groups claim that their headmen aid them in finding accommodations and jobs. Their help is sought during illness, at the time of death, and in the settlement of disputes. Many of these functions are also performed by friendly and burial associations, church groups, cotenants, and friends outside formal groups.

The economy of Koforidua is characterized by a high degree of job specialization. Less than 1 percent of the adult population considers itself unemployed. Complaints are frequently heard from the growing number of middle and secondary "school leavers," who long to secure high-paying, prestigious jobs. Their complaints are against underemployment. Farming and other forms of physical labor do not appeal to these aspiring civil servants and professionals.

Men and women have had different economic opportunities to exploit. Since 1911, the proportion of female farmers has dropped from 81 to 7 percent of the total female labor force, while the number of females engaged in trading has increased from 9 to 73 percent. For males in the labor force, the proportion of farmers has decreased from 13 to 5 percent; traders from 26 to 13 percent; and craftsmen from 37 to 33 percent. Civil servants or clerks have increased from 8 to 14 percent, and businessmen have increased from 3 to 10 percent. Although commerce, education, and wage employment are more important than subsistence farming to the economy of the town, about 5 percent of the total labor force farm in addition to their main occupations.

Since half the population is sixteen years old or younger, it is not surprising that more than half the population has attended or presently attends school. Between 1911 and 1948, despite the influx of illiterate immigrants, the proportion of those able to read and write English remained relatively constant, at about 15 percent of the total. Based upon the level of schooling attained, and bearing in mind that English is the language of instruction from the start, I estimate that 25 percent of the population in 1968 could read and write English. Although Koforiduans recognize that advanced education tends to raise income, it is difficult for most families to support an individual above middle school, or past the mid-teens. Only 8 percent of the population who have attended school have reached the secondary level, and less than 1 percent have attended the university.

In 1911 only 9 percent of the population of the administrative district encompassing Koforidua considered themselves Christian. At present, 54 percent of the townspeople state they are members of an "established" Christian church, and a further 11 percent belong to the growing number of churches that incorporate Christian and traditional West African religious beliefs. Although participation in "purely" traditional religious observances may be decreasing, membership in a nontraditional religious organization does not necessarily imply commitment to European Christian ideals. For example, membership in a nontraditional religious group has a limited impact upon the form of marriage contracted. Ninety percent of the marriages are contracted with reference to traditional norms, 3 percent take place in Christian churches, and 5 percent under the provisions of Islam. There is great variation within the category of customary marriage, and the number of couples who complete the ideal requirements is probably decreasing, and yet those who base their family relations upon nontraditional models are the exceptions.

The town's political system is a complex of institutions and agents representing diverse interests and sources of power. Although stripped of their ability to pass ordinances, collect taxes and rents, and authoritatively settle most criminal and civil cases, the Ashanti paramount chief (*omanhene*) and the traditional political office holders[5] have managed to retain considerable political power. Their informal control derives as much from their wealth as it does from their unquestioned responsibility for legitimating the position of head of family (*abusia panyin*) and acting as the forum of first instance for complaints against the family heads. For most Ghanaians, access to wealth and other sources of mobility are controlled by the head of the family, and the courts continue to support the right of the family heads to allocate the family's resources. Thus the traditional Juaben political hierarchy remains a potent force in contemporary society. However, much of the day-to-day administration of the town, including the maintenance of roads, markets, and public services, is in the hands of a municipal council.

During the period of my fieldwork (January 1968 to June 1969) the council's membership included individuals who had distinguished themselves in public life and had been appointed by the ruling N.L.C. (National Liberation Council).[6] This administrative body collected municipal taxes and rents from market stalls. The district and regional administrative authorities formed a hierarchy concerned with problems of general health, education, and social welfare, including the maintenance of the government hospital, sanitary inspection, agricultural problems, transportation, and public registration of land, births, and deaths.

Extensive communication networks exist among these various political functionaries despite their varied bases for authority. Juaben Koforiduans can approach their municipal, regional, or district administrators either directly or with the assistance of a member of their traditional political hierarchy. Non-Juaben ethnics can also apply directly to "government" administrators, or they can approach Juaben traditional authorities with the assistance of their own ethnic, or hometown, headman. The role of the ethnic headman in Koforidua, a creation of immigrants' needs and an inheritance of British colonial policy, has persisted partly as a result of continued immigration and the continued political influence of Juaben Ashanti traditional authorities.

Despite housing shortages and the creation of new social strata based upon an expanding wage economy, most people in Koforidua continue to define social relations in a kinship idiom. Individuals occupying positions of authority (such as landlords, teachers, employers, senior colleagues, religious leaders, and political incumbents) are treated deferentially and receive loyalty and respect in proportion to the extent to which they provide solicitous care for their "juniors."[7] Coincident with their right to expect loyalty and service, the seniors are under an obligation to help manage conflicts involving the juniors. The dispersal of the extended family has not diminished the importance of life crises as the time when the family expresses its continued corporate nature. For example, funerals are occasions for dispersed family members to recognize both the end of an individual's life and the perpetuation of the family. Continuity is assured by the distribution of the deceased's property and the selection of his "successor."

The birth and naming of children and the deliberations concerning marriage provide other occasions for reinforcing and negotiating the values of the extended family. Despite the urban conditions in Koforidua the essentially corporate character of the family has been maintained. Where family members are not available to fill the roles because of the process of urbanization and wage employment, nonkin substitutes enter junior-senior relationships based on the values of kinship.

SYSTEMS OF CONFLICT MANAGEMENT

Koforiduans use two different Twi words to describe contentious behavior: *entokwa* (an argument) and *asem* (a case). The most distinctive feature of an argument is that it proceeds by direct confrontation, or what we have called *conflict*. A case, on the other hand, is what we have labeled a *dispute;* it involves a third party in its management. This distinction is sometimes blurred. A dispute in which a third party is called upon to intercede on one's behalf to beg the pardon of the offended person is usually referred to as a mere entokwa. The omission of begging forgiveness is often sufficient justification for the transformation of an argument of this type into an asem. The focus of my research, as well as this paper, is on dispute.

Four categories of remedy agents are used in the management of disputes: the court, quasi-judicial agencies, private hearings at home, and the supernatural. With respect to the first of these categories, I will focus on the Magistrates' Court Grade II, one of the four government courts in Koforidua. The meaning that Koforiduan litigants impute to the actual or threatened resort to this lowest jurisdictional court can only be understood by describing it in comparison with available alternative institutions. Our understanding will to a large extent rest upon a consideration of the morality of litigation.

In addition to the courts, there are several legislatively constituted government agencies that are charged with the disposition of certain types of cases. Later in this article, I shall describe one of these quasi-judicial agencies, the reconciliation committee of the Department of Social Welfare and Community Development, and the ways in which it deals with conflict cases. "Home" dispute management implies that it takes place in the compound (*fie*, "house") or other private place. The Twi word for this type of hearing is *afiesem* (house case). Supernatural agencies that act as third parties in the management of cases include shrines, churches, and specialists in the manipulation of supernatural power.

The description of each remedy agent which follows includes the agent's source of power and jurisdiction, its accessibility, the likelihood of public exposure in its use, its economic and psychological cost to the users, and its effectiveness. The description of the physical setting of each agency has been published elsewhere (Lowy 1974) and is therefore brief.

MAGISTRATES' COURT GRADE II

The Koforidua magisterial district (1960 population 54,000) as well as the law administered in it are established by statute. The grade II court, the court of lowest jurisdictional level, is empowered to hear cases involving contract, tort, or the ownership, possession, or occupation of land where the amount of the claim does not exceed $360.[8] It also has jurisdiction over civil matters between landlord and tenant, as well as over family law matters such as divorce and succession to property under customary law. During the one-month sample period 61 percent of the cases were civil and 39 percent were criminal. Most of the civil claims during my period of observation were for amounts below $50. During the twenty-one months preceding my observation, almost 96 percent of the civil cases were for debts. The next largest single category was defamation, followed by land and other family matters. In addition, the grade II court can entertain any criminal case punishable by a fine not exceeding $240 or one year's imprisonment. During the year of 1968, its criminal caseload was divided almost equally between theft and assault cases.

The court has been at its present location since about 1950. It is well known and accessible to the general public. Its central location and open-walled construction allow an average of seventy-five to 100 spectators, including workers, market women, and children, to enjoy the daily procession of cases. Participants' remarks are held up to public scrutiny and frequently elicit laughter and murmurs of approval or disagreement. The issues and participants become the topic of gossip throughout the town.

Court personnel are on duty from 8:00 a.m. to 5:00 p.m., Monday through Friday, and they hear cases from 9:30 a.m. to 3:00 p.m. An individual can initiate a civil case through the court registrar by paying a fee based upon the amount of the claim and the number and location of witnesses. About a third of the plaintiffs employ a letter writer[9] to prepare the statement of claim, which must be in English, the official language of Ghana. Another third of the plaintiffs prepare their statements themselves, and about a third enlist the aid of a lawyer or a member of the court staff. The prehearing costs to a plaintiff using the court for a civil case include court fees and the cost of hiring specialists. About two-thirds of the plaintiffs are required to pay less than three dollars. The remaining third spend between three and ten dollars. Generally, costs range from one dollar (for an individual who prepares his own claim for an amount of less than ten dollars) to seventy dollars (for someone who hires a lawyer to act as a representative in a claim for more than $100).[10] Total costs given to the plaintiff computed after the end of the case in court averaged $10.66 (excluding the high and low amounts). During the period of my fieldwork a daily average wage for an unskilled worker was approximately seventy cents.

Criminal cases are instituted through the police. Although there are over 100 police officers stationed in Koforidua, most criminal complaints arise from the presentation of a complaint by an aggrieved party at the central police station. Both parties frequently arrive armed with charges and countercharges. Statements are made to a police officer, and an investigation, which includes the search for missing parties and witnesses, begins. Sixty-four percent of the complaints made to the central police station during 1968 were later heard by a magistrate. Although there is no direct cost to the complainant in reporting a case, a maximum fine of fifty dollars may be imposed if he makes a frivolous or vexatious complaint. The greatest cost to the parties is the time required by the police to take statements, locate witnesses, and determine whether or not to proceed with an investigation. Normally drunks and alleged thieves are immediately detained by the police. Drunks are brought to court soon after achieving sobriety, while alleged thieves remain in custody. Those charged with assault and less serious offenses are bailed.

The staff of the court exhibit social characteristics that distinguish them from their clients. They are usually younger, better educated, and more socially mobile than the parties to disputes. Their ethnic heterogeneity, their unfamiliarity with several of the languages commonly used in the area, and their formal dress and manners clearly set them apart and result in a psychological cost to litigants which is both difficult to measure and impossible to ignore. The differences between lawyers, prosecutors, and magistrate on the one hand, and the litigants on the other are even more striking. The swift airing of cases (average time: twelve minutes),[11] the magistrate's overt concern with efficiency, the court restrictions limiting discussion to legally relevant issues, the deference demanded by court personnel, the intimidating arrangement of courtroom space, and the written records kept on the proceedings all combine to create confusion and to exact additional psychological costs from the users of this agency. The following exchange between the magistrate and a defendant accused of insulting his neighbor is an extreme example of the result of some of these factors:

Magistrate: Then why do you plead guilty?
Defendant: I am liable because I did not insult him.
Magistrate: I don't understand.
Defendant: If I had abused him, I would go and beg him.
Magistrate: Then why do you plead liable?
Defendant: Because I am before the court, I plead liable.
Magistrate: Then you are liable!
Defendant: I say so because I have to give the court respect.

My attempt to assess the effectiveness of Koforidua's dispute management agencies begins with the recognition that the user's goal is most important. Furthermore, I understand that evaluations of this kind are limited by the time perspective adopted by the analyst. Because I began systematic observation of court cases only five months before my departure from the field situation, I have confined myself to short-term posthearing results (between one and four months). Plaintiffs using the grade II magistrates' court were quite emphatic about their goals: (1) to maximize their monetary payoff, or (2) to elicit an apology from the defendant or an amicable settlement of the situation outside the court. Given these divergent aims, I thought it wise to inquire whether and to what extent the parties complied with the decision rendered by the magistrate; whether either party was dissatisfied enough with the conclusion of the hearing to institute a similar complaint in another forum; and whether the litigants were willing or reluctant to publicly greet each other after the hearing.

The last indicator needs further explanation. In Koforidua, as I suspect in most Ghanaian towns, greeting behavior is elaborate and stylized. The initiator and the proper form of a conversational opening are highly correlated with the sex, age, and social relationship of the pair. There are rare contexts (such as during the performance of toilet functions) in which greetings are inappropriate. However, the failure or the reported unwillingness of an individual to greet another is indicative of severely strained social relations. Therefore, an inquiry into potential greeting behavior provides a shorthand method of judging the short-term impact of the court hearing on social relationships.

In all civil cases, appeal from a decision is possible to the high court.[12] In addition, all questions of law are reserved for the opinion of the high court. The fee for filing a motion for leave to appeal costs one dollar, and an additional one dollar if granted. As a practical matter, plaintiffs rarely appeal a civil case, and defendants do not wish to incur further debts through court costs. Out of 198 civil cases heard during a month-long sample period, an appeal was taken in only one case.

Appeal from a conviction in a criminal case is free, and can be made to a circuit court on a question of fact or a question of mixed law and fact. The motion can be entertained only if the fine, costs, or compensation is not less than ten dollars; if the accused has been ordered to do or not do a specific act; or if the appellant has been sentenced to imprisonment. An appeal cannot be made if the accused was convicted on his own plea of guilty.

Slightly less than half the 128 criminal cases heard during the sample period involved a plea of guilty by the accused. As a practical matter those who do not plead guilty rarely appeal an adverse decision. During the sample month, not one appeal was made. Although an appeal to an upper-level court is rare, the use of another agency for appeal is more frequent. I could not obtain statistics on appeals to other agencies or on compliance and continued social relationships for the total sample of 326 cases I heard. Instead I chose to use an extended case approach to investigate these questions in seventy-four cases (forty-six civil cases and twenty-eight criminal cases). Almost 9 percent of these civil cases, and 14 percent of these criminal cases were later heard by another remedy agent *after* an initial court hearing. Three months after the initial hearing, only 21 percent of the civil defendants had paid all their debts or had otherwise complied with the court's order. And only 17 percent of the civil plaintiffs were willing to greet the other party afterwards.

By contrast, the defendants in criminal cases, almost always paid compensation for loss or injury, undoubtedly to avoid incarceration. Afterwards, 29 percent of plaintiffs in criminal cases were willing to greet the other party.

Short-term posthearing "effectiveness" is a complex social-psychological phenomenon. Decisions of the court are infrequently followed completely in civil cases, and almost invariably followed in criminal cases. Appeals to other agencies are not common, but are much more frequent than resort to a higher judicial level. Finally, we must conclude that the establishment or continuation of social relationships is not a frequent consequence of hearings in this forum.

THE RECONCILIATION COMMITTEE, A QUASI-JUDICIAL AGENCY

One governmental agency that is an alternative to the courts is the reconciliation committee (of the Department of Social Welfare and Community Development), which was established in 1965 to hear cases ". . . where a father neglects to provide reasonable maintenance for his infant child or when a man alleged to be the father denies that he is the father of the child." In such cases "the mother of the child may apply to . . . persuade the father to make reasonable provision for the maintenance of the child . . ." (Maintenance of Children Act 1965). By statute the father's provision is not to exceed ten dollars per month. An order for maintenance may continue until a child reaches the age of seventeen, and may be extended until the child is twenty-one if he is continuing a course of study.

During the committee's first two full years of operation (1966–1967), 112 complaints were made to it by Koforidua residents. Complete information was available on seventy-eight of these cases. Seventy-four percent of these were complaints of nonmaintenance; 9 percent were brought by men seeking custody of their children, 8 percent by women seeking to have a man declared the father of a child or to provide their child with a name. An additional 9 percent of the cases involved such issues as debts between spouses, petitions for divorce, and failure to marry.

Complaints are generally received directly by the officials at the welfare department, though they may also be filed by letter or may be referred to the office by the regional minister. Still others are reported to welfare officers when they visit towns and villages in the district. There is no filing fee, and funds are provided to pay the transportation of any witnesses called.

About three-quarters of the complaints reach the hearing stage. After receiving a complaint, the officer is charge of the case invites the respondent to a hearing. If he refuses, an explanatory letter may be sent to his employer.

If a respondent still fails to attend, the officer cannot force the complainant to take the matter to court. He is permitted, however, to help the complainant prepare a court summons, and may act as a witness in such a court action.

Members of the reconciliation committee are chosen by the chief welfare officer from among prominent men and women in town, and they serve at his pleasure without pay. Three civil service officers, two men and one woman, handle maintenance cases. Their social characteristics are very similar to the members of the court staff. The prominent citizens are older, wealthier, less well educated, and less likely to leave Koforidua than are the civil servants, who are subject to transfer to other parts of the country.

Hearings of the reconciliation committee are held on Fridays beginning at 10:00 a.m. Although the officer in charge sets an informal limit of eight cases per day, no more than four per day were heard during my period of observation. Complaints here are more completely aired than during a court hearing (average time: fifty minutes). Spatial arrangements are less intimidating, and traditional signs of respect for authority in manners and dress are generally absent. The litigants usually wear their working clothes.

The hearing room is situated at the offices of the Department of Social Welfare and Community Development, away from the commercial heart of the town. Although a veranda runs around the front and back of the building and there are two open windows, the record storage room where hearings are conducted is relatively private. However, parties in cases not yet called and those waiting to file complaints can hear the proceedings through the back window.

The plaintiff and defendant are seated close to each other and to the board members. The welfare officer, who takes notes at the proceedings, sits behind the parties and is not visible to them. Hearings are usually conducted in Twi, and none of the participants is placed under oath. Questioning proceeds in a quiet and unhurried manner. A decision is achieved by the committee's trying to help the parties reach a consensus. The welfare of the child is continually stressed by the board members. Custody and maintenance issues are almost always decided in a pragmatic manner: preference is given to the parent who has the immediate or long-term resources to provide the child with the best diet, medical care, education, and life opportunity. The values supporting these goals are made quite explicit during the proceedings. For example, a young mother was advised to forgo a maintenance allowance and send her children to live with her ex-husband in a large town rather than let them remain with her mother in a small village. A female committee member said to her, "An old lady like this—you want [her] to train your children nowadays? . . . Only yesterday I saw a child having convulsions here in Koforidua. What could you do if this happened in a village?"

After the hearing is completed, the written decision is sent to the district welfare officer for confirmation. The confirmed maintenance order is then sent in writing to the two parties. The parent who is ordered to pay the maintenance allowance is told to do so directly to the welfare department for at least the first six months after the hearing.

At the conclusion of the hearings I witnessed, the parties seemed relaxed and in good spirits. Since I did not conduct intensive interviews of the litigants, my assessment of the effectiveness of the agency is limited to the frequency of compliance with the committee's orders, and the number of appeals to other agencies which followed from the decision.

Information was available about compliance with the committee decision in seventy-two cases. Over a six-month period of institutional follow-up, full compliance was reported in about 20 percent of the cases. Partial compliance (where some of the money was paid) was reported in an additional 28 percent of the cases. Fifty-two percent of those so ordered did not comply with the decision of the Committee. However, about 13 percent of these individuals took custody of the children rather than paying the amount of maintenance agreed upon.

Only thirty-two of the 112 complaints received by the committee contained information about posthearing appeal. Of these five (15 percent) were heard at the grade II magistrates' court; about the same number were heard again by the reconciliation committee or by afiesem, an informal hearing in a private home. Four other cases were scheduled to be heard by another agency, but the litigants did not appear. The remainder of these cases were not appealed.

AFIESEM (HOUSEHOLD CASES)

The jurisdiction of afiesem is not regulated by statute. However, this method of settlement is legislatively recognized as a legitimate alternative in all civil suits and in nonfelonious criminal cases. Once the defendant has submitted to a decision by sitting through a case and de facto assenting to the agreement, the latter can be enforced in court. In such instances those who were present and received a portion of the hearing fee are morally obliged to testify to the conclusions in court.

The issues in household cases are usually family matters: inheritance, divorce, land boundaries, compound maintenance, assault, and insult. The landlords in 58 percent of the 178 compounds I surveyed said they settled disputes between their tenants. Of the 43 cases reportedly settled by afiesem in the year previous to my fieldwork, almost 35 percent were marriage and family matters, 32 percent involved compound maintenance, 23 percent were assault and insult, and 10 percent were miscellaneous.

Cases involving marital disputes and insulting behavior are also heard by headmen of tribal and hometown unions as well as by church elders. Similarly, heads of corporations, voluntary associations, and government agencies may also serve in a dispute-resolving capacity regarding their personnel.

Afiesem are heard at a home, in a private compound. Cases which have substantially the same procedure and are variously known as "arbitration" or "reconciliation" are conducted in private offices and houses. All contain the basic elements of privacy and lack of explicit coercion. Of nine cases I observed at four different subchiefs' compounds, the average attendance was fifteen. Besides witnesses, supporters, and the litigants themselves, most afiesem have a president, his spokesman, and a panel of counselors.

In Twi, the person who schedules an afiesem, invites the accused to attend, and acts as the primary mediator during the course of a hearing, is referred to as *odiasem* (literally, the person who eats the case). In English the person is invariably known as the president. The *okyeame* (literally, "the linguist"), or spokesman, adds dignity to the assembly, helps maintain decorum, and is frequently a skilled inquisitor; he shares several of the attributes of the *okyamehene*, or talking chief, one of the most important members of an Ashanti ruler's court. The members of the panel are variously called *beguafo* (helpers) or *panyinfo* (elders). They offer advice to the litigants as well as help the mediator formulate a consensus that will effectively cope with the matters in conflict. Their knowledge of accepted practice as well as of Ashanti proverbs is especially useful to help cajole a disgruntled party into verbalizing his agreement to a proposed solution.

Although afiesem are frequently ad hoc groups, there are also regularly held afiesem in which the panel members tend to remain constant. Afiesem personnel are older than the litigants and are usually considered elderly (above fifty). The social characteristics (such as residence and education) of the disputants closely approximate those of the personnel of the afiesem. It is not unusual for one or both of the litigants to be a relative of a panel member.

The usual time for a hearing is around either 6:00 a.m. or 7:00 p.m., after the morning or evening bath. Saturdays are good days to settle cases, since many people neither work nor attend church then. A hearing is usually scheduled as soon after the alleged offense as witnesses can be assembled.

In the complaint procedure the aggrieved party or a representative reports his case to the president directly or through the spokesman. After paying a "complaint" or "messenger" fee, the party waits to be informed of the response of the other person and the date and time of the hearing. The fees paid are nonrefundable, even if the person called does not attend the hearing. Refusal to attend is an insult to the president, who may urge the plaintiff to take the case to court, where the president himself may act as a witness. Complaint fees begin at forty cents and vary with the prominence of the president. Members of ethnic associations, church groups, and corporations who hold afiesem do not receive complaint fees. However, gifts of eggs, vegetables, or drinks are made to the president for calling someone to answer a charge. A person rarely completely ignores such a call. If he does not ultimately intend to attend the hearing, he will send messengers with excuses for not attending.

At an afiesem the use of space is not intimidating. The two parties sit with their supporters and are encompassed by a circle of participants when speaking. Traditional gestures of respect and everyday clothes are conspicuous.

The procedures followed at hearings vary with the individual who is called upon to act as president. Notes are generally not taken. Parties and panel members speak in the language in which they are most comfortable or in the language that they share with the other participants. Witnesses are generally asked to leave the hearing and are called to tell what they know only after the party who has called them to witness has testified. All the participants are present at the general period of discussion which follows the cross-questioning of parties and witnesses. The participants are usually quite enthusiastic, and often attempt to shout each other down. The president and other panel members, through skillful questioning of the parties and their witnesses, are usually able to steer the discussion onto issues on which there is a good chance for finding agreement between the litigants. Then the relative faults of the parties are announced, and a tentative solution is offered by the president. If his solution is accepted, the case may take no more than forty minutes. However, his initial proposals are usually rejected, and counter-suggestions by the parties are offered. Besides the immediate implementation of monetary settlements, one or both parties are required to provide some token symbolizing the conclusion: money, matches, or a quantity of an alcoholic beverage which is then divided among the assembly.

At the conclusion of the meeting, the plaintiff and defendant are advised not to continue their quarrel or to boast of their winning the case. Proverbs and past personal experiences are frequently cited in support of these proscriptions. Often both are asked to swear an oath that they no longer have a case and to shake hands.

The time spent on an afiesem allows more complete airing of grievances than do court or reconciliation committee hearings. Two hours was the average time of the fifteen cases I witnessed. Adjournments without decision are rare; the issue is called to be settled that day. If a land case requires the panel members to visit a disputed boundary or property, the case may be settled at the property the same day or at a meeting held soon afterwards.

Afiesem seem effective, as awards, damages, and fees are generally paid immediately. For a large sample of cases I could not determine the frequency of appeals to other remedy agents, either before or after a decision was announced. However, of the seventy-four court cases I selected for intensive interviewing, 24 percent had previously been heard by another agency, most of them afiesem. Twelve percent of the complaints made at the welfare department had also previously been heard at afiesem.

SUPERNATURAL AGENCIES

The practice of using the supernatural in the management of disputes came under legislative attack in the early days of British colonial administration. The operation of shrines and other agencies for detection of wrongdoers or for supernatural attack was outlawed; their operators could be held liable for defamation of the character of individuals who were named as offenders. However, this entire class of operations was left out of the 1960 criminal code. Supernatural agencies have continued to be used, among other things, to determine who within a group of suspects is the thief, witch, or sorcerer who is creating problems for the complainant.

There are three supernatural agencies which are frequently employed in Koforidua. The most readily used sorcerers are Muslim holy men called mallams. They frequently live in the *zongo*, a neighborhood that is predominantly occupied by Muslim immigrants and their descendents. Their homes serve as their workshops.

Informants said mallams receive ten or twenty cents for a first consultation fee. Some receive as much as eight dollars to make a rival sick. However, seventy cents to two dollars is probably closer to the normal amount for such services. Some mallams require advance payment, but others ask for payment only after results are achieved. These remedy agents are most often called upon to produce charms, which are frequently passages from the Koran written on paper. Mallams are also supposed to be able to detect the guilty party from among a group of suspects. One practitioner explained his method as follows:

> Two young boys strip off their shirts and face one another. Two slender sticks are balanced between their breasts. Then the suspect comes to the boys with a single stick broom and places it between the sticks; the boys constrict the sticks around the broom, and, if the suspect cannot lift the broom from between the sticks, then he is guilty. While the broom is between the sticks, the mallam recites from the Koran.

Another popular form of thief detection available to Koforidua residents is a specialty associated with the Ewe ethnic group called *aka*. One current practitioner and another eyewitness described a case brought to him for resolution about eight years before.

A tenant in a house noticed that some of his property had been stolen and suspected a cotenant. The sorcerer was called to the compound.

He assembled the materials for making *aka*—a pan, red palm oil, and some secret implements. He (the *akaman*) made the fire and put the pan on it, and it boiled. He said some magical words, then he called the inmates of the house. They put their hands in the boiling oil one by one, and did not get burned. The fourth person who tried, the fire rose up and burned him (because he was guilty).

Ghanaian shrines derive their power from a diverse group of spiritual entities. Some of these gods are local spirits inhabiting unusual geological formations; others are more personal in nature. The number of shrines is always in a state of flux, since their powers and therefore their clientele are subject to rapid change. The proper ritual manipulations necessary to activate or utilize the god's power are closely guarded secrets that are usually inherited and may be sold to others. For example, one relatively wealthy informant was plagued by an undiagnosed ailment. He returned to his hometown in order to consult the keeper of a local shrine. The ailment disappeared after treatment, and the man was able to buy from the priest the knowledge of how to manipulate the power of the god. He began to operate a "branch" of this shrine in Koforidua. This new priest described the manner in which thieves are caught by his god: "The people come [here]. We pour libations. After [that], if one of the parties is indeed guilty, he begins to shake and tremble as the spirit enters him. The individual readily admits guilt."

Major shrines are easily identifiable on the periphery of town; minor ones, such as the one described above, are inconspicuously housed in private compounds. People consult them at any convenient time during the day. Employing a sorcerer or the priest of a new shrine to detect a thief may cost between $1.30 and four dollars.

If a mallam, shrine, or other agency fails to "catch" the thief, then the sorcerer may utter a curse, asking the god to seek out and kill or harm the thief, along with anyone else who may have benefited from the money or the object that was stolen. The curse may be invoked even if no specific person is suspected. Such a curse is a serious matter; the thief must return the goods in order to have the curse removed.

In addition to sorcerers and shrines, spiritualist churches offer parishioners supernatural aid in managing their conflicts. Members of these churches pay dues of ten to twenty cents per month. If a congregant wants supernatural aid against an enemy or help in winning a court case, he reports the matter to the priest. If the priest thinks the cause is just, he will ask the entire congregation to pray for the supplicant on "watchnight." Although this service is free, supplicants often give additional contributions for such help. And if a case is won in court, a part of the award may be given to the church.

The personnel of supernatural remedy agencies are invariably older than most of their clients, since acquisition of the requisite knowledge comes only after many years of study. Furthermore, younger people are not likely to have accumulated enough wealth to buy the knowledge of others. The psychological cost to the person who seeks to invoke a supernatural remedy agent is difficult to estimate. Although traditional signs of respect and formal attire are uncommon, the proximity to sources of supernatural power, as well as the esoteric ritual employed, undoubtedly cause fear in the client.

The effectiveness of supernatural agencies is high among those who have a strong belief in their efficacy. In fact, during my month-long sample period, several court cases were instituted in order to have curses removed. Much to the plaintiffs' discomfiture, the court considered itself impotent to manage such disputes, since legislative control of the use of supernatural agencies and their operators had been removed. I have argued elsewhere that this gap may contribute to the continued use of charms and countercurses (Lowy 1975).

This descriptive review of some important conflict management agencies available to the Koforidua population forms the context in which the use of the grade II magistrates' court can be understood.

THE MEANING OF COURT USE

In this section I will be concerned with how Koforiduans *use* the magistrates' court, grade II. Koforiduans talk about initiating a court case in two ways: "Me ko court" (I will go to court) and "Me ko court straight" (I will go directly to court). The first statement implies that the court will be used *as only one step* in a broader strategy of dispute management. "Court straight" expresses the intention of using the court as *the first and only agency* for the management of the particular dispute.

The meaning Koforiduans attach to the strategies of court use is primarily derived from a consideration of morality. A common proverb asserts, "If you pursue [follow] your sweet case, you do wrong." Plaintiffs who are obviously correct in their claims are thought to act immorally if they attempt to use a "sweet case" unfairly against their adversary. Agencies of dispute management, all other things being equal, fall along a continuum from most moral to least moral as follows: afiesem, quasi-judicial agencies, grade II magistrates' court, and supernatural agents. The proverb implies that a plaintiff who invokes an agency with a low moral ranking before attempting to satisfy his claim through a higher-ranked agency has acted improperly. Disapproval of the immoral maximization of personal advantage in the use of remedy agents is reflected in many other areas of social life as well.[13]

Neither short-term economic cost nor short-term effectiveness provides a reliable guide to the comparative morality of remedy agent usage. For this we look to the source of the power utilized to confront the defendant (accused) and the degree of public scrutiny. Another proverb can help to explicate the morality of power: "A child is to [is able to] break a snail, not a tortoise." No matter how hard a child tries, he will not be able to break the shell of a tortoise because he lacks the strength. Similarly, in social relationships, there are natural limits to one's ability to force compliance with one's wishes. A child can break a snail shell because it is soft. In the moral pursuit of a conflict, one should avoid sources of power which go beyond the natural limits of force and are likely to produce resistance to one's claim (i.e., one should keep the shell soft). The public scrutiny of improper behavior is likely to produce a defensive shell which only unnatural force can break.

Remedy agencies that are publicly accessible and involve the greatest public scrutiny must rely on coercive power. They are among the less moral agencies, whereas the more moral agencies restrict widespread public attendance and announce outcomes based upon the agreement of the parties. The use of supernatural power is the least moral. It acts reflexively and secretly: defense against it is impossible or difficult, and thus it typifies the immoral maximization of personal advantage.

Given the immoral rating of the magistrates' court grade II, as against alternative agencies, we are in a better position to understand the differences between the two ways in which the court is used. First, let us examine these two patterns of court usage, the broad strategy versus the narrow strategy, from the perspective of social structure, which has been so useful in village studies. To what extent, if any, are major social structural variables, as expressed by the plaintiff or the relationship between the litigants, associated with the two patterns of court use? The answers are mainly negative.[14] I examined my seventy-four extended cases and found that the migrant status of the plaintiff, common ethnicity of the litigants, sociological age, participation in a wage-earning occupation, literacy, and formal education are not significantly associated with the two patterns of court use. There was a *slight* association between the sex of the plaintiff and the pattern of use; women plaintiffs are more likely than men to use the court "straight." This difference may reflect a bias against women who are in conflict with men in the afiesem, which is regarded as the most moral agency.

Most ethnographic studies of village law identify the social relationship between litigants as the most significant influence in differential remedy agent usage. In my ethnographic study of urban law, I found that this variable was also significantly associated with the differential use of a single agent. I sorted the cases according to my judgment on the following criteria: (1) the presence or absence of important social relationships between the litigants which were significant in the past and important to perpetuate; and (2) the presence or absence of social ties between the litigants which could facilitate the moral resolution of the issue in conflict. If both were present, I characterized the relationship as multiplex; if both were absent, I characterized it as simplex. I placed cotenants; lineal, collateral, and affinal kin; friends; customers of long standing and coemployees in the multiplex category (forty-one cases), and I placed first-time customers and strangers prior to the incident in the simplex category (thirty-three cases). I found that a larger number of litigants who were enmeshed in multiplex relationships used the broad strategy (the court in combination with more moral agencies) than did litigants who had only simplex relationships.

It is likely that this tendency reflects the litigants' intention to continue their social relationship and the existence of concerned intermediaries who could provide a moral agency to help settle the differences between them.

Therefore the social relationship between parties is significantly associated with the pattern of use of the grade II magistrates' court in Koforidua. However, I came to realize that the association I found between patterns of court use and the kinds of social relationships existing between the parties made sense because I had accepted the notion that courts are primarily used to achieve rational economic ends. My underlying assumption was based on an industrial-capitalistic ideology, rooted in an intellectual tradition stretching back to Max Weber.[15] However, this assumption significantly distorted my understanding of the ways in which Koforiduans use their court.

A very popular Ashanti proverb states that "a good name is worth more than money." In Koforidua a *clear* moral distinction exists between a person or a family's wealth and its prestige (reputation). It is certainly not true that the accumulation of wealth is considered unimportant, but in the abstract its accumulation is morally inferior to the protection or advancement of one's reputation for highly valued behavior.

Starting from this ideological perspective, I categorized the goals of the plaintiff in the seventy-four extended cases. In forty-six of these cases, when asked, the plaintiff explicitly and vehemently described his reason for using the court as a desire to maximize his monetary payoff. On the other hand, in twenty-eight cases, the same question elicited the plaintiff's explicit desire to "teach them [the defendants] sense" or to change the defendant's low esteem for the plaintiff. For these cases I categorized the goal as "prestige." Several plaintiffs replied that they were using the court so that the defendants would "know themselves." I believe my informants were expressing a social as well as a strictly individual concern that the defendants *learn* how they had acted improperly in order that they might improve their behavior in the future. All civil complaints made to the magistrates' court grade II, must specify a monetary claim. An examination of the claims made by plaintiffs whose goal was categorized as prestige frequently revealed a grossly exaggerated monetary claim. Invariably such claims contained specific reference to a desired change in the future behavior of the defendant.

If a plaintiff's goal is prestige, we would expect him to invoke more moral agencies either before or after the court hearing in order to encourage the defendant to render an apology or, at the very least, to have him recognize the correctness of the plaintiff's position. The achievement of such a goal would be inhibited by public scrutiny and the threat of government force, whereas the limited public accessibility and lack of coercion at more moral agencies is more likely to facilitate the vindication and social learning sought by the plaintiff. I found that plaintiffs whose goal is the maximization of their monetary payoff use the court "straight" much more often than do plaintiffs with a prestige goal. If maximization of money is of primary importance, the moral imperatives operating in a private agency are less likely to achieve that outcome than are the courts.[16] The threat of public recognition that one belongs to a family that can neither pay its debts nor meet its monetary obligations increases the likelihood of monetary payment at court. A defendant may be expected to refuse to appease the plaintiff over nonmonetary issues in a publicly coercive situation, but to pay his monetary commitment under similar conditions, because, in the abstract, the pursuit of wealth is morally inferior to the pursuit of good name.

It is important to note that an ideological variable was more strongly associated with the use of the magistrates' court than was the social structural variable, although both were found to be significantly associated with court use. The chi-square statistic of 20.8 means, we can say, that the probability of the distribution of cases in which the plaintiff's goal was by chance associated with court use under the conditions of this test is less than or equal to one in 1,000. The probability that the distribution of cases in which the relationship between the parties was by chance associated with court use would produce a chi-square value of 5.1 is less than or equal to twenty-five in 1,000. These statistics tell us that we can be very sure that the relationships are significant, we can then ask which association is stronger.[17] In Yule's Q statistic, zero represents complete independence between two nominally scaled variables, and 1.0 represents complete dependence. The Q values of the relationship between the parties is equal to .563, whereas the goal of the plaintiff is .843. Since the comparison between the two sets of associations is based on the same number of cases ($n = 74$), we can represent the strength of the two relationships by simply comparing the percentage differences between these two dichotomized, nominally scaled variables. Of those cases in which relationships between the parties were simplex, 78.7 percent used only the court, while of those in which multiplex relationships existed between the parties 53.6 percent used only the court, a difference of 25.1 percent. Of the plaintiffs with a prestige goal 32.1 percent used only the court, while of those with a monetary goal 84.2 percent used only the court, a difference of 52.1 percent. The greater the percentage differences, the stronger the association between the variables.

CONCLUSIONS

There is a saying in Koforidua: "If you pull the string too tight it will break." How far may one go in the legitimate pursuit of his interest before his action becomes reprehensible? In this paper I have explored the conditions under which "immoral" agencies of dispute management are used when more moral alternatives are available. First, I compared the sources of power, likelihood of public exposure, economic and psychological costs, and effectiveness of representatives in four major types of conflict management agencies. I then ranked these institutions from most moral to least moral, focusing upon the likelihood of coercion and public scrutiny in their use. Correlating nominally scaled strategies of court use with nominally scaled social structural categories, I concluded that the social relations between the litigants are significant in accounting for their choice of strategies. However, I was able to improve my understanding of the differential use of the comparatively immoral agency of the courts by focusing on the question of whether the goals of the plaintiffs were monetary or prestige-oriented.

I believe these conclusions have important implications for legal anthropology. Those who attempt cross-cultural studies of the use of remedy agents must be acutely sensitive to ideological bias as well as to the moral ratings that the litigants give to the available agents of conflict management. Perhaps our own limited legitimate institutions for third-party help and an ideology which leads us to justify the invocation of courts on the basis of economic maximization have kept us from seeing more clearly how and why other people pursue interpersonal disputes.

NOTES

1. The research upon which this work is based was supported by the National Institute of Mental Health grant number MH-11211.

2. See Danzig and Lowy (1975) and Felstiner (1974, 1975) for an elaboration of these issues in the United States. Smith (1972) discusses the issue in the African context.

3. The development of Koforidua is discussed in more detail in Lowy (1971) and McCall (1956, 1960, 1962). Ghana achieved independence from Britain in 1957.

4. This statement is compatible with Schildkrout's (1974) observation of the irrelevance of the headman among second-generation Mossi in the Kumasi *zongo*. Sanjek's (n.d.) lucid description of the pragmatic use of ethnic affiliation in Accra is applicable in Koforidua.

5. Detailed descriptions of the traditional offices have been written by Rattray (1929), Busia (1951), and Wilks (1967).

6. The government of Ghana was returned to civilian rule in 1969. Prime Minister K. A. Busia's government was ended by a coup in January 1972. Since that time the National Redemption Council, under the leadership of Col. I. K. Acheampong, has led the government.

7. See Tessler, O'Barr, and Spain (1973) for a clear description of a system of clientage among the Kanuri of Nigeria in the context of changing social conditions.

8. For the sake of convenience, I have converted Ghanaian currency values, which are reckoned in cedis and pesewas, into their approximate 1968 U.S. dollar and cents equivalents.

9. Letter writers are functionally equivalent to local notary publics in United States communities. Their numbers and influence in the process of conflict management appear to be on the wane, as a result of growing literacy and an increase in the availability of lawyers.

10. It is not common to hire a lawyer to pursue a civil complaint when the claim is under $100. I have discussed the strategic use of lawyers by litigants in Lowy (1973).

11. In contrast, Mileski (1971) has reported that 72 percent of cases handled by one local-level urban court in the United States were heard in one minute or less.

12. The discussion of appeal in civil cases is based on the Courts Decree 1966. In criminal cases I have referred to the Criminal Procedure Code 1960.

13. A proverb states: "You must let your neighbor cut nine before you cut ten." This value on equitable distribution is invoked in the context of the family as well as in the relationship between citizens and traditional political authorities.

14. Migrant status, $\chi^2 = .501$, $p \geq .4$; ethnicity, $\chi^2 = .92$, $p \geq .3$; age, $\chi^2 = .009$, $p \geq .9$; occupation, $\chi^2 = .62$, $p \leq .50$; literacy, $\chi^2 = .46$, $p \geq .5$; sex, $\chi^2 = 3.6$, $p \leq .06$. The chi-square statistic is clearly reviewed by Freeman (1965: 213–27). The p values represent the probabilities of the chi-square statistic occurring as a result of sampling variation in a population. Generally a value of .05 or less is necessary to reject the null hypothesis (i.e., reject the hypothesis that the two variables are not associated).

15. The importance of economic rationality in the formation of courts is discussed by Trubek (1972).

16. A similar logic has been used to explain patterns of court use in Japan; see Ohta and Hozumi (1973).

17. The logic of this relationship is discussed by Blalock (1972: 294). The same author explicates the use of Yule's *Q* on p. 298.

SEVEN

DISPUTING OVER LIVESTOCK IN SARDINIA

Julio L. Ruffini

SARDINIA is, except for Sicily, the largest island in the Mediterranean Sea. It is approximately 170 miles long from north to south and ninety miles wide from east to west.

The island is composed largely of mountains and upland plateaus intersected by small rivers, most of which dry up in the summer (Guido 1963: 23–26). Most of the high mountainous land, the Barbagia, is in the central and eastern part of the island, the highest and most inaccessible region being the wild and bare peaks of the Gennargentu range, which rise to 6,000 feet. This zone is mainly of granite, with sharp, craggy summits and wide valleys. The vegetation is generally patchy scrub dotted with oaks scattered over pasture land. The area is poorly watered (Guido 1963: 26).

Although Sardinia is now integrated into the social and cultural life of the Italian nation, it maintains a strong sense of separateness, symbolized by its own language, which is not comprehensible to continental Italians. In many respects the age-old historical pattern of relations to its political and economic masters continues today.

Sardinia has been occupied and controlled by a long series of foreign powers that did little for the local inhabitants, but exploited their resources—the Carthaginians, Romans, Vandals, Byzantines, Genoese, Pisans, Spaniards, and Piedmontese. In 1861, Sardinia became part of unified Italy. In earlier times, the nature of the terrain and the poorly developed systems of transportation and communication, in conjunction with the indifference of the rulers, meant that the mountainous interior zones were relatively uncontrolled by the central governments. In this historical situation of neglect and exploitation, a number of indigenous responses to problems of social control were created, including a shepherds' legal system.[1]

THE SETTING

Mountainous Barbagia, called "an island within an island," is the heartland of pastoral Sardinia and the region where the legal system of the Sard shepherds described in this essay prevails. The region's economy remains almost entirely pastoral.[2] Shepherds are found all over the island, but most of them are from the Barbagia and other zones of the east-central mountains.

Here tens of thousands of shepherds, from several score of villages perched high atop bare rocks, follow their flocks of sheep and goats on the perennial search for scarce pastures. Most of these shepherds are transhumant; they migrate with their flocks each winter from their cold and snow-bound mountain homes to lower and warmer coastal and plains areas throughout the island. They may travel as many as ninety miles from home, and they may be gone for three to nine months of the year. It is not only the climate that necessitates their annual migration. The shepherds of the highest zones own vast flocks of animals, far too many for their sparse pastures, and so they are forced to seek pastures elsewhere. They obtain these pastures in a number of ways, by a variety of rental and sharecropping arrangements with peasants and landowners, and more recently by purchase.

Many of the winter pastures consist of stubble and other remains of harvested crops. In the mountains the vast majority of pastures consist of unimproved, wild grass growing on rocky soil, amid clumps of oak trees and low brush. Only in recent years have some shepherds had enough good land to sow with hay for winter feeding, and seldom do they plow and sow meadows. Consequently, the sheep are not kept in stalls and fed forage—hay and grains—but wander endlessly over vast stretches of wild, lonely mountain pastures.

This system of pasturage requires the constant attention of the shepherd. The animals, if not watched constantly, may die by falling off cliffs or may be eaten by predatory animals or stolen by thieves. The shepherd must remain close to his animals for an even more important reason. Unlike many other pastoral economies, where sheep are raised only for their wool and meat, and therefore huge flocks can be maintained by a few men, in Sardinia the sheep and goats are kept to be milked. The milk, which is made into cheese and shipped to Italy to be sold throughout Europe and America, has to be obtained twice daily from the ewes. Consequently, a shepherd must remain close to his animals, and the number he can maintain by himself is limited.

Nevertheless, even with a small flock—150 to 200 ewes—a shepherd can earn a good living. The cheese made from the milk of these sheep, which feed only on wild grass and wild aromatic herbs, is in great demand, and the sheep are excellent producers. The shepherd augments his income from milk and cheese by the sale of male lambs and wool. However, the vast majority of shepherds are not prosperous. Most of them do not own their own pastures, or all the pastures they require, and they must pay extremely high rents for additional land.[3] They are also forced to sell their milk or cheese at prices fixed by the dairies and cheese merchants. This economic squeeze, along with the grave risks of stockbreeding in a zone with a harsh climate and poor soil, results in a highly risky life for the shepherd.

In the last few years the government has provided money to build some solid shelters for the shepherds in the countryside. These shelters serve as storage barns for feed and provisions (recently the government has subsidized purchase of grains during periods of drought), sleeping quarters for the men, and dry places for the production and storage of cheese. Most shepherds do not have these facilities, however, and continue to rely on the thatched stone huts of their ancestors.

Apart from their transhumance, the shepherds are gone from home weeks at a time, alone with their animals in the mountains. They must milk their animals twice a day and then either transport the milk to distant dairies or to roads where the dairy trucks pick up the milk, or make the cheese themselves. Winter is a particularly difficult time, as it is lambing season and scores of lambs may be born, often at night, while the shepherd is often still in the cold, wet mountains. The shepherd lives close to nature, and in Sardinia nature is harsh and unfriendly.

Since the shepherd lives in the open, far from town and its amenities, he is also at the mercy of his fellow man. If he does not maintain friendly relations with all and at the same time earn the wary respect of all, he is vulnerable to predatory attack. If he leaves his animals unguarded for long, or at regular, predictable periods, he may lose them to thieves or enemies. If he makes enemies, he is alone in the country and he and his animals are vulnerable to attack. This vulnerability of the shepherd—alone in the mountains with no police protection—is a very important reason for his behavior in disputes over livestock.

SOCIAL AND POLITICAL ORGANIZATION

Sardinia is an autonomous region of Italy, with its own parliament, authorized to pass legislation that does not conflict with Italian law. In contrast to the past, the Italian government devotes much money to the island, generally to buttress the burgeoning governmental structure and to encourage industrialization and tourism. Sardinia is also a recipient of Italian mass culture—movies, music, clothing styles. It is no longer a forgotten backwater.

Sardinia is divided into four provinces, each named after its capital city. Cagliari, the southern province, is largely agricultural and industrial and is the most populous.[4] Oristano, in the west, is largely agricultural. Sassari, in the north, is commercial, agricultural, and pastoral. Nuoro is central and mountainous, and mainly pastoral. The provinces are headed by prefects, who are appointed and are part of the central state bureaucracy.

The lowest administrative unit is the commune—city, town, or village. There were 354 communes in Sardinia in 1966. Of these, 212 were considered by the Sard regional government to be mainly pastoral (Brigaglia 1971: 332). About 98 percent of the Sard population lives either in cities or small rural nucleated settlements. Only 2 per cent lives dispersed in the countryside (L. Pinna 1971: 45). Most Sard communes are small and rural, with populations ranging from 1,000 to 5,000. The rural communes follow the typical Mediterranean pattern of a nucleated village surrounded by vineyards and orchards, vegetable gardens, and pastures.

Typically, the land used by a commune forms concentric circles about the settlement. In the nearest circles the land is used for vineyards, orchards, and vegetable gardens. Beyond these is the land used for grains. In the furthest circles, and comprising most of the land, are the pastures. Dotted throughout these pastures, in the mountains and valleys, are thousands of sheepfolds, the enclosures where the sheep, cows, and goats are milked, cheese is made, and other routine work of the shepherds is performed.

An important principle of organization below that of the village is that of the neighborhood. The *vicinato* (*ikinatu* in Sard) is a principle of organization of great importance in the Sard village. *Vicini* (neighbors) have definite and precise rules of behavior and mutual expectations. One's vicinato is carefully delimited geographically. A precise number of houses on each side of one's own and a certain number across the road constitute one's vicinato.

Basically, neighbors expect to help each other with such chores as breadmaking, to visit each other and exchange gifts, and to attend each other's life crisis ceremonies. They can also be depended upon for aid in other crises, such as sickness.

The concept of vicinato extends also to the countryside, where a shepherd has similar relations to the vicini of his sheepfold, who are expected to establish and maintain relations of trust. They help each other at shearing time, visit each other (an important function in the lonely countryside), and watch each other's animals during a shepherd's absence. Vicini of the sheepfold can also be called upon for information and assistance in searches when theft of animals has occurred. Above all, they are expected to refrain from stealing each other's animals.

The most important group in Sard rural political and social organization is the family. The family is generally nuclear, but very often, in pastoral areas, the flock management unit consists of the father and sons until the death or retirement of the father, after which the brothers continue to work together, at least until their own sons are mature. Efficient flock management requires several hands and, typically, flocks are managed by two to four or more adult brothers. Very often these brothers live together in a building, even though they may not share the same hearth.

Sons expect to receive equal amounts of the family estate when they marry. Shepherd brothers who marry continue to manage their animals together after division. Failure to divide the inheritance equally often results in bitter disputes (L. Pinna 1971: 53–60).

The structural tension between brothers and other close relatives, either actual or potential, means that the individual cannot always rely upon the support of a large kinship group. Even when kinship ties are strong, Sards consciously attempt to expand their ties within the village and in other villages. They do this through ties with vicini. Patron-client relations and ritual kinship (sponsorship of baptisms, weddings, and other religious events) are also extremely important in rural Sardinia as means of strengthening and creating social bonds. Friendship networks are also crucial in political and social organization.

All these types of social ties—kinship, ritual kinship, patron-client relations, neighborhood, friendship—are used by the Sard shepherd to strengthen his position as he competes for survival and advancement in a harsh environment. They are all of major importance in the Sard legal and political systems and play a central role in management of conflict over livestock. The importance of these social ties, as well as other institutions and processes which operate in disputes over livestock theft, is illustrated in the following case.

The Case of Zuanne's Stolen Sheep

Zuanne Piras was a young shepherd from the village of Nurache, high in the wild and desolate mountains of the Barbagia.[5] He and his brother Antoneddu had been managing the family flock of 300 sheep, five cows, and twenty pigs since the recent retirement of their father. This number of animals could be expected to provide a good income, but the brothers owned only a small amount of land, and they were required to pay high rents for sufficient pastures. In good years they did well and were more than able to pay their debts. In bad years they were fortunate to break even.

At some times of the year, the brothers divided the flock, Antoneddu taking the young, unproductive ewes and the cows and pigs to low-lying grassland in a neighboring commune, while Zuanne remained, during the summer at least, with the productive ewes in the high plateau above Nurache. Efficient flock management and the availability of pasturage required this separation periodically, aside from the long trip to the distant coastal areas during the winter. It also meant, however, that one man could not relieve the other for trips to the village. They had to stay with their animals or rely on a relative or friend from the village to come out with supplies or to relieve them for a time while they went to the village. Antoneddu had a sheepfold neighbor in the valley whom he could trust to watch his animals for a few hours or a day, but Zuanne's sheepfold was in a very isolated area. His nearest neighbor was far away, over a steep hill. Consequently, he seldom went to the village unless a third brother, who owned a bar in town, or his cousin, who was unemployed, came to relieve him.

One evening after the milking, however, Zuanne could not restrain himself from visiting the village. It was a religious holiday, a *festa*, and there would be singing, dancing, and feasting. He promised himself that he would return early in the morning in time for the milking. And so, putting all the ewes in the stone walled enclosure, he mounted his horse and headed for the village.

The next morning when he returned, tired after a sleepless night of merrymaking, he found the sheepfold deserted—over 200 sheep gone. He was thunderstruck. Rent for pastures had to be paid, and how could they do so without milk to be made into cheese? Zuanne followed the tracks for a while on foot to see in which direction they went. Then he returned to his horse and set out to follow the tracks farther. They led along a low-lying ridge that wound downward, then skirted a valley and proceeded gradually up another mountain.

This zone was particularly desolate, and so he rode a great distance without passing any other sheepfolds. The first sheepfold he did encounter belonged to a good friend of his, but no one was about, as the shepherd was temporarily pasturing his flock elsewhere. Continuing to follow the tracks, Zuanne came to another sheepfold, belonging to a fellow villager, a man whom he knew only casually. This man was friendly and sympathetic, but he told him he had not observed anything, as he had been asleep and his sheepfold was several hundred yards from the path.

Soon the terrain became stonier and it was difficult to follow the tracks, which appeared now to be intermingled with those of other flocks. The sherpherds Zuanne now encountered along the way were strangers to him, members of the neighboring enemy village of Orgheri. The Orgheresi and Nurachesi have, for centuries, accused each other, and rightly, of stealing each other's animals. Some of these shepherds Zuanne knew casually. They were friendly but insisted that they knew nothing. Others were less friendly and also claimed to have seen or heard nothing. Zuanne did not ask to inspect their sheepfolds because he could see that the tracks did not lead to them.

In time Zuanne lost the tracks. He knew that he was not a skilled tracker, but that Ziu Andria, a wily old shepherd in the village, was an expert, and later Zuanne would ask him to help. Now, however, he had done all he could by himself, and so he returned to the village.

Nurache currently had no company of *barracelli* (local official armed patrols of shepherds who protect livestock) because of a dispute with the provincial prefect over choice of captain. Last year Ziu Andria had served in this position. Meetings of shepherds were being held to attempt to form a company, and some shepherds were talking alternatively of forming *soci* (unofficial mutual aid societies of shepherds designed to assist victims of theft). But at the moment, neither existed. Consequently, Zuanne had to rely on his core action set—his kinsmen, friends, and neighbors.

Most of the members of Zuanne's core action set were themselves shepherds—some of the 500 shepherds of Nurache, who possessed a total of about 50,000 sheep. Zuanne could not immediately mobilize these supporters, however, as most of them were in the mountains with their animals. Nevertheless, when he returned to the village he looked for as many of them as he could, in the hope that some would be home for a visit or for chores while their relatives guarded their flocks.

As soon as Zuanne reached home he tethered his horse and told his father the news. His father went to a bar to telephone another bar in the neighboring commune of Pala, to request a friend there to proceed to Antoneddu's sheepfold to inform him. Then he went to find Ziu Andria, a close friend, to seek his aid in following the tracks. In the meantime, Zuanne went to the *piazza* and to all the bars in the center of the village, looking for kinsmen, neighbors, and friends.

He found only two shepherd supporters—a neighbor and a friend whose son was Zuanne's godchild. They were in the village resting as their flocks were being guarded by their numerous kinsmen. Many shepherds had come to town for the festa, but most of them had by now returned to the countryside.

Many retired shepherds were in the village, however, and with little to do, they were eager to help. Zuanne found four of them: one who was a cousin of his mother's, two who were close friends of his father's, and a fourth who was a popular former lieutenant of barracelli who knew many people throughout the zone and was widely regarded as a skilled mediator in disputes over livestock.

A number of Zuanne's core action set were not shepherds, but worked in the village or in Nuoro, the provincial capital, as bartenders, clerks, day laborers, or construction workers. Some of these were ex-shepherds and would be valuable to him now. Again, however, they would be at work. Zuanne did, however, find some more supporters—a butcher, a shopkeeper, a student, and an unemployed man—all close kinsmen, neighbors, or friends.

Meanwhile Zuanne's father had found Ziu Andria and two more friends. In a matter of an hour, then, seventeen men, including a few piazza hangers-on, were gathered in the narrow cobblestoned lane behind Zuanne's house. They stood about for a while, talking earnestly in knots of three or four men, as Zuanne paced back and forth among them, anxious and fearful. Soon they left for the piazza, where they split into groups and got into four cars. They drove several miles into the mountains on the paved road, and then turned off into a dirt road, treacherous with deep holes and huge stones, until they came to the area of Zuanne's sheepfold. From this point they could no longer proceed by car. As the number of horses and donkeys in Nurache had fallen sharply in recent years, the only possible form of travel was by foot.

With Ziu Andria's skilled help, the men were able to follow the tracks for a much greater distance than Zuanne had done by himself earlier that morning. At times it was difficult, as they were traversing zones of rock where they lost the tracks temporarily until they could search the whole area for reemerging traces.

The many shepherds they encountered were of little help. Almost all of them, even the Orgheresi, were known by at least some of the group, but they gave no reliable information. One or two did provide information, but Zuanne's father and Ziu Andria suspected that the information was designed to set them on a false trail.

After several hours of exhausting travel, the men went to Orgheri and fanned out to all the bars. All had some friends there, even though the village as a whole was regarded as the enemy. Each sought his friends or acquaintances in the bars and piazzas, and made inquiries. They achieved nothing immediately, but obtained a number of promises that information would be sought.

After a few hours in Orgheri the group split up. Some took the bus back to Nurache, in order to return to their normal duties, but they promised to help again. Others remained in Orgheri, drinking and making inquiries. The rest went into the countryside beyond Orgheri to attempt to pick up the traces again and to inquire at sheepfolds. By the end of the day, however, they had definitely lost the tracks and had obtained no further information. Reluctantly the tired men returned to Nurache.

In the following days some of these men, along with others who had not been able to help the first day, continued their searches in the zones where they thought the animals might have been taken. They inspected sheepfolds in the countryside and visited friends in a number of villages, spending long hours accepting hospitality in their homes and bars as they made their inquiries. They received no solid information, but by now many people knew of the stolen animals and they hoped they might in time receive some information.

During the next week groups of Zuanne's core action set drove to the countryside and inspected the sheepfolds of shepherds in the suspected zones. After a time they received hints that the animals might be found in certain areas, but these leads were found to be false.

Zuanne, Antoneddu, and their father, along with other close kinsmen, sought the help of several important men in Nurache: Ziu Bainzu, who was the largest landowner and highly respected and liked throughout the zone; Ziu Michele, an ex-shepherd who was now a merchant of cheese and lambs, and widely known throughout the zone; Ziu Pepeddu, a prosperous shepherd who, along with his three brothers and many sons, owned more than a thousand sheep and many cattle, as well as his own pastures; Antonio Mele, a butcher who traveled widely and knew many shepherds, including some who needed the services of a butcher who asked no questions; and Ziu Bobore, a prosperous shepherd who had been captain of barracelli for many years and who had many relatives and friends who were politically important in Nuoro and the zone as a whole. All promised to see what they could do, keep their ears open, talk to *their* friends. One of two even went out several times on the searches.

All to no avail. Two weeks went by. By now Zuanne despaired of finding the animals. Many of his supporters had dropped out of the search, pleading other commitments, although new supporters joined from time to time. Zuanne hoped that the thief would contact him to offer to return the animals for a price, as he had no hope of finding the animals himself. But there was no communication from the thief.

Just then Zuanne's fortunes improved. His mother's brother, Ziu Pepe, a cheese merchant, had been on the continent on business most of this time. But now he returned and was free to help. So, one day Ziu Pepe and his brother-in-law (Zuanne's father) went to see a friend in Orgheri who, Ziu Pepe knew, was active in cattle theft and might have some information.

As they reached the main street of Orgheri they saw the friend, Luisi, driving along with his oxcart. As soon as Luisi saw them he stopped his cart and greeted him. "Ziu Pepe, here at Orgheri? Are you here for need or for pleasure?" Ziu Pepe replied, "No, not such a happy visit." Luisi's face dropped, and he called over a young man and told him to take the cart home. Ziu Pepe told Luisi he had a problem.

Luisi took the two men to a wineshop, asking the owner if the room upstairs were vacant. It was and so he asked the bartender to bring up a bottle of wine. After he left they closed the door, had a glass of wine, and then Luisi said, "Tell me the thing that would be the reason for your visit." Ziu Pepe told him there had been the theft of a flock two weeks before and his friend said, "And whose sheep are they?" Ziu Pepe responded, "The owner is my sister." "Your sister! And why did you wait so long to come?"

Ziu Pepe told him he had been very busy, and besides, others were looking. "Now I have no hope but you," he told his friend. Luisi said, "Yes, but it is late now." (Ziu Pepe said to me, "Of course, it was my brother-in-law's fault, he didn't know where to go, whom to see, he placed reliance on people in the bars he talked to, so much time was wasted.") "But," said Luisi, "I will do my best. I will do what I can."

Ziu Pepe knew that Luisi had friends among the animal thieves and receivers in Mugrone, a commune beyond Orgheri, and that he would go there. Ziu Pepe had another friend in Mugrone, and he telephoned this friend and told him, "Luisi will be coming to Mugrone soon to talk to people. See to whom he talks and tell me." His friend at Mugrone did so, and later told Ziu Pepe that Luisi had talked to one of the biggest landlords of Mugrone, a man who received stolen animals and falsified the documents of ownership. The stolen animals had actually passed through Luisi's hands, but he had not known that Ziu Pepe was involved. (If Ziu Pepe had not taken the precaution to have Luisi observed by another friend, the likely outcome would have been an extortionate demand: Zuanne would have had to pay for the return of his animals, negotiated through Luisi. But now Ziu Pepe and the owners of the stolen flock knew who had the animals, and so they were in a much better bargaining position.)

During the night, seven or eight armed men, including Ziu Pepe, went to the property of the rich landlord, deep in the countryside of Mugrone. They surrounded the sheepfold during the predawn milking. Zuanne and Antoneddu crept up to the enclosure to look at the sheep. They returned saying, "These are our animals."

It was still dark when the servant shepherds finished with the milking. As one of them went to get a horse, the hidden men emerged and said to the servant, "Where are you going?" "To get the mare to bring the milk in." They said, "Now, go get the owner." The man went to Mugrone.

The proprietor came that afternoon, bringing with him the ownership papers for the animals, all in order. They talked. ("Word, threats, they were dangerous moments. These are dangerous situations," Ziu Pepe told me.) The rightful owners demanded that the animals be returned to them, and, as is the custom, more animals, up to double the number, to compensate them for their loss of income and trouble. The other showed his documents, all in order. The owners said, "Yes, we can see you have the papers all in order, but we know these are our animals."

But the proprietor was not willing (Ziu Pepe said), to return the animals "in good spirits." So they threatened him. They told him, "If you do not return these animals, we will leave, but before too long you will have to come to Nurache looking for your own stolen animals." Back and forth the threats flew in this vein. Finally the group said, "We will leave now, but we know where the animals are, and whom to bludgeon." (It will be noted that at no time did the owners consider resorting to the police. Regardless of other considerations, they would have had difficulty in proving they were the rightful owners. The identification markings on the ears of the sheep had been altered to agree with the thief's documents. They no longer accorded with the markings on the documents of the rightful owners. If the rightful owners had resorted to the police, they might have been charged with making threats and attemping extortion.)

As they were leaving, the proprietor said, "No, stop, stay longer. I will kill a sheep for us to eat." They replied, "No, we won't go, but you must return the stolen sheep, and then we will kill one and all eat together. They are ours. Otherwise you will be coming to Nurache. We will strike a blow against you from which you won't recover. And you won't be able to recover your animals then." But no agreement was reached.

When the proprietor returned to Mugrone, he went to a man from Nurache, who had married a cousin of his and now lived in Mugrone. This man was also a friend of Ziu Pepe. The proprietor told the story of the threats to this man, who told him that the men with whom he was dealing were to be taken seriously, were not joking, were men of their word. They would carry out their threats, and (Ziu Pepe told me) the proprietor owned many animals.

The proprietor decided to reason with the rightful owners to avoid action against himself. He sent word to them, and the two sides arranged a meeting to come to an understanding. The proprietor would have liked to make an extortionate demand, but it was too late for that, as his identity and the whereabouts of the animals were known. The rightful owners would have liked their animals returned plus an equal number of the proprietor's for expenses. They were not in a strong enough position to obtain this, however, as the proprietor was rich, powerful, and influential. The result was a compromise. The proprietor said he would return the animals with the documents in order. The owners accepted this offer and then went to see Ziu Pepe.

Ziu Pepe advised them to be sure that all the documents were in order and also the markings on the animals' ears. Ziu Pepe told them to be sure that the new markings were good, dry, not wet and bloody, indicating recent alteration. Otherwise, if the *carabinieri* (state military police) came to inspect the sheep and saw suspicious signs of tampering, they could go to jail.

One night soon after, Zuanne was at his sheepfold when two men brought him the sheep. But their ears were bloody and the ownership marks were obviously newly cut. The owners went to Ziu Pepe for advice, and he told them to return the animals immediately, or they would go to jail for certain. They did so.

The proprietor contacted them again, but they, following Ziu Pepe's advice, told him that they would not accept the animals in that condition. So the proprietor offered to pay them for the animals, and offered a good price, over what could be expected. The owners accepted, and made peace with the proprietor.

They used the money to buy more ewes, and were content. They called together all the people who had helped them on the searches and had a huge feast. "And so," said Ziu Pepe, "everything went very well."

LIVESTOCK THEFT

Livestock theft has probably been a salient feature of Sardinian history as long as pastoralism has been practiced. Any period of Sard history that is well documented discloses the incidence of theft of animals. Certainly in recent centuries it has been extremely widespread, and regarded locally and nationally as a major problem. It is difficult, if not impossible, to be very precise about the number of animals stolen. Official figures exist, but their value is limited, as very many, if not most, animal thefts are never reported to the authorities.

Sardinia has always been a poor region, especially in the rural zones. In periods of acute misery and poverty, livestock theft was widely viewed as a means of survival. It has also long been viewed as a means of enrichment and social advancement. It is seen locally as a legitimate and natural act of valor on the part of shepherds, especially young ones. Given these factors, it is not surprising that in an island with about 3,000,000 sheep alone, livestock theft should continue to be regarded as a serious problem.

Aside from the economic threat, livestock theft is serious because it may result in disputes that escalate to feud, violence, and even murder. Consequently, the Sards attempt to regulate livestock theft through their own legal and political systems, in an effort to minimize its disruptive effects.

The state authorities are also concerned about escalation of livestock theft and, in addition, its potential links with banditry. Suspected livestock thieves may have to become outlaws to avoid arrest. Outlaws, to support themselves, steal animals. As Pirastu (1973: 143) states it, "Theft of animals has nearly always been . . . the first link in the chain of banditry, original cause of vendetta, conflict between families and groups, or reprisals, and sometimes of homicides."

LEGAL PLURALISM

Anthropologists have made significant contributions to the study of legal pluralism—the existence within one political system of a number of legal systems (Graburn 1969; Kuper and Kuper 1965; Nader and Yngvesson 1973; Pospisil 1967). Legal pluralism is best exemplified by the colonial systems established by European states throughout Africa, Asia, and the Pacific islands. Here the colonial powers had to contend with a myriad of ongoing indigenous cultures and social structures, including legal systems. The new nation-states which have emerged since the end of World War II have, to a large extent, inherited this situation of legal pluralism.

Some scholars, notably Sutherland (1949), have also studied legal pluralism as it operates in a complex Western society that is presumably homogeneous in law but may have different law for different classes or categories of people under the same legal jurisdiction (e.g., one law for "common criminals," another for "white-collar offenders"). Some legal anthropologists have argued, also, that all functioning subgroups of a society have their own legal systems, each different in some degree (Pospisil 1967).

Sardinia provides an excellent example of a particular form of legal pluralism, in which two strong and thriving legal systems operate within the same society—that of the Italian state, and that of the Sard shepherds—but in which the legitimacy of the latter is not recognized by the state.

It might be expected that a Sard shepherd would be able to use either or both of these legal systems in his effort to settle disputes, resolve conflicts, defend his interests, or score against an opponent. In many areas of conflict Sards do indeed employ the mechanisms of the state legal system. In one crucial and important area, however—in disputes relating to animal theft[6]—Sard shepherds almost universally prefer to avoid the state legal system in favor of their own. There are a number of reasons why they prefer to choose one legal system over the other, and this paper attempts to examine the constraints upon Sard shepherds' freedom of choice in this area.

The Sard material highlights a recurring theme in the literature of legal pluralism: that the crucial issue of choice and alternatives, so prominent in thinking about legal pluralism, is a double-edged sword. For, while the Sard shepherd has the opportunity (and certainly the wit and agility) to manipulate both systems so that they afford him a wider range of alternatives than either alone would, he is also trapped in a dilemma, a conflict between radically opposed systems of values and behavior so that conformity to one will cause him to suffer the negative sanctions of the other. In this dilemma of choice between opposing legal systems the ancient Sard proverb (G. Pinna 1967: 98)—*lezzes meda, populu miseru,* "many laws, miserable populace,"—takes on a somewhat different, but equally poignant, meaning.

THE ITALIAN STATE LEGAL SYSTEM

The national legal system is represented in Sardinia by the *carabinieri* (national military police) and the *pubblica sicurezza* (national police). Also present is the Italian court system, with its legal personnel (judges, lawyers, bailiffs), formalized codes of procedural and substantive law, norms and values, and system of sanctions (prison, probation, forced residence, fines). The national legal system is unitary, formal, and impersonal. Delicts are expressly defined, and so are the means by which they must be handled by all levels of legal personnel. The law is a body of specific prohibitions accompanied by specific procedures for dealing with infringements of the law.

Livestock theft is, according to the state legal system, a crime punishable by a series of penal sanctions, including prison. It is the duty of police officers to prevent livestock theft, apprehend thieves, arrest them, and compile evidence against them to be used in court proceedings. Disputes between parties over livestock are to be settled in court. Police are not dispute settlement agents.

The courts are not corrupt, but Sards generally agree that they are inefficient and understaffed. Delays are of legendary and awesome proportions. The nature of many Sard disputes, including disputes over livestock, is such that it is difficult, often impossible, for a judge to gain a clear picture of the situation. Crime may occur in the countryside with no witnesses. It is often the word of one man against that of another. It is easy to establish alibis and provide oneself with supporters who will claim to be witnesses.

Cases can be quite complex, with years of historical ramifications. The courts, with their harassed urban personnel, are ill equipped to cope with many of these cases. Thus judicial decisions may be seen by one or more of the parties to be arbitrary, unpredictable, and unrelated to reality. Furthermore, the decisions do not serve to reconcile the disputants. They do not establish peace between them but may actually cause further deterioration of relations between disputants and their supporters, who may have had to testify against each other.

Everyone to whom one speaks in Sardinia agrees that the judicial system has serious defects. The personnel of the system, the media, and organs of national public opinion, however, insist that this admittedly imperfect legal system is the only legitimate system for dealing with criminal activity, including livestock theft.

The major state legal effort against livestock theft is represented by the carabinieri. The carabinieri are outsiders in the rural communities where they work and are usually not Sards. They generally remain in one zone for only a few years before transferring to what they invariably consider more desirable stations.

The carabinieri, as part of their work, attempt to maintain a position of aloofness toward the local population, so that their dignity and impartiality cannot be compromised. They see themselves as outsiders who represent an impartial and impersonal legal system. When they act in the area of livestock theft and its related activities, they operate with a set of norms, rules, and procedures, all clearly defined by the national legal system.

They do not see themselves as locals enmeshed in the cultural and social life of the community. On the contrary, they see the shepherds' community as alien and hostile, a community they have to control and supervise, but one that is alien to the national Italian culture and its legal system. Carabinieri often conceive of shepherds as synonymous with criminals, guilty until proven innocent. Consequently, when carabinieri act in cases of livestock theft, they do not see themselves as mediators, arbitrators, or conciliators between disputants.

The attitude of the carabinieri toward the rural Sard population is reciprocated. In rural, and especially pastoral, communities the hostility toward the carabinieri is marked.

Consequently, the investigations of the carabinieri are hampered by a general unwillingness on the part of the rural population, and shepherds in particular, to cooperate with them in cases of livestock theft. Shepherds do not want to become involved in court proceedings against other shepherds, who might be imprisoned as a result of their testimony. They generally feel that disputes over livestock should be settled within the shepherd community rather than in the courts.

Because of these factors the carabinieri are not able to integrate themselves into the local friendship networks to obtain information. They sometimes employ police informers, who generally are not effective because they are unable to regularly integrate themselves into the networks. Consequently the police have to rely on patrols in the hope of apprehending thieves with stolen animals or butchers with stolen meat.

These patrols often find stolen animals, but usually the animals are wandering about freely and the thieves are not discovered. The patrols also further embitter shepherds whose sheepfolds they inspect. Moreover, these patrols are carried out during the day; the carabinieri seldom venture into the countryside at night, when livestock are usually stolen.

SARD SHEPHERDS' VALUE AND LEGAL SYSTEMS

A number of Sard legal scholars have written on the topic of the shepherds' value and legal systems.[7] What emerges from the writings of these and other scholars, as well as from my own fieldwork, is a well-defined, discrete system of values and norms of behavior in situations of conflict, with institutions and processes that can be called upon when needed. The ultimate sanction in the system is the threat of attack.

The shepherds themselves conceive of two distinct, competing legal systems, their own and that of the state, which they feel is alien, oppressive, and not responsive to the needs of their daily lives. The state law is imposed from without, while their own law emerges from their own social structure and is thus seen as "natural." The shepherds reason that the laws of the state are suitable for the towns and townspeople, where life is more "civil," but that in the harsh environment of the shepherds, laws must be flexible and more attuned to reality (G. Pinna 1967: 26–27).

Consequently, Sard shepherds continue to resort to their own indigenous legal system. The usual procedure for settling disputes is negotiation between disputants or mediation. Mutually acceptable agreements are effected, based upon normative rules and assessment of relative power. The community (village and shepherd) knows about the general provisions of the agreement, and the sanction of public opinion buttresses the agreement.

If the disputants are not able to effect an agreement, the dispute may escalate to feud or vendetta, or the disputants may continue, for years, to be in a state of enmity without resolution, in which they avoid each other. This lack of resolution of a dispute is disliked, as the disputants fear that they may at any time be the victims of attack, even years after the start of the dispute.

The preferred solution, therefore, when negotiation or mediation fails or even at the outset, is arbitration. The use of local arbitrators in many types of disputes is still widespread, because it is inexpensive and local arbitrators are familiar with the situation.

Arbitrators are called *sos homines*, "the men," with the connotation that they are mature men, dignified, able, and respected. In the most simple and frequent form of arbitration, *tres homines*, there are three arbitrators. Each disputant chooses one, and these two together choose the third, a man regarded as independent and objective. The disputants swear to accept the majority decision, and apparently they usually do, except in cases of suspected favoritism on the part of the arbitrators. Usually disputants are of the same or similar social class, but often richer people use arbitration in disputes with poor people, who feel more confident with this system than with state courts (G. Pinna 1967: 117–18).

The worldview of the Sard shepherd has been described as profoundly pessimistic (G. Pinna 1967: 21). He conceives of life as a constant battle, against man and against nature (Brigaglia 1971: 20, G. Pinna 1967: 21). One has to be strong to defend one's interests in a society in which resources are seen to be insufficient and competition and conflict are viewed as inevitable. As Cagnetta (1963: 62) expresses it, the shepherds have only one rule: "He who does not deceive is deceived himself. He who does not dominate is himself dominated."

The qualities that are valued are courage, sagacity, wiliness, astuteness, values that are summed up in the words *su abile*, the capable man, and ***balentia***, bravery, or *su* ***balente***, the brave, able man. An important and crucial component of balentia is skill as well as courage. A man who is foolhardy is not respected. He can be dangerous to himself, his associates, and his family, and may not be reliable. If he is killed or imprisoned, his family may be left without support.

The man who is *furbo*, clever, wily, one who can "get away" with something, is respected. A man who steals animals is courageous, but he is not admired for that trait unless he is also skillful. If he is caught, he is inept and not worthy of admiration (unless he is caught through the information of "spies"). Such a man deserves his fate, as he is not clever and skillful enough. If a thief successfully evades apprehension, however, he is both courageous and astute, and he has a right to the animals or a price for their return.

Pigliaru notes the Sard shepherds have values concerning the types of actions a man of ability should take, which are, lamentably, often regarded as criminal by state law (Brigaglia 1971: 167). Livestock theft is a case in point.

According to the experts, and my own data, livestock theft is viewed by shepherds of the Barbagia not as a crime, but as a "normal element" of pastoralism. It concerns only those directly interested—the victim and those who have close ties with him. Livestock theft is, for the shepherd, a traditional and normal practice. One steals to enrich himself. One also steals to prove one's valor—balentia—the fundamental virtue of the shepherd. The ability to steal animals has always been, in the Barbagia, a matter of pride (*L'Unione Sarda*, July 29, 1970, p. 8).

Livestock theft is not seen by the shepherds as a criminal offense, except under certain circumstances. If a thief steals from a ritual kinsman, friend, or neighbor, it is considered wrong (G. Pinna 1967: 49–50); it is also considered wrong if he steals the family goat or if he steals under circumstances meant to offend (Brigaglia 1971: 195–96). Otherwise, the theft is considered normal. In a case of "normal" theft, the victim attempts to obtain the return of the animals through his social networks within the shepherd community. He does not resort to the machinery of the state legal system, as that could be dangerous and expensive as was demonstrated in the case of Zuanne's stolen sheep. It would also create enmity, while private accords eliminate these dangers (G. Pinna 1967: 49–50).

Pigliaru, Gonario Pinna, and other writers give much evidence to support the existence of these attitudes as well as the legal machinery concerned. It is not possible here to discuss this any further. I merely wish to emphasize that to the shepherd of the Barbagia, livestock theft is not regarded as a crime, but as the source of a dispute, which should be settled amicably without recourse to the state. The positive attitude of shepherds toward animal theft—one proves his worth by stealing animals; one can become rich by stealing animals; a poor man can eat only if he steals—is an extremely important factor in the way the indigenous legal system copes with livestock theft.[8]

The shepherds' political and legal systems as they relate to coping with the problem of livestock theft will be described briefly in terms of a number of structural characteristics: the levels or types of social organization which shepherds can mobilize to deal with the problem; the institutions—patterned forms of behavior and expectations—that they can mobilize to settle disputes over cattle; the values and goals that motivate actors within the shepherds' legal system; and the processes employed by shepherds to deal with livestock theft.

LEVELS OF ORGANIZATION

Within the shepherds' legal system are three subsystems of management of conflict over livestock which can be viewed as levels of organization, each incorporating a greater degree of community participation and responsibility. These three are ego-centered core action sets, mutual aid societies (*soci;* singular: *socio*), and organizations that combine the functions of insurance companies and armed patrols for self-protection (barracelli).

A shepherd who is the victim of livestock theft, acting on his own, with the support of his core action set, has the moral support of his village. All who hear of his plight may be expected to offer expressions of sympathy and solidarity. But only his closest supporters (kinsmen, ritual kinsmen, friends, and neighbors) will be actively mobilized to search for the animals and the thief and to support the victim in his often threat-laden negotiations with the thief. If the victim is ultimately unsuccessful in finding his stolen animals, he cannot always be sure that all the shepherds of the village, as distinct from his core action set, will contribute to restore his flock to its original size.

Furthermore, not all shepherds are equally able to mobilize action sets. Not all are equally popular. Not all have large, prosperous families with many members free to help the others. Not all have been in a position in the past to help others so that they may effectively call for a return for previous favors. Consequently, the use of core action sets, while almost universal in lifestock theft cases even when higher levels are simultaneously brought into play, is not always sufficient.

Soci, or voluntary mutual aid societies, are therefore often formed to provide more security for individual shepherds and to broaden the degree of community support. Soci may be composed of a number of shepherds from one village who agree to form them, or they may be commune-wide, all shepherds of the village being members.

In either case, the processes and institutions used by shepherds at the socio level of organization are the same as those used in the core action set level (and on the barracello level). The essential difference is that the entire village community of shepherds, or segments of it larger than the core action set, are formally committed, before the fact, to support a victimized shepherd. When a shepherd is victimized, the entire socio is mobilized to support him. All members (or representatives of all families) help search and provide support in the delicate negotiations. If the animals are not returned, all contribute to the restoration of the lost flock.

The barracelli differ from the other two subsystems in that they act not only after the fact but continually, all year long, with armed patrols designed to prevent theft. The community of shepherds of a village which elects to have barracelli is committed in the form of dues payments as well as preventive patrols. Furthermore, the barracelli, who are both state officials and shepherds, have more strength than shepherds alone, for behind them is the constantly menacing presence of the state. In the institution of the *barracellato*, the two legal and political systems meet, if not always in easy compatibility.

Companies of barracelli are a curious combination of local insurance companies for livestock and crops, and rural armed constabularies. The companies are organized yearly, on a communal basis, where the local proprietors decide to form them. Once a company is formed, all proprietors must insure their crops or animals, as the case may be, with the company. The barracelli, or members of the company, are generally the proprietors themselves, and they form an armed unit whose purpose is to patrol the countryside to prevent theft or vandalism.

While these associations are voluntary on a communal basis, once they are formed they are regulated by the communal councils, the provincial prefects, the Sard Region, and the Italian government. The barracelli, though an indigenous and unique Sard institution, are recognized by the Italian legal code[9] and regulated by the various levels of Italian governmental machinery.

Whenever the barracelli exist in a given commune, they represent the highest indigenous organizational level of formality and community involvement and solidarity. Yet it is important to realize that the people who become barracelli are shepherds and day laborers—the same people who participate in the core action sets and soci in the absence of companies of barracelli. They conceive of themselves as shepherds protecting their property. They do this in the same ways they did as actors in core action sets or soci, using the same processes and institutions, and with the same methods and motivations. The state, however, views the barracelli as public agents with the responsibility to enforce the state laws, in town as well as in the country, and as representatives of the Italian legal system. Under this mandate the barracelli are expected to keep the peace in town (breaking up fights, for example), help search for bandits, and arrest suspected livestock thieves. These duties the barracelli are loath to perform, as they violate the legal principles of their own communities.

The barracelli patrol the territory of the commune to prevent theft of animals insured with their company. If thefts do occur, all the barracelli participate in the search for the stolen animals and the thieves. If they are unable to return the stolen animals to the victim, they must pay him 75 per cent of the animals' value.

The barracelli are not paid salaries for their work. At the end of each year the treasury (consisting of the dues paid) is divided on the basis of the number of each member's tours of duty. If the barracelli have been successful in preventing thefts, each barracello has a considerable sum of money to supplement his income and defray the cost of his insurance. If the company has been inefficient and has had to pay for many thefts, the barracelli may have little or nothing. Legally they are responsible for paying victimized proprietors from their own pockets if the treasury is empty.

The barracelli, then, are motivated to prevent theft and return stolen animals, both because the animals are their own and because they will suffer financially if stolen animals are not returned. They are not motivated, however, to *arrest* thieves, which they are empowered and expected to do by state law.

INSTITUTIONS OF SETTLEMENT WITHIN THE SARD LEGAL SYSTEM

Friendship

Friendship, *amistade,* is a concept frequently used by Sards in a wide range of contexts, not only in reference to livestock theft. Sards of all strata, but particularly shepherds, consciously establish and maintain extensive friendship networks throughout the geographical zones of their activity. Together with consanguineal, affinal, and ritual kinship, and patron-client relations (which are often expressed in the idiom of friendship), friendship networks provide shepherds with a measure of security, information, and potential support.

Transhumant shepherds are highly mobile. The need to find pastures for their flocks requires them to seek friends and patrons throughout the island, in many communes. Ties which begin as relations of landlord and tenant are often transformed to ties of kinship, real and ritual, and they form the basis for further contacts as shepherds seek to establish nuclei of trusted supporters in each area. From these friends they can obtain information on pastures, rents, and prices, potentially useful social gossip, information on potential victims of theft if they are inclined to steal, support in their disputes with others, and companionship. Above all, friends are used by victims of livestock theft to attempt to find the stolen animals or establish contact with the thief, and by the thief to establish contact with the victim, if he desires to negotiate the return of the animals for a price. In a society in which it is necessary to establish an acceptable identity and be vouched for when in a strange town, and where it is impossible to obtain information or support from a stranger, a friend is an absolute necessity.

Friendship in Sardinia consists of an overlapping network, extending from the village to other communes and to other sheepfolds in the mountains. These networks, often linked by casual acquaintances, extend through entire zones, and form, in the minds of the shepherds, social maps with which they can chart their journeys. These networks are consciously established, and the need to maintain and reinforce them by prestations, reciprocal hospitality, and expressions of goodwill and friendliness, is consciously recognized.

Aside from the shepherds themselves, a number of others who play key roles in disputes over livestock have occasion to establish wide networks. Middlemen, buyers of cheese, milk, lambs, and wool, travel far and wide in their business and know many people. Butchers do also, and they are also potential receivers of stolen animals. Wealthy landowners often own land in a number of communes and employ servant shepherds from a number of communes. All these people, in addition to shepherds, may become links in the chain of friendship used in disputes over animals. Sometimes these links play an active role beyond seekers and providers of information; they become mediators.

Mediators play an important role in the process of negotiations between disputants over livestock. They are links in the friendship networks, employed by either the victim or thief, or both. People with wide networks, prestige, influence, and appropriate personalities are called upon or volunteer to be mediators. In every commune there are a number of people who everyone knows are the men to go to with a problem. They are respected men who cherish and value their role and reputation as men who can accomplish things. Typically they are rich landlords or merchants, but sometimes they are prosperous shepherds.

Their role is crucial because often agreements are reached without the victim and thief coming into contact, or the identity of the latter being known to the former. The mediator acts as a friend to both in the delicate negotiations.

The role of mediator or, for that matter, that of friend anywhere along the network between victim and thief, is not without its dangers. Often one doubts if he can trust his friend, and information given to a friend can result in reprisal. A friend to one man may be a spy to another. One shepherd expressed it this way: "Friendship is fine, but there are dangers also. There have been many killings because of this, because of spies. It is fine for a friend to say that somebody stole the animals, and the thief says, 'Yes, I have the animals, here they are,' but then the spy gets shot." The goal, obviously, is to effect an agreement suitable to all, so that a "friend" is not considered a spy or traitor by a disgruntled participant.

Accommodation

An accommodation (*acconzamentu*) is the Sard term for a verbal agreement between disputants to resolve their dispute amicably, with or without the aid of Sard mediators, conciliators, or arbitrators, and without recourse to the state authorities. It is also the term for the final agreement itself. Accommodation is closely related to friendship: it is the hoped-for result of the processes of friendship and depends upon it for its effectiveness. Simultaneously, a successful accommodation creates a new, or recreates an old, relation of friendship between the disputants. If an accommodation is to occur, the victim and the thief must be able to communicate, if not directly, then through intermediaries. The contact may be initiated by either the victim or the thief, but in either case it is established through the mechanisms, idiom, and ideology of amistade.

If no contact is made—because the thief either had to flee unsuccessfully without any animals, or fled too successfully and does not wish to negotiate with the victim, no dispute can be said to exist between them and no accommodation will occur. Accommodation, then, occurs when the parties are in contact, through a situation of apprehension *in flagrante;* through successful searches and inquiries on the part of the victim, soci, or barracelli, utilizing friendship networks; or through the efforts of the thief himself to initiate contact, also through friendship networks.

These accommodations are patterned forms of behavior which occur within the framework of Sard pastoral culture and society. They emerge from the indigenous system of values and social relationships, and reflect the real economic and ecological facts of life. They are forms of settlement between people who share the same basic outlook and values and recognize that they live in the same society—*in* it not only physically, as the carabinieri do, but morally, emotionally, economically. The people making the accommodations live and work in the same society. So do their children, parents, brothers, cousins, friends. The well-being of the shepherds depends directly on the opinion others have of them. They are vulnerable to attack because they own animals, a form of wealth which is highly vulnerable. Consequently, they are willing to employ the institution of accommodation, even though, as we shall see, it often is not equally advantageous to both parties to a dispute.

The fact that disputing parties agree to an accommodation implies that all are reasonably satisfied with its outcome, even if each party is not equally happy with the degree of his gain or loss. The pessimistic outlook of the Sard shepherd predisposes him to expect less than the best solution. Even if one party feels that the details of the accommodation are not in his favor, he recognizes that, given the circumstances, the result is the best he can obtain.

The type of accommodation achieved may be related to factors of relative power (measured by the ability to inflict damage) and consequently to relative bargaining power, as well as to situational factors. Thus, while each accommodation is similar to others of its type in broad structural features, each is unique in content as a result of the differential situational factors associated with it. In this way the Sard legal institution of accommodation is directly related to economic, political, and cultural factors and is, therefore, closely attuned to the reality of the relations between the disputants, unlike proceedings carried out in the state courts.

Some accommodations are relatively advantageous either to the thief or the victim (asymmetrical accommodation), while others are more equally balanced in terms of cost and gains for both parties (symmetrical accommodation). The agreements finally hammered out also depend on such factors as the length of time that has elapsed between a theft and a confrontation; the relative costs to each party; and, most importantly, whether or not the thief has been able to conceal his identity and the whereabouts of the stolen animals.

Some accommodations are effected immediately between victim and thief when the thief is caught in the act. Usually in this situation the thief is allowed to flee as long as he leaves the animals to be restored to their owner. The victim keeps his animals and, as he has not been greatly inconvenienced, he is content to allow the thief to leave unharmed. Barracelli typically behave the same way. Their goal is to prevent theft, not to punish thieves.

Most accommodations occur some time after the theft. In one type, the thief is discovered, either through physical clues or through friendship networks. In such a case the thief must return the stolen animals, as he has been caught with the goods. He does not have the moral support of the community, as he obviously is not a successful thief. Because the victim has suffered through the loss of his animals and access to their products while he has had to continue to pay rent for pastures, the thief is expected to return the stolen animals plus a number of his own, often double the number of animals stolen, depending on the extent of the victim's loss. The accommodation may be effected through the barracelli or sos homines, or through negotiation or mediation. The outcome in all cases is affected by the willingness of the thief to comply with the conditions of the agreement which, in turn, is affected by his assessment of the dangers to himself if he does not comply.

Barracelli often enforce this type of accommodation, as their presence in a case means, first of all, that the supposed thief has been found out. The successful thief initiating contact with the victim for purposes of extortion would not bring in the barracelli. The presence of the barracelli tips the balance in the victim's favor. He is no longer relying only upon his core action set but upon the whole moral force of the village community on his behalf. Often the barracelli themselves arbitrate the details of the terms, or they may play a more passive role, allowing the thief and victim to negotiate in their presence. The exact nature of the participation of the barracelli in this type of accommodation varies with the circumstances, but in all cases their presence supports the position of the victim.

This kind of accommodation is not limited to situations in which the barracelli are present. However, the ability of a victim to enforce the terms of an accommodation is problematic if he is engaged in a dyadic (one-to-one) relation with the thief.

In the other type of asymmetrical accommodation, that favorable to the thief, the outcome is what may be called extortionate. In this situation, the thief has successfully hidden the stolen animals and his own identity. He is in a strong bargaining position because the victim is in no position to retake his own animals or retaliate against the animals of the thief.

After a waiting period, the thief initiates contact with the victim through his network of friends and intermediaries, or he allows his friends and intermediaries to be approached by the investigating friends of the victim. The typical result of the ensuing negotiations is that the stolen animals are returned to the victim, who pays a sizable sum of money to the thief. Obviously this type of accommodation occurs only when the thief is willing to return the animals to the owner for a price. In reality, of course, thieves often steal to keep and use the animals themselves, consume them, or sell them to "fences." In such cases, no dispute exists between the thief and victim if the identity of the former is not known to the latter.

A number of variables may affect the relative positions of strength and thus the outcome of accommodations, but the factors that seem to be most salient and most consistent in my data are whether or not the thief has been successful in eluding pursuit or unmasking; the relative degree of cost expended by both parties; and the relative ability of each party to retaliate or escalate the conflict, that is, the relative vulnerability of each party to reprisal.

No matter what the variables, however, and no matter what the situation, an accommodation of some sort is the valued goal of participants and the shepherding community as a whole. Disputes of this sort should be settled "among friends," or "among ourselves." Recourse to the state authorities is considered to be wrong, except by the barracelli under certain circumstances (for example, if a thief has failed to carry out the terms of an accommodation felt to be reasonable). Recourse to state authorities is considered a dangerous escalation of the conflict by introduction of a new and forbidden weapon, not an attempt to resolve it, and therefore it calls for retaliation.

FACTORS RELATING TO USE OF THE SARD LEGAL SYSTEM

Ecological Factors

The nature of Sard pastoralism—the use of wild, unimproved pastures in mountain, foothill, and lowland areas; the inadequacy and insufficiency of pastures in any given area; the prevailing land tenure system, whereby shepherds do not own most of the land they need—results in widespread and far-ranging movements of men and animals. This means that a shepherd must be concerned about his personal reputation and social networks over large areas of the island, not merely in his own village. He is dependent upon the friendship and goodwill of others throughout the zone of his activity as well as in future potential zones of activity.

Because of the prevalence of nucleated settlements and the need for the shepherd to be constantly with his animals as they graze, the shepherd spends long periods of time in the country. Here local law, not state law, prevails. Furthermore, the police of the state legal system cannot protect the shepherd in the country, while the shepherds' system can if he obeys its rules. He is less vulnerable to attack if he has an honorable reputation, which he is unlikely to have if he resorts to the state legal system inappropriately.

While transhumance creates and necessitates social networks that can be mobilized when needed within the shepherds' legal system, the constant movement of men and animals creates and aggravates the bitter relations between the shepherds and the state authorities. The latter are frustrated by the mobility of the shepherds and find them difficult to control. Their attempts at regulation cause bitterness among the shepherds.

Because of the nature of Sard pastoralism and the geography, livestock theft is both possible and frequent. Animals cannot always be guarded. It is always possible to steal *somebody's* animals, when the opportunity presents itself to the ever-alert and peripatetic shepherds. Because livestock theft is such a constant fact of life, it has to be dealt with in such a way that neither it nor the efforts made to cope with it disrupt excessively the pastoral community's social and economic life.

Because of the ecological as well as the social and cultural situation, the carabinieri are not able to function well in cases of livestock theft and disputes over animals. Police are efficient in coping with auto theft, and in such situations shepherds turn to them for aid, but the geography of Sardinia renders them relatively ineffectual in cases of livestock theft. This fact is another reason why shepherds avoid use of the state legal system. Its use carries negative sanctions and is relatively less productive.

Land in Sardinia is limited, but animals are not. The path to social and economic power lies through conversion of wealth in livestock into wealth in land. This has long been accomplished, and continues to be accomplished, by theft of animals.

Sardinia is poor, and there has always been an impetus to steal, not only for purposes of advancement, but also for purposes of survival. Consequently, there is, except in special cases, considerable sympathy for those who engage in livestock theft. This sympathy results in strong support for amicable settlements of disputes over animals, rather than recourse to the state system with its prison sanctions.

Because of transhumance, a shepherd cannot safely ignore the feelings of a man who lives far from him. He may have to visit that man's home village, and that man may come to visit his home village. His relatives, friends, and neighbors may have friendly relations with this stranger. In this way, both the actuality and potentiality of social links exist between individuals throughout the island. Within this far-flung community, determined socially and culturally rather than geographically, the mechanisms and institutions of the Sard legal system operate.

Social Factors

Disputants over livestock conceive of themselves as members of a community ("we shepherds"), though shepherds from other villages are not considered to be as close as shepherds from the same village, unless special ties exist between them. It is noteworthy that a feature of dispute settlement is the establishment of peace and friendship between the parties, symbolically creating close ties where they did not exist before. Thus, Sard shepherds fit into the general model relating to the tendency toward amicable restitutive settlements within tightly knit communities. In Sardinia, however, the community is not limited to the village boundaries but corresponds to the shepherds' social map of the countryside.

While ongoing face-to-face relations typically do not exist between disputants, their potentiality is recognized. Additionally, pressure to settle disputes comes from those who *are* members of the village and in daily face-to-face relation with the disputants. Because of collective responsibility, retaliation against anybody within a village is common. If the victim of theft knows only that the thief is from a certain village, he retaliates by stealing from anybody there. Since all are vulnerable to such reprisals, all exert pressure on the individual disputant to enter into negotiations and make mutually acceptable arrangements, knowing that general escalation of thievery may result from failure to negotiate.

An important social factor which supports the use of amicable accommodations within the Sard legal system is that the mechanism and process which brings the disputants together—amistade—involves many links along the social network of the pastoral community. For example, the victim receives his information concerning the thief from others, who would not have provided the information unless they trusted the victim to settle amicably rather than resorting to the state legal system. To call for arrest is to embroil one's informants.

Shepherds are mutually dependent upon each other. Their dependence is both positive (the need for mutual services, actual and potential) and negative (restraints against theft of each other's sheep). Shepherds need information, help in crises, routine help at certain periods of the annual cycle, and suitable mates for their children. Because of these needs they must maintain honorable reputations.

The shepherd who maintains an honorable reputation receives positive sanctions. If he does not he is ostracized, shunned, not helped when he needs it. Worse, he is vulnerable to attack. One important criterion of honor is predictability. One should be able to predict that another will be willing to effect accommodations when a dispute occurs, and not resort to the state legal system when that is inappropriate. To do so is to disturb the system of expectations one has concerning his fellows.

Cultural Factors

Due to the numerous reasons for the sympathetic attitude toward the livestock thief, there is strong pressure to effect amicable settlements in disputes over animals. The victim, unconcerned with the righteous desire for retributive justice, is content to have his animals restored to him. The shepherd is not always indifferent to matters of abstract justice. On the contrary, when his honor is offended he seeks vindication, not an accommodation. Livestock theft, however, does not constitute an offense to one's honor in the shepherd's legal and value systems. Consequently, he is not interested in punishing the thief, but in restoring his property.

The shepherd's self-perception and his perception of the personnel of the state legal system also are of crucial importance in his general avoidance of the state legal system. The shepherd views all shepherds, no matter how much he may compete with them for scarce resources, as fellows. He views the police and court officials as threatening outsiders.

Retaliation

The essential factor in the shepherd's use of the Sard legal system, however, is that all sides to a dispute over livestock are economically and physically vulnerable to retaliation and escalation if they do not settle harmoniously. Even the rich and powerful, as is illustrated in the case of Zuanne's stolen sheep, are vulnerable. All are shepherds or own animals, which can be stolen or killed. Unlike the police, even the barracelli are vulnerable to vendetta if they break the pastoral code by resorting to the state with its prison sanctions.

SUMMARY AND CONCLUSION

Pastoralism is an important aspect of the Sardinian rural economy. Many thousand shepherds care for the approximately 3,000,000 sheep and 400,000 goats, which form about one-third of the Italian total, in addition to large numbers of cattle and pigs. Many of these shepherds are transhumant; they move seasonally with their flocks and herds from their homes in the mountainous interior, often to distant lowland pastures throughout the island, forming, in the process, a perpetual movement of men and animals.

Because of the nature of the Sard topography and other ecological factors, the threat of livestock theft is ever present. At the same time that each shepherd must cope with the threat of theft of his own animals, a variety of factors operates to encourage him to steal the animals of his fellow shepherds.

While animal theft is generally regarded as justified under certain conditions, it is recognized by the pastoral community that such theft can be the source of interpersonal and intercommunal strife, with the danger of escalation from mutual theft to quarrels, feuds, and violence. Consequently, the Sard shepherd community has evolved a number of institutions and processes, within its indigenous legal-political system, to regulate livestock theft and to minimize the risk of escalation.

The indigenous shepherds' legal system has a range of roles, mechanisms, procedures, norms, values, rules, and agencies for dealing with disputes over livestock theft. Groups that can be activated to cope with problems concerning animal theft range from ego-centered action sets to voluntary mutual aid societies organized on a group or village basis, to village-wide livestock insurance associations that have police powers, to respected elders who are mobilized to intervene between the disputants. The disputes themselves can be handled by direct negotiation between disputants or by mediation, conciliation, or arbitration.

Institutions that can be mobilized in the indigenous legal system include amistade (networks of friends) and acconzamentu (the ritualized amicable settlement of disputes). The actors participating in these institutions are guided by a clearly defined system of rules for appropriate behavior in disputes over livestock. At the same time, the rules are flexible as to the *content* (who gets what) of settlements in order to reflect actual or potential positions of power, while the *structure* (the form or procedure) of the dispute management process is fairly uniform. Regardless of the specific details of individual cases, the goal of participants within the indigenous legal system is to effect amicable settlements, which, while not necessarily regarded as "just" by all disputants, are accepted by them as reasonable and realistic attempts to restore harmony. The goal is to avoid escalation either from the feared state legal system or from feuds between the disputants.

The Sard shepherds' legal system, viewed by the pastoral community as legitimate and competent, is, however, an informal legal system in that it is not recognized or granted official status by the Italian state legal system, which insists upon exclusive jurisdiction over disputes involving animals and livestock theft. The state legal system has its own roles, mechanisms, procedures, norms, values, rules, and agencies for dealing with these disputes. State military police are given the responsibility of preventing livestock theft and arresting thieves. They engage in periodic patrols to search for offenders and stolen animals. State courts are empowered to adjudicate disputes over livestock, both civil and criminal. Police and other judicial actors within the state legal system define livestock theft as a crime rather than merely as a dispute between individuals, which is the shepherds' view.

Ideally, the Sard shepherd who is a disputant in a case involving animals is free to choose to use either or both legal systems. In fact, however, a number of constraints act upon his freedom of choice. The state legal system defines some of the procedures used in the shepherds' legal system as illegal. Nevertheless, the Sard shepherd almost always prefers to ignore the apparatus of the state legal system and to mobilize that of the indigenous system. A range of ecological, economic, cultural, and social factors act as constraints upon the shepherd's freedom of choice and cause him to resort to his own legal system in disputes over livestock.

NOTES

1. The fieldwork upon which this paper is based took place in Sardinia from August 1972 to June 1973. I also engaged in fieldwork in Sardinia during the summers of 1969 and 1970. Funds for this research were obtained mainly from the National Institute of General Medical Sciences, Training Grant Number GM-1224. Field work in 1970 was also funded by the Wenner-Gren Foundation for Anthropological Research, and the University of California, Berkeley. I gratefully acknowledge these sources of support. My fieldwork took place in the Barbagia and in the foothills to the west. Because the subject matter of this paper is a delicate one, I have decided to change the names of the villages in which I worked, as well as the names of the people who participated in the case discussed. This decision means that I cannot thank by name those men and women who so kindly and generously helped me in the field. They were many, and my debt to them is immense. I am also grateful to

Laura Nader, Harry Todd, and Grace Buzaljko for reading and commenting on earlier drafts of this paper.

2. Over the last few decades the official figures for the number of sheep in Sardinia have fluctuated between about 2,500,000 and 3,000,000. As of the 1961 census, there were 2,860,000 sheep, 31.2 percent of the national total; 408,000 goats, 29.8 percent of the national total; and about 200,000 cattle, 2.1 percent of the national total (Brigaglia 1971: 173). Figures on the number of shepherds vary considerably. Luca Pinna (1971: 46) speaks of 60,000. Mori (1966: 413–14) mentions 50,000. Later figures cite 23,000 shepherding "firms," with 35,000 shepherds (*La Nuova Sardegna*, November 2, 1972, p. 3).

3. In Nuoro province, where the Barbagia is located, about 60 percent of land used for pastures is rented by shepherds, while only 40 percent belongs to the shepherds themselves (*La Nuova Sardegna*, November 2, 1972, p. 3).

4. The population of the island as a whole is 1,300,000 (L. Pinna 1971: 45).

5. This case, designed to be illustrative, is taken from an actual case that is recorded in my field notes. The actual case as reported here, however, begins essentially where Ziu Pepe enters the picture. The material prior to that is taken from other cases in my data. Some of these events were witnessed by me. The others were reported to me by informants. The processes described in this illustrative case are typical, as exemplified by numerous other cases and written sources.

6. This paper focuses on livestock theft rather than on the total range of disputes in pastoral Sardinia. Livestock theft is of major importance, and a study of processes concerning it leads inexorably to a study of much of the society as a whole. The institutions and processes described in this paper are often utilized in other kinds of disputes, such as abusive pasturage (trespassing). Because of the focus on disputes over theft of animals, the paper ignores the role of women, as the latter play no significant role in this area of disputing in the Barbagia.

7. Antonio Pigliaru, until his recent death, was a legal scholar at the University of Sassari, born in the Barbagia. He described a putative shepherds' legal system, with its own norms, values, personnel, procedures, and sanctioned by feud and vendetta. Pigliaru postulated a shepherds' legal code of twenty-three articles. The first ten consisted of general principles (e.g., an offense must be vindicated). The second part, consisting of seven articles, described offenses. Livestock theft is not regarded as an offense. The third part, six articles, dealt with vendetta (Brigaglia 1971: 194–97).

Gonario Pinna, a practicing lawyer with many years' experience defending shepherds from his native Barbagia, has also written extensively on the topic of the Sard shepherds' legal system and their legal attitudes and values. His writings, more empirical and detailed, and well rooted in the daily social and economic life of the shepherds, support the thesis of Pigliaru.

8. I do not mean to imply that all Sard shepherds are livestock thieves. First of all, the fact that a shepherd does not view livestock theft as a crime does not necessarily mean he indulges in it himself. The attitudes and practices described here are

well documented for many transhumant shepherds from the Barbagia. Even among them, however, there are many shepherds who consider themselves, and are regarded by others, as "serious" and "honest." While some shepherds freely admitted to me that they stole, or had stolen when they were younger, most spoke of *others* as thieves (usually those of other villages, while the shepherds of their own village had given up animal theft). Values are complex and situational. The same informant may, under different circumstances, express widely divergent opinions on the same topic. But, granted that not all Sard shepherds, or even most of them, are thieves, the evidence is strong that most shepherds of the Barbagia would adhere to the values described in this section concerning *other* shepherds who *do* steal animals.

9. The present law concerning the barracelli, a revision of earlier ones, was written in 1898.

EIGHT

DISPUTE SETTLEMENT AND DISPUTE PROCESSING IN ZAMBIA: INDIVIDUAL CHOICE VERSUS SOCIETAL CONSTRAINTS

Richard S. Canter

THIS PAPER analyzes choice making in the law in the Lenje chieftaincy of Mungule, situated in the Central Province of Zambia. Choice making will be examined from the point of view of the individual and the societal constraints that circumscribe and sometimes directly inhibit his legal options.[1]

In order to explore the interacting elements of individual remedy agent choice and societal constraints, I have found it necessary to distinguish between dispute settlement and dispute processing. By dispute settlement I mean the form of resolution (conciliation, mediation, or adjudication) which individuals choose in order to terminate a conflict, at least in its present manifestations. All other things being equal, the form of dispute settlement chosen by an individual relates to the strength or weakness of his local-level kinship, his residential and social networks.

Legal networks in Mungule are egocentric, and they do not exist in an ongoing form. They arise extemporaneously through links that an individual maintains within the chieftaincy. Corporate groups (family, village, chieftaincy) are part of an individual's legal network, but the network generally also contains noncorporate links that an individual can activate. These will be examined below.

The corporate nature of an individual's legal network is most clear in intrafamily disputes. In nonfamily disputes the corporate character of the legal network is less distinct. Yet, despite the varied nature of these networks, all public remedy agents represent corporate units. This generalization brings us to the second feature of Mungule law and society to be examined: dispute processing.

Dispute processing relates to the total range of accepted remedy agents conceived and used by the people of Mungule. Whereas dispute settlement focuses on the form chosen to settle a conflict, dispute processing examines the process followed to reach a particular form of resolution. I will explore the possibility that the dispute processing system has been adapted to reinforce boundary maintenance, that is, to force individuals to process if not settle disputes within significant corporate group boundaries that form the basis of local-level political power. In short, each higher level of the dispute processing system supports the jural authority of lower levels, thereby maintaining the strength of lower-level corporate units.

THE SETTING

Chief Mungule's area lies immediately northwest of the Zambian capital of Lusaka. An area of 532 square miles, it is one of six chieftaincies of the Lenje-speaking peoples of the Central Province. The eastern border of Mungule is formed by the railway line which connects the cities of Livingstone in the south and Lusaka in the east with the copper belt in the north. The chieftaincy has been affected by its closeness to this main transportation artery of central Africa ever since the construction of the railroad in the first decade of the twentieth century.

According to initial estimates of the latest Zambian census (1969), the population of Mungule was nearly 28,000 people. This is almost double that given in the 1963 census, which reported the population as 15,636 (Regional Plan for the Mungule Area: 4). In terms of ethnicity 65 percent of the population are indigenous Lenje; 35 percent are peoples of other ethnic origins from elsewhere in Zambia and central Africa who have migrated to Mungule since the early 1950s because of the area's potential for cash cropping.

The major cash crop of Mungule is maize. For most Lenje it is the only cash crop. Maize is sold to the government in standardized bags that hold thirty-seven pounds of shelled maize. Cash crop production varies from year to year depending on the weather. The average production of maize for male heads of household in my census sample varied from 29.5 bags in a poor year to 65.4 bags in a good year. Today, planting is done almost exclusively with oxen. Few farmers use fertilizer; almost all practice crop rotation, alternating different crops from year to year.

Cattle keeping in Mungule, like most areas of Zambia, is not directed to the sale of cattle for cash income. They are kept for potential cash security, for use in ceremonies, and for bride-wealth payments. The Lenje claim that formerly they had much larger herds but that as a result of endemic cattle rustling and decreased grazing land, their herds are smaller today. My own census sample showed an average of 8.6 cattle per Lenje household and 10.4 per non-Lenje household.

Nonagricultural enterprises in Mungule include stores, bars, and grinding mills. The owners of these enterprises are also part-time farmers. Small stores sell staple goods of salt, sugar, kerosene, bread, and limited types of canned goods. Most large stores sell soft drinks and bottled beer as well.

Most government services have their headquarters in the chief's village, located on the area's main graded road, which connects with the all-weather Great North Road. In the chief's village are the local court for the chieftaincy, the only medical clinic, the main bus stop, the only gas pump, and the main depot of the Grain Marketing Board.

Although the Lenje infer that the entire Lenje group migrated from the Congo, linguistic and cultural evidence implies a long history of residence in the Central Province of Zambia. In the main, Lenje oral tradition focuses on the arrival in what is now the Central

Province of the legendary Chief Mukuni, who is said to have been of Luba origin and to have come from the Congo. Portuguese sources mention the presence of a Chief Mukuni in that area as early as the seventeenth century. A century later other Portuguese sources refer to trade with the "Arenje," a name that appears to be a corruption of Lenje (Sutherland-Harris 1970: 231–42). Linguistically, the Lenje are classified with their neighbors, the Ila and the Tonga, as the Bantu Botatwe (the three peoples) (Torrend 1931). This classification denotes only a dialect difference between the three groups, suggesting long-term residence and contract. From archaeological evidence it has been established that the Tonga, the Lenje's southern neighbors, have resided in the Southern Province of Zambia for perhaps 1,000 years (Fagan 1966: 93). Historically, the most striking feature of Tonga political organization is its lack of centralized authority. It seems highly unlikely that a group like the Lenje, had they arrived with a centralized form of political organization, would have adopted the language of a politically decentralized neighboring people.

Further evidence that the Lenje are long-time residents of Zambia's Central Province, and not unlike their neighbors, can be gleaned from an examination of their nineteenth-century political organization. Though characterized by centralized, hereditary leadership, precolonial Lenje political organization bears some striking resemblances to the acephalous structure of the Tonga society. The basic organization of the Mungule chieftaincy indicates the possibility that the Mukuni conquest imposed hereditary leadership on a preexisting Tonga-like society, organized on a village, neighborhood, and clan basis.

In precolonial times, before British control, the Mungule chieftaincy was organized under the *chumbu* (area of power) system. The chumbu was a group of villages whose headmen recognized the overriding authority of the chumbu leader, who resided in one of the four to seven villages that comprised his area of power. Chumbu leaders, who in turn recognized the authority of the chief, were believed to be descendants of the first person to migrate to the area.

If the concept of chieftaincy was imposed by the people of Mukuni on a preexisting Lenje form of social organization, the linguistic and social structural affinity between the Tonga and the Lenje becomes more understandable. The most likely explanation for the similarities between the two groups is that they have both long resided in Zambia as neighbors but were affected differently by the historical events of the fifteenth to seventeenth centuries.

Although my informants speak of Mukuni's residence among the Lenje as though it encompassed a single chief's lifetime, I suspect that the events attributed to Mukuni involve the succession of a number of men who inherited the title. In any case, legend in Mungule has it that at some point Mukuni departed from Lenjeland to become chief of the Toka-Leya near Victoria Falls. Brelsford (1965: 72) also verifies the Toka-Leya's belief in this event from the present Chief Mukuni of the Toka-Leya.

The departure of Mukuni from Lenjeland, if we interpret the legend literally, or a change in the nature of political power, if we interpret the events figuratively, may in either case correlate with the beginning of trade relations between the Lenje and the Portuguese. At some point the Mukuni chieftaincy became decentralized and his administrators/chiefs established independent local power. This may have been in the eighteenth century, when Portuguese trade in copper, slaves, and ivory enhanced the power of the local administrators by making it advantageous for the groups under their administration to have centralized trade centers (chiefs' villages). It may have been at this point in time that the six independent Lenje chieftaincies emerged (Mungule, Chitanda, Chipepo, Chamuka, Liteta, and Mukubwe).

The concept of chieftaincy among the Lenje seems well established in the nineteenth century, and yet there was a strong distinction between the Benemukuni (the rulers from outside) and the Lenje (the ruled). From informants who describe life in precolonial Mungule, one gets the impression of people well aware of having a chief but in their day-to-day existence somewhat remote from his view as well as his authority. People talk of a two-day walk to the chief's village, where they went to settle important cases and exchange ivory and slaves for trade goods brought by the Mbundu of Angola. Day-to-day life seems to have focused on the village and the chumbu (Lenje institutions), while the chieftainship (a Benemukuni institution) was recognized but not of daily importance. Eventually these local administrators of the Benemukuni amassed sufficient local-level power to become independent chiefs. They in turn, during the nineteenth century, began to expand their domains within and without the Central Province through satellite communities under subchiefs.

Whatever the exact relationship between the Benemukuni and the Lenje in pre-European times, the Lenje were forced to work through Benemukuni leaders in order to cope with the superordinate authorities of the British colonial system. This may have given the Benemukuni a "structural" strength that they did not enjoy before European conquest. By the same token, as the Benemukuni took on an undisputed, integral political role in colonial times, there was less reason for them to emphasize the differences between themselves and the Lenje. The concept of hereditary leadership assured Benemukuni succession. Today there is no distinction between these formerly separate groups, mostly because in the twentieth century their interests have become indistinguishable.

KINSHIP AND DESCENT

The following is a brief description of the groups formed by Lenje concepts of kinship and descent. By *kinship,* I mean the group which is formed with reference to an ego, and determined by his recognition of relatives whom he considers to be members of his primary kinship network. Since kinship networks are egocentric, membership and status are variable. By *descent* I mean the group formed with reference to an ancestor, connecting only a limited number of ego's relatives. Here membership and status are absolute. With this distinction, Lenje kinship, like all kinship, can be characterized as bilateral, and Lenje descent as matrilineal. Bilateral kinship obtains from the principle of the *lekoto,* best translated as the family. Matrilineal descent obtains from the principle of the *bashikamukowa,* best translated as the clan. For any given ego the recognition of his lekoto is flexible, while recognition of his bashikamukowa is fixed.

Within the Lenje system of kinship and descent, ego's primary status is determined by his mother's bashikamukowa; his father's mukowa is important but secondary. With exceptions that will be detailed below, ego's mother's bashikamukowa determines his name, inheritance rights, and incest rules and his rights and status vis-à-vis other Lenje and sometimes non-Lenje. His father's clan, though less important, participates in his life crises and the division of his estate and in defining his social responsibilities.

In spite of the importance of the matrilineal line, Lenje kinship behavior exhibits an increasingly bilateral tendency. This tendency is rationalized by the Lenje as both recent and idiosyncratic. Each case of non-bashikamukowa inheritance is described as unique. Though a man may favor transferring a good deal of property to his son, he expresses this decision as his unique choice. Culturally he will uphold the predominance of bashikamukowa inheritance. One gets the strong impression that the Lenje carry in their minds a matrilineal model that is scarcely affected by actual cases of bilateral inheritance.

In terms of residence this paradox is even more striking. Though the Lenje say they are eclectic in residence rules, they claim a basic matrilocal orientation. However, my census data reveal that matrilocal residence hardly exists. No woman head of household in the census was residing in the village of her birth. Some female non-heads of households were, but they were sisters of headmen and therefore categorized themselves as dependents. The situation might best be summed up by classifying the Lenje as matrilineal in terms of belief and bilateral in terms of behavior.

Though matrilineal in belief, Lenje kinship principles show a high degree of flexibility, which allows continuity in belief as well as adaptability in usage. Here I will focus on the power kindred, a kinship unit that goes undefined by the Lenje, but one that I believe has evolved as a political unit through the manipulation of contemporary kinship principles. The power kindred is an extended family unit originally associated with descent from a chumbu leader. By its control of village fission it has extended its territorial control over large areas of Mungule by allowing breakaway villages to be formed only by bashikamukowa and lekoto members of the founder of an original village. Inheritance of village headmanships, like inheritance of names, is ideally matrilineal (brother or sister's son or sister's daughter's son). Patrilineal and affinal fission occurs from father to son and sister's brother to sister's husband; yet after one or two generations inheritance reverts to brother or sister's son or sister's daughter's son. Today the matrilineal descent principle has been reinstated as the office of village headman passes from generation to generation.

A contemporary function of the power kindred is to staff offices not associated with the traditional political organization. For instance, the two elected officials of the local court are members of two of the dominant power kindreds in Mungule. Their tenure is dependent on nomination by the chief, approval of the people, and agreement of the government. They must be reaffirmed every three years by popular vote. To ensure continued support of their candidates in government offices, power kindreds form many local-level alliances, which link the Lenje elite into mutually dependent political networks.

CONTEMPORARY POLITICAL ORGANIZATION

Political networks are an adaptation to the political and economic changes brought on by the colonial and independence governments. During the twentieth century the locus of power within the chieftaincy has changed, but the change has been within a narrow range of roles and offices almost exclusively controlled by the Lenje elite. In its simplest form the power structure is a political network involving the roles and offices of chief, headman, and important power kindreds represented by former chumbu leaders. From this network are recruited the personnel who inherit traditional offices and who staff the new offices that are part of the bureaucratic structure of the Zambian nation-state.

During the early stages of my fieldwork in Mungule, my interest in law and politics led me to observe almost exclusively the power positions of chief, headmen, and power kindred leaders. Although the traditional power elite was the most obvious local-level political force, I expected that by 1970 there might be significant new political networks, economic interest groups, or factions made up of immigrants or the more educated younger members of the chieftaincy—people who were not associated with traditional roles and offices. There were, but they lacked significant political power, and had absolutely no jural authority.

The Power Elite

Rapid social and economic change throughout this century has reinforced the power potential of traditional roles and offices. Faced with rapid change, the traditional elite by its adaptability has maintained its prominent position by absorbing into preexisting roles and offices the power contingencies of a changing rural society.

Through mutual support, the traditional power elite has monopolized and maintained local-level power in the following spheres: (1) influence, (2) land allocation, (3) control of village fission, (4) village residence, (5) political privilege, and (6) national government support. All the above give the Lenje elite the edge in maintaining old and adapting to new forms of local-level power.

In a milieu of rapid change, mutual support might also be seen as mutual dependence. Some of the more obvious support/dependence relationships are the following: The chief is dependent on chumbu leaders and village headmen to help him implement national government policy decisions. In turn, the chief must have government support in order to ensure his position. Though the office of chief seems highly esteemed among the people, individuals who occupy the office are not assured of continuous tenure. In 1957 the then Chief Mungule was deposed. In 1971 an attempt was made to depose the new chief. The chief has become dependent on the local court members because they are the only office holders who are backed by the force of the national government. Court members in turn depend on the chief for nomination and support. Village headmen must seek the chief's approval to expand their power base and that of their heirs. Headmen and family authorities need the sanction of the court to maintain and back their jural authority.

With the exception of that of the village headman, all local-level roles and offices are constitutionally defined. But no constitution can define how roles and offices will be adapted by individuals who are the products of a variety of forms of local-level political organizations and different economies and who have experienced varying degrees of social change.

In Mungule, the Lenje elite has adapted to change by monopolizing political power. It has done so by maintaining the locus of power within a small range of roles associated with tradition. Power is monopolized over the 35 percent of the population which is not Lenje, and over Lenje who do not have traditional rights to local power. During the past half-century, under different forms of superordinate political control and within a rapidly changing social and economic environment, rarely has this monopoly been broken.

The Judicial System

A description of the Zambian judicial system, which is supported by the national government, is only a partial description of the legal levels considered by an aggrieved person seeking to process a dispute in Mungule. The government-supported court system consists of a local court for the entire chieftaincy, the magistrates' court, and the high court. For civil cases the local court is the lowest level of the government's judicial hierarchy. Until 1968 the local court was presided over by the chief and two assessors. Today only the two assessors, now called court president and court assessor, hear the cases. Both have been court members since the 1950s. Every three years, they must be renominated by the chief and reelected by the people, and their tenure is subject to the approval of the central government.

The coercive powers of the local court derive from the national government. Primarily, the threat of being cited for contempt of court backs the decisions of the local court. Ultimately, flogging or jail are the little used but real sanctions which cap the authority of its decisions. The will of the court is enforced by two court messengers who are paid by the national government but are under the direction of the court member. Local court decisions may be appealed to the magistrates' court in the urban center of Kabwe. Of the 532 cases that came before the Mungule local court in 1970, twenty were appealed to magistrates' court, and in only one case was the local court's decision overturned. This statistic is not known to the people of Mungule, but the general sentiment exists that for civil cases the local court is in spirit if not in fact the high court of the chieftaincy.

THE DISPUTE-PROCESSING SYSTEM

To a resident of Mungule the dispute-processing system is perceived as a wide range of remedy agents whom he can call upon in hierarchical order before he appeals to the local court. When considering the range of remedy agents available at the local level, I think it is useful to make a distinction between private and public dispute processing (see table 8.1). The distinction relates to the choice between a remedy agent who is not associated with a recurring dispute settlement agency and institutionalized dispute settlement agencies that are associated with family heads, village headmen, and the local

TABLE 8.1
CHOICES IN THE DISPUTE-PROCESSING SYSTEM

Choice	*Remedy Agent*	*Forms of Dispute Settlement*	*Boundary Maintenance**
LOCAL			
	Private Dispute Processing		
1. Ignore conflict	None	None	Avoid
2. Avoid use of third party	Self	Self-help	Defy
3. Avoid use of public forum	Individual with high prestige	Conciliation	Avoid
	Public Dispute Processing		
4. Mubandi (family moot)	Family head or kinship group	Mediation	Reinforce
5. Nkuta (village moot)	Village headman	Mediation	Reinforce
NATIONAL			
6. Local court	Government-supported local judges	Adjudication	Support or maintain
7. Magistrates' court	Government-supported national judges	Adjudication	Restate

* For a discussion of boundary maintenance, see the conclusions to this chapter.

court. Private v. public dispute settlement is further distinguished by whether an individual attempts to mobilize his legal network or attempts to process a dispute without such help.

Private Dispute Processing

Non–Dispute Processing. There is a complex set of motivations which individuals use to justify the nonprocessing of a dispute. Most relate to the social costs the individuals would incur if the case were brought to a public forum, even when there is a high expectation that the decision would go in their favor. Another significant motivation, which is never expressed, is that an individual may be "saving" the dispute for some future case. This is especially true in marital cases. A woman seeking a divorce will catalog a long history of grievances, some of which may have never been aired at a hearing before. I have no way of determining the frequency of this type of choice. By ignoring the conflict the individual receives less public attention, and the dispute often remains strictly private. I did observe enough examples of non–dispute processing to know that it is not a highly unusual occurrence. The following examples will illustrate.

A progressive immigrant farmer had loaned an important traditional political leader about sixty dollars (forty kwacha in 1971) and was promised repayment after the crops were harvested. Four years went by, and repeated requests for repayment were ignored. Since there were several witnesses to the loan, the farmer was sure he could force repayment by bringing the political leader to court. He rationalized his inaction by stating that the consequences that would follow bringing the case to court would cost him more than sixty dollars.

A man traveling in a distant part of the chieftaincy noticed a cow that had been stolen from him a year before. He demanded the return of the cow, but chose not to seek additional compensation for the theft. He claimed that the thief was a clan relative of his senior wife, and that she had prevailed upon him not to press the case.

During a marital dispute a man tied the hands of his wife with a rope and locked her in a hut, where she remained for several hours until his relatives heard her cries and released her. Though marital disputes are common and generally invoke minor interest among outsiders, this case brought a great public outcry because the wife had been tied and locked up. So high was the public indignation that the village headman publicly admonished the husband, and told him what a good case his wife had against him. Six months after this dispute occurred, the wife still had not brought a case against her husband either at the family or village moot or the local court. In the future should the wife seek a divorce she would undoubtedly cite this incident to validate her claim.

Self-Help. There are two types of self-help in dispute processing which occur in Mungule: individual and community-wide. The first type occurs with some regularity; the second type is rare. The frequency of individual self-help can be seen in the high percentage of assault cases which come before the local and village courts. The resort to assault generally negates whatever legitimate grievance a plaintiff might have had against the defendant. The typical part of the decision in an assault case is for the judge to tell the defendant "you had a good case against him, but you took the law in your own hands and now it is you who must compensate him."[2]

Dispute Processing through Third Parties with High Prestige. There are two forms of private dispute processing in which a noninstitutionalized third party is sought but a public forum is avoided. These forms might best be characterized as "conciliation," since the decision is not binding and it avoids public awareness and pressure in the settlement of a dispute. No witnesses are heard, and the decision is pronounced only in the presence of the individuals involved in the dispute. Because of the lack of group participation, this form of dispute settlement offers the greatest potential for compromise.

Almost any individual with high prestige in the traditional or national political structure may be asked to attempt to resolve a dispute that has not yet been brought before a public remedy agent. The choice of a third party with high prestige may depend on some preexisting ethnic, kinship, or social tie with the disputants. Personal acquaintance coupled with high prestige combine to give noninstitutionalized remedy agents effective "personal" power in the processing of a dispute. No fee is expected for conciliation cases. Even local court judges in their off hours attempt to process disputes privately without the enforcement powers that characterize their decisions given from the bench. An attempt at conciliation may be the first step an individual chooses in processing a dispute. If conciliation is unsuccessful, the dispute may move to institutionalized public remedy agents.

Public Dispute Processing

Once an individual decides to bring a dispute to a public forum, societal constraints and expectations shape the process if not the form of dispute settlement. So long as a dispute remains private, the individual has a choice of remedy agents. Once a dispute reaches the public sector a complex set of factors affects the choice-making process.

The most obvious difference between family, village, and local courts is their "technical" enforcement power. Local court decisions are backed by the political force of the nation-state, but family and village decisions are not. I have used the term "technical" enforcement power because, as will be seen below, I have come to believe that the terms "mediation," to characterize family and village dispute settlement, and "adjudication," to describe local court dispute settlement, are useful in general, but they do not denote some of the more subtle aspects of enforcement associated with each type of settlement. Under certain circumstances a mediated family or village settlement can take on aspects that appear more like adjudication, as when a decision is backed with the threat of banishment. Banishment as an implied threat is frequently used in mediated decisions. It may be for a specific time, or forever. In family cases the disputant is usually forced to live with the other side of his family. A typical way this is done can be seen in the following case.

A young man who had been living with his father's matrilineal relatives was believed to have been stealing from them over a period of time. The case came before the local court as a slander case between the young man and his aunt (his father's sister), who had publicly accused him of stealing from her. A witness (the father's brother) told the court what had been decided at the family moot: "What we can only do—this is our only son—if he makes a mistake [steals again] we should say, 'OK, your father's side fails to go along with you. You go and try your mother's side.' Then we send him to his mother's side."

Village banishment operates in the same way but with less consideration. Although all headmen agree that they can banish someone from their villages, the means are idiosyncratic. Ultimately, since banishment is not backed by the national government, a headman generally uses a strategy that involves making a village resident's life so unpleasant that he or she is forced to leave.

The point is that, although family and village decisions are in the main not backed by the political force of the nation-state, mediated decisions can under extreme circumstances be backed with an absolute sanction—banishment, enforced by the family and village members. Likewise the local court, characterized by adjudication, may ignore the political force that underlies its decision-making powers and may render a decision that is left to the enforcement of the aggrieved party (see p. 268 below).

I will now describe and analyze the social process and dispute settlement forms associated with the family and village moots and the local court. I will focus on the role of the third party, the types of inquiry, the procedural style, and actual enforcement powers.

The Family Moot (*Mubandi and Nkuta*). The word *mubandi* is best translated as "discussion." The neutrality of the term belies the forcefulness with which families attempt to settle disputes by this means. The dispute settlement authority of the family derives from traditional and contemporary jural power associated with the bashikamukowa. In the past the bashikamukowa had corporate responsibility for the legal rights and obligations of its members. Today, corporate responsibility might best be expressed as corporate concern. From the point of view of both the individual and the community, corporate concern is assumed. The community will rely upon and sometimes hold responsible the kinship group of an individual embroiled in a dispute.

Today senior kinsmen will consider attempting dispute settlement for members of their lekoto as well as their bashikamukowa. Still, as a corporate group, the bashikamukowa is the only unit which exercises exclusive jural rights. For inheritance the bashikamukowa is considered the only legitimate legal authority. Inheritance cases do come before village and local court, but the cases will involve only a technicality such as who was the rightful owner of a piece of property involved in an estate. In terms of who can inherit what, only the bashikamukowa can decide.[3]

It is the jural authority still vested in the bashikamukowa by the community which underlies its authority as a potential remedy agent beyond inheritance cases. There are two steps that individuals follow when they first attempt to process a family dispute publicly. First, an individual will inform his close relatives of his legal involvement in a dispute. Here he begins to mobilize his legal network for support. It is this step that is called mubandi ("discussion"). It was often unclear to me whether an individual only intended to seek support or whether he or she was asking to have the dispute processed at the family level. The reason individual motivation is unclear is that once senior kinsmen are informed of an intrafamily dispute, they often set the direction of the legal process by advising how the conflict should be handled.

Generally, senior kinsmen advise that all geographically close bashikamukowa and lekoto members be informed that there will be a family hearing at a specific time and place. When this happens, people will refer to the hearing as a family nkuta ("compensation"), the second step in family dispute processing. I have witnessed cases when a mubandi became a nkuta on the spot by the dictates of the senior kinsmen. The only difference I can discern between the social process of mubandi and the legal process of nkuta is that in the former advice is given which sometimes settles a dispute, while in the latter there is an expectation that an actual decision will be forthcoming.

A family nkuta is carried out in a formal setting. In a convenient space in the compound of a senior kinsman, male and female relatives sit in separate groups, more or less in a circle. Senior male kinsmen sit on stools, while younger men and all women sit on the ground. If it is a marital dispute husband's and wife's families are both present. The visual attention of the participants is focused on the senior male kinsmen. The disputants generally sit in front of their senior kinsmen, so that many in the group only see their backs. One senior kinsman presides and attempts to keep order in the sense that he gives everyone who wishes to speak a chance to do so.

First, the disputants give their testimony. No attempt is made to keep them on the issue for which the nkuta was called. All grievances, past and present, are documented, debated, argued, and denied. Everyone present can give his opinion, and it is often difficult to decide whether the participants are testifying or judging the case or cases. No time limit is set on the speeches of the disputants, the witnesses, or the interested parties. Most cases I observed took half a day, and during this time no one was allowed to consume alcohol.

When everyone has had his say, senior kinsmen begin to sum up the case, attempting to draw a consensus from the often diverse opinions of family members. They focus their attention by citing conflicts between the disputants in the past. Eventually they give a definitive opinion that is intended to settle the case of the moment. The decision of the nkuta may involve compensation or it may involve an order, such as, "Go back to your husband," or, "Go see a witch doctor, who will determine if you have charms on your body." Although the decision focuses on the immediate dispute, it not only takes into account the present conflict but attempts to settle past grievances. Family dispute settlement handles conflict over time, and is flexible enough to settle a series of disputes only one of which is the justification for the family nkuta.

Although one senior kinsman presides, it is questionable if he is the third party except in terms of procedure. It might be more correct to view the kinship network as the third party, as the decision reached is likely to be an attempt at mediation based on the consensus of the group. Family decisions are in the main backed by the moral force of the kinship network. Decisions of the mubandi and nkuta are specific as to moral obligations based on kinship. Family loyalty, obligation for past care, sentiment, and shame are the often used arguments in which family decisions are framed. Banishment is the ultimate threat. The senior kinsmen always emphasize that members of the bashikamukowa and lekoto are not supposed to have disputes, and if they do they are supposed to be settled within the group. Although obviously the disputants do not always comply, the relatively low percentage of cases between consanguineals which reach the local court (6 percent; see table 8.3) speaks of a high degree of success in intrafamily dispute settlement through family and village dispute processing.

The above description of family dispute processing describes

Lenje expectations. Mubandi and nkuta are the first steps in public dispute processing. That they will precede village and local court dispute processing is assumed by village headmen and local court members. Since all headmen and court members are Lenje, they expect that members of other ethnic groups will in similar fashion first inform their families and then attempt family dispute settlement, if this is possible, whatever the nature of the primary corporate kinship unit. With many immigrants (e.g., Rhodesians), it is either impossible or impractical because of geographic distance. In such cases the court is more likely to impose an independent decision in a family case, where it is unlikely to do so in cases where individuals have strong local-level kinship networks.

The Village Moot (*Nkuta*). Members of a village are expected to inform village headmen of their extrafamilial legal disputes. Again it is often unclear if a litigant is following expected procedure or is seeking a mediated village settlement. At the time a headman is informed, he may attempt to process the dispute or advise that it be taken to the local court. A headman's offer to mediate is rarely refused by a village resident, whether he intends to appeal the headman's decision or not. Since the headman as remedy agent is also the same person who allocates farmland, determines the grazing area for cattle, tells village members where to build their compounds, and is a potential witness if the case is heard before the local court, it is unlikely that a village resident will reject the headman's offer to mediate.

What is less difficult to assess is the headman's choice of options in dispute processing. Although he may volunteer to mediate a dispute, he may also refuse to do so and may force a case to the local court, in spite of a village resident's desire to have a case mediated. Headmen are likely to reject for mediation the following types of cases: (1) cases involving individuals with extremely close kinship ties who have a long history of conflict; (2) cases involving the headman himself or other members of the political elite; (3) cases in which the headman has insufficient power to summon a party to a case (e.g., one of the litigants lives in an urban area); and (4) disputes that have previously been heard before the local court but have flared up again. The role of the village headman in directing cases toward a mediated or an adjudicated settlement often removes from individual choice the type of settlement which will be achieved. Here choice of remedy agent becomes remedy agent's choice. Like the bashikamukowa in inheritance cases, the village headman has an absolute domain over intravillage land dispute cases. There were no intravillage land dispute cases in the local court sample during the period January 1–April 1, 1971. In fact, land dispute cases in any form rarely go beyond a mediated settlement. This is due to the Lenje belief that only traditional political authorities have the expertise to handle land disputes. Since they allocate land, only they can know the boundaries of an individual's land.

There was only one intervillage land dispute case in my local court sample. Such disputes are handled by the headmen of the two villages if the disputants are not the headmen themselves; by the "council of headmen" if the dispute involves two headmen; and by the chief if it involves the headmen of several villages.[4]

Besides his domain in land disputes, the village headman is a potential remedy agent for all other types of civil cases, including divorce. If a village headman handles a divorce case, the litigants and headman later appear before the local court in chambers, and a certificate of divorce is granted without a formal court hearing.

Though the village moot is in many ways different from the local court, in terms of types of civil cases heard and rules applied to a given dispute, there is otherwise little discernible difference. The social setting within which a village nkuta takes place contrasts with both the family nkuta and the local court. The participants in a family moot are either bashikamukowa or lekoto relatives of the disputants with the exception of a witness or two who may not be relatives. Other village residents avoid a family moot, even when it takes place within view and hearing range; they listen from a discreet distance, but they do not interfere.

At a village moot, however, everyone feels free to participate. Observers may include the kinsmen of both disputants who know the case from either mubandi or family nkuta, any village resident who knows either party, and interested others. This is true for both Lenje and non-Lenje cases.

In an intravillage dispute the village headman invites two other headmen of his choosing; most often one is a former chumbu leader. In intervillage disputes the headmen of the two villages decide between themselves on a third headman, again usually a former chumbu leader. The use of at least three headmen at the village nkuta is said to be a recent innovation dating from the year after independence, 1965. I was told that after independence the chief called the "council of headmen" to a meeting, where he proposed that in the future all village moots include at least three headmen.

The village headman in whose village a case is heard presides over the hearing. The case is heard just outside the village nkuta building which is in the headman's compound. Rarely can this small building, about eight feet in diameter, accommodate the large number of people who choose to observe and participate in the mediation of a dispute.

The hearing begins with the testimony of the plaintiff and then that of the defendant. Again, no attempt is made to keep testimony to the case at hand. Individuals are likely to range widely over past and present issues. In this way the case in point is put in a contextual setting. After the testimony of the disputants, anyone present is free to argue, contradict, elaborate, and put forth tentative solutions. Besides the village headmen, the most prominent participants at the village moot are the local village elders. Most often they include the senior kinsmen of the disputants. Irrespective of kinship relationship, village elders, male and female, Lenje and non-Lenje, discuss the problems of the case with great authority, generally stressing ideal behavior and the need for an agreeable solution. Their opinions seem to carry great weight with the village headmen and the participants in general.

As at the family nkuta, many people who wish to give an opinion do not seek, as the village elders do, to forward a solution. Here, too, individual testimony amounts to individual judgment. Eventually the three headmen discuss publicly the merits of the case. They put forth tentative solutions and assess the reaction of the disputants, their kinsmen, and the observers. Anyone may comment on the tentative decision, though here it seems that the headmen take into consideration the reaction of the disputants' senior kinsmen, who will be important in "enforcing" a mediated decision should the disputants agree. Finally the local headman announces a decision or states that no acceptable decision seems possible. In the latter situation he may advise the plaintiff to buy a summons calling the defendant to the local court; this document will cost him about twenty-five ngwee (forty U.S. cents in 1971). Agreed-upon decisions of the village nkuta do not necessarily signal the settlement of a dispute. Theoretically nothing save social pressure constrains either disputant from having the case heard before the local court.

The Local Court. The most formal setting for dispute settlement in Mungule is the local court, situated in the chief's village. The courthouse, a square, red brick building with a tin roof, is divided into two rooms, the courtroom and the chambers of the court members. The sides of the courtroom have permanent openings, which allow large numbers of people who cannot be seated inside to observe cases from without. I have seen as many as 150 people attending a case, forty seated indoors on wooden benches and the rest grouped around the outside of the building.

In the front of the courtroom is a three-foot high cement platform where the court president and court assessor sit, wearing black robes, on either side of a large photograph of the president of Zambia. At ground level is the desk of the court secretary, who records a synopsis of each case. He sits facing the court members, with his back to the audience. On the opposite side of the desk, facing the observers, sits one of the two court messengers. At the extreme right and left of the courtroom, just behind the court secretary's desk, are two wooden boxes with chest-high railings. In the right box stands the plaintiff, in the left the defendant. They face the court members, their backs to the audience.

The court hears cases three days a week, and processes as many as ten cases in a given day. There is nearly military decorum in the courtroom. Observers must remain silent unless called to testify. Should someone speak up during a hearing, he will be unceremoniously removed from the court. Plaintiff and defendant must stand erect in the boxes. Should they lean on the railing, they will be placed in the correct posture by the court messenger. Everyone present within the courtroom, except the chief should the latter be an observer, must rise at each entrance and exit of the court members. Any defiance of the court's authority can land an individual in the jail, which is conveniently situated fifteen feet from the court. The more casual behavior of participants at family and village moots stands in marked contrast to the formal decorum of the local court.

Equally contrastive is the court procedure. Rarely does the court call more than one or two witnesses, and it is highly unusual for a case to take more than three-quarters of an hour. The reason local court hearings are so brief as compared to family and village moots is that the court will deal with only one dispute at a time. Though the court insists that litigants stick to the case at hand, it does not use the concept of judicial ignorance. The court does use its personal and past knowledge of litigants to determine fault. Statements like the following are commonly made by the court members: "As if you were a person without mistakes!" "You have been married to this woman for a long time; you were her first husband." "Just recently you were accused of adultery with Pauline, the wife of teacher Kapansa."

The court is quite willing to settle a series of disputes between individuals, but the disputes must be brought before the court one at a time. Thus the court has far less flexibility in balancing a whole set of wrongs between litigants than do the family and village moots. The court is aware of this difference and often advises a litigant whose testimony covers several disputes to take his case to a family or village moot.

The court reaches its decisions in private. The court members and the court secretary retire to chambers, and within three to five minutes the members return to render a decision. Once a decision is reached it is up to the litigants to work out compliance with the decision. Since most local court decisions involve compensation, the litigants go outside the court with the court messenger and work out a plan for payment of the compensation. In this way an "adjudicated" decision can become a "compromise in compliance" between the litigants, who are given a decision backed by force, but are left to decide the actual means of compensation themselves. This act shows tremendous variability. If the aggrieved party demands immediate compensation and it is not forthcoming, he can return to the court in a matter of days and charge his opponent with contempt of court. Then, and only then, will the court enforce its decision. During the three-month period I observed the local court, there were only eight contempt of court cases out of a total of 150 cases. These eight cases are not included in the analyzed sample below because they were then classified as criminal cases.

Normally, the litigants agree to a series of payments over a three- to nine-month period. I have limited data, gathered in the summer of 1973, which reveal that for some cases observed in 1971 the compensation had still not been paid. I would say tentatively that the correlation for these data relates to the ties between the litigants; the closer the ties, the less likely it is that compensation will be paid.

For all practical purposes, the local court is the most formal level of dispute settlement in Mungule. Its decisions are backed by force rather than social pressure. Fault is assessed in terms of a specific dispute. For all its formality, local court procedure allows for some flexibility in dispute settlement, since compliance with court decisions is left to the litigants. Thus, even with an adjudicative decision, individuals can, if they so desire, work out a compromise settlement, given the type of relationship they have had in the past or they wish to have in the future.

ANALYSIS OF CASE MATERIAL

Given the different forms of dispute settlement which make up the dispute processing system in Mungule, I will now analyze the cases gathered at the local court to explain the differential use of remedy agents among various groups within the chieftaincy. For civil cases the local court is statistically the last appeal level for the people of Mungule, since few cases go to magistrates' court. I analyzed the cases I observed at the local court for which I interviewed the litigants and cross-checked the data ($N = 79$). The types of cases which made up the local court sample were described by the plaintiff, as shown in table 8.2.

TABLE 8.2
CIVIL CASES BROUGHT BEFORE THE LOCAL COURT, JANUARY 1–APRIL 1, 1971

Divorce	15	Assault	11
Nonsupport	1	Theft	4
Paternity	3	Debt	2
Abduction	5	Slander	8
Rape	1	Cattle trespass	5
Desertion	2	Land rights	1
Inheritance	2	Fraud	1
Sorcery	1	Breach of contract	5
Adultery	11	Negligence	1
		TOTAL	79

Kinship Relations of Litigants

The first question to be asked of the data, in terms of kinship relationship, is simply, who are the people who use the local court? Of the sample 53 percent had no kinship ties, 39 percent were affines, most of whom were involved in marital disputes, and 6 percent were consanguineals.

TABLE 8.3
KINSHIP RELATIONS OF LITIGANTS

None	42
Wife-Husband	19
Husband-Wife	3
Parent-Child	1
Siblings	1
Child-in-law/Parent-in-law	6
Siblings-in-law	3
Cousins	1
Aunt-Nephew	1
Uncle-Nephew	1
Unknown	1
TOTAL	79

Other important findings that emerge from the extended case (N = 52) data give a clearer explanation than the variable of kinship.

Cases between nonkinsmen generally do not have a long history; they are based on relatively short-term conflict. Cases between affines are generally marital cases in which the partners have already attempted conciliation and mediation; adjudication signals a final phase in which one party desires to have the relationship terminated or is threatening termination. Cases between consanguineals which reach adjudication always have a history of long-term conflict which rarely involves the specific issue that brings the case to the local court.

Here it might be useful to note a nonstatistical finding about disputes between consanguineals. I have no way of stating the actual incidence of disputes between close relatives. From observing family and village moots my impression is that they occur not only with a good deal of frequency, but with high frequency. Perhaps this is more understandable when one considers the things that close kinsmen come into conflict about—inheritance of property and, among the Lenje, inheritance of offices. Both types of conflict generate a great deal of hostility that may be manifested in cases other than inheritance. Perhaps the cultural belief that death from witchcraft is likely to occur between members of the bashikamukowa is a reflection of the high potential for conflict between consanguineals. In one case in which the two litigants were sisters, the defendant was accused of having killed her brother-in-law through witchcraft. Her defense was "How could I have bewitched someone who wasn't of my own family [bashikamukowa]?"

Sex of Litigants

The variable of the litigants' sex (table 8.4) shows some interesting patterns, though I believe that it tells us as much about the roles of men and women in Lenje society as it does about choice of remedy agent. Nearly 60 percent of the cases that came to the local court were cases in which both litigants were male. By contrast, in only 5 percent of the cases were both litigants female. In another 5 percent the plaintiff was male and the defendant female, and in 30 percent the plaintiff was female and the defendant male. In this last category, eighteen of the twenty-four cases were brought for divorce. This does not necessarily mean that only women are seeking to terminate a

TABLE 8.4
SEX OF
LITIGANTS

Male-Male	47
Male-Female	4
Female-Female	4
Female-Male	24
TOTAL	79

marriage. Rather it is an implicit cultural belief that the dominant position of men minimizes the possibility that they will find it necessary to take a woman to court. A not atypical example can be seen in the following dialogue between the court president and a husband brought by his wife for a divorce.

C.P.: Not to waste time, I want to find out how many times you have been in court with your wife?
H.: I think it is the second time.
C.P.: She always summons you, you never summon her, so we think that there is something cooking.
H.: How can I summon a woman? It is not necessary to summon a woman.

The variable of sex of litigants also relates to the legal status of women. Although a woman can initiate a civil court case, she is supposed to be represented in court by her legal guardian. I use the word "supposed" because the rule seems to be in a process of change. Whereas in marital disputes the woman is invariably accompanied by her guardian (father or uncle, depending upon whose house the woman was married from, and sometimes by her mother if the mother is very old), in nonmarital cases the court no longer insists that a woman bring her guardian. The situation can best be summed up at this point in time by saying that for marital disputes women are treated as legal minors, but for nonmarital cases they are considered to have legal majority.

The fact that male-male conflict occurs in 60 percent of the cases while female-female conflict occurs in 5 percent of all cases should not necessarily be taken as an index of greater male-male conflict. It should be seen as a reflection of the authority men have over women, and the power men have to force women to settle cases at the family or village level.

I often had the impression, when observing female-female conflict at the village and family levels, that male kinsmen and male remedy agents viewed female-female conflict in the same way they viewed disputes between children. Most cases seemed slightly embarrassing to the males and were explained in terms of stereotyped beliefs about the "nature" of women. Even at the local court this attitude was prevalent in discussing the behavior of women: "It takes a few days for them [women] to cool down," or "All woman thinking is the same." On the other hand, all male-male conflict, no matter how minor, was treated with great seriousness, and the potential for escalation was feared.

One more nonstatistical finding about sex as it does relate to choice of remedy agent should be noted. Almost 80 percent of the "conciliation" cases that I observed, mostly by chance, involved women as the aggrieved party. Most were marital disputes in which women chose a nonkinsman of high status (headman, chief, court member, ward councillor) to intercede in the conflict. Several women told me that they know they would receive little support from their families, who would tell them to respect their husbands. Therefore they chose a third party to hear their grievance outside a public forum. In short, women believe—and observed cases bear out—that men are publicly favored at the family and village levels in marital disputes. Women tend to choose private third-party conciliation to minimize the favoritism shown to men in public forums. This is true so long as reconciliation is the strategy. When a marriage has been through many conflicts that have been conciliated and mediated, a woman chooses adjudication when she desires termination of the marriage or threatens termination.

Residence of Litigants

The variable of residence adds another dimension to our understanding of choice of remedy agent (table 8.5). Of the total sample (N = 79), nearly half (48 percent) of the cases heard at the local court were between litigants who resided in the same village. This finding should not be interpreted as reflecting a high incidence of intravillage conflict that must be settled by adjudication. Rather, it is partially a consequence of the types of cases brought to the local court. Twenty-six of the thirty-eight cases that involved individuals of the same village were marital disputes. Outside of these, less than 20 percent of the total number of cases involved litigants from the same village.

TABLE 8.5
RESIDENCE OF LITIGANTS

Residents of same village	38
Residents of different villages within Mungule	31
One litigant not resident of Mungule	9
One litigant not resident of Zambia	1
TOTAL	79

In 87 percent of the cases, both litigants were residents of Mungule, and in 13 percent one litigant was not a resident of the chieftaincy. Without further explanation these findings could be misleading. The jurisdiction of the Mungule local court is defined by the boundaries of the chieftaincy. Cases occurring within the area are heard at the local court; cases occurring outside the area must be heard at the geographically appropriate local court. One case I observed was originally heard at the local court in another Lenje chieftaincy. When the court members realized that the events had occurred in Mungule, the case was transferred to the Mungule court, although a good deal of testimony had already been taken.

Again it may be illuminating to place the variable of residence in a nonstatistical framework. When I was pursuing extended case material on the local court sample, I was struck by the fact that I rarely, if ever, had to walk or drive a great distance to interview both litigants in the same case. Given the forty-five-mile distance from the eastern to the western border of Mungule, cases seem to occur between individuals who reside within a relatively short distance of each other. About five miles would, I believe, account for the typical distance between the parties' residences in nearly all the litigation cases in the local court sample.

The final variable I shall explore in terms of choice of remedy agent is ethnicity. This, I believe, is the crucial variable for understanding choice making in the law in Mungule.

Ethnicity of Litigants

Of the total sample, both litigants were Lenje in 22 percent of the cases (see table 8.6). In other words, the Lenje, who make up 65 percent of the population, were involved only with each other in some 20 percent of the cases settled by adjudication. Another 20 percent of the sample involved a Lenje plaintiff and a non-Lenje defendant; 9 percent involved a non-Lenje plaintiff and a Lenje defendant; and 49 percent were cases in which both litigants were non-Lenje. Put another way, nearly 80 percent of all adjudicated cases involved either one or both litigants from immigrant groups who make up 35 percent of the population.

TABLE 8.6
ETHNICITY OF LITIGANTS

Lenje-Lenje	17
Lenje-Other	16
Other-Lenje	7
Other-Other	39
TOTAL	79

The most obvious conclusion is that the Lenje are less litigious with each other than they are with the immigrant population, and less litigious than the immigrant population is with itself. Given the fact that the Lenje outnumber the immigrant population by nearly two to one, the numbers are striking. I propose to explain the above findings in terms of social, kinship, and residential networks, and their relation to the choice or constraints for mediation and adjudication.

After I had recorded the three-month sample of cases at the local court, I became aware of the need for a village-level sample in order to understand the differential use of the court by the Lenje and non-Lenje. Since it probably would have taken at least a year to get an adequate observed sample at the village level, I chose the following strategy. I interviewed five of the village headmen in my census sample, and asked each to recall all the village nkuta cases he had heard from the rains of 1970 to the rains of 1971. In all, I recorded sixty-seven cases. Of these, forty-eight were Lenje-Lenje cases. Put in population statistics, the Lenje, who are 65 percent of the population, were involved in 72 percent of the village mediation cases. The figure may be conservative since the percentage of Lenje per village varies, and since they were underrepresented in the villages of my census sample in terms of their proportion in the chieftaincy as a whole.

When I had calculated these findings in the field, I decided to discuss them with the remedy agents and the people. They were not in the least surprised, and offered many explanations to back my numbers. "We [Lenje] understand each other; therefore it is easier for us to agree." "We [Lenje] respect the headman; therefore we listen to his advice." "We [non-Lenje] fear favoritism, so we go to the court." The non-Lenje point of view was well described by a nonresident Gwembe Tonga man from the Southern Province of Zambia, who was trying to bring an adultery case against a man of Mungule. The Tonga man's father-in-law, a local resident, claimed that he had not made the proper marriage payments and therefore was not legally married. The village nkuta agreed with the father-in-law, and so the Tonga man appealed to the local court. His rationale was "The court doesn't know my father-in-law, and they don't know me." He did, in fact, receive a "limited" award from the local court.

CONCLUSIONS

Folk explanations aside, I will now offer an analysis of both dispute processing and dispute settlement in Mungule. Irrespective of kinship, social and residential networks, and ethnic identity, the people of Mungule perceive a range of remedy agents by which they can process a dispute. What is significant is that the range of remedy agents that make up the dispute-processing system is conceived and used in a hierarchical order. This order has been established by the remedy agents themselves, who insist on hierarchical dispute processing. They have determined the system, if not the form, which must be used.

Though the various remedy agents relate to different forms of dispute settlement (i.e., traditional [family and village] and national [local court and magistrates' court]), they have adapted, at the local level, a unified system for dispute processing. I believe that the dispute processing system in Mungule has been adapted to maintain the boundaries of significant corporate groups that support the power of the traditional Lenje elite. Assuming that boundary maintenance is the key feature of the dispute processing system, one can see the following consequences of the hierarchical system (see also table 8.1).

In private dispute processing, individuals and groups either avoid or defy the significant corporate groups of which they are members. By ignoring a conflict an individual uses no remedy agent, chooses no form of dispute settlement, and avoids activating his kinship, social or residential network. One can also avoid the activation of networks and yet privately process a dispute. This form is conciliation; one chooses a remedy agent of high status or prestige, but not in his public role (which would require network activation). Through self-help, individuals and groups defy boundary maintenance by processing a dispute outside the expected system.

In terms of boundary maintenance, the expectation is that intrafamily disputes will first be processed at the family mubandi/nkuta, thus supporting the corporate integrity of the bashikamukowa. Family dispute processing reinforces the corporate boundaries associated with Lenje concepts of kinship and descent. Likewise, village dispute processing reinforces corporate boundaries at the residential level. For non-Lenje immigrants, it forges a residential corporate identity. Since for most civil cases the local court upholds all the above expectations save self-help, it too supports or maintains boundaries. Court members expect that a case will not come before the local court until it has first been processed by the group or groups that have corporate concern for the litigants. The local court maintains boundaries by reaffirming the decisions of lower-level forms of dispute settlement, and by calling lower-level remedy agents as "expert witnesses." Appeal to magistrates' court, a little-used option, seems to restate boundary maintenance by that court's almost exclusive backing of local court decisions (of the twenty cases appealed in 1970, only one local court decision was overturned).

Given a hierarchical, boundary-maintaining dispute-processing system, how do we account for differential use of the system by different groups within Mungule? From the above statistical analysis of local court dispute settlement, it is clear that the indigenous Lenje tend to mediate, while the immigrant non-Lenje tend to adjudicate. Ethnicity is the crucial variable in the choice of different forms of public dispute settlement.

In Mungule, ethnicity is far more than just a label to denote different ethnic identities. To be Lenje in Mungule is to have a wide network of kinship, social, and residential ties. One's basic kinship group—bashikamukowa and lekoto—is likely to reside within a five-mile radius. By marriage and clan affiliation one has real and fictive kinship ties with a great many local people. One is likely to have been born in the chieftaincy, and therefore to have strong social ties with age mates, schoolmates, and friends. Traditional political and jural authority is understood in the context of oral tradition, legend, and myth. The chief and headman's legitimacy is historically known, not merely accepted. To be Lenje in Mungule means that cases are heard in one's mother tongue. All the above factors increase the likelihood that the remedy agent will have a long personal knowledge of a Lenje litigant's behavior and his kinship, social, and residential networks.

In varying degrees to be non-Lenje in Mungule is to be physically removed from a significant part of one's primary kinship group, to have social ties with less time depth, to have been born in another part of Zambia or, in the case of the Rhodesians, in a foreign country to which one can no longer return. It is to speak a language that at best is only intelligible to the Lenje or at worst requires translation because the remedy agent and local people do not understand it. To be non-Lenje is to be forced to accept the legitimacy of traditional Lenje authorities, to whom respect must be expressed even though it is not necessarily felt.

In conclusion, ethnicity as a variable is but a surface explanation of the sociocultural factors that determine the nature of dispute settlement. A complex set of factors—kinship, social and residential networks (or the lack thereof), the litigant's relationship to the remedy agent, the efficacy of local-level power, the fear of bribery and favoritism—all coalesce into the variable of ethnicity. As the crucial variable, ethnicity tells very little; in an ethnographic context, it explains a great deal.

NOTES

1. Fieldwork in Zambia on which this research is based was supported by the National Institutes of Health (National Institute of General Medical Science) training grant number GM-1224.

2. Community-wide self-help in dispute processing is a new phenomenon in Mungule; it is a reaction to certain types of criminal cases which must otherwise be taken out of the community to magistrates' court. I observed two instances of community-wide self-help or mob violence in 1970, both in response to cattle rustling. This choice of dispute settlement was related to the frustrations the community felt with the procedures and rules associated with magistrates' court; it was an attempt to apply local-level concepts of law in opposition to the national government's concepts of judicial settlement.

3. The undisputed jural authority of the bashikamukowa in terms of inheritance became apparent to me when I asked hypothetical questions to village headmen and local court members. The court president's reaction to the probability of an inheritance case coming before the court was typical. He felt that it was impossible; it had never happened, and he doubted that it ever would. The only possibility he could foresee was that the chief or he himself might visit the bashikamukowa informally and "advise" the members on the importance of coming to a decision. He could not imagine that anyone but the bashikamukowa itself could be responsible for settling a member's estate. Similarly, he stated that the court would back with its enforcement powers the decision of the bashikamukowa. Although it had yet to happen, he said that the court would also force an individual to inherit a name should he resist beyond the expected degree.

4. The one intervillage land dispute case which did come before the local court illustrates the reluctance of the court to become embroiled in disputes associated with lower corporate units (villages) that have their own forums for dispute settlement. This case involved a defendant who was the son of a village headman and a plaintiff who was a Bemba immigrant from northeastern Zambia. The two village headmen who had heard the case (one of whom was the father of the accused) had

ruled in favor of the Bemba immigrant. The son refused to abide by the decision, and the Bemba man appealed to the local court. The local court similarly ruled in favor of the Bemba, and in its decision stated to the Lenje plaintiff, "If you think that the court hasn't settled the case accordingly, you can appeal [to magistrates' court]. After all, from your own headmen we have not heard that Filemon [Bemba] was wrong."

NINE

DISPUTING ISSUES IN SHEHAAM, A MULTIRELIGIOUS VILLAGE IN LEBANON

Cathie J. Witty

THIS DISCUSSION is based on eighteen months of research in a rural agricultural village in the central Beqaa' Valley of Lebanon. My fieldwork was undertaken to describe the range of choices available to individual villagers in the settlement of disputes, and to correlate information regarding the local management of conflict within the functioning of the national legal system. Because Lebanon provides such a visibly plural society, this discussion of local conflict in a multireligious, economically diverse community is also geared toward understanding the legal needs of such a community as the community defines them.

The purpose here is to describe the elements of kinship, political organization, and economics which modify and constrain dispute management procedures. This perspective lends insight into the types of constraints which operate to limit the scope and jurisdiction of the national legal system. Formal legal codes in Lebanon, based as they are on French concepts of property, equity, and contract, have been superimposed upon a highly diverse society whose system of law is traditionally based on reciprocal obligations defined by kinship, marriage, factionalism, and strict codes of honor and shame. By focusing on local legal processes, this discussion considers the ways in which villagers define, interpret, and limit the legitimacy and jurisdiction of the national legal system.

The villagers of Shehaam have modified their traditional processes of dispute settlement and conflict management to take into account the presence of the formal legal structures of the nation-state. These villagers have not successfully assimilated the procedures of the formal legal system, however, or the legal principles upon which they rest. Rather, they have incorporated the formal system of courts, judges, police, and prisons into their own traditional legal framework. They have made some concessions to the state's jurisdiction to prosecute statutory breaches at the village level, but this is a recognition of political facts, not procedural imperatives. Villagers still resolve 85 percent of all their interpersonal disputes through traditionally based mediation and intermediation processes.[1]

THE SETTING

Shehaam is an agricultural village located in the central Beqaa' Valley of Lebanon. The total population of the village during the winter months (October to May) is 900. A summer influx of population reunites families and provides some extra labor in the village households and fields.

Shehaam is one of a string of villages dotted along the foothills on the western fringe of the central Beqaa'. Unlike the neighboring villages, which are predominantly Muslim, Shehaam has a mixed Christian and Shia Muslim population.[2] The village faces east, overlooking the agriculturally rich valley gradually sloping below; the mountain highlands above Shehaam support a variable number of seasonal nomads and shepherds who come from northern Lebanon, Syria, Jordan, and as far away as eastern Turkey.

None of the mountain springs in these highlands (5,500 to 6,500 feet above sea level) feeds into the inhabited village area. The introduction of a piped water system in 1968 has led to the proliferation of small family vegetable gardens and the planting of fruit trees that lend some shade to the parched hillside. Water in this dry, wind-blown land is life; the control of water resources within the village has many political implications. Not all plots of agricultural land have equal access to water, and this situation leads to a number of temporary, shifting alliances among individual farmers who try to increase their crop productivity by sharing limited supplies of water.

Shehaam contains a regional civil police station with eight policemen and a police chief in residence; none of these officers are village residents. Shehaam's station has jurisdiction over eight other Shia Muslim villages in the surrounding area as well. The village also contains a government school (grades 1 through 9), which draws teachers and pupils from all religious groups in Shehaam as well as some pupils from small neighboring villages.

The village population is a mixed community of Shia Muslim, Greek Orthodox, Greek Catholic, and Maronite peoples. My census, taken in the spring of 1973, revealed the religious affiliations shown in Table 9.1.

TABLE 9.1
RESIDENT VILLAGE POPULATION BY RELIGION AND NUMBER OF HOUSEHOLDS

Religion	Households (N = 136)	Individuals	Total Population (N = 900)
Shia Muslim	47	81 men 84 women 192 children*	357
Maronite	38	52 men 50 women 136 children*	238
Greek Orthodox	29	37 men 47 women 93 children*	175
Greek Catholic	22	27 men 42 women 61 children	130

*Children = persons under 20 years of age

Households are composed primarily of nuclear families. Residence is ideally patrivirilocal at marriage. Newly married couples initially live in the husband's natal household, but most prefer to build separate houses for their growing families as soon after marriage as is financially possible. Whenever possible, one male, usually the eldest son, remains permanently in the original family home so that some extended households are found. Residents in such households may include, for example, widowed relatives, the son's parents, grandparents, and unmarried siblings.

Not all families in Shehaam own productive farmland, although all families own their home sites in the village. Families who do not own farmland either work on the land of their affines and neighbors during the harvest season or seek other types of work outside the village in nearby towns. Landless families may also raise donkeys and cows, which they rent to others for use in farm work. They also sell milk and cheese, which they process from the cows or a few goats and sheep. A few families who own tractors work for hire on a day-today basis as well.

Most of the people who own substantial amounts of productive agricultural land are members of the Christian community. Only one Muslim family owns substantial amounts of agricultural land; other Muslim families own some land, but not in large amounts. They must supplement their family incomes with other wages. Over 70 percent of the land that is registered for Shehaam is owned by Christian families, although they comprise only about 60 percent of the total village population. There is a wide range of variation in the amounts of land owned, yet nearly all the Christian families work plots of land for subsistence and profit during the growing season. In contrast, over half the Muslim families (twenty-eight of forty-seven) must earn substantial parts of their total income working as skilled and unskilled laborers. This unequal distribution of land has a long history and is based on the politics of land surveys, land registration, and the turbulent history of the area.

Shehaam's economy is primarily based on mixed cash crop agriculture—wheat, hemp, potatoes, and sunflowers. Families who own land satisfy their own annual food needs by planting and harvesting wheat, potatoes, and other vegetables, and selling any surplus in nearby market towns or to seasonal Bedouin nomads in the valley. These same families grow sunflowers (which are sold directly to the government) and hemp (which is sold green to local distributors for export).

Any village in Lebanon with over fifty inhabitants is entitled by law to elect a mayor (*mukhtaar*). Shehaam has two mayors, one for the Christian community and one for the Muslim community. Mayors were traditionally powerful political figures in the village, but since independence and the growth of centralized authority in Lebanon (1943), their formal duties have become mainly administrative; they certify births, deaths, and weddings, and generally represent villagers officially to government and groups outside the village. Their formal position puts each mayor in contact with other local elders, with administrative officials in the region, and with a wide range of external political networks. The mayors are often consulted by villagers in times of personal quarrels or crisis, and their assistance in minor disputes, quarrels, and political situations plays an important role in tempering violence, disagreements, and protracted disputes among villagers.

There are some differences in the acceptance and adoption of Western cultural and political values between the Christian and Muslim populations, but these are generally reflected more in degree than substance. The older Muslims still tend to dress in the traditional Arab robes, skirts, and headdress, although the younger people, both Muslim and Christian, prefer Western skirts, jackets, and slacks.

Most of the adult population, young and old, are intensely interested in the activities and destiny of the larger Arab world. During the frequent periods of social and political upheaval in Lebanon and the Middle East at large, villagers in Shehaam listened constantly to the news from various world centers on portable radios. Reactions to these broadcasts varied, but Christians fended to sympathize to a greater extent with Lebanon as a nation-state committed to progress and Western-oriented development than did the majority of Muslims.

To a large number of Muslims, the traditional values of honor, justice, generosity, and dignity are still valid, and they feel that such values have been forgotten or largely ignored by the Christians in the Lebanese government. This sentiment tends to incline the Muslims of Shehaam in favor of support for the broad-based Arab politics in preference to strictly Lebanese national politics. According to local tradition, a man should be strong and unyielding in the defense of his dignity, his family, and his God. Such feelings regarding the protection and application of traditional values exclude no one, not even those in the national government (see Rothenberger 1970).

THE SOCIAL ORGANIZATION OF SUPPORT GROUPS

The Community

Some knowledge of local kinship and marriage patterns is necessary for understanding legal processes within the community, because most situations involving authority and decision making begin with individuals and their family groups. Discussions of conflict strategy may take place with various agnates and affines who maintain supportive relations, but the exact content of alliance and support relationships varies with the type of problem, the range of kin involved, and the relative status of individual members within the lineage. Furthermore, the number of alternatives that are open to an individual in any given situation are dependent not only on the network of alliances which the family has within the village itself, but also on the range and density of its network of relations beyond the village boundaries.

The family (minimal lineage) is every individual's first source of social identity. Family membership is a personal, ascribed alliance common to each villager. But going beyond the personal level, the family is incorporated into the villagers' functional and conceptual levels of community and aggregates of communities.

Every villager in Shehaam is a member of five levels of self-defined communities. The primary religious affiliation is important in some situations, whereas at other times (during Christian-Muslim disputes and in the designation of preferential marriage partners) the secondary religious organization (Christian v. Muslim) takes precedence. Against outsiders, the third level of organization, the village, becomes the critical level of reference and identity. A set of common beliefs, institutions, sentiments, and a sense of "belonging together in a settled place" binds a number of diverse groups and individuals throughout the central Beqaa' Valley into a regional community (*HaDaara*) which is larger and more inclusive than the preceding three levels. The final level, ***wlaad al-balad***, children of the country, is a more nebulous aggregation, but serves to separate the traditional, indigenous population from Westerners and foreigners.

When I use the term "community" throughout this discussion, it will specifically refer to one of these types of self-defined communities and will be labeled accordingly (e.g., Christian community = secondary-level organization, Orthodox community = primary-level). In two respects these various types of communities have common functional properties: they are all situationally utilized in response to a challenge from some opposing individual or social group, and they are all conscious sources of social and personal identification with a common situation and culture (shared values).

The Family

The term "family" is used to refer to what is, strictly speaking, a minimal lineage—the smallest group that recognizes common descent and operates as a corporate group at the local level. There are thirty-six such families in Shehaam (twelve Muslim, ten Maronite, eight Orthodox, and six Catholic). All these are unrelated minimal lineages, except among the Orthodox and Catholic population; with the exception of one family in each group, the minimal lineages in these two communities are all members of the same maximal patrilineage. In other words, twelve of the fourteen Catholic and Orthodox families are all related at a higher level of organization—the patrilineage.

It is necessary to consider the full complement of thirty-six families in discussing politics and conflict within the village, for it is the clearest way to understand the factional splits and alliances which characterize local political life. It is the family as a unit which functions as the decision-making body in matters of general family concern and which contributes money and other types of support during disputes. It is to this group that an individual must first look when a marriage partner is desired. Rarely does an individual household operate as an independent unit in these types of social situations, and in business associations this generalization can be made as well. Defection from the family on some important decision or issue may give rise to an enduring factional split.

The Lineage

Patrilineage is used here to refer to the next highest level of identification for all individuals. Links of ancestry and group identity are derived from one's membership in a particular lineage; a woman upon marriage keeps the name of her natal patrilineage. Children always take the name of their father's patrilineage. The patrilineage is not absolute, but is the network against which other types of ties are articulated. Bilateral ties of kinship and marriage create important, strategic links between individuals, families, and lineages. Although the ideal Middle Eastern model is one of patrilineality and patrivirilocal residence upon marriage, matrilateral ties mitigate the exclusive importance of patrilateral kinship in areas such as political strategy and economic assistance. There is no ultimate concentration of power and authority in any one form of local kinship group; rather, there exists an interlocking network of matrikin and patrikin which extends over a large geographic area and maintains sources of power and authority which can be tapped in many ways.

Networks of Alliance

Each person in Shehaam is the focal point for a set of bilateral kinship ties extending over a wide area and intersecting with similar sets of ties radiating from different centers. The relations between individuals which are based on or rationalized as bonds of kinship vary in frequency on a geographic scale; the nearer the interacting units are physically to one another, the more frequent the contact.

The most common point of intersection between two families or villages is a married woman who has left her natal village to live virilocally, but who maintains ties with her own family and village. There are, however, even in this ideally patrilocal society, males who take up uxorilocal residence upon marriage to women outside Shehaam. Where the number of males is low in one area, alliances with other lineages in other villages not only serve to bolster alliances through women, but can also serve to bring men into a depleted family for economic as well as political support.

The frequency of kinship contacts outside the village but within the region can be demonstrated to vary directly with the geographic distance between persons. However, the quality and intensity of these contacts do not necessarily vary directly with distance. Distant affines are often called upon in times of serious need when defense or influence is required beyond the village boundaries. The best friends to have in distant places are relatives. Because the patrilineal ideal tends to be more strongly realized in the village, where political relations are centralized and dense, those ties which link families to the political environs beyond the village are more likely to be matrilateral.

These links mean that the alternatives for dealing with economic, political, and social arrangements are greatly enhanced in the personal way that is characteristic of Middle Eastern society. Because it is generally women who leave the village and live virilocally upon marriage, the vast network of ties, patrilateral and matrilateral, from her natal family come with her to her husband's family. In this sense it is the women who bind the families of the area together, and it is this factor that gives a woman the power to enhance or cripple the political assets of her own lineage and the lineage of her residence after marriage. Women not only operate their own political structures, but also directly influence the formal modes of interaction and decision making among men. More importantly, they draw from their bilateral networks within the patrilineage, and specifically from the varied associations with women in the family, the power ultimately to determine the political viability of any given family and any given household. A simple example of the operation of channels of support and influence through a bilaterally extended kinship situation will illustrate the strategic effectiveness of such ties.

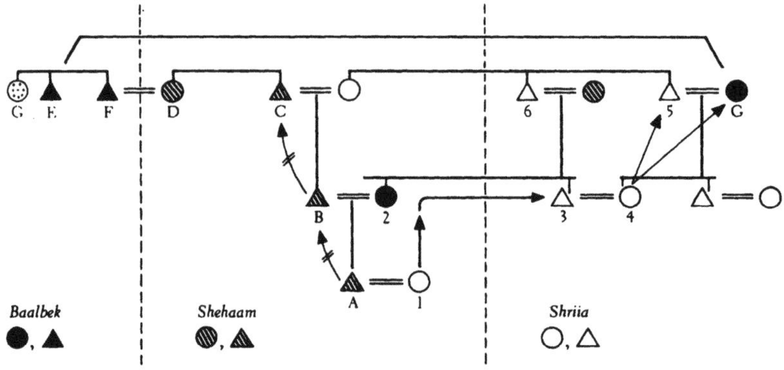

Figure 9.1. Interfamily Action Set

In fig. 9.1, person E was in the process of changing a number of his contractual agreements regarding stubble wheat grazing in the valley. The figure is a representation of the chain of influence activated by a particular individual in order to solve a particular problem; it is an action set from which nonessential kin, those not directly involved in the discussions and strategies, have been removed. Although all family members are informally involved in the family's political affairs, it is only specific individuals with specific ties whom a person selects when he or she needs influence brought to bear on other individuals or groups.

The initiator of the maneuver to be outlined was A, who, although he had direct affinal ties through his patriline to E, found this avenue blocked because of an ongoing dispute between the brothers E and F on one side, and D, C, and 6 on the other. Through an ingenious and lengthy series of discussions and calculations, A manipulated his strong ties matrilaterally, even though they extended into another village some three miles distant (Shriin). These matrilateral relatives spoke formally to E on A's behalf and convinced him that A was not a party to the economic dealings which had alienated E from D, C, and 6. This maneuver was successful in large part because E's sister in Shriin (person G) was married to one of A's matrilateral relatives, and her arguments, when ultimately thrown in alongside the others, finally persuaded E to grant the grazing rights to A. (A's family is one of the few that still keep small numbers of sheep in the village.)

Initially, in this situation A had attempted to have his patrilineal grandfather (C) present his case to E, but found that his grandfather refused to do so. Although patrilateral links were more structurally direct in this case, matrilateral ties were utilized to produce the desired result, even though they were more extended geographically and affinally.

This brief discussion illustrates the flexibility inherent in bilateral ties of marriage and kinship. The patrilineal ideal is not in question, for men as well as women identify themselves formally with the parameters of the patrilineal model. But people, in fact, relate to each other bilaterally; such bilateral linkages are not only useful and ubiquitous, but are frequently crucial in the survival of the household and family. The ability of a family to compete with other families for support and influence is quite realistically a measure of its success and failure in political, and often economic, terms. It is specifically one's links through the maternal or affinal line which determine the degree of connectivity and communication in this regard.

FACTIONAL POLITICS AND SCARCE RESOURCES

Nearly all political activity in Shehaam is covert. The political organization of the village is complicated even further by the existence of numerous factions operating across and within the formal kinship structures. The term "politics" is intended here to cover a broad spectrum of activities, including manipulation of administrative power for personal gain, negotiation of contract, secret agreements to increase one's political bargaining power, and the winning of allies through persuasion and pressure.

The basic necessities of agricultural life in Shehaam—land, water, crops, and to a lesser extent animals—are limited commodities. With the increasing pressures for modernization, social mobility, and increased production, there is tension and disagreement within and between families over the proper allocation of these precious economic resources.

Factional disputes cannot be analyzed solely in economic terms, however. Theft of crops within a family, for example, may lead to violent arguments and physical assault which will be discussed and mediated by the villagers as matters of honor and family responsibility. Furthermore, diverse personal animosities (resulting from slander, jealousy, insult) are often vented against economic resources and property rather than against individuals. Crops may be stolen or damaged, or animals slaughtered because, informants state, many individuals receive more satisfaction for alleged wrongs through overt acts of hostility directed at property (i.e., a form of self-redress).

A faction has been defined as "a coalition of persons recruited personally according to structurally diverse principles by or on behalf of a person in conflict with another person or persons, with whom they were formerly united, over honor and/or control of resources" (Boissevain 1974: 192). As Boissevain has explained, a faction is focused around the person who recruits it.

The factional networks found in this village are a type of nongroup which has been discussed in relation to network analysis (Boissevain 1968, 1971, 1974). Such nongroups are characteristic of the core membership of an individual's support group in Shehaam. The core membership, aligned through kinship, forms a flexible but relatively stable network. Sometimes core members are recruited not on the basis of kinship but of some other set of criteria, usually political power or economic resources; in these cases relations are based on reciprocity, but are not bound by moral obligations that characterize kin-based core relations.

Oppositions develop between core members, and when this opposition becomes manifest in open conflict and dispute, the core membership is splintered and a new faction results. This new faction may remain in opposition to the original core or may join it again in a coalition at some later date, a coalition that is focused around a different, and usually overriding, issue. In order more clearly to understand the differences between formal political structure and political processes, it is important to distinguish between the extended network of social relations which exists through time (kinship and marriage) and the coalitions, personal support networks, and action sets which emerge situationally to accomplish specific tasks. The activities of factions and their internal action sets may cross-cut structures of permanent social relations, such as the family.

Support networks are those personal networks that operate within the village boundaries. They are egocentric and focus on a given person's interconnected chains of persons who comprise a network of support, alliance, and communication. The action set will be used to illustrate local political activity because it is useful as an analytical and descriptive device. The action set captures any set of individuals who have coordinated their activities around a specific goal. As it is used in this discussion, an action set is considered to be focused on the center—the core group that recruits the followers. Action sets have a defined goal that is separate from other bonds of affection or interest among its members; they are recruited through diverse principles; they have a measurable density and a common identity; and finally, they are in competition with rival units of the same order.

As noted above, the traditional Arab family is ideally a patrilineal corporate unit in which rules of descent govern membership and alliance. It would seem that there has developed in Shehaam since the mid-1940s a type of lineage fragmentation which has led some members of a family to switch loyalties and unite with traditional enemies, as well as with traditional allies, in order to inflate the power of a factional network. Such occurrences are highly situational, issue-oriented, and of short duration.

To say that minimal lineages or descent groups are the main structural bases of factional alliances would be an oversimplification. Factions exist within families and may be initiated by any male head of household. Women do not initiate factional divisions within the family unit, but they are certainly instrumental in determining the range and character of the factional alliances, the intensity of conflict, and the maintenance of competition. Men and women coordinate their political efforts in factional alliances and co-participate in the broad range of daily behavior, boundary maintenance, and social strategy which are an integral part of factionalized political activity. Women compete and maneuver within parallel political structures of their own, however, and in this sense have factional alliances of their own which overlap with those of the family unit. Frequently a woman's personal support alliances coincide with those of the patrilineal entity, but often there are exclusive or additional areas of influence within the political realm of women which can combine with, work in opposition to, or remain exclusive from, the network of male political organization.

As every adult is a potential creator of personal support groups within and between family and religious structures, people sometimes find themselves in direct opposition to siblings and other patrilateral kin. Although the families in Shehaam number thirty-six, the factional alignments that were formally recognized by villagers at the time of this study numbered approximately forty-five. Numbers alone do not tell the story, however, for while a family itself may form a factional unit in opposition to other families, some factions contain members from two or more different families.

Thus, such factionalism in Shehaam is relatively common. Fig. 9.2 and the accompanying discussion below illustrate one typical fac-

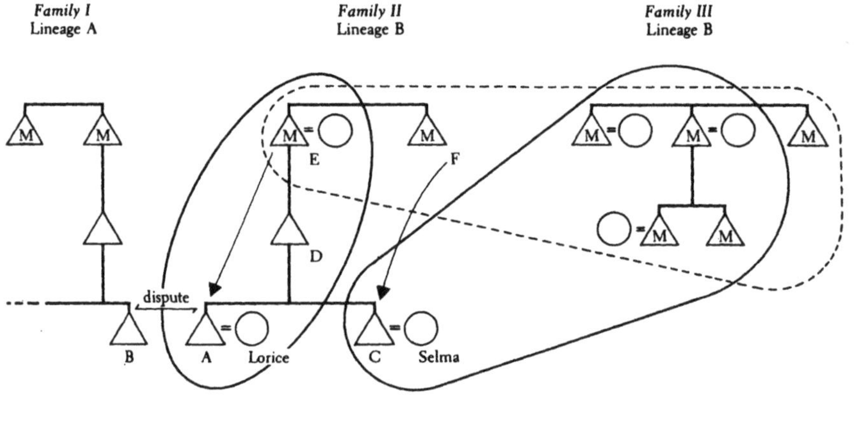

Figure 9.2. Interfamily Factional Divisions. (M) indicates mediators in the dispute.

tional division of this order. The family groups shown in fig. 9.2 depict a gradual shift in alliance and authority over time. The large dotted loop represents a factional alignment that existed several years previous to the present dispute but was informally disbanded once the original goal had been achieved. One of the parties to that dispute (F) remained friends with those members of family III pictured in the diagram. Then a new dispute occurred:

Persons A and B had a verbal argument and a physical fight, although no serious injury was sustained by either. A's father began to press him almost immediately after the incident to settle the argument that evening. A's brother, C, however, argued against this action and was supported in his arguments initially by persons E and F, his paternal grandfather and his grandfather's brother. All persons involved in this dispute, with the exception of B, were members of the same patrilineage.

Persons A, B, and C had been sharing farm labor and equipment when the fight between A and B occurred, but in the days that followed, C became irritated with his brother (A) and his father (D) because of their refusal to demand an apology from B, who had initiated the argument and insulted the family name.

The mediators in this case were elders from families I, II, and III (indicated by the letter "M" in the triangles). Although this dispute was mediated and resolved, it created a permanent rift within family II. Person C publicly withdrew his support from his father's house, and with his father's brother's (F's) advice and counsel, began sharing labor and farm equipment with the persons indicated by the solid-line loop in family III. This shift occurred over a strong and vigorous protest from Persons A and D, supported by E, who wished to hold the family together at any cost. But because A, D, and E deeply distrusted those individuals in family III and suspected that they had stolen some of their best crops during the previous two years, the opposition of loyalty and affiliation finally split family II into conflicting groups indicated in the diagram by the solid-line loops.

The authority for formal decisions now runs in two channels within this family, as indicated by the arrows. A subsequent minor dispute between A and F required formal mediation involving neutral, extrafamilial mediators, an action that would not have been necessary if the channels of communication, influence, and authority within the family had remained united and intact.

This intrafamily fragmentation process cannot be completely understood, however, by focusing solely on the precipitating dispute between A and B, or on the broader-based opposition between the elder family patriarchs (E and F). Disagreements between brothers and cousins occur frequently, but usually they do not lead to such serious oppositions as are seen in the above example.

The women of this familial configuration played an integral part in the eventual outcome. C's wife, Selma, because of her relatively advanced education and because she was not born in Shehaam but had come to the village upon marriage, is closely associated with the women of family III. This association is not only in terms of social compatibility and cooperative household activity, but also in areas of child rearing and interests outside the household. Selma wants her children to be well educated and able to leave the village if they wish. To this end, she has gone into economic partnership with two women from family III in a joint venture to sell milk and cheese throughout the area. E, her husband's grandfather, disapproves of this activity. Selma, as a result, stands in direct opposition to E's authority over her husband, and also to the women related to and allied with A's wife, Lorice. Although it is not proper for Selma to oppose her husband's patrilineal elders directly, her opposition to A's wife is a reality of the daily routine.

Thus, Selma and F are in agreement when A disputes with B. It is these two individuals (Selma and F) who eventually persuade C that A is not taking proper action against the insult that has been made against his family name. These arguments, plus support from a patrilineal elder (F) and a desire to continue Selma's economic ventures in cooperation with family III, make the division between siblings almost inevitable (from C's point of view).

This case serves in many ways to illustrate how traditional values of leadership, respect for elders, and authority act as constraints upon individual action, even if those actions are taken primarily to maximize personal gain. In this particular case, C was greatly influenced in his choice of allies in an economic dispute by his patrilineal relative, F, and by his wife. Because F is well known and respected in the surrounding community as well as in the village, he is an elder of position and stature. This fact, combined with F's strong, aggressive personality, not only worked in this case to influence and counsel C, but also to alienate F's own brother, E.

Although E had previously been allied with F in the factional activities of several years ago, in this case he abandoned those ties entirely and worked to influence A, directly and through an intermediary, D. He was strongly motivated by the insult to the family name which had been incurred by B during the argument with A, but also by jealousy of his younger but well-respected brother (F). E used the argument of family honor and solidarity as a strong local traditional value in an attempt to outweigh the respect and strength of F. The result was to divide the family unit politically.

Although the precipitating dispute occurred in the third generation between A and B, the polarization of the family members can only be understood through a depth of several generations and by considering the political and economic alliances of all members of the participating households, including those disputes, personal characteristics, values, status systems, and political spheres (male and female) which go together to make up the overall family organization. If such extended relationships through time were not considered in this case, for example, one might incorrectly conclude that the economic dispute between A and B alone caused the split within family II. Such a focus would also eliminate the influence of women in the village political system and strengthen the belief that only men are involved in political rivalry and competition. Disputes over scarce resources *can* override traditional ideas of obligation, support, and alliances within the patrilineage, but this example shows how other factors also work cooperatively to complicate tense and competitive social situations.

LOCAL BELIEFS AND VALUES

A brief discussion of traditional values regarding status and its concomitant power will help clarify changing authority roles within the family and the competition over scarce resources.

Ideally, high status and authority accrue to all adult males in the family. Status here refers to the rights and obligations of any individual relative to others and to whatever scale of worthiness is valued within the group; authority refers to the publicly recognized right to exercise power.

Authority is exercised daily within the household, in political debates and gossip in the village, and through economic relationships with neighbors and kin. Theoretically the men of the household hold the ultimate authority for decisions, but women and men really compete for status and the consequent authority. Women can achieve high status and exercise authority over other individuals within and beyond the household.

Status can be thought of as existing along two separate continua (female and male) that overlap and articulate with one another. A woman's status among other women is maintained by her own personality, alliances, and actions and by the relative status of her natal lineage, as well as the lineage with which she is aligned through marriage. Likewise, a man's status is a function of his lineage membership and his political and economic astuteness. Ranking is worked out in relation to other men with whom he is in contact.

Age is probably the most important criterion of status for both men and women, but marriage and the responsibility of a family also contribute strongly to one's status in the community. Generosity is also considered a status indicator; villagers say that a man, to be just and honorable, must be able to abstract himself to a certain degree from the pressures and interests of his kin and give generously to all those in need, "down to the last sheep in the fold."

For every individual in Shehaam there is a sense of belonging to the regional community. A person of respect and status must first be a person from the community (HaDaara). The shared values of the regional community, villagers say, make a person respected, informed, capable, and just, when wisdom is required in political matters or when the goodwill of the community is reaffirmed through mediation. The most important element of the community concept in relation to dispute settlement is simple. It is within the confines of the regional community that the authority code, values, and status indicators of the villagers derive legitimacy. The regional community is not a finite, bounded geographical area, but a conceptualization by villagers of a cultural and social area in which the same values are shared and where personal relationships are of a long-standing and respected nature.

The ability to temper wealth with the above qualities is an important index of status, although the political and economic influence of wealth can never be disregarded. A wealthy family is rarely considered of low status; a poor family may achieve very high status on the basis of the attributes described above. Villagers recognize that such ideals as wisdom of age and generosity are conditional and constantly need to be reconciled with the competition and tension that are realities of agricultural village life.

OFFICIAL DISPUTE-HANDLING AGENTS

The Mayor

Although the position of mayor is officially an administrative office, as outlined above, it holds a great deal of prestige and influence within the village, and several factions have been initiated over the election of the local mayors. Each mayor is officially the nucleus of mediation forums in his secondary religious community in Shehaam, and thus each has added potential for expanding his personal networks outside the village boundaries as well.

As a powerful and influential male elder, each mayor is actively involved in the peacekeeping and mediation procedures within the village and region. In a dispute between members of the secondary religious communities (Christian and Muslim), the two mayors usually work together gathering facts and information about the dispute and acting as mediators along with family elders to be sure that such intercommunity conflict does not escalate to serious proportions.

When a dispute involves a large group of elders in the mediation process, a mayor is often present in his role as senior male of the family. He is also often brought into minor disputes, quarrels, thefts, and cases of minor property damage and stolen animals which occur in the village. For most villagers, their mayor is an influential and neutral third party who can advise, calm, and often settle problems directly.

President of the Municipality

The only other elected official in Shehaam is the president of the municipality (*ra'iis al-baladiyyi*); he is elected for a term of six years and officially administers municipal funds in the village and environs. The president's range of influence is expanded in the same manner as that of the local mayors. Individuals are constantly consulting him and trying to influence him to release money for special projects they would like to have financed in the village, such as paving the road in certain parts of the village or supplying new electrical lighting.

The ra'iis plays another important role in village affairs because he controls the allocation of water within the village and supervises the maintenance of the local water system. Although there are various control centers on the piplelines throughout the village, these are padlocked and are to be opened only by the ra'iis or an employee of the water company.

Disputes over water are particularly common during the dry summer months. Frequently, individuals will break open the padlocks and allow themselves more water than has been assigned to their household. There are usually strained feelings over the water supply, since many families feel that personal and factional grudges and some favoritism are involved in the allocation of water. Some individuals break locks and are never asked to repair them, while others are advised to make such repairs quickly; similar kinds of seemingly discretionary actions regarding the maintenance of the village pipe system cause anger among various networks of allies in the village. Since most of the ra'iis's administrative duties are subject to judgment and discretion, and since water is always in short supply, there is a constant flow of factional energy directed toward control and influence of his office.

VILLAGE DISPUTES

Types of Disputes

It is clear from table 9.2 that there is a wide range in the types of disputes between villagers in Shehaam. These cases range over a ten-year period (1963–1973), and all were settled within the village through mediation.

In the corpus of 196 cases, theft (fifty cases) and physical assault (total of forty-two cases) are by far the most prevalent. Insult ranks third (eighteen cases) and actually ranks closer in frequency to theft and assault than these figures indicate because many insults are not successfully mediated and thus are not included in this tabulation. Such insults continue to rankle and are a primary source of factional hostility. The relative distribution of cases illustrates in a statistical way that economic resources—water, land, animals, and property—and honor and prestige are the basic issues that involve most individuals (and factions) in disputes.

Women are more active participants in disputes involving theft of animals, insult, debt, and slander. One-third of the physical assault cases with injury were between two women, however; women do actively fight and argue when their or their families' honor is at stake. Most of the cases involving women as one of the parties (25 percent) occurred within the village boundaries rather than in the fields.

In the instances in which women were involved in animal theft (six cases), the thefts were either the result of personal arguments and political rivalries between individual women or extensions of rivalries between families as a result of factional tension. The main plaintiffs against women are other women (67 percent); in only two cases did a man formally accuse a woman of stealing certain of his animals. These figures reflect the fact that the status and political systems for men and women are complementary and intersecting. Although most overt political competition is within sexual categories (male-male, female-female), direct confrontation between women and men does occur because the needs and goals of individual men and women are never mutually exclusive.

Men usually prefer to deal formally with other men in dispute settlement processes. But even when women are actively involved as parties to a dispute, the mediation process is formally managed and organized by the men of the respective families. The control by men is to protect the women's interest, say the men, in order that women will not be subjected to or intimidated by deviousness, false arguments, or coercion.

All the women (twenty) whom I interviewed who had been involved in mediated disputes were perfectly content to let the men handle disputes publicly. Women repeatedly stated three reasons for this: (1) they felt that men could argue strongly in public, whereas

TABLE 9.2
LOCALLY MEDIATED DISPUTES IN SHEHAAM, 1963–73

Type of Case	Number	Percent	Plaintiffs*	Defendants*	Police Action	Inter-Christian	Intra-Muslim	Mixed
Theft (N = 50)								
Animals	28	14.3	22M, 6M	26M, 2F	1	10	10	8
Property	8	4.1	8M	8M	1	4	4	—
Crops	14	7.1	14M	14M	—	6	5	3
Physical assault (N = 27)								
No injury	4	2.0	4M	4M	—	1	1	2
Injury	23	11.7	15M, 8F	15M, 8F	7	6	8	9
Physical assault with weapon	15	7.6	15M	15M	2	4	4	7
Insult	18	9.2	15M, 3F	13M, 5F	—	6	7	5
Illegal use of water	13	6.6	13M	13M	2	5	3	5
Debt	11	5.6	9M, 2F	7M, 4F	—	4	5	2
Property boundaries	11	5.6	11M	11M	2	5	5	1
Illegal use of land	10	5.1	8M, 2M	8M, 2F	3	4	4	2

Property damage	8	4.1	6M, 2F	6M, 2F	—	3	3	2
Crop damage	8	4.1	7M, 1M	7M, 1F	—	2	3	3
Marital disputes (N = 8)								
Argument, insult	2	1.0	2M	2F	—	1	1	—
Assault	2	1.0	1M, 1F	1M, 1F	—	1	1	—
Fight	4	2.0	4M	4F	—	1	3	—
Slander	7	3.6	2M, 5F	1M, 6F	—	4	2	1
Hit and run (N = 4)								
Death	1	0.5	1M	1M	1	—	1	—
Injury	3	1.5	3M	3M	1	1	2	—
Forgery (N = 5)								
Checks	3	1.5	2M, 1F	2M, 1F	1	2	1	—
Deeds	2	1.0	2M	2M	—	2	—	—
Homicide	1	0.5	1M	1M	—	—	1	—
TOTALS	196	99.7†			21	72	74	50

* Male = male, F = female
† Rounding error

women were hesitant to do so in front of neighbors and strangers (although they argue vigorously elsewhere); (2) men were more knowledgeable and skilled in mediation discussions because they took part in them frequently; and (3) mediation gave the men something important to discuss and do in their leisure time.

A substantial number of the total of mediated disputes are interreligious in nature (fifty of 196, or 26 percent). The classification here deals only with the Christian-Muslim distinction and does not differentiate between the primary Christian communities. Every effort is made to resolve interreligious disputes informally and internally without resort to local police or court authorities (cf. Rothenberger, above, and 1970).

Interreligious conflict is the biggest threat to village and community unity, say informants, and for this reason every effort is made locally to mediate such conflict through a process which reintegrates relationships within the village. Villagers feel that the participation of outside authorities, such as the police and external codes of law, does not serve this purpose, but rather tends to perpetuate hostility by fining, punishing, or imprisoning one of the disputing parties.

Mediation

Not every dispute rallies the same kin and allies to one's defense, either in numbers or classificatory type. The range of supporters involved depends on relationships within the family unit, the structure of the litigants' personal support networks, and the nature of the dispute.

The seriousness of a dispute may be gauged by observing the daily routine of the households involved. If the men from two households are not speaking, for example, the dispute is probably minor and will work itself out in a matter of days. But if the women of the two households are not speaking, the dispute is much more serious in scope and will require protracted mediation to resolve.

When a serious incident occurs, male relatives of the disputing parties meet spontaneously, dyadically or in groups, as soon as news of the incident spreads. Not all male relatives necessarily convene; this is the first stage at which factional splits within families, support networks outside the family unit, and the types of dispute act to select out individual supporters and mediators.

If the dispute is between members of the same family, only close agnates and affines within an individual's support network will gather to discuss and advise in the dispute. Other extended family members may be asked to join, but at the discretion of the individual directly involved in the dispute. Family arguments should be resolved within the privacy of the family unit if possible, villagers say.

In a dispute between husband and wife, the man and woman look to others of their sex within the household for support. If this does not yield results, the woman will consult with her own parents, aunts, uncles, and siblings if they are resident in the village. These relatives will visit the husband and some of his close relatives in order to effect a compromise or agreement. If this process fails, the woman usually leaves the household and returns to her family, and her husband must then negotiate with her family before she will agree to return.

If the dispute is between members of two different families, then close agnates and affines in each individual's support network, as well as all other members of the support network, will gather to discuss and formulate strategies.

As these men begin to gather, the extent of the violence and injury are the first facts to be clearly determined. It is important that the two primary actors in the dispute do not see one another personally at this point in order to contain resentments and strong feelings and avoid a further outbreak of violence or verbal insult. If one or more parties have been hospitalized, discussion is postponed until the injured can be consulted.

If none of the parties is hospitalized, the male elders will first go to the home of the victim or injured party or the eldest person involved in the dispute, and listen to his account of the incident. The elders will then move to the home of the opposing party and follow the same procedure of listening and asking some pointed questions when accounts are confused or contradictory. They continue the discussion and fact finding back and forth in this manner until the facts of the case begin to emerge in a clear fashion. In cases of general community concern such as homicide, injury, or protracted violence (feud), when the integrity of the whole community is said to be threatened, male elders from throughout the entire village and surrounding communities will converge at the location of the dispute in order to participate in the procedure.

After the impromptu discussion shortly after the dispute erupts, the next step is to collect and weigh the evidence and review the history of the disputants and their families. Then, during lengthy discussions lasting days, weeks, or even months, the mediators weigh the merits of the particular case. It is important that all persons discussing the case have knowledge of a large range of disputes which have occurred in the area, for it is from this corpus of precedents that criteria of guilt, intent, circumstances, and payment are derived. Women and men participate fully in these extensive debates and discussions leading to resolution, as this period of the process occurs at random times throughout the days that follow the initial incident.

At some later date arrived at through informal consensus, the disputants, their family and supporters, and the mediators convene at the home of the injured or elder disputant. The incident by this time has been discussed privately to both sides' satisfaction; the amount of payment has been agreed upon through informal compromise, and a willingness to settle the incident has been privately expressed. At the final meeting the two groups meet and review the dispute, their points of view, and the activity that has led to final mediation of the matter. The payment in compensation is passed from one family to the other during the course of these discussions, and when the discussions are completed to everyone's satisfaction, coffee is served and the matter is considered closed.

Because every elder in the village and surrounding area feels it a duty to respond to conflict and violence in a conciliatory role, the containment value of informal village mediation is quite high.

If one's political or economic rivals are felt to be getting out of hand, there are several strategies to be considered by every villager. A person can create a minor dispute, escalate a preexisting hostility to violence, or force a public confrontation through gossip, insult, or open disclosure. Immediately, relatives, political allies, and quite possibly some neutral and respected third parties will step in to calm and stabilize the inflammatory situation. Contrary to the manifest function of settling disputes, mediation can also be effectively used to undermine opponents' strategies and raise, or at least temporarily stabilize, one's political position at any given time.

Furthermore, during the time required successfully to complete the mediation process, the family protects the accused individual from harm or verbal abuse. Such actions serve to reaffirm for accused individuals the traditional statements regarding social and political status, namely, that one's jural rights and political status reside in the power and unity of the family. By providing protection and shelter in times of crisis, the family binds its members continually to the power and authority structures which are its ideological basis. Factions and personal support networks also provide the same kind of support with a broader political base to individuals in times of conflict.

Mediation generally has an integrative function in terms of the village community. By attempting to solidify the divisive tendencies of factions and competition over scarce resources, mediation acts to strengthen the individual villager's sense of community at various levels of organization—religious, village, regional.

DISPUTES OUTSIDE THE VILLAGE

Not all disputes between village members are contained and resolved within the local mediation process, and not all disputes involve villagers as both parties. When a dispute occurs with an outsider, the forum usually moves to the next higher and external level, that of the local police or the regional court system.

Outsiders are not members of the local community by definition, and therefore derive none of the status, respect, or authority congruent with that position; because shared values are assumed not to exist, such disputes are usually handled directly by the police or court authorities.

One alternative in dealing with outsiders is to try to establish relationships through personal support networks and then to mediate the conflict through this aggregation of interested individuals. If individuals from different religious groups or regions are in dispute, they may seek to avoid the local legal authorities by trying to locate or establish such overlapping networks of support. This is why the density and extensiveness of the family support networks outside the village can be so important, and why bilateral affiliations will be increasingly important to social and political survival.

A number of features from the police records over a nine-year period (1965–73) are rather striking. Out of the total of 160 cases involving villagers, only twenty-eight, or 18 percent, involved village members as both plaintiff and defendant (table 9.3). That is, only 18 percent of the police cases were the result of individuals in Shehaam filing formal complaints against one another. Conversely, 82 percent (132) of the cases made a matter of public record in this forum were between villagers and persons or institutions from the outside.

TABLE 9.3
POLICE CASES: DISTRIBUTION OF PARTICIPANTS, 1965–73
(N = 160)

Participants in Cases	*Number*	*Percentage*
Between persons (N = 87)		
Both parties villagers	28	17.5
Only one party a villager	59	36.9
State v. individual	73	45.6
TOTALS	160	100.0

This distribution is skewed somewhat because cases brought by the state against particular individuals involving administrative matters are included in the "outsider" category. Therefore, numerous civil cases involving building, repairing, expanding households, or operating a business in the home without a government permit are included in this 82 percent. It is not only significant that most police cases involved villagers and "outsiders," but additionally, that seventy-three of the 132 cases (55 percent) recorded between villagers and outsiders were cases initiated by the state against individuals in the village.

State-initiated cases predominantly involved administrative control of civil wrongs (forty-nine of seventy-three cases, or 67 percent). Civil wrongs in this instance are broadly defined to include the following: building without a permit, illegal sale of tobacco, illegal possession of weapons, illegal opening of water pipes, blockage of a public road, disturbing the peace, and operating a business without a permit.

Within the village, crimes against persons (48 percent) and against property (52 percent) were distributed in nearly equal proportions. Furthermore, over a nine-year period, only six cases (21 percent) were actions between Christian and Muslim households in Shehaam (table 9.4).

TABLE 9.4
POLICE CASES BETWEEN INDIVIDUALS WITHIN THE VILLAGE, 1965–73
(N = 28)

Category *	*Type of Case*	*Frequency*	*Religion of Disputants* †
B	Physical assault	4	3 S, 1 D
A	Illegal use of property	4	2 S, 1 D, 1 S§
A	Theft	3	3 S
B	Personal injury	3	3 S
C	Unauthorized building	3	3 S
A	Suspected theft, search	2	2 S
A	Crop damage	2	1 D, 1 S§
B	Assault with weapon	2	2 S
A	Right of usufruct	1	1 D
A	Property rights	1	1 D
B	Attempted murder	1	1 D
C	Digging without permit	1	1 S
C	Insult	1	1 S

* Categories of cases:
A = disputes involving scarce resources
B = violent crimes against persons
C = minor, miscellaneous disputes
† Religion of disputants:
D = different religious group, Christian or Muslim
S = same religious group
S§ = Christians, inter-sect (i.e., Orthodox v. Maronite)

It is important to note here that this total number of cases (twenty-eight) is less than half the number of cases recorded in the same period against outsiders (fifty-nine). Two factors appeared quite early in reading these police cases: problems within the village were only dealt with infrequently by the police at this level, and disputes between Christians and Muslims were certainly resolved outside this public arena.

A look at the cases involving outsiders (table 9.5) highlights this situation. As in table 9.4, the outsiders' cases are arranged in descending order of frequency of occurrence. The general value of this type of comparison is in outlining areas of demarcation in the origins

TABLE 9.5
POLICE CASES BETWEEN INDIVIDUALS AND INSTITUTIONS OUTSIDE THE VILLAGE, 1965–73
(N = 59)

Category *	*Type of Case*	*Frequency*	*Religion of Disputants* †
A	Property damage	9	3 S, 6 D
A	Theft	7	2 S, 5 D
A	Illegal use of property	7	2 S, 5 D
B	Physical assault	7	3 S, 4 D
A	Fraud	5	2 S, 3 D
A	Crop damage	4	4 D
A	Forgery	3	3 D
B	Injury	3	2 S, 1 D
C	Debt	3	2 S, 1 D
B	Hit and run	2	1 S, 1 D
C	Illegal use of public land	2	1 S, 1 D
C	Unauthorized building	1	1 S
C	Verbal threat	1	1 D
B	Threat with weapon	1	1 S
B	Assault with weapon	1	1 S
C	Misconduct	1	1 S
A	Opening water pipes	1	1 S
B	Attempted murder	1	1 S

* Categories of cases:
A = disputes involving scarce resources
B = violent crimes against persons
C = minor, miscellaneous disputes

† Religion of disputants:
D = different religious group, Christian or Muslim
S = same religious group

and frequencies of public disputes. This sample contained very few complaints between villagers of different religious affiliation in contrast to the collected corpus of village-mediated cases. This finding indicated that the formal arena (police, courts) was not used frequently to resolve disputes, but was used for some other purpose. Most disputes between individuals, and particularly those that threatened the solidarity of the village internally (Christian-Muslim), were primarily resolved informally through mediation.

THE VILLAGE AND THE NATIONAL LEGAL SYSTEM

The village's system of conflict management and dispute resolution articulates with the national system in a very limited way. Although the discussion has been necessarily brief, several patterns are evident.

The existent formal legal system is used as one alternative in a much broader range of strategies which individuals employ to separate, alienate, and isolate their particular opponents from their contingent of supporters. The very presence of the formal legal system and its concomitant enforcement agencies is manipulated in order to place opponents in positions of weakness and conciliation and to threaten them with external force. As such, the national legal system has been integrated into the rural, traditional legal processes rather than the rural population having been integrated into the legal structures of the more inclusive nation-state. The choices, networks, and systems of alliance, kinship, and marriage which are part of the everyday life of a villager in Shehaam must be given more weight in future considerations of modernization, development, and planned social change.

An understanding of the variables and constraints which influence villagers in their use and perception of the formal legal system must become a part of the legal planning process. Villagers actively utilize the legal system as a threat to some internal status quo. Civil complaints that appear in police or court records are most often initiated by the state against individuals and are enforced by the local police. These actions are received as a matter of course in Shehaam.

The villagers deal with this type of state action as routine, bothersome contrivances by the state to collect additional revenue.

Criminal sanctions pressed by the state against individuals are a more complex matter, as the village has its own principles and procedures for dealing with actions punishable within the national criminal code. Villagers generally agree that the state has the authority to prosecute violations of its national civil and criminal codes. They do not agree that this authority should penetrate into criminal or civil matters between families in the village or community if its aid is not actively sought by one of the disputing parties.

The consequences of such conflict in principles of authority and jurisdiction are juxtaposed in two ways. First, the villagers, by defining the basis of authority differently than the state, tend to view state prosecution at the village level as distant and disruptive. By their insistence on having the choice of activating the court system at their own discretion and according to individual needs, villagers state clearly what is also clear in the village case materials: rather than using the courts directly, they have modified the local legal processes and absorbed the courts and police into their own political organization, economic competition, and mediation procedures.

The nation, on the other hand, defines its legal problems as problems of enforcement, uniformity, and consistency. Alternative remedy agents outside the formal system of laws, courts, and professionals are untenable. The fact that villagers do appear occasionally in the courts is evidence, say judicial administrators and legal scholars, that a broad cross-section of the population is using the legal system. The national legal system is unconcerned for the most part about village-level constraints and decision making, and has no clear idea of why villagers appear in the courts or why they consult legal professionals.

Villagers agree that their lives are subject to, but not governed by, laws deriving from the national legal system. They do not feel that the court system is adequately equipped to handle such issues as family honor, the unity of the community, just compensation, and the containment of disputes. They further argue that the courts are unduly expensive (hence exclusive), do not save money in the long run, and are unprepared to handle many cases because the administrative "outsiders" lack knowledge of the complexities and subtleties of community relationships and values.

The people of Shehaam argue that rules of evidence are restricted within the formal court proceedings. The social and political history of a case, which they feel bears directly on questions of premeditation, fault, obligation, and definitions of "reasonable" behavior, is not allowed to be developed in sufficient depth. Pleadings are subject to various interpretations and consequences, and require the technical expertise of a lawyer; lawyers, unless they are relatives, are uninterested in the social or political merits of a case, and charge prohibitive fees for even routine consultation. Rules of fault in accident and injury, particularly in regard to the concept of negligence, vary markedly between the local and national levels.

CONCLUSIONS

An understanding of the reasons why people use the courts and formal judicial system must become a priority in planning, adapting, and modernizing legal systems. People do not automatically use legal systems just because they are there. They have specific personal, political, and legal reasons for using such a formal system. The poor and the powerless cannot use the legal system to their own advantage; they have neither the technical knowledge nor the money to gain access to the formal legal machinery. Formal definitions of crime and jurisdictions must be synonymous with or complementary to the informal definitions that make up the social and legal world of the users of the legal system. Without such overlap and consistency, the formal legitimacy of a legal system will not transcend the values and principles of the people who must use it.

People in Shehaam prefer to use village and regional mechanisms for settling disputes because they have the knowledge to manipulate and use such mechanisms to their own advantage and they have ready access to these mechanisms because of their multiplex networks throughout the community. Villagers see no value or legitimacy in sending an offender to jail; if that offender and his or her family has mediated and repaired relations within the community, the rights of the community have been exercised and reaffirmed.

To have several systems of legal principles and values operating with legitimacy within the same polity could be viewed as a social and legal asset rather than as a liability. The focus of planners and scholars on change and assimilation—drawing everyone into the operation of the national legal system—should be reevaluated. The problems of legal pluralism might be turned into assets if legal pluralism were analyzed at all its different levels. A resolution of village needs, regional needs, and national needs might well require the integration of mediation and adjudication into one model of dispute management.

NOTES

1. Research on which this paper is based was carried out during 1972 and 1973 through a grant from the National Institute of Mental Health; the author gratefully acknowledges the Institute's generous support during the period of field research and writing. I am particularly grateful to Dr. Harry Todd of the Medical Anthropology Program, University of California, San Francisco, and to Drs. Bud Winans and Sue-Ellen Jacobs of the University of Washington, Seattle, for their critical and editorial comments during the preparation of this paper.

2. For an explanation of the origin of the Shia (or Shii[c]a) Muslim sect, see Rothenberger 1970.

TEN

VILLAGE OR STATE? COMPETITIVE LEGAL SYSTEMS IN A MEXICAN JUDICIAL DISTRICT

Philip Parnell

CENTRALIZATION, a process concomitant with development of state power, and the process by which a growing state duplicates its institutions through structural self-imitation, may eliminate state responsiveness and accountability to the people it controls or represents. State bureaucratization of social functions (once performed by local communities as territorial units) creates a closed system of institutional social relations that are unaccountable to relationships outside the bureaucracy. The absence of accountability does not result solely from structural duplication, but is largely a result of the development of interactional classes, for example, of bureaucrats and professionals, whose personal networks exclude those with whom they have no institutional relations. As the state grows, the relationship between state institutional and non-institutional communities is similar to that in culture contact, with one system of social relations breaking down and assimilating the functions of another.[1]

The processes by which community functions are assumed by the state influence the effectiveness of social control procedures, especially when modern state and local indigenous legal jurisdictions overlap. In such contact situations, at least two overlapping cultural oppositions are generated: community/developing state and indigenous/modern, the indigenous/modern opposition often providing the idiom through which community/state oppositions are expressed.

The Zapotec judicial district of Loani in the state of Oaxaca in southern Mexico represents such a situation of culture contact. There state and local legal systems co-participate in the settlement of about sixty disputes yearly. Through contact between state and local institutions and through the participation in village social networks of individuals who occupy positions in state institutions, Loani villages and state courts are placed in a competitive relationship. One asserts customary jurisdiction over local disputes, the other jurisdiction dictated by the state. Here I will examine the effects of that competitive relationship on the operation and integration of institutions in both the state and local legal system.

Residents of the judicial district of Loani may choose from a number of institutional alternatives in their attempts to settle or prevent the escalation of disputes. Some of these alternatives are informal (e.g., gossip and feud) and derive from village social organization and relationships among villages of the mountain district; others are formal (e.g., the village court, the state-operated district court, and the state supreme court in Oaxaca City and its associated judicial agencies). Village courts, like gossip networks, respond to village organization and values; state courts respond to state laws and state codes of judicial procedure.

Two dispute-processing systems operate in Loani: the community system and the state system. The community system consists of formal and informal means of settling disputes. The state system, through the structure of appeals, ties the formal village court into the state courts and judicial agencies.

The operation in Loani of two legal systems representing different levels of organization introduces a number of oppositions into the processes of dispute settlement. These oppositions are organizational as well as legal, political, and stylistic. They organize village and state legal institutions into competing camps and contradictory systems of dispute settlement.

Each of the forty-three villages in Loani is a corporate unit that values its legal and political autonomy. Use of state legal agencies by local villages or courts affirms the legitimacy of the state system and challenges the authority of local institutions. On the other hand, the ability of local courts to seal off disputes within the village legal structure is a test of local judicial authority and efficacy as well as a gauge of local autonomy.

The style of dispute settlement in village courts derives from village organization and values; state court procedure derives from the tradition of nation-states which organizes political units into a structure of power and tribute. The respective levels represent a conflict between what Lambert characterizes in colonial Africa as "judgment by agreement" as oppossed to "judgment by decree" (Epstein 1954: 1). Collier succinctly contrasts the nature of justice achieved in local and state courts in Chiapas, Mexico: disputing parties who use local legal institutions may achieve restitution and reconciliation; those who choose the state are faced with the prospect of revenge and continuing hostility (Collier 1973: 228).

Ottenberg (1967) draws on his study of the introduction of a British model of local government into southern Nigeria—a "radically different cultural milieu"—to conclude that the interaction in a society of two political systems with different political styles and types of organization will inevitably lead to breakdown of self-regulatory processes. He asserts, as Merton (1949) does, that "the functional deficiencies of the official structure generate an alternative (unofficial) structure to fulfill existing needs somewhat more effectively."

Here I am concerned with direct confrontation between the two legal and political structures in Loani, when disputes are not sealed off on the local level but instead become embroiled in the state system. Here, I am not only concerned with how the oppositions inherent in the intermingling of the two political structures channel disputants to one legal system or the other; rather, I am more interested in how those oppositions affect the operation of local legal institutions once *both* legal systems are involved in a battle to maintain jurisdiction over resolution of a dispute. Disputes that are being resolved simultaneously in both systems clearly expose these oppositions, and raise questions of how disputants and legal authorities will react to them. Such disputes are not only a direct challenge to the autonomy and equilibrium of the local political unit, but are also a test of the legitimacy, efficacy, and authority of institutions within both legal systems, in that they place the two systems in direct competition with one another.

The effects of this competition between or among legal levels with overlapping jurisdictions on the processes of dispute settlement may be either beneficial or adverse. Competition may increase the efficiency of each institution; it may also increase the likelihood that one if not the other institution will be successful in controlling a dispute: if compromise is not effective, then force and decree may be. The responses of Loani legal levels to competition suggest, however, that when institutional alternatives exist in different legal systems—systems which are rooted in contrasting cultural norms and traditions—their co-participation in the management of the same dispute disrupts the operation of *each* institution, decreasing its effectiveness, and strengthening barriers to cooperation between levels.

Thus, once a dispute enters the state system, a new, totally distinct unofficial process of appeals (an "operational," as opposed to an "official," appeals structure) is generated—a new appeals process that is less effective in controlling the dispute than were the local institutions in which the dispute arose. In such situations, the competitive relationship that is established by the conflict between state and village systems has a greater impact on the development and processing of disputes than do any other factors (such as the nature of the dispute or the relationship between parties).

When both systems become involved in the same dispute, therefore, state mechanisms of coercive control and village mechanisms of normative control become appended one to the other by individuals occupying positions within both organizations. The strategies by which this appending is achieved or avoided constitute the unofficial or *operational* system of appeals in Loani. When this appending is direct (i.e., achieved through personal contacts and the choices of disputants) and is not mediated by village or state courts, it becomes a primary force in altering the structure of political and legal relationships between the village and state; it may also act to intensify political conflict and the stratification of power within the villages.[2]

In the following discussion, by examining overlapping and competing claims to jurisdiction over disputes as exemplified by two case studies of homicide in Loani villages, I shall attempt to answer two major questions: (1) why do so few disputes travel from local villages to state courts; and (2) why are state courts incapable of resolving so many of the cases they receive.

THE SETTING

The forty-three villages of Loani lie in the Sierras about halfway between Oaxaca City and the state of Vera Cruz. Forty-one of these villages are Zapotec-speaking; one village on the outskirts of the district speaks Mixe, and the natives of Villa Laba, the district seat, are monolingual Spanish speakers. Loani villages fall into overlapping geographic and economic regions. Villages within each region are interrelated through the market networks that they share. Ralu'a, studied by Laura Nader (1964b), is a major village in one region, and Villa Laba is the hub of another. Both villages became regional meeting places by dominating the connections with and access to modern state and national movements. Each of the two centers hosts a weekly market, is a communications node, and supports a secondary school open to students from district villages.

All villages in Loani are interconnected by paths, and some by dirt roads maintained by village-based citizen work groups. Two dirt roads from Oaxaca City, the state capital, provide passage for buses to some villages on the outskirts of the district, and for trucks, jeeps, and motorcycles to others further into the Sierra. Ralu'a and Villa Laba are also connected to Oaxaca City by regular flights of two small commercial aircraft. However, during the nine-month rainy season, both overland vehicular and air communication to outlying villages of the Villa Laba region is unreliable.

The major occupation in the district of Loani is agriculture: Beans, maize, squash, chile, sugar cane, and maguey are the subsistence crops of the small-scale farmer. Most farmers, individually or collectively, cultivate coffee as a cash crop. Economic variation among district villages, as well as among individual farmers, is primarily due to (1) the extent of coffee holdings, and (2) the level of technology utilized in coffee production. Technological variation generally correlates with use of technological assistance from the developmental Papaloapan Commission in Oaxaca City.

POLITICAL STRUCTURE

Each Zapotec village in Loani is a cohesive corporate unit. Most villages are compact nucleated settlements, rather than scattered family dwellings dispersed among individually cultivated plots of land. Schmieder (1930) attributed the nucleated pattern of Zapotec settlements to cooperative clearing of large tracts of land and later division of each tract into individual family plots. Most Zapotec farmers now maintain permanent family dwellings within the central settlement as well as huts or lean-tos on areas of current cultivation (see Nader 1964b).

The Village

A basic characteristic of the mountain Zapotec village is the strong resistance by its natives to outside violation of the political and territorial boundaries of their community. Although natives of the villages (except those of the district seat and of Mixe Tonapec) refer to themselves as Zapotecs, their shared name and linguistic characteristics do not foster common identity. Identity is derived from the individual community and, in Loani, plays a significant role in preventing rather than creating political coalitions among mountain Zapotec villages.

Loani villages are tied together politically by a state-imposed administrative and judicial hierarchy. Depending on their size, villages fall into three different political classifications, from largest to smallest: the *municipio*, the *agencia*, and the *rancho*. Although all villages have their own elected governments and courts, each agencia and rancho falls under the administrative and judicial jursidiction of a specific municipio.

Relations between an agencia and its municipio are typically strained. Municipal overstepping, in the name of the state, of customary norms that regulate behavior on community boundaries may foment intervillage feuds that result in a shifting of district political ties. Two such feuds within the last twenty years resulted in realignment of two agencias with the municipality of Spanish-speaking Villa Laba, accomplished through direct requests to the Mexican federal government.

The District Seat

Natives of Villa Laba trace the founding of their village and their descent to the Spanish of the conquest. From among Villa Laba's approximately 700 permanent residents, five extended families are said to descend from the Spanish founders. The surnames chosen by Villa Labans to represent those families may vary according to the status of native sons. The Spanish-speaking Villa Labans identify with modern state and national movements rather than with the culture of their indigenous neighbors. Their idiom for village egotism, formulated in competition with other district villages, is politics and ethnicity. Native Villa Labans apply a well-defined negative identity to all natives of bilingual and non-Spanish-speaking villages.

As a result of Villa Laba's ties to and identification with the state, the district seat, in contrast to the primarily agricultural Zapotec villages, is occupationally heterogeneous. The village houses state administrative and judicial agencies for the district of Loani, and six district administrators, usually from Oaxaca City, maintain temporary residence there. Native Villa Labans fall into five major occupational categories: state employee, merchant, craftsman, landed farmer, and day laborer. Most adult male members of "Spanish" families are landowners and work as schoolteachers or state employees. Most adult female members of "Spanish" families are schoolteachers in the district or telegraph operators in Mexico City.

Community boundaries to outside involvement in village affairs are not as well defined in Villa Laba as in most Zapotec villages of the district. They are, rather, negotiated in village *juntas* and in direct confrontation with the state. The negotiators are two Villa

Laba political factions: the "progressives," made up of schoolteachers, state employees, and successful merchants; and the "conservatives," farmers and day laborers led by one schoolteacher and a retired district administrator. Progressives align with modern state movements. Conservatives defend local autonomy and oppose state projects and institutionalization. Progressives have dominated Villa Laba government since the middle 1950s. One of two case studies examined later illustrates how, in 1974, conservatives came to power in the district seat following violation of Villa Laba community boundaries by the state.

Native Villa Laban employees, who are considered well-to-do, a wealthy Villa Laban merchant, and a Villa Laban moneylender participate in the personal networks of district personnel stationed in the district seat. Five Villa Laban families maintain personal ties with relatives and associates in Oaxaca City who wield political influence in state offices. Three Villa Labans are influential within the district agencies where they work. Most Villa Laban teachers and merchants occasionally post bail for and informally counsel Zapotec villagers involved in district court cases. Two Villa Laba residents who are natives of Zapotec villages (one a farmer and the other a primary-school teacher) act, by reason of their bilingualism and literacy, as brokers between Zapotecs and district personnel.

Every Zapotec falls under the jurisdiction of district agencies and faces the possibility of having to deal directly with them. For many Zapotec villagers, experience with state values and institutions is primarily limited to direct confrontations with district offices and with native Villa Labans. In these confrontations, individual and collective strategies for maintaining and breaking through bondaries between the village and the state are developed and tested.

JUDICIAL STRUCTURE

The judicial line of appeals in the district of Loani flows from agencia and rancho to municipio, and from municipio to the district court in Villa Laba. A case may be appealed from the district court to judicial agencies in the state capital; from there to the state superior court in Oaxaca City; and ultimately, from there to the federal supreme court in Mexico City. A case may be initiated in the district court by any individual or village of the district. Cases may also be initiated in Oaxaca state judicial agencies or the state superior court; however, these agencies as well as the superior court refer the case to the Loani district court if it involves citizens of Loani. A case may not be appealed to the superior court until it has been tried in the Loani district court.

The Loani district court occupies three rooms in a long rectangular municipal building in the central square of Villa Laba. The district judicial structure consists of two offices—that of the prosecutor for the state and that of the judge. The prosecutor occupies one room with his secretary. The judge occupies two other rooms with his auxiliary personnel: a secretary; a court executor who is also a secretary; and the civil registrar, who records births, deaths, and marriages.

The district judicial structure is replicated in village courts. The municipio elects an *alcalde*, who is the subordinate of the district judge, and a *sindico*, who is the subordinate of the district prosecutor. According to state law, a village dispute is first taken to the sindico, who, if he cannot successfully resolve the dispute, sends it on to the alcalde. The alcalde may then refer the dispute to the prosecutor in Villa Laba. If the prosecutor determines that a crime, or *delito*, has been committed, he refers the case, with formal accusations, to the district judge. Once a case reaches the district court, the village sindico and alcalde become local investigators for the district court. They are aided by the *regidor*, or chief of village police.

Other investigative personnel at the disposal of the district court are the *perito practico* and the state judicial police, a group of "confidential agents" who are at the service of the state judiciary during investigations of cases. They are on assignment by shifts in Oaxaca City. In Villa Laba, the perito practico is a village resident trained by correspondence as a paramedic who, as an avocation, performs autopsies and sometimes conducts on-sight inspections in place of the district prosecutor. There are three paramedics in Villa Laba who are regularly used by the district court. A Villa Laba practico is paid by villages of the district when he assists them in homicide investigations; however, most villages use resident paramedics in such cases to avoid the high fees charged by Villa Laba practicos.

Personnel of village courts are elected local citizens, but residence requirements are not applied to personnel of the district court. During the period of my research, the district executor and the civil registrar were, and traditionally had been, residents of the district seat, but since the early 1960s district judges have not been residents of the district. They are drawn from a pool of district judges rotated by the state superior court among Oaxaca districts.

District courts in Oaxaca are rated by court personnel on a scale from most profitable to least profitable, profit being taken from civil cases. The number of civil cases a district court receives is directly related to the level of urbanization within the district. Agricultural Loani is known as the least profitable of all Oaxaca districts. Court personnel profit from civil cases by extracting fees for the preparation of documents. One secretary of the Loani district court reported that, while working in the court of a district which borders on Loani, he had earned more than $240 a month in fees for civil cases. A former executor of the Loani court, who complained that Loani court personnel did not share bribes with him, once pocketed $800 in ten days as secretary in another district. By contrast, an agricultural day laborer in Loani generally earns from $1.20 to two dollars per work day.

Because Loani has a low profitability rating, its district court is often left without a judge. In the absence of a judge, the court secretary assumes his duties. District judges have formal legal training; court secretaries learn of state laws and procedures on the job. The 1974 Villa Laba court secretary/judge boasted twenty years experience as executor and secretary in another district. Examination of Villa Laba district cases over a ten-year period suggests that judges and secretaries implement the same court procedures.

The district court differs from village courts both in style and in the type of outcome which it imposes on a dispute. Village court dispute settlement is based on compromise outcome and is restrictive, whereas the district court judge imposes a win-lose or zero-sum outcome on the dispute. Laura Nader (1969b) has described the style of court proceedings for the village of Ralu'a. When disputants are gathered before the village court, court officials attempt to promote discussion or debate among them in their Zapotec dialect. Disputants may vent their spleen before the court, a procedure which, when followed by mediation, defuses the dispute rather than increases hostility. By mediating among disputants and urging them to enter into a compromise solution, village court officials attempt to "reestablish the balance" that existed among disputing parties and within the village before the dispute arose. Punishment of offenders of the community usually consists of small fines and up to three days in jail. Jail terms are spent performing services for the village, such as carrying rocks for construction, repairing walls, or filling in rain-washed gullies. Fines enter the village treasury.

In contrast to village court officials, the district court official imposes a fine or sentence on an accused who he determines is guilty according to state law. Fines enter a state fund. Guilt is determined primarily on the basis of testimony delivered individually and in privacy before the judge by parties and witnesses. All testimony is recorded by the secretary. A district judge converses with disputants only to clarify accusations and evidence; he, unlike his village-level counterpart, does not attempt to clarify among disputants the normative or moral basis for considering an act as wrong. He does not attempt to state or clarify the social basis of court enforcement of specific duties and obligations among village residents.

Within the investigative process, district court procedure requires performance of the *careo*, a discussion held before the court between the accused and, individually, his accusers. This step in district court procedure replicates village court style. However, in the district court context of adjudication which excludes compromise, the careo has no effect on the outcome of the case, except through revealing new evidence. Participants in careos I have observed or have read of in transcripts do not talk directly to each other and make no changes in previous testimony.

When a disputant takes his accusations to the district court he escalates the dispute. He precludes "making the balance" through discussion and mediation, and invites continuation of the dispute through future retaliation by his opponents. A Zapotec teacher who frequently counsels disputants in district court cases stated that once a dispute reaches the district court "*no hay discúlpame*," there is no "forgive me."

Two junta-settled offenses against the community which occurred in Pagui, a Zapotec village of about 300, illustrate local views in dispute settlement. In Pagui, each village official is entrusted with the safeguarding of a portion of the village treasury. The two crimes involved, in each instance, the misuse by a village official of his portion of the treasury. Each official was present and tried in a town meeting open to all male citizens. In one of the juntas, which I attended, the accused official did not speak. For three hours citizens discussed the nature of the crime and its proper punishment in front of the official. The junta became heated as individual citizens stood to shout their views and then walked out of the meeting to cool off. Each junta decided that the village would take something from the property of the guilty official equivalent to the sum he had squandered. One official lost the tiles which formed the roof of his house. A work group harvested and sold for the village treasury the other official's coffee crop.

Structural variation occurs in village courts throughout the district. Essentially, any elected village official may, and sometimes does, participate in dispute settlement. The village administrative heads—*presidentes municipales* in larger villages and *agentes* in smaller ones—often serve as mediators or adjudicators. Cases are sometimes rotated among village officials until balance is reestablished among disputing parties. Some cases that affect an entire village are discussed and tried in a town meeting. I also found four villages with tenured political bosses who adjudicate most disputes and control appeals to Villa Laba. In two villages converted to Jehovah's Witness, Witness courts have been established as an alternative to the municipal court. An older resident of one Zapotec village in the Ralu'a region mediates all his village's difficult cases, although he is not an elected village official.

Determination of which types of cases will be tried in village courts and which will be sent to the district courts is arbitrary, although certain patterns occur throughout the district. In general, most cases referred to the district court by Zapotec villages or by the district prosecutor are those (1) that involve death; (2) that involve an injury that draws blood or is not immediately curable within the village; (3) in which the accused is a repeated offender of village norms; and (4) in which, as some village court officials explained, the parties to a dispute *no entran al razón* (do not enter into justice) and *siguen en pleito* (continue in dispute). Misdemeanors that are appealed to the district prosecutor from village courts may be settled by the prosecutor. Approximately 50 percent of cases consigned by the district prosecutor to the judge from 1968 through 1973 were initiated by the disputants in the office of the prosecutor rather than in village courts.

Once a case has reached the district court judge a general procedure is followed, regardless of the type of crime under consideration. The case is consigned by the judge to the district prosecutor and an investigation, the *primeras diligencias*, is conducted by village court officials. This investigation is conducted either before or after consignation of the case to the district prosecutor, who represents the state against the accused.

After consignation the district judge calls the parties to the case to Villa Laba through a letter to the village alcalde. Once the parties are present in Villa Laba, the judge detains the accused and takes his testimony, as well as the testimony of witnesses. The judge then sends the case to the district prosecutor, asking if he prefers further investigation. The district judge may, at any point in the investigation, order that further testimony be taken in the village court. Once the investigation is completed, the judge formulates his decision. He notifies the parties to the case of his decision and gives them the opportunity to appeal. If he finds the accused innocent, the judge sends the case back to the prosecutor, asking if he conforms with the decision or wishes to appeal. The district prosecutor may send the case to his superior in Oaxaca City, the state attorney general, for advice, or he may conform or appeal at his own discretion.

The district prosecutor generally appeals to the superior court if the district judge finds the accused innocent. If the judge finds the accused guilty and the accused appeals, the superior court, when it upholds the judge's conviction, usually reduces the sentence pronounced at the district level. The district court, as a rule, levies the maximum sentence on a guilty party.

The preceding discussion outlines the formal judicial procedure followed in Loani courts, but it does not convey the ambiguity that actually exists in district court procedure. The district court is dependent on the cooperation of Zapotec court officials and individual disputants in its investigation of a case. When cooperation is not forthcoming from village court officials, witnesses, or parties, the district court personnel, at their own discretion, may terminate the case at any point by placing it in the archives. They may also threaten fines against village court personnel for lack of cooperation. At the last resort, the court may enlist the aid of the state judicial police. To my knowledge, between 1963 and 1973, judicial police were only twice asked by the district judge to enter Loani villages. Usually the court terminates a case without the use of force.

Individuals may influence district court personnel who participate in their social networks to terminate a case. Rotation of district court personnel leaves some cases forgotten in court archives. Most cases in which a prisoner is held in Villa Laba after conviction end with the prisoner's escape before his compliance with the court sentence. After an escape, accusations are made against Villa Laba village officials for accepting bribes to aid the escape. No such accusations were verified in any case between 1963 and 1973, by either court officials or myself.

The primary terminator of district court case investigations and prosecutions is the mountain Zapotec village in which a dispute has arisen—even when the village court itself has been instrumental in sending the case to Villa Laba. The actual district court investigation makes the state an active presence in the local-level legal structure. This presence is, as illustrated before, a challenge to village autonomy and to the maintenance of customary village boundaries. More directly, it is in conflict with a community's views of its own rights in the control of community-based affairs.

A district court investigation and prosecution does not merely conflict with Zapotec court style and aims in worldview or through comparison. It directly impedes the operation of Zapotec village courts as well as other village institutions that settle disputes. The ways in which conflicts and contradictions between levels take form in competition over the settlement of disputes is examined in the following two cases involving murder. The first case, "The Murder of the Political Boss," was investigated simultaneously by the district court and by me. The second, "A Case of an Unlikely Death," is drawn from district court documents.

THE MURDER OF THE POLITICAL BOSS

March 13 marks the first day of Villa Laba's largest celebration, the annual fiesta of its patron saint. On March 12, 1974, the people of Villa Laba were making final preparations for the fiesta's first program, a presentation of dances, speeches, and poetry by primary school students from nearby Zapotec villages. That night R. Luis Maldonado, a schoolteacher, the political boss of Villa Laba, and the most powerful political figure in the district of Loani, was murdered. The next day, when news of Luis's death reached residents of Villa Laba, the village entered a state of crisis and paranoia, which resulted in the strengthening of divisions among Villa Laba's political factions and a shifting of power.

On the morning of March 13, Jose Maldonado J., Luis's father, appeared in the district court. The district prosecutor recorded the following declaration:

"Yesterday, my son, Professor Luis Maldonado, lending his services to the primary school of Loaga, being drunk, left his house around 10:30 p.m. to walk to Loaga. I asked him not to go because it was late. He answered that the trip to Loaga was pressing because his students had to prepare for the fiesta and needed his help. I told him he could leave at 5:00 in the morning and arrive in Loaga at 7:30 a.m. to prepare his students for the trip to Villa Laba, but he didn't want to listen to me. He left that night for Loaga, not allowing anyone to go with him, carrying his 22-caliber rifle, a machete, and his pistol. Just a few minutes ago I learned that he was found dead inside a hut on the 'Ranch of Cipriano' along the path to Loaga. At the moment I don't know who is responsible for his murder, but I plan to investigate it and will return to this office later to add to my declaration. If my son was murdered, it's because he has been the initiator of many projects for the benefit of the village and for this reason he has many enemies."

Following Jose's declaration, the district prosecutor and all the court officials walked down the path leading to the river of Loaga and the Ranch of Cipriano, an abandoned adobe hut thirty minutes' walk above the river crossing. During Jose's declaration, word had spread quickly throughout Villa Laba of Luis's death. Men from the village ran out of their houses and farmers left their fields to fall in line behind the court officials as they headed to recover Luis's body. They found him lying on the dirt floor of the hut with four machete wounds in the head, neck, and abdomen. After the prosecutor's inspection of the body and the hut, which yielded no clues, the men of the village hoisted their leader's body onto a wooden plank, covered it with a sheet, and carried it up the mountain to Villa Laba. They cleared a room in Luis's home and placed the body on a table, which was soon surrounded by mourners and Luis Maldonado's family.

The district prosecutor returned to his office and typed out a description of Luis's injuries and an account of his inspection of the hut. He sent a telegram to the state attorney general, informing him of the murder, and officially opened an investigation into the death. That day the court investigation assumed a strategy that continued until the identification of the murderer. Court officials did not actively prosecute the case. They called no witnesses and refused to answer questions of Villa Laba citizens concerning information they had on the assassination. Court officials merely continued with their daily work and waited.

The villagers of Villa Laba also embarked on their own investigation. On the afternoon of March 13, small groups of men and women filled the village paths and the central square. They all talked quietly and confidentially, speculating on who had killed their political leader. Their speculation did not initially run to one individual but to groups and villages. It was possibly the people of Yagila who, between 1952 and 1954, had feuded with Villa Laba; or the people of Villa Grande, who were in competition with Villa Laba for leadership in the district. The people of Villa Laba, in their conversations, agreed that the murder had been premeditated.

The afternoon of March 14, the district prosecutor summoned Luis's wife to his office. He recorded the following testimony from her:

"The afternoon of March 12, R. Luis Maldonado was lending his services to the rural primary school of Loaga. That day he was called by the federal school inspector of this zone to a meeting of all the zone's teachers.

After the meeting he made a few purchases in the village and then returned home where, between 8:00 and 9:00 p.m., he ate supper. Since he had instructions from the inspector to bring his students from Loaga to Villa Laba the next day, he left for Loaga around 10:30 p.m., carrying a 22-caliber rifle, a wool bag containing forty-five bullets, a mountain knife, and medicine.

"The next day, around 11:00 a.m., a messenger from Loaga arrived at Luis's house with musical instruments and materials they were going to use today in the fiesta program. The messenger said Luis had not arrived in Loaga. The declarant then sent one of her sons to advise her father-in-law of the message so that he would look for Luis. After a long search they found his body in the Rancho of Cipriano about one kilometer and a half from Villa Laba. . . ."

To the district prosecutor's questions Luis's wife answered:

"When Luis left the house he took his two dogs, who returned about an hour and a half later. So possibly her husband was killed around 11:30 p.m. in the abovementioned place. When her husband talked with the declarant he said that various people in Villa Laba resented him for village projects he had been working on and for advice he was giving to village authorities concerning completion of the technical school. Luis was actually head of the school's committee of patrons. Also, when her husband was presidente municipal of Villa Laba, he constructed the concrete municipal building which houses village offices and the district court. He brought electricity to the village and constructed the road connecting Villa Laba with Padua. For all these projects he received congratulations from the governor of the state. Because of completion of these projects, people who are not friends of progress have been distributing anonymous sheets which attack her husband. Up to this moment she does not know who killed her husband, but will investigate it and then return to add to her testimony."

The day of Luis's wife's declaration, following the initial shock of Luis's murder, village gossip—or the public voice, as it is called—began to change the focus of its speculation. Other people in Villa Laba besides Luis's father and wife believed that one of their own citizens, or a group of their citizens, had killed Luis. This opinion was not spoken openly, but was whispered in homes and kitchens into individual gossip channels. Speculation centered around Cipriano (owner of the hut where Luis was murdered), Cipriano's cousin, and a core group of traditionalists who opposed Luis's political stance and his leadership in village projects.

One of the village elders, when he first learned of Luis's death, stated that it was bound to happen: Luis had led a valiant life. He was referring to the many fights Luis had initiated with other village residents who had opposed him. In 1972, while drunk, Luis had attempted to strangle the 62-year-old Cipriano. The dispute was handled by Villa Laba's presidente, but Cipriano had been vocal in his dissatisfaction with the fine levied against Luis. Luis had also fought with Cipriano's cousin.

Both Cipriano and his cousin had criminal records. Cipriano had robbed and killed a mail carrier in 1938. He was put in Villa Laba district jail, but escaped. No one had attempted to reapprehend him, although he walked daily throughout the district seat. In that murder, Cipriano had used a machete and, although his guilt was determined by the district court, he was never rejailed. Both Cipriano and his cousin, like many other Villa Laba citizens with records of violence, participate actively in the daily lives of their villages, their criminal pasts unknown, forgotten, or not considered important.

The Villa Laba public voice also accused the village's core group of traditionalists, a few of whom had been seen talking together the night of the murder. Three lived along the path to Loaga. They were farmers, the poorest citizens of Villa Laba, and all had participated in writing and distributing in the streets and paths of the district seat sheets of paper signed "Anonymous." They attacked progressivist projects and called on the people of Villa Laba to unite against exploitation by the state government and by Villa Laba citizens who profited from state-supported village projects.

Not all the traditionalists were poor. Among them was one of the wealthiest men in Villa Laba, who had been the most prestigious state-employed official in the district of Loani, using his position to fill his pockets and purchase land in the district seat. He was opposed to change in Villa Laba and had written a number of "Anonymous" sheets. One of the sheets contained the following poem addressed to Luis Maldonado:

The negotiation is over now
For the technical school.
Maybe now you're going to understand
What is left to our secondary school.
But don't bother yourself for that reason,
I treat you like my son-in-law.
I will plant you in a grave
And give you a ticket to Hell.

Although the popular public voice was trying Cipriano, Cipriano's cousin, and the traditionalist faction, a smaller gossip channel, limited to a few of the village's older women, was developing a different version of the murder. A woman who lived just above Villa Laba's entrance to the path to Loaga had, the night of the murder, seen a man walking into the village with blood on his machete, shirt, and hands. He had stopped to wash in one of the creeks that run through Villa Laba, and had then continued into the village. She knew that the man was from a village called the "Land of Roots," a settlement about seven hours' walk from Villa Laba. That village was also ruled by a political boss of Villa Laban descent. The day Luis's body was discovered, the stranger had gone to a dry-goods store owned by a Villa Laba progressive, second in political power only to Luis. There he had sold two burlap bags of coffee, and then headed back to his village. This information did not become general knowledge in Villa Laba through the public voice. Only female friends of the old woman were privy to her observations.

Throughout the week following the assassination, conversation centered on the murder. The popular version carried by the public voice entered into the gossip channels of the district court through the civil registrar of Loani, a Villa Laba native and resident; through the executor of the district court, who was Luis's brother; and through the presidente municipal of Villa Laba. Officials in Oaxaca City also began to investigate the murder. On March 23, the district prosecutor sent a letter to the state attorney general in which he stated that he had made no progress in his investigation. The attorney general then sent an order to the head of the state judicial police. Two agents of the judicial police were dispatched from Oaxaca City to investigate the assassination.

On the evening of April 3, some Villa Laba rumors became formal testimony in the office of the district prosecutor. The confidential agents of the judicial police had called in Luis's father, the presidente municipal, and a Villa Laban teacher who had worked with Luis in Loaga. The Villa Labans designated Cipriano, the cousin, and the core group of traditionalists as the murderers of Luis. They cited popular village gossip and past actions of the accused parties as reasons for their accusations. That same evening the state judicial police formulated a list of possible assassins, whom they planned to take to Oaxaca for interrogation.

On the morning of April 4, the presidente of Villa Laba dispatched village police to warn some of the accused to hide because the judicial police would, that morning, attempt to apprehend them. The presidente did not warn Cipriano, the cousin, and two other members of the traditionalist group who had vocally attacked Luis in village meetings. That morning, the four men who had not been warned were brought by the judicial police to the office of the district prosecutor. Their hands were bound with rope, and they were placed in a truck that took them to the top of Villa Laba's mountain. From there, they walked eight hours along a rain-rutted path to Villa Grande, where they boarded a truck to Oaxaca City. With the actions of the state judicial police, the village of Villa Laba was again thrown into a crisis.

The public voice expressed sympathy for the accused who had been taken away to Oaxaca City. The people of Villa Laba, although they had been the original accusers, voiced fear for the future and lives of their abducted *paisanos*. "Why didn't they go to Yagila or Villa Grande to look for the murderers? Why are they punishing Villa Laba?" became the mood of the public voice. People spoke of the hardships the accused would experience during their interrogations. More specifically, the public voice contained fear that the Villa Labans would undergo torture in Oaxaca City and confess to the murder whether they were guilty or not. That night, a secret agent of the state judicial police, who was working in Villa Laba as head of the construction crew for the technical school, discussed state tactics of interrogation in Tia Pia's restaurant. A number of citizens of the village crowded into Tia Pia's and listened to three hours of stories of how judicial police tortured witnesses into "telling the truth" or signing confessions.

Tia Pia was a native Villa Laban and the widow of a former district prosecutor and secretary of the district court, who had died in 1964 of overdrinking. She was a major terminal for Villa Laba gossip and participated in the older women's gossip channel. Tia Pia was a friend of Cipriano, who had been taken away by the state judicial police. She often prepared breakfast for him in exchange for a few ears of fresh corn. Tia Pia was also, at the time, having a secret affair with the presidente of Villa Laba. The day after Cipriano and the others were taken to Oaxaca City, Tia Pia was sitting in her kitchen with her Zapotec servant, discussing the murder of Luis. Following the discussion, in which Tia Pia and her servant exchanged the women's versions of the murder, Tia Pia put on her shawl and, after looking up and down the street, walked alone toward the Villa Laba municipal building. She walked past the village offices where the presidente was talking with other citizens, and then headed for a secret place where she and the presidente often met. There, Tia Pia related to the presidente the older women's version of the death of Luis. She told him about her friend's observations of the man from the "Land of Roots."

Later that day, village authorities and personnel of the district court pieced together their knowledge of the public voice and Tia Pia's revelation. They then apprehended Jeronimo Gonzalez, a resident of a village near

Villa Laba who made frequent trips to the "Land of Roots." On the night of the murder, Jeronimo, after selling coffee in Villa Laba, had left the district seat and had headed in the direction of the "Land of Roots" with his fourteen-year-old helper, Carlos. On the day Tia Pia confided in the presidente, Jeronimo was back in Villa Laba to participate in the weekly market. In the office of the district prosecutor, Jeronimo told the story of how and why Luis Maldonado had been murdered in the Ranch of Cipriano.

On the night of March 12, Jeronimo left Villa Laba with Carlos for the "Land of Roots." As they were walking toward the Loaga river crossing, it began to rain. In the path, just above the river, they ran into Pablo Velasco, a stranger who was returning to his home in the "Land of Roots." The three decided to return to the abandoned adobe hut they had passed along the path. When Pablo entered the hut, he found Luis Maldonado sleeping inside. Luis woke up and surprised, grabbed his rifle, asking Pablo where he was from. Pablo, frightened, at first didn't answer. Luis then asked again, threatening Pablo with his gun. Pablo answered, and then Luis, drunk, began to insult and threaten him. Pablo left the hut and told Carlos to go down the path to his donkey and bring him his machete. When Carlos returned, Pablo sent him to wait for him along the path and then addressed Jeronimo: "Now we're going to see how *macho* you from Balea are," and warned Jeronimo never to reveal what he was about to do. Pablo, angered with Luis's threats, walked back into the hut and murdered him. Jeronimo had not known who Luis was nor where he was from.

Jeronimo was jailed, and young Carlos was summoned from Balea by the district prosecutor. He corroborated Jeronimo's testimony and testified that Jeronimo had not participated in the murder. The prosecutor then sent a telegram to the attorney general in Oaxaca City and consigned the case to the judge of the district court. The judge, through the prosecutor, notified the head of the Oaxaca state judicial police that he had issued an order for the apprehension of Pablo Velasco. The police did not attempt to apprehend Pablo; a search would have led them through the mountains and villages of Loani's roughest terrain. Their investigation was suspended with the formal jailing of Jeronimo, and the family of Luis took over the investigation. They sent descriptions and other information concerning Pablo to relatives and Villa Labans throughout Mexico with the hope that they would see or apprehend him in his flight from Loani.

Representatives from the factions of Villa Laba addressed a village meeting four nights after Jeronimo's apprehension and testimony. The general theme of the speakers was that wounds had formed in the village, but that people needed to forget the events of the past few weeks and return to normalcy. The village, however, did not do so. When those who had been taken to Oaxaca City came back, the core of traditionalists expanded their voice in village affairs. They attacked the views and actions of the progressive presidente, and in the next village elections they took over the village government, which had not been in their hands for eighteen years.

In June 1974 the district prosecutor requested the attorney general to transfer Jeronimo to the state penitentiary. The prosecutor claimed that the district jail did not provide enough security for the continued confinement of Jeronimo. In early July, as papers were being prepared for Jeronimo's transfer, he escaped from the Villa Laba jail. He fled to Yecovi, a small village near the "Land of Roots." There, unbeknownst to the villagers of Villa Laba, he was given refuge. But at the time my research ended, in December 1974, the actual murderer of Luis had not been apprehended.

ANALYSIS OF THE MURDER OF THE POLITICAL BOSS

The murder of Villa Laba's political boss took place against a backdrop of the struggles among the political factions of the district seat, and between Villa Laba and the state judicial system. The case charted, first, the cooperation of Villa Labans with state judicial authorities and, later, villagers' resistance as the state investigation generated a feeling of persecution. This feeling overrode Villa Laba's internal political conflicts and inspired a unified effort by the villagers to resist prosecution of village citizens by judicial agents from the state capital. The shifting alignments are illustrated in the relationship between the informal village-level investigations of the murder, conducted through individual networks, and the formal investigation, conducted by the district court and the state judicial police.

Four lines of reasoning evolved in Villa Laba's public voice during the state investigation. Two of them were prevalent in all Villa Laban gossip networks. The first was based on general village knowledge and was discussed openly in gatherings of citizens on the streets and in the bars. It developed from the history of inimical relations between the district seat and the Zapotec villages. This line of reasoning charted past power struggles between the villages and postulated a unified effort by an "enemy" village to eliminate Villa Laba's most influential leader.

The second line of reasoning, also general knowledge and discussed openly, derived from conflicts between Villa Laba's major political factions, the conservatives and the progressives. Gossip that related specific acts or statements of the conservatives to the murder of Luis was not general knowledge but was fabricated by the progressives. The progressive fabrications entered slowly into the general public voice and were discussed only in limited gossip networks, since the members of the networks were aware that anyone possessing knowledge of these fabricated relationships faced the possibility of being called as a witness in the district court investigation.

The third rationale included a number of personal motives for murdering Luis Maldonado. It implicated both Villa Labans and mountain Zapotecs who held grudges against him. Grudges held by certain Villa Labans were general knowledge and were discussed openly in street gossip groups. Gossip which linked Luis specifically with Zapotecs in other villages was transmitted through personal ties between Villa Labans and Zapotec villagers.

The fourth line of reasoning was factual and was based on a Villa Laban woman's sighting of the murderer the night of Luis's death. This line of reasoning was individual and was confined, through fear of involvement, to the witness's personal gossip network.

The Operational Structure of Appeals

The district court based its case on the second line of reasoning and the parts of the third which were discussed openly. Some testimony in the court investigation was factual, specifically that which detailed grudges held by certain Villa Labans against Luis. However, the basic court case that established a conservative conspiracy to murder Luis was fabricated as it passed through gossip channels.

The way in which the district court case developed, as well as its effects on the village of Villa Laba, were products of the transactional networks of district court personnel which, in Loani, are confined to progressive state employees, local politicians, and merchants.[3] The selective nature of these networks erects a structure of privileged access to the court, for through them individuals may pass information to the court concerning specific investigations or may lay the basis for future investigations. The reciprocal nature of the court's transactional networks, as well as their political and professional basis, eliminates for the privileged the danger of involvement in a formal district court investigation by providing an informal mode of testifying.

Villa Laban networks are an extension of the district court and in essence provide a district-wide structure of appeals which the court may utilize in conjunction with the formal state structure. The informal structure stretches as far into Loani as Villa Laban networks reach. As Zapotec village networks have extended to state personnel as well as to Villa Laban state loyalists, so have village gossip channels—a mode of social control generally confined to a local village in Loani. The informal structure operates in two directions: the villager may utilize it to pass on information, or the district court may use it to plug into a public-voice investigation of a village crime. Either use of the voice has the same consequence: a change in power relations on the local level through the direct involvement of a state institution and through validation of only one of many possible village views of a dispute.

When the formal legal structure is not productive in a case investigation, the district court may initiate a passive strategy of waiting for information to enter into its gossip channels. The court may also apply an active strategy through stepping up its formal investigation and forcing villagers to surrender factual information on the dispute, formally or informally, in order to defend community boundaries. The court initially applied the passive strategy in its search for the murderer of Luis, allowing the village of Villa Laba to conduct the investigation through the public voice. For the court, waiting proved successful through inducing the flow of information, verified by more than one state employee since it had sprung from their gossip network, from which the court could make, in conjunction with state judicial police, formal accusations. The formalization of Villa Laban gossip by the court undermined the role of gossip as an investigative and rehabilitative mode of social control and escalated Villa Laban factional disputes by taking them beyond the point of forgiveness.

Political Crisis

By translating accusations of the public voice into formal accusations, the district court ended its waiting game and began an active prosecution, through the judicial police, of individuals who had been accused in the progressive gossip channels. The beginning of this stage of the court investigation initiated a period of crisis in Villa Laba.

When the judicial police took residents of Villa Laba to Oaxaca by force, they overstepped village barriers to outside participation in local affairs. The control that residents of the district seat were accustomed to exercising over district court investigations was eliminated by the involvement of state judicial police. Use of force by the state police as well as the sizable number of citizens taken to Oaxaca generated a feeling of political persecution among the residents of Villa Laba, and they moved to a defensive posture. The progressive public voice turned to accusing the state rather than the local conservatives of violent action. It also began to defend those whom it had previously accused, saying that they should not be punished for old grudges and conflicts.

A compromise with the state took form in the public voice. Knowledge which had previously been confined to personal gossip channels rose into the general public voice. Personal information on grudges held by individual mountain Zapotecs against the political boss became more widespread, and knowledge of the fourth line of reasoning entered the district court network.

On the basis of the fourth line of reasoning, founded on one Villa Laban's sighting of the bloodied murderer the night of Luis's death, the district court apprehended one of the murderer's companions. Through his testimony the court developed the full history of the homicidal incident. Since the factual clue that led to the companion's apprehension entered the district court through the operational structure of appeals, the individual who originally held the clue was not called to witness in the court investigation. When the district court began to develop the case on the basis of the fourth line of reasoning, resistance to the court investigation shifted to the accused and their villages.

Restoration of Equilibrium

Release of the Villa Laban prisoners by the state judicial police marked the restoration of strained equilibrium between the state and the district seat. However, internal disequilibrium among Villa Laban factions, which was a result of state involvement in the murder case, continued. Conservatives, through the public voice, began to conduct an investigation into who among Villa Laban employees had been responsible for the formalized accusations against them. The progressives, however, successfully confined this information to their own personal networks. Conservative leaders began to speak more often and with less intimidation in village juntas. In the first village election following the crisis initiated by Luis's death, a leader of the conservative faction, for the first time in eighteen years, was elected presidente of Villa Laba.

THE CASE OF AN UNLIKELY DEATH

On January 11, 1968, Angela Bautista, a twenty-three-year-old housewife from Arroyo Chico, walked to Villa Laba to inform the district prosecutor of the death of her husband. The prosecutor recorded that Angela declared:

"On the afternoon of Wednesday, January 10, the authorities of Arroyo Chico called a general meeting of all citizens to present an account of the past year's finances. Her husband, Ernesto Bautista Garcia, was attending the meeting. The meeting was suspended that afternoon so the citizens could return to their homes to eat supper, but was resumed during the evening. Around 7:00 p.m. Angela went on an errand to the central square, where some boys from the village informed her that her husband, Ernesto, had been placed in jail. Angela returned to her home and told her mother-in-law that when the meeting ended they should take some supper to Ernesto because he was in jail.

"Around 9:30 that night Angela and her mother-in-law left their house for the jail in the central square, but on the way they ran into a group of men whom they didn't know. They said good evening to the men and continued on their errand. When they arrived at the jail, Ernesto was not there. The two women finally located him surrounded by a group of men on the village basketball court near the municipal building. Approaching the group, Angela and her mother-in-law saw that Ernesto was lying on the court dead. Ernesto's mother immediately went to the municipal building and asked the authorities if they had called Ernesto to the meeting in order to kill him. The authorities answered 'no' and said that they were preparing an account of the death to send to the district seat. After passing once more by Ernesto's body on the basketball court, Angela and her mother-in-law, crying, began to walk toward their house. On the way, they ran into a group of men whom they could not identify because it was night.

"The men asked the two women why they were crying. Angela answered that they were crying because Ernesto was dead, that the authorities had murdered him. The men explained that the authorities had not murdered Ernesto but that he had been killed by gas from a generator that was located in the jail. The men added that the sindico had covered the wrought-iron jail door with two sheets of aluminum siding because the generator was drowning out what he was saying during the meeting. When Angela arrived at her house, she asked Ernesto's brother whether he or she should go to Villa Laba to advise the authorities of what had happened. Ernesto's brother told Angela and her mother-in-law to go to Villa Laba while he took care of Ernesto's body."

In answer to a question posed by the district prosecutor, Angela stated that she did not think the authorities had killed Ernesto. She believed it was definitely the generator that had deprived him of life. Angela's mother-in-law then gave a similar account of events to the prosecutor. She added that Ernesto did not have difficulties with anyone in Arroyo Chico and that he was an honest boy. She stated that she did not think anyone had killed him, and she attributed his death to gas from the generator.

With the declarations of Angela and her mother-in-law, the prosecutor prepared a letter to the sindico of Arroyo Chico. He enclosed a copy of the women's declarations and instructed the sindico to begin an investigation into the death of Ernesto Bautista Garcia. The prosecutor told the sindico to take testimony from anyone who might know about the death and to perform an autopsy on Ernesto's body. Prompted by the prosecutor's letter, the sindico immediately consigned the investigation to the alcalde of Arroyo Chico. With the sindico's consignation of the case, the alcalde began to take testimony. The sindico, a thirty-six year old farmer, made this statement to the alcalde:

"Last year's authorities gave to the authorities of this new year an act dated December 30, 1967, which ordered Ernesto Bautista Garcia to serve in the village police force because he had not complied with a previous order to serve. Taking into account the contents of the act and finding the village citizens gathered in a meeting on the porch of the municipal building, I ran into Ernesto and informed him he had been ordered to serve in this year's police force. Ernesto refused to serve, and so I notified the presidente of his refusal. Since he had so many matters to attend to in the meeting, the presidente ordered that Ernesto be held in jail until the meeting was finished. When the meeting was over, more or less around nine o'clock, the presidente ordered me to take Ernesto out of jail in order to hear his case. However, the policemen I ordered to bring Ernesto returned and told me that they had found him dead in jail, and that just a few moments before finding his body they had seen Domitilio Alcantara and Urbano Vargas standing in front of the jail chatting with him. I then ordered the police to remove Ernesto from the jail in order to try to help him. The police took Ernesto's body to the basketball court to give him air, but his body did not react. From the basketball court they took the body to the corridor of the municipal building, where Ernesto's grandfather tried to revive him. Since the body showed no signs of life we put it in the courtroom of the municipio."

The alcalde then read to the sindico the declarations that Angela and Ernesto's mother had made before the district prosecutor. The alcalde asked the sindico if it were true that he had covered the jail door with two aluminum sheets in order to block out the noise of the generator. The sindico replied to the testimony:

"It isn't true that I covered the jail door with two aluminum sheets. There wasn't any need to because, although there was a generator in the jail, it wasn't functioning. During the meeting we lit up the porch with gasoline lanterns. It's true that Ernesto's mother came to see us asking if we had killed her son. We indicated to her that we were then taking care of her son's death in order to advise the authorities in the district seat."

Following the sindico's declaration, the alcalde of Arroyo Chico heard testimony from six more men who had been present at the village meeting. All the men confirmed that the generator in the jail had not been in use the night of the meeting and that the corridor had been lit with gasoline lanterns. Also, all six men denied that the door of the jail had been covered with aluminum sheets during the meeting. Domitilio Alcantara and Urbano Vargas, who according to village police had been standing in front of the jail talking to Ernesto during the meeting, also testified. They stated that around 8:30 p.m. they had run into Ernesto's brother on the basketball court. His brother gave them some cigarettes and matches and asked them to give them to Ernesto, who was in the jail. They went to the jail and called for Ernesto, but he didn't answer. They couldn't see him because the jail was dark. They then gave the cigarettes to the village authorities. In answer to the alcalde's questions, the two stated that there had been no aluminum sheets in front of the jail door when they went to look for Ernesto.

After taking testimony in the case, village authorities prepared Ernesto's body for burial and arranged for an autopsy to be performed at the cemetery. They asked two citizens of the village to serve as witnesses in identifying the corpse. The two men testified that they recognized the body because they were paisanos from Arroyo Chico. They said that Ernesto was eighteen and that they didn't know if he had had any illnesses. They gave the names of Ernesto's parents and said they knew nothing about the cause of Ernesto's death. The perito practico, Alfredo Flores, a Villa Laban farmer who, for a price, performed autopsies for the nearby villages, then began his examination of the body.

In his report, the perito practico stated: "The thorax cavity opened, the lungs were found to be in a normal state; the abdominal cavity opened, the organs were found to be in a normal state; for which, in the judgment of the *perito practico*, the death of Ernesto Bautista Garcia was due to a cardiac arrest."

The autopsy having been completed, the presidente ordered the body buried. The presidente then returned to the municipio and prepared Ernesto's death certificate, which he sent to the alcalde. The alcalde then sent the results of his investigation to the district prosecutor in Villa Laba.

The prosecutor immediately consigned the investigation, or *primeras diligencias*, to the judge of the district court. He requested the judge to take the case through to completion, ordering all witnesses to come to Villa Laba to ratify their declarations. He also asked the judge to submit the autopsy report and all other pertinent documents to the Third Judge of the district, located in Oaxaca City, who assists district judges in case investigations, so that he might receive an opinion about Ernesto's autopsy from doctors assigned to the superior court. The prosecutor also gave the district judge a piece of paper he had found in Ernesto's pocket, a paper signed by the previous year's authorities of Arroyo Chico, certifying that Ernesto had served in the village police force in 1966 and should not be asked to serve in 1967. The paper instructed village authorities to name another citizen in Ernesto' place.

The district judge notified the superior court in Oaxaca that he was opening an investigation into the murder of Ernesto Bautista Garcia of Arroyo Chico. He also sent the perito practico's autopsy report to the Third Judge in Oaxaca, asking him to forward it to the court doctors. The district judge then sent a letter to the alcalde of Arroyo Chico ordering him to notify all who had testified before him to come to Villa Laba to ratify their declarations. On January 17, 1968, the witnesses from Arroyo Chico went to Villa Laba and signed their declarations. None had anything to add to or change in their testimony.

Nine months later, on September 7, 1968, the district judge received a letter from the Third Judge in Oaxaca which included the coroners' opinion on the death of Ernesto. The coroners concluded from the alcalde's investigation and the perito practico's autopsy—not from their own examination of the body—that "the cause of the death of Ernesto Bautista Garcia was a cardiac insufficiency of pathological origins." Having received the coroners' opinion, the district judge did not proceed further with the case. It lay inactive for nearly three years until, in May 1971, a new district judge, clearing house, reopened it by sending it to a new district prosecutor to ask how he wished to proceed in the investigation.

The prosecutor replied in a written communication that since the coroners had previously determined that Ernesto's death was due to pathological origins, no crime had been committed. He asked the judge to close the case. Conforming with the prosecutor's request, the district judge, on May 18, 1971, closed the investigation into the death of Ernesto and archived the case.

ANALYSIS OF THE CASE OF AN UNLIKELY DEATH

This case is illustrative of many that pass through the district court. Here, the district court investigation is a search for a key in the case—any fact or the first fact that happens to surface, not as a clue but as an explanation that will provide a reasonable justification for terminating the case investigation.

In many investigations, the district court may find the key to resolution in a fact associated with the crime or in an act that occurs during the investigation. Resolution through the latter generally results from lack of cooperation of Zapotec villagers with the district court investigation. In the face of lack of cooperation the district court may achieve resolution by officially archiving the case or unofficially forgetting about it. As I stated before, lack of cooperation is not the only means Zapotec villagers have for resisting the district court investigation. They may also provide the district court with a fabricated fact that may serve to terminate the district-level investigation. It is up to the villagers to decide whether the key they provide the court will be fact or fiction.

In the case of Ernesto Garcia's unlikely death, the key to resolution was provided by one of the district seat's perito practicos. It was confirmed, on the basis of second-hand information, by practicos assigned to the superior court in Oaxaca City. However, the public voice, as it was presented by Angela Bautista to the state prosecutor, indicated that there were two other possible resolutions: (1) that Ernesto was murdered through tacit agreement among village authorities and the male citizens, or (2) that Ernesto died of gas-fume inhalation resulting from the sindico's act of covering the jail door with aluminum sheets.

Although Angela had originally stated that she suspected the village officials of killing Ernesto, her later testimony protected both the village government and her fellow citizens from involvement in the case. In court she stated she did not believe village officials had killed Ernesto, and she said she could not identify the men who told her he had died from gas-fume inhalation. The latter claim is unlikely, given the face-to-face nature of life in the small village of Arroyo Chico.

The village government covered itself through homogenization of testimony in its own investigation and in that of the state prosecutor—a common occurrence. The testimony of defendants or complainants before district court officials often has a word-for-word similarity, resulting from unified resistance to the court investigation and previous agreement on a story that will provide the court with a key to resolution and at the same time protect the village. Homogenization of testimony, in many cases, is the effect of gossip on the remembered impressions and perceptions of witnesses as well as on witnesses' unwillingness openly to contradict local public opinion. The purpose of village testimony in the case of Ernesto's death was to protect the sindico from prosecution, for the district court could have charged him with accidental homicide.

Most cases that pass through the district court have resolutions similar to that of the case of Ernesto's death rather than that of the case of the murder of the political boss. The district court generally does not have the interest to move the case—as it did the political boss's—either by the waiting tactic or by triggering the feeling of political persecution and making the public voice enter into its transactional networks.

The differences between the two cases illustrate some of the main reasons why Zapotec villages are able to resist the district court. Unlike the Villa Laba prosecutor (in the murder of the political boss case study), the alcalde of Arroyo Chico did not include the family of Ernesto in his investigation. Although the village boundaries were violated by Angela and her mother-in-law, both of those villagers in their testimony to the district prosecutor protected fellow villagers from prosecution by denying motivation or reasons for accusation. The Arroyo Chico investigation of the death did not give the district court informal channels of communication to utilize in gaining key information.

CONCLUSIONS

The two legal levels in Loani, the state legal system and village legal systems, are interrelated within two structures: the formal state structure of appeals and an informal operational structure of appeals based on personal ties among state personnel, residents of the district seat, and Zapotec villagers. Within the state legal system, village and state judicial institutions are arranged vertically in a line of appeals. Access to institutions travels up this line of appeals from local to state judicial institutions but in practice does not travel downward from state to local institutions or from village municipio to agencia. Competition between levels inhibits use of state institutions by village institutions or residents and inhibits cooperation by village courts with district court investigations and prosecutions.

As village courts, through direct contact with state institutions, have elaborated their procedures to protect their customary jurisdictions and local autonomy, some villagers have extended their transactional networks to individuals in Villa Laba and Oaxaca City who are involved in modern state movements. The extension of individual transactional networks into state institutions on the district level provides an informal structure that individuals and institutions participating in the network may activate when the formal legal structure does not serve their aims.

The informal operational structure is similar to the local-level legal system in that relationships within it are particularistic (personal) and often functionally diffuse.[4] The permanence of the operational structure of appeals derives from continuity in the transactional networks of Villa Labans and from inclusions in their networks of *positions* in district-level institutions, rather than merely specific individuals who occupy them at any one time.

The informal structure, unlike the state structure of appeals, provides two-way bilingual channels of communication between the district court and local communities. It allows the litigious plaintiff to balance the legal ledger in his favor as he initiates a district court case and provides channels through which facts and gossip may be volunteered or surrendered to the district court without consequent involvement in a formal court investigation. It also provides channels of communication which the district court may tap or activate by applying investigative strategies developed through competition with the local legal systems.

As a district court investigation proceeds through both formal and informal legal structures, competition between state and local levels affects the capability of Loani legal systems to settle disputes. When the barriers that isolate the local legal systems are transgressed by the district court through the individual transactional networks that extend to the district seat and into the district court:

1. An imbalance is created within local lines of gossip. Transactional networks of district court personnel consist primarily of state employees. The occupational homogeneity of these networks opens a path of privileged access to the district court. The activation of gossip networks that extend from a village to the district court distorts power relationships in the village in favor of individuals with ties to the state. Through giving credence to one line of gossip over another on the basis of personal ties, the operational structure disrupts the equilibrium in local lines of gossip and makes gossip a disruptive force within the village.

As a result of the disruption of the local judicial system by the active participation of the district court in village disputes:

2. Local court procedure is involuted to resist the involvement of outside judicial agencies in village affairs.
3. Village courts falsify case investigations sent to the district court in an appealed dispute.
4. Village courts actively ignore or resist district court investigation.
5. Individual participants in disputes homogenize their testimony, if it has not already been homogenized through gossip, in order to direct the outcome of district court investigations.
6. Individual participants in the dispute actively ignore or resist the district court investigation.
7. Individual participants in the dispute escape from the district jail.

As a result of the practices of village judicial institutions and residents in resisting state involvement in localized disputes:

8. The district court cannot investigate a village dispute, or it processes a falsified or one-sided version of the dispute.
9. The district court does not take to a point of resolution over 70 percent of the cases it processes. Village resistance also reduces the caseload of the Loani district court.

Also, as a result of village judicial practices formulated in response to district court investigations:

10. The district court changes its procedural mode of operation and triggers a feeling of political persecution within the village in which the dispute arose in order to make local gossip enter into district gossip networks.
11. The district court accepts without active investigation any version of a dispute which offers a key to resolution congruent with state codes of judicial procedure.[5]

The effects of competition between the state and villages in Loani are contradictory. Participation in the formal structure of appeals tends to strengthen village courts as they develop and test strategies to assert their authority and protect local autonomy. Extension of village transactional networks to the district seat, as well as to Oaxaca City, gives state institutions an operational foothold in village life and challenges the balance of power within local communities. Through the participation of local and state courts in dispute settlement, barriers to cooperation between them are strengthened. When village networks that extend to state institutions operate in dispute settlement, institutional cooperation is precluded and, for the state, unnecessary.

The question remains whether Loani villages will be able to maintain their corporate nature as they increase their participation in the legal, economic, educational, and political life of the state and nation—whether the territorial community will break down as the institutional community grows, or whether it may take a new form in the urban-rural networks of Mexico and the United States. Law in Loani, however, signifies that when the developing state attempts to integrate local community and state legal systems, the overlapping of jurisdictions leads to competition rather than cooperation between them, and thus to a breakdown in the abilities of both the state and community to exert social control. As long as the local community retains its cohesive nature, its ability to prevent the escalation of disputes and maintain the peace lies in the elaboration of its own modes of social control in opposition to state institutions. The state may counteract this resistance by proffering to individuals privileged access to its institutions and by manipulating power relationships within the community.

NOTES

1. The research upon which this research is based was supported by a training grant from the National Institute of Mental Health administered through the Center for the Study of Law and Society, University of California, Berkeley campus.

2. It must be noted, however, that the comparison of village and state as two distinct systems of political power may be misleading. While it is analytically useful

to present the structures as distinct in norms, purposes, and internal organization, this mode of explication may cloud the fact that as they participate in dispute settlement, the village and state are a single process. The dualism lies in the impact of this process on the abilities of members of each group to apply their own strategies in the struggle for jurisdiction.

3. Jeremy Boissevain (1974) describes an individual's transactional network as follows: "Then there is a circle of friends who are important to him in a more pragmatic sense for economic and political purposes and the logistics of daily life. As these contain strategic persons who may be useful to ego, he keeps his relationships with them warm so he can gain access to the friends of his friends."

4. Ottenberg (1967: 33) describes a similar situation in Southern Nigeria where the British attempted "to apply a system of government whose rules were highly universalistic and functionally specific in a region where particularistic values and functional diffuseness predominate despite differences in the cultural and political organization of the traditional ethnic groups. . . . What has happened is the Southern Nigerians, in local government and in association with it, have continued to carry out traditional patterns of behavior that are particularistic with diffuse role relationships."

5. Some pressures for closure come from procedural rules that require reporting of all steps taken in the processing of a case to judicial agencies in Oaxaca City. Litigious plaintiffs also complain in writing or in person to the superior court in Oaxaca City when the district court does not follow through in a case investigation. The district court is directly accountable to the Tribunal Superior in Oaxaca City. Case statistics are compiled annually by the state attorney general's office. However, an assistant to the state attorney general claimed that outgoing attorneys general burn reports from state districts which were submitted during their terms of office. State statistical reports are based on those statistics provided by the districts. With the help of an assistant to the state attorney general, I conducted a search for the reports and found only two complete annual collections of the original telegrams sent by district court officials reporting case statistics.

REFERENCES

Abel, Richard. 1973. "A Comparative Theory of Dispute Institutions in Society." *Law and Society Review* 8(2): 217–347.

American Heritage Dictionary of the English Language. 1969. Ed. William Morris. Boston: American Heritage and Houghton Mifflin.

Aubert, V. 1963a. "The Structure of Legal Thinking." In *Legal Essays: Festskrift til Frede Castberg*. Oslo.

—— 1963b. "Competition and Dissensus: Two Types of Conflict and of Conflict Resolution." *Journal of Conflict Resolution* 7(1): 26–42.

—— 1966. "Some Social Functions of Legislation." *Acta Sociologica* 10: 98–120.

—— 1969. "Law as a Way of Resolving Conflicts: The Case of a Small Industrialized Society." In L. Nader, ed., *Law in Culture and Society*, pp. 282–303. Chicago: Aldine.

Ayoub, V. F. 1965. "Conflict Resolution and Social Reorganization in a Lebanese Village." *Human Organization* 24(1): 11–17.

Bailey, F. G. 1960. *Tribe, Caste and Nation*. Manchester: University Press.

—— 1965. *Decisions by Consensus in Councils and Communities. Political Systems and the Distribution of Power*. A.S.A. Monograph No. 2. London: Tavistock.

—— 1969. *Strategems and Spoils: A Social Anthropology of Politics*. Oxford: Basil Blackwell.

—— 1971. *Gifts and Poison*. Oxford: Basil Blackwell.

Barnes, J. A. 1954. "Class and Committees in a Norwegian Island Parish." *Human Relations* 7: 39–58.

—— 1961. "Law as Politically Active: An Anthropological View." In Geoffrey Sawer, ed., *Studies in the Sociology of Law*, pp. 167–96. Canberra: Australian National University Press.

Barth, F. 1966. "Models of Social Organization." Occasional Paper No. 23. London: Royal Anthropological Institute of Great Britain and Ireland.

—— 1973. "Descent and Marriage Reconsidered." In J. Goody, ed., *The Character of Kinship*, pp. 3–19. London: Cambridge University Press.

Barton, R. F. 1919. "Ifugao Law." *University of California Publications in American Archaeology and Ethnology* 15(1): 1–186. Reprinted 1969. Berkeley and Los Angeles: University of California Press.

—— 1949. *The Kalingas: Their Institutions and Custom Law*. Chicago: University Press.

Berman, H. J. 1958. *The Nature and Functions of Law*. 3rd ed., 1972. Brooklyn: Foundation Press.

Berndt, R. M. 1962. *Excess and Restraint: Social Control among a New Guinea Mountain People*. Chicago: University Press.

Berthoud, G. 1972. "From Peasantry to Capitalism: The Meaning of Ownership in the Swiss Alps." *Anthropological Quarterly* 45(3): 177–95.

Best, Arthur, and A. Andreasen. 1976. *Talking Back to Business: Voiced and Unvoiced Consumer Complaints*. Washington, D.C.: Center for the Study of Responsive Law.

Black, Donald. 1976. *The Behavior of Law*. New York: Academic Press.

Black, Henry Campbell. 1951. *Black's Law Dictionary*. 4th ed. by the publisher's editorial staff. St. Paul: West.

Blalock, H. 1972. *Social Statistics*. New York: McGraw-Hill.

Bohannan, P. J. 1957. *Justice and Judgment among the Tiv*. London: Oxford University Press for the International African Institute.

—— 1965. "The Differing Realms of Law." In L. Nader, ed., *The Ethnography of Law*. *American Anthropologist* (special publication) 67(6) (2): 33–42.

Boissevain, J. 1968. "The Place of Non-Groups in the Social Sciences." *Man* 3: 542–56.

—— 1971. "Second Thoughts on Quasi-Groups, Categories and Coalitions." *Man* 6: 468–72.

—— 1974. *Friends of Friends: Networks, Manipulators and Coalitions*. Oxford: Blackwell.

Bott, E. 1957. *Family and Social Network*. London: Tavistock.

Boulding, K. E. 1962. *Conflict and Defense: A General Theory*. New York: Harper & Brothers for the Center for Research in Conflict Resolution, University of Michigan.

Brelsford, W. V. 1965. *The Tribes of Zambia*. Lusaka: Government Printer, Zambia.

Brigaglia, M. 1971. *Sardegna, perche banditi*. Milan: Edizioni Leader.

Bromley, H. M. 1967. "The Linguistic Relationships of Grand Valley Dani: A Lexico-Statistical Classification." *Oceania* 37(4): 286–308.

Busia, K. 1951. *The Position of the Chief in the Modern Political System of Ashanti*. London: Oxford University Press.

Cagnetta, F. 1963. *Bandits d'Orgosolo*. Paris: Buchet/Chastel.

Campbell, J. K. 1964. *Honour, Family, and Patronage*. Oxford: University Press.

Canter, Richard. 1976. "Law and Local Level Authority in Zambia." Ph.D. dissertation, University of California, Berkeley.

Collier, J. F. 1973. *Law and Social Change in Zinacantan*. Stanford: University Press.

—— 1975. "Legal Processes." *Annual Review of Anthropology*, ed. B. J. Siegel, 4: 121–44. Palo Alto: Annual Reviews.

Colson, E. 1948. "Rain Shrines of the Plateau Tonga of Rhodesia." *Africa* 18(3).

—— 1953. "Social Control and Vengeance in Plateau Tonga Society." *Africa* 23: 199–212.

—— 1974. *Tradition and Contract: The Problem of Order*. Chicago: Aldine.

Conn, Stephen. 1977. "The Extra-Legal Forum and Legal Power." In R. D. Fogelson and R. N. Adams, eds., *The Anthropology of Power*. New York: Academic Press.

Cox, Bruce Alden. 1968. "Law and Conflict Management among the Hopi." Ph.D. dissertation, University of California, Berkeley.

Cox, Bruce Alden and G. S. Drever. 1971. "Some Recent Trends in Ethnographic Studies of Law." Law and Society Review 5(3): 407–15.

Danzig, R., and M. J. Lowy. 1975. "Everyday Disputes and Mediation in the United States: A Reply to Professor Felstiner." *Law and Society Review* 9(4): 675–94.

Ehrlich, E. 1936. *Fundamental Principles of the Sociology of Law*. Harvard Studies in Jurisprudence, vol. 5. Cambridge: Harvard University Press.

Epstein, A. L. 1954. "Juridicial Techniques and the Judicial Process." Rhodes-Livingstone Papers No. 23.

Epstein, A. L. 1967. "The Case Method in the Field of Law." In A. L. Epstein, ed., *The Craft of Social Anthropology*, pp. 153–80. London: Tavistock.
—— 1969. "The Network and Urban Social Organization." In J. C. Mitchell, ed., *Social Networks in Urban Situations*, pp. 77–116. Manchester: University Press.
—— 1974. "Introduction." In A. L. Epstein, ed., *Contention and Dispute*. Canberra: Australian National University Press.
Evans-Pritchard, E. E. 1940. *The Nuer*. London: Oxford University Press.
Fagan, B. M. 1966. *A Short History of Zambia*. Lusaka: Oxford University Press.
Felstiner, W. L. F. 1974. "Influences of Social Organization on Dispute Processing." *Law and Society Review* 9(1): 63–94.
—— 1975. "Avoidance as Dispute Processing: An Elaboration." *Law and Society Review* 9(4): 695–706.
Forman, Sylvia. 1972. "Law and Conflict in Rural Highland Ecuador." Ph.D. dissertation, University of California, Berkeley.
Frankenberg, R. 1957. *Village on the Border: A Social Study of Religion, Politics, and Football in a North Wales Community*. London: Cohen & West.
Franklin, S. H. 1969. "Bauern, Worker-Peasants, and Family Farms in Federal Germany." In *The European Peasantry: The Final Phase*. London: Methuen.
Freeman, L. 1965. *Elementary Applied Statistics*. New York: John Wiley.
Friedman, L. M. 1969. "On Legal Development." *Rutgers Law Review* 24: 11–64.
Friedman, L. M. and R. V. Percival. 1976. "A Tale of Two Courts: Litigation in Alameda and San Benito Counties." *Law and Society Review* 10(2):267–301.
Fuller, L. 1968. *The Anatomy of Law*. New York: Praeger.
Galanter, M. 1974. "Why the 'Haves' Come Out Ahead: Speculations on the Limits of Legal Change." *Law and Society Review* 9(1): 95–160.
Gibb, H. A. R. 1962. *Mohammedanism: An Historical Survey*. 2nd ed. New York: Galaxy.
Gibb, H. A. R., and J. H. Kramer. 1961. *Shorter Encyclopaedia of Islam*. Ithaca: Cornell University Press.
Gibbs, James L., Jr. 1963. "The Kpelle Moot: A Therapeutic Model for the Informal Settlement of Disputes." *Africa* 33: 1–11.
Gluckman, M. 1955. *The Judicial Process Among the Barotse of Northern*

Rhodesia. Manchester: University Press for the Rhodes-Livingstone Institute.
—— 1961. "Ethnographic Data in British Social Anthropology." *Sociological Review* (n.s.) 9: 5–17.
—— 1963. "Gossip and Scandal." *Current Anthropology* 4(3): 307–16.
—— 1965. *The Ideas in Barotse Jurisprudence*. New Haven: Yale University Press.
—— 1969. *Ideas and Procedures in African Customary Law*. Ed. M. Gluckman. London: Oxford University Press for the International African Institute.
Government of Ghana. 1960. Criminal Procedure Code, Act 30.
—— 1965. Maintenance of Children Act.
—— 1966. Courts Decree. National Liberation Council Decree, 84.
Graburn, N. H. H. 1969. "Eskimo Law in Light of Self- and Group-Interest." *Law and Society Review* 4(1): 45–60.
Guido, M. 1963. *Sardinia*. London: Thames and Hudson.
Gulliver, P. H. 1963. *Social Control in an African Society: A Study of the Arusha, Agricultural Masai of Northern Tanganyika*. Boston: University Press.
—— 1969a. "Introduction to Case Studies of Law in Non-Western Societies." In L. Nader, ed., *Law in Culture and Society*, pp. 11–23. Chicago: Aldine.
—— 1969b. "Dispute Settlement Without Courts: The Ndendeuli of Southern Tanzania." In L. Nader, ed., *Law in Culture and Society*, pp. 24–68. Chicago: Aldine.
—— 1971. *Neighbours and Networks*. Berkeley and Los Angeles: University of California Press.
—— 1973. "Negotiations and Mediation." Working Paper (no. 3) from the Program in Law and Society, University of California, Berkeley.
Gusfield, J. R. 1967. "Moral Passage: The Symbolic Process in Public Designations of Deviance." *Social Problems* 15: 175–88. Reprinted in L. M. Friedman and S. Macaulay, eds., *Law and the Behavioral Sciences*, pp. 308–21. New York: Bobbs-Merrill.
Hahm, Pyong-Choon. 1967. *The Korean Political Tradition and Law*. Seoul: Hollym.
Hirschman, A. 1970. *Exit, Voice, and Loyalty: Responses to Decline in Firms, Organizations and States*. Cambridge: Harvard University Press.
Hitti, Philip K. 1949. *The Arabs: A Short History*. Chicago: Henry Regnery.

Hoebel, E. A. 1954. *The Law of Primitive Man: A Study in Comparative Legal Dynamics*. Cambridge: Harvard University Press.

Howell, P. O. 1954. *A Manual of Nuer Law*. London: Oxford University Press.

Hunt, Eva, and Robert Hunt. 1969. "The Role of Courts in Rural Mexico." In Philip K. Bock, ed., *Peasants in the Modern World*, pp. 109–39. Albuquerque: University of New Mexico Press.

Koch, K.-F. 1967. "Conflict and its Management among the Jalé People of West New Guinea." Ph.D. dissertation, University of California, Berkeley.

—— 1970. "Structure and Variability in the Jalé Kinship Terminology: A Formal Analysis." *Ethnology* 9(3): 263–301.

—— 1974. *War and Peace in Jalémó: The Management of Conflict in Highland New Guinea*. Cambridge: Harvard University Press.

Kuper, H., and L. Kuper, eds. 1965. *African Law: Adaptation and Development*. Berkeley and Los Angeles: University of California Press.

Leach, E. R. 1968. "Social Structure: The History of the Concept." *International Encyclopedia of the Social Sciences*, ed. D. L. Sills, 14: 482–89. New York: Macmillan and Free Press.

Llewellyn, K., and E. A. Hoebel. 1941. *The Cheyenne Way: Conflict and Case Law in Primitive Jurisprudence*. Norman: University of Oklahoma Press.

Lowy, M. 1971. "The Ethnography of Law in a Changing Ghanaian Town." Ph.D. dissertation, University of California, Berkeley.

—— 1973. "The Use of Counsel and Cross-Examination in a Ghanaian Court: A Report from the Berkeley Comparative Law Project." Paper read at the 1973 American Anthropological Association meetings.

—— 1974. " 'Me Ko Court': The Impact of Urbanization on Conflict Resolution in a Ghanaian Town." In G. Foster and R. Kemper, eds., *Anthropologists in Cities*, pp. 153–77. Boston: Little, Brown.

—— 1975. " 'The Shrines are There': The Treatment of Sorcery in a Ghanaian Court." *Kroniek Van Afrika* 1: 38–46.

Macaulay, S. 1963. "Non-Contractual Relations in Business." *American Sociological Review* 28: 55–66. Reprinted in V. Aubert, ed., *Sociology of Law*, pp. 194–209. Baltimore: Penguin Books (1969).

Maine, Sir H. S. 1963. *Ancient Law: Its Connection with the Early History of Society and Its Relation to Modern Ideas*. Boston: Beacon Press. Originally published 1861.

Mauss, Marcel. 1906. *The Gift: Forms and Functions of Exchange in Archaic Societies.* Reprinted 1967. New York: W. W. Norton.
McCall, D. 1956. "The Effect on Family Structure of Changing Economic Activities of Women in a Gold Coast Town." Ph.D. dissertation, Columbia University, New York.
—— 1960. "Koforidua: A West African Town." *Journal of Human Relations* 8 (3, 4).
—— 1962. "The Koforidua Market." In P. Bohannan and G. Dalton, eds., *Markets in Africa,* pp. 667–96. Evanston: Northwestern University Press.
McCarthy, Carl P. 1974. "The Consequences of Legal Advocacy: OEO's Lawyers and the Poor." Ph.D. dissertation, University of California, Berkeley.
Merton, R. K. 1949. *Social Theory and Social Structure.* Rev. ed. 1957. New York: Free Press.
Metzger, D. 1960. "Conflict in Chulsanto: A Village in Chiapas." *Alpha Kappa Deltan* 30: 35–48.
Mileski, M. 1971. "Courtroom Encounters: An Observation Study of a Lower Criminal Court." *Law and Society Review* 5(4): 473–538.
Moore, S. F. 1969. "Law and Anthropology." *Biennial Review of Anthropology,* ed. B. J. Siegel, pp. 252–300. Stanford: University Press.
Mori, A. 1966. *Sardegna.* Turin: Unione Tipografico-Editrice Torinese.
Nader, L. 1964a. "An Analysis of Zapotec Law Cases." *Ethnology* 3: 404–19.
—— 1964b. "Talea and Juquila: A Comparison of Zapotec Social Organization." *University of California Publications in American Archaeology and Ethnography* 48(3): 195–296.
—— 1965a. "Choices in Legal Procedure: Shia Moslem and Mexican Zapotec." *American Anthropologist* 67(2): 394–99.
—— 1965b. "The Anthropological Study of Law." In L. Nader, ed., *The Ethnography of Law. American Anthropologist* (special publication) 67(6)(2): 3–32.
—— 1969a. "Introduction." In L. Nader, ed., *Law in Culture and Society,* pp. 1–10. Chicago: Aldine.
—— 1969b. "Styles of Court Procedure: To Make the Balance." In L. Nader, ed., *Law in Culture and Society,* pp. 69–91. Chicago: Aldine.
Nader, L., K.-F. Koch, and B. Cox. 1966. "The Ethnography of Law: A Bibliographic Survey." *Current Anthropology* 7(3): 267–94.

Nader, L., and D. Metzger. 1963. "Conflict Resolution in Two Mexican Communities." *American Anthropologist* 65: 584–92.

Nader, L., and J. O. Starr. 1973. "Is Equity Universal?" In R. Neuman, ed., *Equity in the World's Legal System: A Comparative Study*, pp. 125–37. Brussels: Etablissements Emile Bruylant.

Nader, L., and B. Yngvesson. 1974. "On Studying the Ethnography of Law and Its Consequences." In J. J. Honigmann, ed., *Handbook of Social and Cultural Anthropology*, pp. 883–921. Chicago: Rand McNally.

Ohta, T., and T. Hozumi. 1973. "Compromise in the Course of Litigation." Tr. P. Figdor. *Law in Japan* 6: 97–111.

Ottenberg, S. 1967. "Local Government and Law in Southern Nigeria." In D. C. Buxbaum, ed., *Traditional and Modern Legal Institutions in Asia and Africa*. Leiden: E. J. Brill.

Parnell, Philip. 1978. "Conflict and Competition in a Mexican Judicial District." Ph.D. dissertation, University of California, Berkeley.

Photiadis, J. D. 1965. "The Position of the Coffee-house in the Social Structure of the Greek Village." *Sociologia Ruralis* 5(1): 45–56.

Pigliaru, A. 1959. *La vendetta barbaricina come ordinamento giuridico*. Milan: Giuffre.

Pinna, G. 1967. *Il pastore sardo e la giustizia*. Cagliari: Fossataro.

Pinna, L. 1971. *La famiglia esclusiva: parentela e clientelismo in Sardegna*. Bari: Laterza.

Pirastu, I. 1973. *Il banditismo in Sardegna*. Rome: Editori Riuniti.

Pospisil, L. 1958. "Kapauku Papuans and their Law." Yale University Publications in Anthropology No. 54.

—— 1967. "Legal Levels and Multiplicity of Legal Systems in Human Societies." *Journal of Conflict Resolution* 11(1): 2–26.

—— 1971. *Anthropology of Law: A Comparative Theory*. New York: Harper & Row.

Pound, R. 1906. "The Causes of Popular Dissatisfaction with the Administration of Justice." *Reports of the American Bar Association* 29, pt. 1: 295–417.

Propp, V. 1968. *Morphology of the Folktale*. L. Scott, trans.; L. A. Wagner, ed. Austin: University of Texas Press.

Radcliffe-Brown, A. R. 1952. *Structure and Function in Primitive Society*. New York: Free Press.

Rattray, R. 1929. *Ashanti Law and Constitution*. Oxford: Clarendon Press.

Roberts, J. M. 1965. "Oaths, Autonomic Ordeals, and Power." *American Anthropologist* 67(6)(2): 186–212.

Rothenberger, John E. 1970. "Law and Conflict Resolution, Politics, and

Change in a Sunni Muslim Village in Lebanon." Ph.D. dissertation, University of California, Berkeley.

Ruffini, J. L. 1974. "Alternative Systems of Conflict Management in Sardinia." Ph.D. dissertation, University of California, Berkeley.

Salim, M. S. 1962. *Marsh Dwellers of Euphrates Delta.* London: Athlone Press.

Sanjek, R. n.d. "Pat-Pat, Pat-Mat, Mat-Pat, Mat-Mat: Mixed Marriage and Ethnic Identity in Adabraka." Unpublished manuscript in possession of author.

Schmieder, Oscar. 1930. "The Settlements of the Tzapotec and Mije Indians." *University of California Publications in Geography* 4.

Schildkrout, E. 1974. "Ethnicity and Generational Differences Among Urban Immigrants in Ghana." In A. Cohen, ed., *Urban Ethnicity*, pp. 187–222. London: Tavistock.

Siegel, B. J., and Alan R. Beals. 1960. "Pervasive Factionalism." *American Anthropologist* 62: 394–417.

Smith, D. 1972. "Man and Law in Urban Africa: A Role for Customary Courts in the Urbanization Process." *American Journal of Comparative Law* 20: 223–46.

Smith, W., and J. M. Roberts. 1954. "Zuni Law: A Field of Values." *Peabody Museum Papers* 43(1).

Spradley, J. 1970. *You Owe Yourself a Drunk: An Ethnography of Urban Nomads.* Boston: Little, Brown.

Stanner, W. E. H. 1966. *On Aboriginal Religion.* Sydney: University of Sydney, Oceania Monograph 11.

Starr, J. O. 1968. "Dispute and Delay: The Functions of 'Slowness' in a Turkish Court." Paper read at the 1968 American Anthropological Association meetings. Unpublished manuscript, in files of the editors.

—— 1970. "*Mandalinci Koy:* Law and Social Control in a Turkish Village." Ph.D. dissertation, University of California, Berkeley.

—— 1974. "Mediation and Status Deprivation: A Preliminary Statement." Presented at Yale Law School, Law and Modernization Conference.

—— 1975. "First Thoughts on Western Law in Islam." Paper read at Middle East Symposium, 1975 American Anthropological Association meetings.

—— 1978. *Dispute and Settlement in Rural Turkey: An Ethnography of Law.* Leiden: E. J. Brill.

Starr, J. O., and J. Pool. 1974. "The Impact of a Legal Revolution in Rural Turkey." *Law and Society Review* 8(4): 553–60.

Starr, J. O., and B. Yngvesson. 1975. "Scarcity and Disputing: Zeroing-in on Compromise Decisions." *American Ethnologist* 2(3): 553–66.

Stirling, Paul. 1965. *Turkish Village*. London: Weidenfeld & Nicolson.

—— 1974. "Cause, Knowledge, and Change: Turkish Village Revisited." In John Davis, ed., *Choice and Change: Essays in Honour of Lucy Mair*, pp. 191–229. London: Athlone Press.

Sutherland, E. 1949. *White Collar Crime*. New York: Holt, Rinehart & Winston.

Sutherland-Harris, N. 1970. "Zambia Trade with Zumbo in the Eighteenth Century." In R. Gray and D. B. Birmingham, eds., *Pre-Colonial African Trade*, pp. 231–42. Oxford: Oxford University Press.

Tessler, M., W. O'Barr, and D. Spain. 1973. *Tradition and Identity in Changing Africa*. New York: Harper & Row.

Todd, H. F., Jr. 1972. "Law and Conflict Management in a Bavarian Village." Ph.D. dissertation, University of California, Berkeley.

—— 1973. "The Social Organization of Dispute Settlement." Paper read at 1973 American Anthropological Association meetings.

—— 1978. "Status and Disputing in a Bavarian Village." *Ethnologia Europaea* 10(1).

Torrend, J. 1931. *An English Vernacular of the Bantu-Botative Dialects of Northern Rhodesia*. London: Kegan Paul, Trench, Trubner.

Trubek, D. 1972. "Max Weber and the Rise of Capitalism." *Wisconsin Law Review* 3: 720–53.

Turner, V. 1957. *Schism and Continuity in an African Society: A Study of Ndembu Village Life*. Manchester: Manchester University Press.

van der Sprenkel, S. 1962. *Legal Institutions in Manchu China: A Sociological Analysis*. London School of Economics Monographs on Social Anthropology No. 24. London: Athlone Press.

Van Velsen, J. 1964. *The Politics of Kinship: A Study in Social Manipulation Among the Lakeside Tonga*. Manchester: Manchester University Press.

—— 1967. "The Extended-Case Method and Situational Analysis." In A. L. Epstein, ed., *The Craft of Social Anthropology*, pp. 129–49. London: Tavistock.

—— 1969. "Procedural Informality, Reconciliation, and False Comparisons." In M. Gluckman, ed., *Ideas and Procedures in African Customary Law*, pp. 137–52. London: Oxford University Press.

Vogt, Evon Z., and Ethel M. Albert, eds. 1966. *People of Rimrock: A Study of Values in Five Cultures*. Cambridge: Harvard University Press.

Wallace, A. F. C. 1966. *Religion: An Anthropological View*. New York: Random House.

Wehr, Hans. 1961. A *Dictionary of Modern Written Arabic*. Ed. J. Milton Cowan. Ithaca: Cornell University Press.

Whiting, B., ed. 1963. *Six Cultures*. New York: John Wiley.

Whiting, J. W. M., et al. 1953. *Field Manual for the Cross-Cultural Study of Child Rearing*. New York: Social Science Research Council.

Whyte, W. F. 1955. *Street Corner Society: The Social Structure of an Italian Slum*. Rev. ed. Chicago: University Press. Originally published 1943.

Wilks, I. 1967. "Ashanti Government." In D. Forde and P. Kaberry eds., *West African Kingdoms in the Nineteenth Century*, pp. 206–38. London: Oxford University Press.

Williams, Nancy. 1973. "Northern Territory Aborigines under Australian Law." Ph.D. dissertation, University of California, Berkeley.

Witty, C. J. 1975. "The Struggle for Progress: The Socio-Political Realities of Legal Pluralism." Ph.D. dissertation, University of California, Berkeley.

Yngvesson, B. 1970. "Decision-Making and Dispute Settlement in a Swedish Fishing Village: An Ethnography of Law." Ph.D. dissertation, University of California, Berkeley.

NAME INDEX

SUBJECT INDEX

Bei Fragen zur Produktsicherheit wenden Sie sich bitte an:
If you have any questions regarding product safety,
please contact:

Walter de Gruyter GmbH
Genthiner Straße 13
10785 Berlin
productsafety@degruyterbrill.com